SHORT-TERM PSYCHOTHERAPY

LEWIS R. WOLBERG, M.D.

with nine contributors

GRUNE & STRATTON New York and London

Books by the Same Author

Hypnoanalysis

Medical Hypnosis

The Technique of Psychotherapy

Second printing, February 1967

Contents

Introduction

LEWIS R. WOLBERG, M.D.

STATISTICS CONSTANTLY EMPHASIZE the great disparity that exists between the number of persons in need of help for emotional and mental disorders and the available personnel trained to administer this help. Oft quoted is the ratio of one psychiatrist to every 16,000 persons in the general population. More than half of all psychiatrists practice in fifteen of the largest cities in the U.S.A. There are ten states which have fewer than fifty psychiatrists, and in many communities there are no psychiatrists at all. What holds true for the dearth of psychiatrists applies also to clinical psychologists and psychiatric social workers.

The foregoing census tells only part of the story; for not more than a fraction of the professionals who are fully qualified to call themselves psychiatrists, clinical psychologists and psychiatric social workers have been trained to do psychotherapy.

Yet humanity dictates, in the face of this professional shortage, that something be done about the constantly expanding patient waiting lists. One solution is increased recruitment and training of qualified personnel. Another is more research into methods of shortening treatment and of making it more efficient.

Investigation of methodologies of short-term therapy have been, to some extent, hampered by the fact that long-term psychotherapy has traditionally been accepted as the most effective approach for problems of an emotional nature, particularly where the objective is reconstruction of the personality structure itself. There is little need to apologize for the protracted period that so ambitious an objective requires. The workings of the human mind are devious and one can meander only leisurely through labyrinths of structure, dynamics and pathology. Resistance is a staunch adversary constantly blocking this journey. Triumph over it can be achieved only by painstaking "working-through," shuttling back and forth from destructive patterns to more healthy modes of reacting. But transferential contaminants continue to obstruct progress, diverting the patient from a reality orientation. Neurotic behavioral patterns, rooted as they are in early conditionings, are, practically speaking, embedded in a neuronal matrix. Their extinction and reorganization require time.

1

These are the common, understandable and apparently reasonable arguments against curtailment of the term of treatment. The difficulty of resolving a childhood neurosis which continues to burden the individual in his adult life, of removing resistance, of resolving transference, of recovering significant memories and establishing connecting links to present-day problems can be attested to by an analyst, even when years of concentrated treatment are dedicated to such tasks. It is hardly conceivable then that these goals, elusive as they are with long-term treatment, could be achieved by abbreviated methods. If our aim is to eliminate the neurosis completely, and to bring about a radical change in the personality, shortening therapy would seem to be out of the question.

The scientific contentions for the extended time in psychotherapy have been reinforced by historic, philosophic and economic propositions. Historically, we have witnessed a gradual increase in the period allocated to persons in therapy. At one epoch, three months of concentrated treatment was considered ample. This limit was gradually raised to six months. When it became apparent that the patient could not be liberated from his neurosis in this period, nine months became the established duration. The latter, the nine month span, was rationalized by some therapists as equivalent to the term of gestation in the human infant. If it required a child nine months to be born, could we expect a personality rebirth in less time? Apparently many individuals required a much longer sojourn in the womb, because we see therapeutic pregnancies that go on for five, six, and even ten years, with both gratifying and not so gratifying results. Part of the explanation for the increased extent is that our concepts of mental health and mental illness have broadened. We know a great deal more than we did several decades ago about personality development and disorganization; and the complexities of the problems involved in therapeutic change have made us assume that time itself was essential in bringing about the essential transformations.

Philosophically, we have justified the expansion of the therapeutic period. We have insisted, first, that it takes time to peal off layers of defense in order to reach the conflictual core of a neurosis. Second, it takes time to enlist the cooperation of the reasonable ego to accept the necessary insights required for change. Third, it takes time to translate these insights into action, to recondition ways of thinking, feeling and behaving that will lead to a more productive adjustment. Fourth, it takes time to evolve a different concept of the self, shorn of neurotic props and defenses, and anchored in self-respect, self-confidence and a firm sense of mastery.

Economically, these philosophic concepts have, for better or for worse, paid off. It is comforting for a therapist to have sufficient leisure to explore an emotional problem unhurriedly; time enables him to correct mistakes without jeopardizing results. In the competitive press, a full case load guaranteed over a long stretch is much less hazardous than a rapid turnover. How much a therapist's theoretical convictions are influenced by financial factors is a hazardous matter to assess.

The scientific, historic, philosophic and economic forces supporting long-term therapy have gradually become amalgamated into a credo to the effect that good results in psychotherapy are possible only after protracted treatment. Technics have accordingly been adapted to an extended time factor. The results have in many instances left much to be desired. First, excessive passivity on the part of the therapist, which is prompted by the idea that he can rely on the magic of time, may cause the patient to flounder around helplessly for years, mobilizing resentments and masochism. Second, prolonged contact between patient and therapist may accentuate the transference neurosis, producing paralyzing dependency and stimulating uncontrollable acting-out. Finally, a deification of insight as the only corrective force in therapy has fostered an avoidance of certain helpful adjuncts in treatment such as the somatic therapies, hypnosis, group approaches and environmental manipulation, on the basis that time itself will eventually act like a detergent, washing away resistances and liberating the emotional understanding essential to cure.

Undermining this credo has been the empiric finding that many patients get well, even though they have been seen for relatively few sessions. In instances where an evaluation of results has been possible, astonishing changes in personality organization have occurred even approaching those hoped for in long-term treatment. Furthermore, it has been possible by spacing sessions appropriately, and utilizing special technics, to achieve changes which we once believed required continuous treatment over an extended span. Indeed, time spent in formal therapy is not the only variable involved in therapeutic gain. It is but one ingredient, and not always the most important one.

A productive search for a serviceable methodology has been emboldened by the pilot project on brief psychotherapy conducted under the auspices of Group Health Insurance, Inc., the American Psychiatric Association and the National Association for Mental

Health, which was sponsored by a grant from the National Institute of Mental Health (Avnet, 1962). In this project, an attempt was made to examine the practicality of a program of insurance coverage for short-term psychotherapy, and to assay the results of a limited number of sessions. Seventy-six thousand subscribers to Group Health Insurance, selected for the study, were told that they had coverage for fifteen office psychiatric visits. A panel of 1,139 participating psychiatrists cooperated in the project which lasted two and one-half years. On termination, fully 75 per cent of the patients treated were rated by the panel as improved or recovered. A complete spectrum of psychiatric syndromes was represented in the project. Sixty per cent of all patients terminated therapy before the allowed number of sessions had been exhausted. Of the 40 per cent who took advantage of the full quota, a good number continued privately beyond the sessions allowed by insurance. As Coleman (Coleman, 1963) has pointed out "these figures seem to indicate that the majority of patients who currently both need and elect to get psychiatric help can benefit from some form of short-term help, and indeed their recovery rate is most impressive. With due allowances for the crudeness of these measurements, this study underscores the benefits and the practicality of short-term treatments as an answer for a very large proportion of the community's psychiatric needs."

With the development of health insurance programs to finance a limited number of psychotherapeutic sessions, interest is being focused on short-term treatment methods. This economic stimulus merely highlights a growing conviction among psychotherapists that there are disadvantages in long-term approaches in many cases. Indeed, short-term therapy may be the treatment of choice.

The potentialities of short-term approaches, however, the particular kinds of patients and problems that are responsive, the parameters of functioning that may be favorably influenced, the depth of reconstructive change, if any, and the permanence of the results have been only incompletely delineated. Even less structured are the methods that have proven themselves to be of value.

In this volume, authorities with vast psychiatric and psychotherapeutic experience have written chapters on various aspects of short-term therapy with the object of contributing to a better understanding of the theory and practice of this important and socially useful expediency. Except for a contribution by Helen Avnet, the chapters are patterned after lectures on Short-Term Therapy given by the contributors in a seminar at the Postgraduate Center for

Mental Health in New York. A questionnaire on various aspects of short-term therapy was distributed to each of the participants in advance of the seminar, inviting them to comment on items related to their talk. Pertinent answers, as well as replies to questions during the lecture, have been included and follow the more formal chapter presentations.

The questions posed to the participants were these:

1. *Selection of cases:* Are there any special kinds of symptoms or syndromes that respond better to short-term than to long-term methods?
2. *Psychodynamic formulations:* Since it is manifestly impossible within the confines of a short-term psychotherapy program to arrive at the definitive psychodynamics in many cases, is it possible to present a general formulation of dynamics that may be meaningful to the average patient?
3. *Goals:* Are goals in short-term therapy limited to symptom relief, or are reconstructive personality changes possible?
4. *Methodological differences between long-term and short-term methods?* Are there qualitative differences in technics in short-term as compared to long-term treatment?
5. *Treating target symptoms:* Psychotropic drugs deal with target symptoms. Are there any special psychotherapeutic technics that can also deal with target symptoms?
6. *Transference neurosis:* Is a transference neurosis desirable in short-term therapy? How may it be managed most constructively, if it does develop?
7. *Handling resistance:* Are there ways of managing resistance in short-term therapy that differ from long-term therapy?
8. *Dealing with dependency:* Since there are many patients who develop intensive dependency relationships and who consequently tend to make therapy an interminable affair, how can we deal with such patients in a short-term approach? Are there ways of bypassing dependency or resolving it, or directing it at therapeutically corrective foci other than a never-ending therapeutic situation?
9. *Dealing with detachment:* Are there ways of breaking through characterologic detachment to involve the patient therapeutically in a few sessions without stirring up too great anxiety?
10. *Dreams:* How does one utilize dreams in short-term therapy? Does one employ them in any way other than that in long-term therapy?
11. *Psychotropic drugs:* How valuable are drugs in short-term therapy?
12. *Supportive approaches:* What supportive approaches are helpful in short-term therapy?
13. *Reconstructive possibilities:* Are there technics that may encourage reconstructive changes in the therapy and post-therapy period?

14. *Counseling with related family members:* Is it helpful to see related family members in short-term therapy? If so, for what purpose?
15. *Psychological testing:* Can psychological testing or other psychological approaches contribute to short-term treatment?
16. *Utilizing social resources:* What environmental resources may be enlisted to help a patient during short-term therapy?

The chapter by Dr. Franz Alexander contains some material, originally presented at the Postgraduate Center, which later was incorporated in a paper published in the American Journal of Psychiatry. Permission to reprint portions of this article was obtained.

How Effective Is Short-Term Therapy?

Appraisals of Mental Health
After Short-Term Ambulatory Psychiatric Treatment

═══════════════════════════ HELEN H. AVNET

(Editor's Note: It is generally acknowledged that short-term therapy is the only practical solution to the dilemma facing mental health planners. But how effective short-term therapy can be in bringing about cure or improvement has been a moot point. Reporting on the pioneer pilot project on short-term psychiatric benefits of Group Health Insurance, Inc., Helen Avnet brings out some important data in follow-up studies that might be helpful in clarifying the effectiveness of short-term therapy. In spite of the fact that most of the 1200 participating psychiatrists were analytically and long-term oriented, and though they were skeptical prior to the project regarding attempted short-cuts in psychotherapy, cure or improvement of 76 per cent was reported by them at the end of the limited treatment period. A follow-up study after an average of two and one-half years following termination showed that 81 per cent of patients reported sustained recovery or improvement. In spite of the lack of scientific instruments to permit of objective measurements, there is impressive agreement by both participating psychiatrists and patients regarding recovery or improvement with short-term methods. On the basis of the data in this study, a gross prediction may be made that four out of five patients receiving this type of therapy will probably feel or report some degree of improvement two or three years later, even with the treatment methods available today, and though rendered by long-term oriented therapists. The fifth non-responsive patient cannot be identified in advance by any known criteria including diagnostic category.

THE CASE WITH THE NEW UPPER PLATE was one of our favorite patients—the man who phoned our project office one day to request the name of a psychiatrist-hypnotherapist. He was gagging because he couldn't get used to his new dentures and this was affecting his digestive system, which in turn was causing a disturbance in his general outlook. He had two sessions with the psychiatrist, who subsequently reported a complete recovery. Our follow-up study elicited a similar report directly from the patient.

Atypical and simple though this case is, it provides a good illustration of the difficulty of evaluating the need for and benefits of ambulatory psychiatric treatment. Certain facts are known—the symptoms, the complete recovery after two sessions of hypnotherapy, the patient's subsequent maintenance of his recovery status and his feeling that the psychiatric project which enabled him to seek treatment was worthwhile. The psychiatrist was not certain, at initial interview, of the need for treatment, but entered a diagnosis of "psychophysiologic autonomic and visceral disorder; gastrointestinal reaction." Do the known facts permit the inference that the treatment was effective? Would the patient have adjusted as satisfactorily without it?

Depending on the psychiatric point of view, both these questions might be answered affirmatively or negatively. Another psychiatrist might have indicated no treatment necessary, while a third might have felt the presenting symptoms to be merely a shield for a deep-seated neurosis requiring "insight" rather than "supportive measures." Much seems to depend on the individual psychiatrist—his training, his flexibility, his general outlook, his own personality—as well as on the patient.

We had a few other light moments during the operation of the project to test the insurability of short-term ambulatory psychiatric treatment, but from where we sat, not many cases were so readily identifiable with clear-cut happy endings. The project was not set up to measure the efficacy of treatment. In view of the failure of the mental health professions to establish criteria for judging success, it would have been presumptuous for insurers to attempt evaluation. By the same token, however, the uniqueness of our experiment and the sparsity of reporting in the field create pressures to report such impressions as we do have. It is a measure of the continuing contradictions, ambiguities, and uncertainties in this whole area, especially in ambulatory treatment, that data gathered to test one hypothesis are sought as clues in the retrospective testing of another.

PROJECT

The project referred to began in 1959, when Group Health Insurance, Inc. of New York offered short-term psychiatric benefits to 76,000 people (about 10 per cent of the membership) who were already insured for most other types of physician services rendered in office, home, hospital. The project was backed by the National Institute of Mental Health, co-sponsored by the American Psychiatric Association and the National Association for Mental Health, and operated by Group Health Insurance.

In two and one-half years of operation, 1115 men, women and children received project benefits.

The project enrolled over 1200 psychiatrists as participants who agreed to accept $20 as payment-in-full per individual 45-minute private session (of which the patient paid $5). Other arrangements were made for group therapy, electroshock therapy, psychological testing, and up to 30 days of hospitalization, but emphasis was on ambulatory private individual treatment and most of the claims were in this category. There was a limit of 15 individual sessions (or alternatively many more group sessions) allowed per eligible member. Payments were made starting with the first visit; there were no "deductibles." Only participating psychiatrists and hospitals were paid.

Although the project sponsors clearly intended to encourage early and limited treatment, no restrictions of any kind were placed on psychiatrists as to types of conditions acceptable for treatment, types of treatment rendered, or spacing of allowed treatment. Even if a psychiatrist decided on psychoanalysis, despite the fact that the patient could hardly get started within the allotted visits, no objection was raised. Actually, project payments did contribute to the cost of analysis in a few cases, but these patients either were already in treatment when the project happened along, or continued afterward.

PSYCHIATRISTS

We originally anticipated that the project might attract as participating psychiatrists, those mainly interested in short-term therapy. We were wrong. We soon learned that most of the private practitioners, at least in the New York area and its environs, are analytically, long-term oriented. With respect to the project, psychiatrists in the area divided themselves into three categories—those who elected not to join, those who joined because of interest in insurance, and those who joined because of interest in insurance plus an active concern with short-term treatment possibilities.

Non-Participants. We never knew how many were in this category, since we had no figures on the total number of psychiatrists in private practice in New York and its environs. There were about 2100 members of the American Psychiatric Association in the area who were invited to join, and of the 900 who did not participate we estimated that at least 200 and possibly many more were in private practice and could have joined had they been so inclined.

We invited non-participants to voice their reasons for not joining. A few expressed enthusiasm for the project, stating that a full schedule or a full-time hospital position prevented participation. The majority of those who answered, however, declared their opposition to short-term therapy as offered by the project. Some stated their objections in terms of the patients' welfare (what to do after the project visits), others simply indicated that they never engage in short-term therapy:

"I do not give short-term therapy."

"Totally inadequate time allotment for psychotherapy."

"I am not convinced of the efficacy of short-term psychotherapy, and therefore restrict my practice to psychoanalysis, consultation work, and drug therapy."

"My practice would not fit into a short-term program."

"I do not wish to join because I think there are too few patients who would receive any kind of real benefit from such a time-limited therapy. I think the plan would merely make a nice situation for news releases but will in actuality accomplish nothing."

"I confine my practice to those who can benefit from psychotherapy and none benefit appreciably by 4 months of treatment."

"Fifteen sessions do not seem sufficient in the majority of cases. This will create problems for the patient and the therapist."

"While most interested in your project, I cannot participate since I limit my practice to psychotherapy which in most cases requires considerably more than the stated number of visits. I do not see how I could justifiably start a patient in treatment and discontinue it. There would be no other resources since clinics are full."

"I feel that it is unethical to drop a patient after 15 sesions and there is no screening process to insure that only short-term therapy cases will come to the office."

"I do long-term psychotherapy exclusively."

"I do analytic therapy—15 hours is only an introduction to such work."

"I'm interested only in intensive psychotherapy and analysis."

"There are too many problems involved in experimental treatments, especially one limited to 15 sessions, the most obvious problem being the disposal of the cases after the visits are over. It's a rare case when 4 or 5 months of treatment are enough."

"I never have such short termed cases. I do hope in the future you will be able to work out an insurance policy to include psychoanalysis."

. . . and so on.

It will be noted that all of the respondents used long-term therapy as their base of comparison in criticizing short-term therapy. No one discussed short-term vis-a-vis no therapy.

Other than the obvious conclusions that (a) long-term therapy is assumed to be effective and (b) the individual patient who cannot obtain long-term therapy (for whatever reason) is not the problem of the individual doctor, there is the implied conclusion that zero therapy is preferable to short-term therapy in most cases. This position underlines the schism that exists between a large segment of private practitioners who cater to the carriage trade and their colleagues who are concerned with the problem of nationally inadequate resources to meet untreated mental illness and who see in short-term or limited therapy the only solution to the practical dilemma facing mental program planners.

Participants. Like their non-participating colleagues, the participants as a group were trained in and practiced long-term approaches to treatment, skeptical of attempted short-cuts. Participation seems to have been associated with interest in attaching psychiatry to the medical insurance universe, rather than with confidence in the short-term aspects of the experiment.

One of the observations we made in the course of reviewing case reports was the frequency with which initial interviews with patients included discussion of their financial ability to continue treatment beyond the number of sessions allowed by the project.

Other evidence of resistance to the short-term approach came from psychiatrists' recommendations for further treatment. The cases in which further treatment was not recommended constituted a minority; and for those patients who completed the allotted project treatments, the recommendation to continue was almost universal (94 per cent).

For about 30 per cent of the treating psychiatrists, the inclination toward long-term therapy or analysis as the treatment of choice was modified for project patients. Many adjusted their usual approach to try for quicker results. They defined their goals sooner, narrowed their treatment objectives, tackled the immediate problem, treated symptoms instead of reaching for causes, became more directive, participated more actively, spaced visits at longer intervals, worked harder. Some used the opportunity as a learning experience and seem to have enjoyed it.

Irrespective of their long-term orientation as a group, or their individual encouragements or discouragements with individual cases, the participating psychiatrists generally reacted favorably to the project itself, as a worthwhile social endeavor pointed in the right general direction. One man commented, "The whole plan appears to me to be a long-needed and necessary thing, far more important than 'CA,' 'MS,' and a dozen other drives to improve public health."

To the extent that such enthusiasm existed for the experiment, the disadvantages of relying on long-term therapists to provide short-term therapy may have been modified. Nevertheless, if we had set out to test effectiveness rather than insurability, our approach would obviously have been different.

PATIENTS

As a group, the 1115 people who used one or more project services were not seriously disabled and would probably appear normal —whatever that is—to those meeting them socially or at work. The major effects of their illness were felt in the home. Less than half had symptoms of such severity as to have a serious effect on their social or working life. You might have encountered them auditing your tax return, interviewing for employment, driving that trailer truck, painting your apartment, acting in the Broadway play you were seeing, delivering your milk, printing the publication you're reading, selling you a car, teaching your child, or processing your insurance claim.

They appear to be a stable group of citizens: Two-thirds of the gainfully employed adults have been with their present employers over 5 years, and 40 per cent over 10 years. Since the psychiatric project, most have the same or a better job, and are earning more.

About one in five of our patients was under the age of 19 at the time of treatment. Most of the others were from 20 to 45. About two-thirds were in family income categories $4000-$8000 at the time of the study; thirteen per cent were over $10,000, and another thirteen per cent reported incomes under $4000. Half were in families of blue-collar workers. There were twice as many single, divorced or separated adults, and three times as many college graduates, as would have been expected if the patient population had been distributed maritally and educationally as the eligible population. Still, married patients and patients with high school or less education dominated.

By and large it was a group which would ordinarily not have sought private treatment from a psychiatrist, and almost 70 per cent of them never had, despite the fact that nearly half the patients reported symptom-duration of two years or more. For these patients, the project was a major factor in bringing them to the psychiatrist.

TREATMENT

All types of problems and symptoms were presented to the psychiatrist and recorded—sometimes without translation ("hits kids"; "sets fires"; "throws rocks"). Most frequently mentioned, however, were terms such as depression, anxiety, neurosis, mental strain, nervousness, phobia. There were numerous problems of marital adjustment and family conflict, and various others involving single status or blighted romance, or problems of post-partum, middle age, or retirement adjustment. Somatic complaints were listed in a number of cases. Relatively infrequent were cases of alcoholism, drug addiction, homosexuality.

Twenty per cent of the patients were classified by the psychiatrists as psychotics. Most of these, as well as practically all other patients, were treated on an individual ambulatory basis. Drugs were prescribed for about 2 out of 5 patients. Hospitalization expenses were incurred by the project for only 6 per cent of all patients. Thus, under the vast majority of current medical insurance policies, only a small fraction of the psychiatric expenses incurred by our project would have been covered.

In actuarial circles the coverage we offered is criticized as being unpredictable, an elective service rendered to patients not overtly disabled by the condition for which they seek diagnosis and treatment. On the other hand, the brevity of the treatment we covered inspires criticism from the non-actuarial contingent—the psychiatrists and the patients themselves.

The "brevity of the treatment we covered" does not tell the story of the length of therapy actually undergone by our patients. On this we experienced the following:

For half the patients, the project maximum was never a factor; they quit before reaching the limit allowed.

Of the other half—those who did use the maximum benefits—57 per cent had additional treatment after reaching the project limit. The number of additional treatments ranged from 1 to 360 over a period averaging 2½ years between project benefits and follow-up report. Half those reporting additional treatments had 70 or more.

Among patients who did not fully utilize their project benefits, 25 per cent reported further treatment. Some of these used non-participating psychiatrists or hospitals, some used psychologists or clinics, some returned for supportive therapy after the project ended.

Overall, 60 per cent of the patients reported no further therapy beyond the project treatment.

Certain factors seem to predispose toward continuation of treatment—those with previous treatment, prior to the project, were somewhat more likely to continue, as were those with major effects from their illness; those in white-collar (except sales) occupations; the maritally unattached (except widows); women aged 20-29; boys; adults under 50; college graduates. Income was not a factor except for children in families with income over $10,000.

The psychiatrists' recommendations were usually followed where further treatment was *not* recommended, usually not followed where it *was* recommended. (It works out this way because psychiatrists usually recommended further treatment, and most patients did not continue.)

TREATMENT APPRAISAL

In attemping to assess what was accomplished therapeutically, we have access to a variety of reported facts and opinions from both psychiatrists and patients (or parents of patients). Initially, we recorded demographic data on the eligible population (age, sex, marital status, family size, occupation, education, income, area of residence). As eligible members became patients we received reports from psychiatrists as to referral source, previous treatment, type, duration and severity of symptoms, need for treatment, medical surgical history, psychiatric diagnosis and prognosis, type and amount of treatment, and, in the final report, whether the patient was continuing, referred elsewhere, whether further treatment was recommended, psychiatrist's judgment as to response to treatment, final diagnosis and prognosis, whether psychiatrist was reporting to family doctor. There was provision of space for comments on every report.

Other sources of information were a follow-up questionnaire sent to treating psychiatrists; and a follow-up questionnaire sent after the completion of the project to all patients (which brought a 77 per cent response from those reached).

None of this information was collected with the thought of assessing therapeutic techniques—long-term, short-term or otherwise. We asked questions and we amassed answers, attitudes, opinions. These are still being studied and will, it is hoped, be presented in some detail elsewhere. In the meantime, leaving aside the facts pertaining to insurability, and directing our attention instead to the state of mental health of the patients, a few tentative gross findings can be reported.

The interval between project treatment and follow-up study of patients averaged about 2½ years for the respondents. We obtained 801 recordable questionnaires from patients, of which all but 18 gave us their appraisal of current mental health status. For 740 of the respondents we also had ratings from their psychiatrists as to their response to treatment.

Neither of these types of measurements is based on objective criteria; both are patently crude. Each psychiatrist's evaluations are presumably objective by his own standards, but since these may differ from those of his colleagues they must be considered subjective in that respect. As for patient appraisals, the lack of standardized criteria is even more of a drawback to interpretation; to which must be added the possibility of distorted reporting, either deliberate or because of wishful thinking. Futhermore, patients' statements as to present mental health status are not necessarily related to treatment; reported changes might have occurred with, without, or despite treatment.

In the absence of alternative sources, however, the comparison of the two ratings will be of interest (table 1):

TABLE 1.—Mental Health Status of Patients,
Psychiatrist vs. Patient Appraisal

Patient Appraisal of Subsequent Status		PSYCHIATRIST APPRAISAL DIRECTLY AFTER TREATMENT				
		Number of Patients				
		Recovered	Improved	Unimproved	Uncertain	No Answer
Recovered	137	25	70	15	14	13
Greatly Improved	279	23	189	19	30	18
Somewhat Improved	218	21	143	23	20	11
Same	98	3	42	17	24	12
Worse	21	2	12	4	1	2
Uncertain	30	3	21	1	3	2
No answer	18	1	8	2	4	3
Total	801	78	485	81	96	61

These source figures can be variously combined and interpreted. The following observations seem to this writer to be noteworthy:

The great majority of the ratings by both psychiatrists and patients are in the recovery or improved columns.

Eighty-one per cent of the 783 patients responding to the question see at least some improvement—17 per cent claim recovery, 36 per cent great improvement, 28 per cent some improvement. This compares with psychiatrists' overall ratings, on 740 patients, of 76 per cent either recovered (10.5 per cent) or improved (65.5 per cent).

Only 19 per cent of the patients say they are the same, worse, or uncertain. This compares with 24 per cent of psychiatrist ratings in the unimproved or uncertain categories. If we omit cases rated uncertain, or not rated, we find 12 per cent of psychiatrist appraisals and 16 per cent of patient appraisals in the unimproved category. The individual cases assigned to these categories by each group of raters do not coincide.

In 53 per cent of the cases rated by both groups, rating coincided—psychiatrists and patients made similar appraisals as to recovery, improvement, unimprovement, or uncertainty. In a third of the other cases, the differences relate to the rating recovery vs improvement: Psychiatrists rated 70 patients improved who later claimed recovery, and 44 patients rated by psychiatrists as recovered labeled themselves improved. Overall, if we combine psychiatrist ratings of recovered or improved we find subsequent corroboration by the patients in 85 per cent of the cases.

The degree of agreement varies. But considering the subjective nature of the evaluation and the fact that no scientific "instrument" was devised to measure changes, plus the time interval between psychiatrist and patient ratings, the coincidence in ratings, if that is what it is, seems remarkable. It could not have occurred without a strong feeling among the majority of both groups of respondents that some change for the better, however minimal we do not know, had taken place.

Areas of disagreement thus largely concern patients self-rated, or rated by the psychiatrists, as unimproved or uncertain:

Fifty-seven of 81 cases (70 per cent) rated by the psychiatrist as unimproved were subsequently rated by patients as recovered or improved.

Sixty-four of 96 cases (67 per cent) rated by the psychiatrist as uncertain were subsequently rated by patients as recovered or improved.

Forty-two of 61 cases (70 per cent) not rated by the psychiatrist were subsequently rated by patients as recovered or improved.

Twenty per cent of the patients were rated "uncertain" or not rated at all, by the psychiatrists, as against 6 per cent in these categories for patient ratings.

On the other hand, two-thirds of the patients self-rated as worse at follow-up, and 80 per cent of those who were uncertain, had been listed as recovered or improved by the psychiatrist.

Of the 98 patients who saw no change in their mental health status, 45 had been considered recovered or improved by their psychiatrists, while 17 were rated unimproved. For this category of patient response the psychiatrists reported relatively more uncertainty or non-response to the question than for any of the other categories. What distinguishes this group from those who said they were worse or uncertain is not readily apparent from our data although there is some indication that certain types of problems—e.g., alcoholism, sexual abnormality or maladjustment, obesity—account for a disproportionate share of patients rating their problem as unchanged.

If we accept at face value the patients' self-ratings of mental status subsequent to psychiatric consultation or treatment, we observe, then, a core group of about 1 in 5 who feel unchanged, uncertain or in some cases worse.

Analysis thus far has revealed no common denominator which might have predicted failure in the face of 4 to 1 odds in favor of improvement.

Diagnosis, for example, is hardly a clue. Those with psychophysiological diagnoses do seem harder to reach, psychiatrically, but they account for only about 2 per cent of our cases. And although 20 per cent of all patients were diagnosed as psychotic, these are not the people who later reported themselves unimproved. In fact, the three classifications which together account for 86 per cent of adult diagnoses—psychoses, neuroses, and personality disorders—each show on self-rating exactly 20 per cent in the unimproved-uncertain categories. Although the terms psychotic and psychoneurotic are frequently used elsewhere to differentiate between major and minor mental or emotional illness, no such clear distinction seems to derive from the diagnostic designations used for our project patients.

Compared with diagnosis, the prognosis listed for adult patients is somewhat more predictive of subsequent self-ratings (table 2). Forty per cent of those with unfavorable prognosis failed to report improvement, compared with only 12 per cent of those given a favorable prognosis. The other 60 per cent of the cases of unfavorable

TABLE 2.—Psychiatrists' Prognosis vs. Subsequent
Patient Self-Ratings of Health Status

Psychiatrist Prognosis	Total	Patient Subsequent Self-Rating	
		Recovered-Improved	Same, Worse, Uncertain
	%	%	%
Adults			
Favorable	100	88	12
Unfavorable	100	60	40
Uncertain	100	75	25
Children			
Favorable	100	88	12
Unfavorable	100	86	14
Uncertain	100	82	18

prognosis, however, did report improvement. For children, prognosis proved completely negative: the percentage reported recovered or improved was the same regardless of whether the prognosis had been favorable or unfavorable.

What about amount of treatment? (See table 3.) Does this seem to influence the ratings? To an extent, yes, but here we encounter the egg-chicken type of riddle: Which came first—the appraisal or the amount of treatment? Some patients stop treatment because they have improved; others because they have not.

Twenty-four per cent of our patients with 6-14 treatments reported no improvement, compared with 15 per cent of those with 15 or more visits. Did more of those in the latter group improve because of the additional treatment? Or were they in this category because they were improving, while those who were discouraged had a greater tendency to drop out? Would more of those in the 6-14 visit category have improved, with additional treatment? We have no answer.

TABLE 3.—Patient Appraisals of Mental Health,
by Amount of Treatment

Patient Appraisal of Mental Health Status	Number of Project Visits			Patients with Post-Project Treatment
	1-5	6-14	15	
	%	%	%	%
Recovered	25	16	13	12
Greatly Improved	34	32	39	43
Somewhat Improved	21	28	33	30
Same	15	16	9	9
Worse	3	3	2	3
Uncertain	2	5	4	3
Total	100	100	100	100

Patients who returned for fewer than 6 sessions under the project, comprising about a quarter of the group, provided much more encouraging news of themselves than could have been foreseen on the basis of their brief project experience. Psychiatrists were generally uncertain or pessimistic about them, reporting improvement in only 46 per cent—quite a contrast to the improvement generally reported for most patients. The self-ratings of this group are therefore an important result of the follow-up study, with 3 out of 5 claiming recovery or great improvement, another fifth somewhat improved, and only 20 per cent unimproved or uncertain. This group on self-rating claimed the highest percentage of recovery, whereas the psychiatrists had assigned this distinction to the patients with 6-14 visits (table 4).

TABLE 4.—Psychiatrist Appraisal vs. Subsequent Patient Self-Appraisal, by Amount of Project Treatment

	Number of Project Visits					
	1-5		6-14		15	
	Appraisal by Psychiatrist Patient		Appraisal by Psychiatrist Patient		Appraisal by Psychiatrist Patient	
	%	%	%	%	%	%
Recovered	5	25	23	16	7	13
Improved	41	55	55	60	78	72
Unimproved-Uncertain	54	20	22	24	15	15
	—	—	—	—	—	—
Total	100	100	100	100	100	100

In reviewing these figures, it should be remembered that the general similarity between the distribution of psychiatrist and patient ratings, for patients with more than 5 project visits, does not necessarily apply to individual cases. As shown in table 1, over half the patients later self-classified as unimproved or uncertain, had been considered improved by psychiatrists, while most patients classified as unimproved by psychiatrists subsequently rated themselves as improved.

Indeed, the more one studies subgroups of patients or individual cases, the more one is convinced of the futility of generalizations in this field of emotional or mental illness. The available data do not permit classification of our patients into "types" who could have been expected to react in any predetermined way as might have been the case if they had, say, measles. We have 60 to 75 variables listed for each patient, none of which occur in the same combination more than once. Each patient's background and history, the psychiatrist he chooses, the problem he presents, the treatment he receives, affect the outcome of treatment. If any pattern seems to emerge from studies of sub-groups of patients (and usually none does!)—there is always an important minority of cases which do not fit the pattern. Thus all our studies of different variables produce none which, in the project for our patients, could have been considered predictive for the course of illness in individual cases.

We can make the gross prediction that 4 out of 5 patients appearing for this kind of treatment will probably feel or report some degree of improvement 2 or 3 years later; but we cannot identify that 5th patient—the one who will feel the same, worse or uncertain of his condition. Neither, apparently, can the psychiatrists.

IMPRESSIONS

The process of attempting judgments on the value of the limited treatment provided by our project inevitably involves unanswerable questions such as what would be the alternative, what is success in treatment, is it fair to judge short-term therapy given by long-term-oriented therapists, to what extent are patient evaluations believable, to what extent would these evaluations have varied if treatment had not been made available?

In a sense, it seems foolish even to argue the effectiveness of abbreviated treatment. Aside from the implication that number of treatments is the factor differentiating between success and failure —a point which has eluded scientific substantiation—there is the practical question as to whether limitless therapy, even if preferable, is the appropriate base for comparison. Certainly, for most potential patients, it is not. The factor of expense usually precludes long elective treatment, whether financed individually or by insurance companies (which, where they cover ambulatory psychiatry at all, are increasingly tending toward limiting the amount covered). The shortage of psychiatric treatment time in many areas is another factor eliminating the option of long intensive individual treatment for all but a small percentage of patients in need of treatment.

Thus, although there is evidently enough effective (cash) demand for long-term treatment to occupy a good share of the time of privately-practicing psychiatrists, thereby permitting indulgence of their preference for the long-term approach, the choice for most patients will be limited individual therapy, group therapy, or no therapy.

It follows that limited therapy *must* be effective for the majority of ambulatory patients. Perhaps this means setting standards for effectiveness at levels which brief therapy can realistically hope to achieve. Perhaps it even means that if the patient thinks he is recovered, greatly improved, or somewhat improved—he may very well be, even though he might also be a continuing candidate for occasional "booster" sessions. If this is a feasible working hypothesis, and if we can ignore the question as to whether long intensive therapy might have been more beneficial in some ways, we may conclude that even the limited treatment afforded by the project was effective.

Despite the fact that it was rendered by long-term oriented thera-pists, and despite our inability to take objective measurements, there were impressive areas of agreement by psychiatrists and patients as to improvement. Psychiatrists, notwithstanding their predilection for "exploration," "reconstruction," "insight," in preference to "sup-portive" measures, "crisis" therapy, relief of "acute symptoms," generally saw improvement in response to any amount of treat-ment beyond 5 visits. Over half the patients reported recovery or great improvement, while another 28 per cent claimed at least some improvement. More than 90 per cent thought the project worth-while, although many would have preferred longer benefits.

A number of patients credited improvement to factors other than treatment, but in general there was enthusiasm rather than skep-ticism for psychiatry, with reservations directed more toward the treatment methods of individual psychiatrists.

If one of the objectives of ambulatory psychiatric treatment is to avoid hospitalization, the project was apparently successful in this respect. Only 4 per cent of the respondents to our follow-up survey stated that they had been hospitalized subsequent to their project treatment. Of these, half had also been hospitalized during the project operating period. Whether we can fairly credit this find-ing to preventive psychiatry and to the project for making it avail-able, we do not know. We have occasional comments indicating that a preventive role was indeed played by the project. On the other hand, our data tend to show that most patients were not suffering from a major mental illness; 20 per cent were diagnosed as psychot-ic, but there is no positive evidence yet that even this diagnosis was necessarily equated, in psychiatrists' thinking, with serious illness. Evaluation of the avoidance of hospitalization requires further study.

Also warranting further study would be the patients who were not rated improved either by psychiatrists or on self-appraisal at time of follow-up. Since the two classifications did not coincide—those rated unimproved by psychiatrists tended to rate themselves im-proved, while the majority of the patients who failed to note any im-provement had been considered improved by their psychiatrists—much might be learned by further investigation. From a humane standpoint, too, it would be desirable to learn whether help of some kind could be advised for the 20 per cent of patients who feel the same, worse, or uncertain since their project contact.

The full story as to what this project to test insurability meant to individual patients cannot be fathomed. Many appreciative comments were received, as well as some which reflected perplexity. The interest of the majority extends beyond their own experience, to that of fellow-patients: Three out of five, in answer to a question, requested a copy of the report on the follow-up study in which they were cooperating.

Suggestions for change in the program most frequently concerned increased coverage. The belief of practicing psychiatrists that long-term therapy is the usual treatment of choice, certainly communicated itself to many patients. Still, the positive values of the coverage as offered must be acknowledged:

It satisfied the acute needs of a large proportion of patients.

It provided, for many patients, the only alternative to no treatment.

It drew into treatment patients who had been procrastinating because of timidity or misconceptions—e.g., the notion that private treatment necessarily involves intensive, extensive analysis.

It provided a learning experience for psychiatrists willing to experiment with treatment concepts foreign to their usual procedure with private patients.

The plan of insurance coverage now being offered by Group Health Insurance provides a further advantage not available under the project: Benefits are annually renewable, thus permitting "booster" sessions for patients requiring spaced supportive therapy.

Historical-Comparative and Experimental Roots of Short-Term Therapy

JULES H. MASSERMAN, M.D.

(Editor's Note: The understanding of the nature of short-term psychotherapy requires a broad vista with historical and experimental perspectives. Historically, men, from earliest times, have labored to overcome stress, evolving techniques for survival that have been passed along to succeeding generations. These include: (1) technical mastery of the physical universe, (2) collaborative friendships, and (3) organization of a transcendent system of beliefs. Most of the methods we employ today not only have their counterparts in, but are identical with the threefold devices employed by our forebears. Out of early modes of dealing with human misery systems of psychotherapy have evolved. Experimentally we may approach the dynamics of what goes on in psychotherapy in a more or less objective way. We may, for example, induce experimental neuroses and then attempt to obviate them by various means: environmental manipulation, the establishing of a trusting relationship, the use of drugs, etc. Thus we may gain an understanding of the forces that produce, and the forces that allay conflict. Examples from the experimental laboratory are detailed by Dr. Masserman. In a somewhat lighter vein, he comments on a number of questions related to short-term therapy.)

In a lecture I once delivered, the Chairman, in a rather complimentary prologue, mentioned that some of my books had been translated into various languages. He then turned to me to say, "and, Jules, if you'll give me the right, I'll also translate them into English." Which brings up a rather important point: namely, that we do attempt to conceal ignorance by jargon or euphemisms in order to gloss over large hiatuses in knowledge and conceptualization. But our challenge is that if we cannot make ourselves clear in the rich heritage of our very expressive and simple English tongue, we probably do not know what we're talking about.

To illustrate, the title of this series is "Short-Term Psychotherapy," with, I suppose, the implication as to what goes on in the various schools. But schools are for minnows and not for scientists who, hopefully, have somewhat broader perspectives of the universe. In

hazy issues we are often tempted to go back to the insight and
clarity of the Greeks. Before we can define short-term psychotherapy, we must ask: "What is psychotherapy?"

Since in psychiatry we deal in so many myths, you may remember that Psyche was the name of a lovely Greek maiden who had
an affair with a mysterious midnight lover until, contrary to their
initial agreement, she one night lit a candle and discovered that he
was none other than the god Cupid. For this transgression she was
condemned by gods and men alike. In this lovely fable, the intellect
or psyche, deriving its inspiration from love, could remain happy
were it not for its nagging spirit of research—something Eve could
have told Psyche about.

But in modern science we must not live only in poetry; we must
deal with processes and transactions, rather than myths referred to
as "psyche," or "mind," or psychopathology, which translated as "a
diseased abstraction." Again, simply change "mind" from a mean-
ingless noun to an operational phrase, and, lo, Anglo-Saxon makes
more sense than Greek. Thus, if we "put our mind" to something,
we're talking about "perception and attention," if we "keep in mind"
something, we're talking about the unique property that living
things have of processing, storing and cross-indexing information
at a level of complexity, though not speed, far greater than any calculating machine; and if we "mind somebody," we're talking about
the whole social process, and the inheritance of culture. And so
"mind" becomes, in the last analysis, a study of behavior: i.e., we
know someone's "mind" only by the way he adapts to his physical
and cultural milieu. In this connection, "therapy" is another highly
significant word, which in its Greek origin, simply means service;
ergo what we really mean by psychotherapy is the service which
one human being can render another, by whatever modality, by
whatever techniques, and in whatever culture the two happen to
coexist.

But in this sense the parameters of brief or long may have nothing to do with the effectiveness of the service. For example, the
more training and experience one acquires as a surgeon, the more
rapid and skillful the operations. In fact, psychotherapy and surgery
can well be compared in an operational sense; in both, the physician first establishes confidence, then surveys the patient's life to
delimit the probable locale of the difficulty. One then explores, but
gently, and *without unnecessary and damaging dissection,* until
the disease process is found. The trouble may have been a con-
genital mistake, a postnatal injury or insult to the tissues, or a more

recent pathologic result of stress or trauma. In any case, one cor-
rects what one can and then, as rapidly, as gently and as skillfully
as possible, reapproximates the tissues so that there will be no wide
open wound which may never heal or, at best, will leave a healed
scar. Both the surgeon and the psychotherapist use nature's reparative powers, and gently help the spontaneous regrowth and readap-
tation of the individual, so that he may recover personal function
and social happiness by every device possible. A good degree of
directiveness is essential in both specialties. Once, in a talk to a
group of Rogerian "non-directive" therapists, I made a terrible slip
of the tongue, and referred to Roger's system as non-corrective therapy. But, in reality, good therapy is about as "non-directive" as good
surgery, and a broad and sophisticated perspective is essential in
making our directiveness as useful as possible.

When we face the broad problems in shortening therapy, there
are a number of approaches that are useful, providing that we
avoid employing biased data to reconfirm our prejudices—a procedure the logical fallacy of which is dealt with mathematically in
the Godel hypothesis. The three basic areas are the historical, the
comparative and the experimental. First, history furnishes a perspective on one's current thought; second, comparison broadens it;
and third, experiment subjects one's ever-contingent postulates to
the disconcerting exeprience of controlled data.

A HISTORICAL-COMPARATIVE REVIEW

Many psychiatrists, despite a professed humility, sometimes give
the impression that in their oracular interpretations of human nature, they commune directly with a god who, somehow, strongly
resembles the psychiatrist. I propose, in all sincerity, that we actually have access to only very mortal wisdoms, and though these
may have been gathered through many ages, I am afraid we sometimes stultify and render them less clear by our formulations,
although mercifully not in our practice. This will be precisely my
theme—that literally, we all labor in a common cause with common techniques derived from centuries of common human experience, and in short-term therapy we certainly employ these techniques.

It is somewhat startling, but it may very well be true that most
of the techniques we use to help ill and troubled human beings can
be summarized under three headings. Forgive me if these sound
somewhat oversimplified, but in a field where there has been so
much overobfuscation, oversimplification is a welcome relief. May

I propose that we can attempt to control our universe in only three ways? First, we can try to control material things, and so reassert our technical mastery of the physical universe. Second, we can co-operate with our fellow human beings and so establish collaborative friendships. Or, third, we can resort to a transcendental system of beliefs, whether we call it science, philosophy, metaphysics, or theology, and so find order and security in an otherwise chaotic universe. That these three methods have been used ever since human life originated, is an historically demonstrable statement. But we have a peculiar attitude toward history, particularly in our current American culture. H. J. Muller has perhaps expressed it most trenchantly in his aphorism that, here in America, our concept of history seems to be confined to the minutes of the last board meeting, and that we neglect the precious lessons not only of half a million years of human development, but of three billion years of biological evolution.

If we now read the earliest records of humanity, the three principles becomes almost immediately apparent. Let us take the oldest record we have of human behavior, say the Mousterian caves of fifty thousand years ago. These primitive people, although equipped with the same brain potential and all of the physical endowments we have today, had only their crude stone axes, scrapers, throwing darts and so on with which to manipulate the universe. At the same time, they had already reached a high level of social development and were gregarious and friendly. They lived in caves, not only in familial groups of enforced friendships, but also in gatherings of clans and tribes. They joined in common endeavors with apportioned roles and organizations. They apparently took care of their aged; they certainly took care of their children or else we would not be here to philosophize about it all. They used, then, the two principal techniques we still use today: the employment of mechanical skills, and the utilization of human communication and fellowship. But, also, a third: a system of beliefs not only in a tomorrow but in a universal order and in a hereafter. How do we know all this? We have, for example, those, by our standards, unlovely but unforgettable little stone statuettes called Paleolithic Venuses, with physical features of unmistakably exaggerated womanhood and motherhood. What do they represent? They are really a kind of tribute to universal gentleness, a form of mother worship epitomized by the ancient goddesses Ishtar, Isis and all the other beneficent mothers of men. In addition to these, we find works of art expressing not only man's creative strivings, but also a trust in man's capacity to determine his own future. You have read of the wonderful drawings and paintings in the caves of Altamira in Spain and Lascaux in France, in which the tribal hunt was represented. There is no deliberate cruelty in these pictographs; they simply showed human beings in a common endeavor for the good of the clan. But they were also placed in alcoves very much like primitive chapels, in remote regions of the common cave, and surrounded by articles of worship. Thus, through form and ritual, they represented man's dreams and hopes in a sense that, if he depicted the future in the poetry of his own imagination, he could thereby control it. L. S. B. Leakey, curator of the Coryndon Memorial Museum in Nairobi, describes similar paintings possibly a quarter of a million years old in the Olduvai Gorge of Africa.

Have we learned very much since then? It seems that the basic principle by which men live, by which they obtain security and which we now employ in what we call psychotherapy, had already been determined. You can very well imagaine a Neanderthal man, troubled or lost, coming home to the cave, being accepted into a society of his fellowmen, being reassigned a role and feeling once again secure—provided, of course, that he fitted into the technological and cultural requirements in the organization of his society, participated in its philosophy and, if you will, in its primitive theological-religious system.

By the time of ancient Egypt many of these techniques had achieved a high degree of reliability. You came to the Temple when you were ill or frightened. There you went through certain rituals which gave you a feeling of mastering physical objects. At the same time, you met with people whose problems were similar to yours and you consulted with them. Also, and most important, you found a haven of refuge in a hospice or "hospital," a special place of healing connected with the Temple. There you were fed and given drugs that "tranquilized," after which you fell into a gentle sleep. During that sleep you had dreams which you did not understand but which the priest explained to you. He then told you what troubled your soul. He also gave you certain kinds of advice which, if followed, would purportedly not only solve your problems here on earth but also in heaven. And so the Egyptians were a very happy people because they had encompassed their difficulties not only here on earth but, through the authority of their bible called the Book of the Dead, in a life hereafter.

By the time we come to the Greeks, there is hardly a technique that we use today that wasn't used in what might be called the

Golden Era of Humanitarian Psychiatry. A Greek who was really troubled, who had difficulty with his family, with his business, with his associates or with his systems of thought, would first of all leave the place where his difficulties had become unbearable. He would repair to a temple of peace called an Asclepiad Sanatorium. This temple of healing was located in some remote region away from trade, war, and stress, in a salubrious climate among beautiful surroundings; it was a haven of refuge from the difficulties and conflicts of daily living.

In them was practiced all that was best, not only from the standpoint of science, but from the standpoint of humanitarian understanding. I have already mentioned that the hospitals were located in places that would be appealing to almost anyone who wished once again to experience aesthetic delight in the communal love of nature. But this was only the beginning. The troubled pilgrim was met not by a secretary or a receptionist, but by a high priest or priestess, representing an authoritative parental welcoming of the prodigal son returning home, where direct and immediate comfort was offered. For example, much attention was paid to the patient's diet: he was fed exceedingly well. Care was taken of his ablutions; he was bathed and he was massaged. He was put to bed to rest, and given medicine to reduce his anxiety. The drugs were called "nepenthics" rather than "ataractics," and there was no technical talk of physiotherapy, balneotherapy, pharmacotherapy, etc.—nevertheless, the purposes were pretty much the same and the effects all the greater.

What, then, was happening to this troubled human being who wanted to escape from the responsibilities and sorrows of adult life? He was literally welcomed back home and permitted to become once again a dependent, secure child, given a good deal of comfort and reassurance and warmth and human acceptance. This, it is true, we still try to do, although some of us, busy with "deeper techniques," very often leave these essential first steps to others. The Greeks, however, were also a great deal wiser than we with regard to the later stages of therapy. They recognized that a precipitate retreat to infantile dependence, though a necessary stage of gathering strength for a new base of operations, may in itself become an escape and a handicap. Therefore, instead of making this mistake (one we often make now in our so-called "anaclitic" therapy in which we literally infantilize the patient indefinitely, or in our misuse of the analytic couch where people may become fixed in a horizontal position for a baby-sit of five or six years, or in various

other kinds of retreats form reality) the Greeks almost immediately began to use a rehabilitative program designed to restore the patient as soon as possible to social functioning. As an example of one of many methods, they began to use what has always been a universal form of communication: music. Now music is one of the most meaningful and transcendent kinds of communication. It mobilizes a sense of belongingness in an orderly universe, a sense of harmony, a progression toward logical solution, a working together through blended effort and a reaching for aesthetic perfection. The Greeks knew this well, and made it part of their philosophy; for example, the Pythagoreans employed numbers and music as the basis of life and reality. And so the patient, before he regressed too deeply, was called back by the harmonious strains of music to more mature thoughts and communications. Music was also combined with the dance and with calesthenics through which the patient could join and renew contact with his fellow human beings.

And much else was done. For example, the patient's personal problems might be acted out in the wonderful plays written by Aeschylus, Euripedes or Aristophanes, in which the most fundamental of human relationships were acted out, such as those of Oedipus, Narcissus, and Medea. These human relationships are deathless and therefore give the plays, even today, their poignant meaning. But the Greeks approached them in a more dynamic fashion than we do because they did not simply sit and watch and criticize. They joined in. There was a chorus; the actor and the audience were very much more in communication and even interchangeable, and so each person felt as though he were acting out each human tragedy and comedy and reaching his own solutions by these vicarious means. Today we call it psychodrama, or associative drama, or the spontaneity stage, or whatnot. Is there anything new in it? As a matter of fact, in Aristophanes' "The Clouds," there is a wonderful scene in which a troubled human being comes to the philosopher, Socrates. Strepsiades, the patient, is told to lie on the couch, to think completely freely and thereby to reach an understanding of his problems by this apparently indirect technique. But Strepsiades doesn't know exactly what his troubles are, except that he doesn't sleep well nights and is tense and anxious. Socrates directs him not to lie on the floor, but on the couch (*klinikos*) and then simply to *say anything that comes into his mind!* Strepsiades begins to talk, of all things, about the moon, and Socrates says in effect: "That's all right, go ahead and talk about the moon if you want to." And it turns out through a series of free associations (circa

390 B.C.) that this brings to mind the fantasy that if Strepsiades could only capture the moon and put it in his pocket, his financial problems might be solved, for if the moon wouldn't wax and wane, the first of the month could be prevented from making its appearance and Strepsiades wouldn't have any debts to pay. And thus it was that the problem was "analyzed" and "insight" acquired; unfortunately, then as now, there was no mention of a cure.

More seriously, the Greeks also acknowledged that there are certain "Divine" areas of thought that should not be desecrated, and even they, scientists that they were, made Socrates drink the hemlock because he dared to question the power of the gods. They recognized that human beings must have beliefs and systems, and whether or not they glorified what was best in humanity, these systems must be respected and not desecrated. They therefore placed their temples of healing next to temples of religion and thereby added the powerful tools of joint beliefs, joint rituals and joint appeals to beneficent Deities—something we do not always do now. And when the patient left the sanitarium, the Greek physician, being humanitarian, was fully willing to collaborate in directing his patient for advice and guidance to the priest of his own choice in mundane as well as heavenly matters. Have we improved on anything much since then?

Then, during the Middle Ages, the Church offered a haven of refuge that humanity sorely needed as a retreat from the difficulties of a very conflicted world. The Church was a center of learning and so also of medicine, and offered a haven of security to which all could adhere. It had to protect its system, of course, and sometimes it was severe and ruthless in protecting its prerogatives, but all churches of various ctaegories and denominations are alive today simply because they fill fundamental needs which will persist as long as men remain human.

When, only three centuries ago, psychotherapy began to pretend to become "scientific," it is interesting that the first two self-designated mental healers were actually downright quacks. The earlier of these, who proclaimed that he could cure a human being without the aid of divine intervention was a chap by the name of Greatrakes the Stroaker, who lived in the seventeenth century. He claimed to stroke (stroake) people in such a way that somehow the noxious humors in their bodies would be forced out of their extremities. During this post-Cromwellian era, he had thousands of people flocking to his clinic to be stroked. Why were they there? Because in a difficult world where many encounters were murderous rather

than gentle, they found somebody who supposedly knew what he was doing, who would pat and comfort them much as though they were children. They would find fellow believers in his system, which was the "science" of the day. With their common belief, their common group activity and a jointly revered "healer," everyone was helped. And so do thousands of people who believe in chiropractic, or osteopathy, or Swedish massage, or Yogi exercises, or yogurt diet, obtain a great deal of comfort from going for their respective brands of "stroaking." Not because the massage or the "adjustments" or the baths or the calisthenics or the rotting proteins have anything to do with the cure, but because the faithful are very much like troubled children who are hurt and frightened, and whom mother reassures and pets and plays with and feeds until they feel better.

A century and a quarter later there lived the founder of a great many of our modern therapeutic techniques—another quack by the name of Anton Mesmer. He, too, had his "science." (Incidentally, I wonder what people will think of our psychotherapeutic "science" a hundred years from now?) What Mesmer noticed, however, was that people could affect each other at a distance; that is, when he himself made certain movements with his hands, he could influence others without touching them. Now, what forces act at a distance? There were only two known at the time: gravity and magnetism. So Mesmer gravely figured that there must be a kind of animal magnetism that had to do with touching an object and then waving one's hands and thus producing remote effects. Since the same sort of gravity-magnetism seemed to set the planets in their course, naturally his so-called science was also connected with the influence of the planets on people, i.e., astrology. (For that matter, Kepler, one of the greatest astronomers of all time, was also an astrologist.) Thus did Mesmer set up a system which was highly successful therapeutically. Under Mesmeric spells, people would fall into trances, dream, have highly emotional reactions, and wake claiming to feel not only very much better, but exhilarated and euphoric.

Mesmer undeniably entranced a great many influential people, and was therefore, for a time, highly successful and fashionable. In view of our highly organized cults of the present day, it is amusing to recall that there were international Mesmeric societies; with international Journals of Mesmerism. If you were properly Mesmerized by a properly Mesmerized person, and you had a certain number of controlled Mesmeric sessions, you could enter the local Mesmeric Society, after which you were an accredited Mesmerist. Then you could treat people according to the Rules; however, if you sought new and better methods, there was a good deal of discussion about your loyalty and therefore your professional qualifications. Of course, Mesmer was quite sincere in his theories, and felt himself martyred by the medical men of the day, who, along with Benjamin Franklin, had called him a quack. Indeed, he died convinced that he had discovered a universal System of Healing—and so he had, in the sense that he had once again tapped a basic human yearning for encounter and relationship. Not "animal magnetism" (later called hypnotism) but the kind of communication that had been practiced in the temples of Egypt. There, too, in a setting of diminished light, with a central altar upon which everybody was concentrated, the priest had intoned a repetitious, monotonous, rhythmic lullaby known to all mothers of troubled children who need reassurance and rest in a trusting security. Intuitively, when we are approached by troubled people, we still talk in this kind of soothing, monotonous, cadenced tone of voice. Predictably also, Mesmer's practice grew to such proportions that he couldn't give individual attention to every patient; thus, he began to deal with them in groups. Mesmer's patients would form a circle, hold hands, feel overpowered by the "magnetism," fall into trances, have an intensive "corrective emotional experience" and leave praising the system and spreading the Mesmeric gospel.

From Mesmer, there arose a great many of the systems that we can now call by their modern names. First, is the wearing of "magnetic belts." Have you any idea of how many belts are sold in the U.S.A. by mail order houses and others? Hundreds of thousands of people still wear this kind of "magnetized" diaper around their middle beneath their clothes and swear that it cures all sorts of diseases.

Second, we have a current school of hypnotists who, in their theorizing if not in their practice, try to avoid the simple fact that people like to be comforted, like to feel safe, like to feel as if they are being treated by a magically wise and powerful person; consequently, some professional hypnotists themselves seem to operate in a sort of trance. In this connection, one of the greatest of hynotists, a physician by the name of Bernheim who taught Freud, wrote perhaps one of the most penetrating commentaries on hypnotism. Cautioned Bernheim: "It's a darn good hypnotist that knows who's hypnotizing whom."

A third derivative of Mesmerism is the Christian Science Church, which invokes some of the most powerful principles of human behavior known to psychiatry. These include first, a system of transcendent beliefs, not only religious but purportedly "scientific"—the two most powerful systems of thought. Second, the Church offers opportunities for an almost universal kinship: three thousand Churches of Christ Scientists, so that one can hardly feel alone anywhere in the western world. Third, the Church offers a very simple, repetitious and assertive dogma, which resembles some aspects of analytic therapy in being completely self-confident in its obscurity. The services consist of readings from Mary Baker Eddy, endlessly reiterated, so that if one learns a few key phrases, he knows all of it. Furthermore, think of the vast power with which Christian Science healers proudly believe they are endowed. I have to see and work with people in order to do something with them in my practice. But then I am a psychiatrist and a psychoanalyst and not a Christian Scientist, who can heal at any distance with what is apparently a divine power. This, of course, is comforting to all concerned but me. Nevertheless, a great many lost, troubled, lonesome human beings join not only Christian Scientist churches but many organizations with similar beliefs and practices and thereby find precious comfort and security. No one can deny the tragedies that can result from the misapplication of such doctrines, but no one can gainsay how much comfort can also be given to hundreds of thousands of people. And as humanitarian psychiatrists, we can neither neglect nor deny anything that concerns our patients.

But there is another derivative of Mesmerism that seems at first sight almost completely scientific: modern-day psychoanalysis. And yet its evolution, too, though a long story and a somewhat discursive one, can be summarized for our present purposes in the light of what we have said. Freud began by using hynotism to command his patients to tell him what was troubling them—i.e., the directed confessional. But since many patients resented this, Freud granted his patients greater freedom, and simply invited them to say anything and everything that came to their minds without fear of condemnation or judgment. And so, of course, they would tell him, often with appropriate histrionics, about what they wanted him to think troubled them. Freud called this process "catharsis," in the sense of ridding the mind of something noxious, and "abreaction" when the emotionality was intense and therefore presumably corrective. And, of course, some patients got better because they thought that here was a man who was interested and understanding, but at the same time not judgmental or punitive; ergo they had, in effect, found a friend. But Freud went on from this to a deeper recognition: namely, that these people must have been chronically troubled long before the arrival of the trivial happenings to which they attributed their current difficulties; in other words, they must have been sensitized by preceding unfortunate experiences, perhaps in childhood. It did, in fact, become apparent that most patients began to talk about their adolescence and eventually their childhood, in the light of events that had rendered them particularly sensitive to hurts and rejections and to corresponding sorrows in later life. Many patients also began to talk about their family relationships and certain unfortunate insecurities, jealousies and conflicts in that sphere. Thus, for a time psychoanalysis consisted of an attempt to recall and reconstruct childhood "traumas," particularly the so-called "Oedipus complex" and other "libidinal conflicts."

Then Freud also began to recognize something that every minister, physician or other advisor had implicitly observed; that the patient inevitably places the therapist in the role of some sort of parental surrogate. The patient thus attributes to the therapist certain characteristics that he does not necessarily possess, and then treats him as a mother, rival, erotic object, a source of suspicion, a protector who must look after the patient indefinitely, or in various other roles involved in the patient's interpersonal relationships. Therapeutically, once the patient recognizes the artificial positions into which he forces not only the therapist but various other people in his life, he may correct these interpersonal misinterpretations by the use of a more realistic approach. Freud called this "transference analysis," by which he simply meant that the patient transfers to his therapist, whether that therapist be a physician, a priest, a friend, a "Dutch uncle," a corner druggist or a hospital aide, certain important human relationships meaningful to the patient and which the therapist should understand and help to correct. This is about where Freud stopped, but by this time he had already rediscovered and reformulated (sometimes unnecessarily fancifully and obscurely) various basic principles of human behavior and clinical therapy that have been operative throughout the ages—and, of course, need still be applied if any form of treatment, including psychoanalysis, is to be effective.

Since then, of course, we psychiatrists have employed a great many other approaches, none of them new. We have rediscovered the efficacy of re-establishing control of the material universe through "occupational" therapy, job training, and so on. We have rediscovered the necessity of progressive social rehabilitations through making a hospital not a place apart from the rest of the universe, but an intimate part of the community. And, finally, we have rediscovered the intimate relationships between psychiatry and the various religious systems. In our own peculiar American way, we immediately commercialized this so that there are now Institutes of Psychiatry and Religion, richly endowed, of course, by our government, but which I am afraid might again become over-institutionalized to the extent whereby they may lose the humanitarian substrata on which they were founded.

Does this brief review give us any feel of the roots of "humanitarian" psychotherapy? I hope so. There is one difficulty with it: we have been able to look briefly at only a skeletal outline, and as I have remarked elsewhere, only an archeologist can be really involved in skeletons. But we can clothe the skeleton with the living tissues of our own human experience, and render it alive and vibrant. Thus all of us from all walks of life may recognize that in our love of our fellowmen we have all, in our dealings with each other, also always been humanitarian psychiatrists.

THE EXPERIMENTAL ANALYSES OF PSYCHOTHERAPY

But there is yet one more heuristic root to the basic understanding of the clinical dynamics of short-term psychotherapy; namely, the experimental. There is one incontrovertible advantage to laboratory work: if one asks intelligent questions, the answers one gets from electrons, from chemical compounds and from animals, though bewilderingly more complex in that order, are nevertheless relatively operational and thereby less subject to obfuscation by a prejudiced observer. The problem is, then, to put the answers in their larger contexts—a task particularly difficult in the vast sciences of behavior. But in this context let us review some of the factual data on experimentally induced deviations of animal behavior.

Shenger-Krestovnikova, one of Pavlov's students, first demonstrated in 1913 that persistent aberrations of conduct can be induced in dogs by subjecting them to adaptational stresses beyond their integrative capacities ("ego span"); interestingly it was Pavlov himself who advocated the use of bromides as the sole therapy of such "experimental neuroses." This work was continued along orthodox Pavlovian lines in the United States by Gantt and extended to pigs and sheep by Liddell (Masserman, 1943).

Beginning some 25 years ago, my associates and I have been particularly interested in elaborating these studies and integrating them with clinical psychiatry (Masserman, 1953(b). Since our results have been reported in considerable detail elsewhere (Masserman, 1943; 1936-1950; 1948; 1953 (a,b,c,d); 1955, 1958, 1961), I shall note here only that we were able to confirm as "biodynamic principles" various fundamental analytic postulates such as: (1) the relationship of so-called instincts to basic physiologic needs, (2) the importance of individual experience in shaping later patterns of behavior, (3) the role of frustration in eliciting seekings for displaced or substitute satisfactions, and, finally, (4) the etiologic importance of motivational conflicts in causing deviations of animal behavior analogous to anxiety states, phobias, compulsions, somatic dysfunctions, regressions and even hallucinatory and delusional phenomena in man. Even more relevant to our present interests, however, were the many methods we tried of alleviating these experimental neuroses once they were established. Of those investigated, some eight general techniques were successful to varying degrees and in various combinations. In briefest summary, and with their clinical connotations mentioned only *pari passu,* they were these:

1. *Change of Milieu:* A neurotic animal given a prolonged rest (three to twelve months) in a favorable home environment nearly always showed a diminution in external evidences of anxiety, tension and in phobic-compulsive and regressive behavior. However, these deviant patterns reappeared when the animal was returned to the laboratory, even though it was not again subjected to a direct repetition of conflictual experiences. To draw a human analogy, a soldier with severe "combat neurosis" may appear "recovered" after a restful sojourn in a base hospital, but unless his unconscious attitudes are altered, his reactions to latent anxiety recur cumulatively when he is returned to the locale of his adaptive conflicts.

2. *Satiation of a Conflictful Need:* If a phobic inhibited animal which had refused food for two days was forcibly tube-fed so that its hunger was mitigated, its other neurotic manifestations correspondingly decreased. Hippocrates is reported by Soranus (perhaps apocryphally) to have utilized a parallel method in human psychotherapy. Hippocrates, it seems, was once called into consultation to treat a strange convulsive malady which was keeping a newly wed bride virginal. Discerning, after a private interview, that she was torn between strong sexual desires neatly balanced by fear of assuming an uxorial role, Hippocrates advised the husband "to light the torch of Hymen" forthwith and thereby satisfy one of her conflictful wishes. The results of the therapy are not recorded.

3. *Forced Solution:* A hungry neurotic cat was prevented from escaping from the apparatus and instead was brought mechanically closer and closer to the feeder until its head was almost in contact with a profusion of delectable pellets. Under such circumstances

some animals, despite their opposing fears, suddenly lunged for the food; thereafter, they needed lesser degrees of mechanical "persuasion" until their food-inhibition disappeared altogether, again carrying other neurotic generalizations with it. This method is a variation of the Hippocratic one mentioned above, but entails a narrower choice and greater degree of activity on the part of the patient. In some ways, the "therapy" is akin to pushing a boy afraid of water into a shallow pool. Depending on his capacities for re-integrating his experiences into new *Gestalten* (in analytic terms, his "ego strength"), he may find that there was, after all, no reason to fear—or he may go into a state of abject terror and thereafter hate not only water, but all pools, all water sports and all future therapists. Because of the latter eventuality, ruthless force is generally considered a dangerous method in dealing with neurotic anxieties.

4. *Example of Normal Behavior:* An inhibited, phobic animal paired for several weeks with one who responds normally in the experimental situation will show some diminution in its neurotic patterns, although never to the degree of complete "recovery." In like manner, problem children do better when they have opportunity to live with "normal" youngsters in an environment that favors "normality"—although more specific individual therapy is nearly always necessary to complete the "cure."

5. *Re-education by a Trusted Mentor:* As noted, a neurotic animal, perhaps by virtue of its regression to earlier patterns of relationship, becomes exceedingly dependent upon the experimenter for protection and care. If this trust is not violated, the latter may then retrain the animal by gentle steps: first, to take food from his hand; next, to accept food in the apparatus; then, to open the box while the experimenter merely hovers protectively; and, finally, to work the switch and feed as formerly without further "support" from the therapist. During its "rehabilitation," the animal not only re-explores and resolves its motivational conflicts, but also masters and dissipates the symbolic generalizations that spring from this nuclear "complex": i.e., its inhibitions, phobias, compulsions and other neurotic reactions. This, indeed, may be the paradigm for the basic processes in clinical psychotherapy. The neurotic patient channelizes his needs for help toward a therapist upon whom he transfers his dependent and other relationships. The therapist then utilizes this "transference" with optimal patience and wisdom to guide and support the patient as the latter re-examines his conflictful desires and fears, recognizes his previous misinterpretations of reality, and

essays new ways of living until he is sufficiently successful and confident to proceed on his own. Whether this be called re-education,
re-training, rehabilitation or psychoanalysis depends more on the
context of the problem, the necessity for thoroughness in anamnes-
tice review and symbolic analysis, and the art, skill and effectiveness in the utilization of the fantasied and actual interpersonal relationships involved, than on any fundamental differences in the
essential dynamics of the respective procedures.

6. *Physio-pharmacologic Methods:* As has thus far been indicated, some of the vectorial processes of psychotherapy can be isolated in principle and demonstrated operationally in the laboratory.
There remains, however, the fact that various physical methods
such as the use of drugs, electroshock and lobotomy have also
proved clinically useful in the treatment of certain behavior disorders. I can here give only the most cursory supplementary review
of further experiments dealing with this subject.

a. *Action of Drugs:* Preliminary tests of the effects of various
sedative, ataractic* and narcotic drugs on normal animals showed
that, in general, such drugs disorganized complex behavior patterns
while leaving relatively simple ones intact. Thus, in one series of
experiments an animal was taught in successive states (1) to open
a food box, (2) to respond to food-signals, including signs reading
FOOD or NO FOOD, (3) to operate the signal-switch, (4) to work
two switches a given number of times in a set order, and finally
(5) to traverse a difficult maze to reach one of the switches. If the
animal was then given a small dose of barbital, morphine, or alcohol, it would become incapable of solving the maze, but would still
work the food-switches properly; with larger doses, it could "remember" how to work only one switch; with still larger doses, earlier
stages of learning would also be disintegrated, until, finally, it lost
even the simple skill required to open the foodbox. Conversely, as
the animal recovered from its intoxication, its learned responses
were reconstituted in their original order. If the animal was then
made neurotic by an adaptational conflict, it developed a new set
of highly intricate and elaborate reactions; i.e., various inhibitions,
phobias, compulsions, somatic dysfunctions and sensorial disturbances. These, too, proved relatively more vulnerable to disintegration by the sedative drugs than did the simpler, preneurotic behavior

---

* A half decade of intensive experimentation has indicated in briefest
statement that most phenothiazine derivatives and related "ataractics" are
on the whole inferior to the bromides, barbiturates and alcohol in amelio-
rating experimental neuroses.

patterns, so that if a neurotic animal was given barbital or morphine,* its anxiety reactions and inhibitions significantly abated. In effect, instead of crouching tense and immobile in a far corner or showing panic at the feeding signals, it could respond to the latter by opening the box and feeding (in a somewhat groggy, but comparatively effective manner) as though, for the time being, its doubts and fears were wraiths forgotten.

b. *Drug Addiction:* In one variant of these studies in which alcohol was used as the nepenthic drug, the animals which experienced relief from neurotic tensions while partly intoxicated were later given an opportunity to choose between alcoholic and non-alcoholic drinks. To our surprise (and, it must be confessed, subdued delight) about half the neurotic animals in these experiments began to develop a most unfeline preference for alcohol, and in most cases this preference was sufficiently insistent and prolonged to warrant the term "addiction." Moreover, the induced dipsomania generally lasted until the animals' underlying neurosis was relieved by the dynamic methods of therapy described above. It would be redundant to discuss the human analogues to these experimental observations.

c. *Protective Effects:* In still another series of experiments we observed that the administration of hypnotic drugs (including alcohol) so dulled the perceptive and mnemonic capacities of animals that they were, while thus inebriated, relatively immune to the neurosis-producing effects of traumatic experiences. In this connection, it may be recalled that many a human being long ere this has been tempted, through subversive experience, to take a "bracer" before challenging some authority, getting married, flying a combat mission, or facing other presumed dangers.

d. *Effects of Cerebral Electroshock:* In briefest summary, we found that when the ordinary 60-cycle current usually employed clinically was passed through the brain of the animal, the resultant shock acted like an intoxicant drug to disintegrate complex and recently acquired patterns of behavior, whether these were "normal" or "neurotic." Unlike most drugs, however, electroshock produced permanent impairment of future behavioral efficiency, even though this could not be correlated with pathological changes in the brain detectable by present methods. Weaker or modified currents (i.e., the direct square-wave Leduc type) produced lesser degrees of deterioration in our animals, but also had less effect on their neurotic

---

* The phenothiazine derivatives and mono-amino oxidase inhibitors proved less effective (Masserman, 1962, 1959).

behavior. All in all, these experiments supported the growing conviction among psychiatrists that electroshock and other drastic
therapies may occasionally be useful in certain relatively recent and
acute psychoses, but that the cerebral damage they produce, however subtle, makes their indiscriminate use replete with temporarily
hidden cost and potential danger.

e. *Lobotomy, Topectomy, Thalamotomy:* Obviously, any cerebral
operation will (1) produce a transient general disorganization of
perceptive and reactive patterns, and (2) result in a more circumscribed hiatus in the patient's responsive capacities—both effects
being of possible therapeutic import in patients resistant to all other
forms of therapy. Indeed, recent studies by a number of workers,
especially Bard (1947), Pribram (private communication), Rioch,
Schreiner et al. (1953) and their respective associates, as master-
fully reviewed in a recent volume by Fulton (1951), have revealed
exciting new possibilities for altering basic patterns of behavior by
specific cerebral lesions. Thus, section of the head of the caudate
or under Area 13 in the posterior orbital gyrus may counteract otios-
ity and release spontaneity and responsive activity, although the
latter may sometimes take the form of vicious rage. Conversely,
lesions in the ventral thalamic-cinglate-hippocampal-amygdaloid
circuits of the visceral brain may tame and quiet even dangerously
aggressive behavior, though perhaps at the cost of peculiarly regressive patterns in which the animal tastes everything within reach
yet fails to learn from adverse experience. *However, the effects of
apparently identical lesions in different animals may vary with
the preceding experiences of each*—a circumstance that underlines
once again the necessity for dealing with each organism, from the
standpoint of both etiology and therapy, as an individual, dynamic
entity. In effect, each person behaves differently from every other
because (1) he was differently constituted at birth and (2) because he has had different experiences; clinically, then, he will
react uniquely to any given cerebral lesion and will also need rehabilitative therapy specially tailored to fit his frame and modes
of action, hide his defects, and best utilize his remaining capacities
for optimal adaptation.

MAN'S PRINCIPLE DISTINCTION FROM OTHER ANIMALS: HIS UNIQUE UR DEFENSES

These, then, are the leads culled from comparative and experimental psychology, rich in their implications of future contributions to clinical theory and practice. And yet, as we have seen,

some of us cling to a sacrosanct belief that whereas the organs, physiology, and nervous system of other animals are disconcertingly like ours, we differ from all other creatures so fundamentally that studies of their behavior are interestingly irrelevant to the problems of psychiatry. True, men differ from animals, but the differences consist mainly (a) in the complexity and versatility with which human beings elaborate both "normal" and "neurotic" behavior, and (b) in their possession of several transcendent articles of faith (axioms, beliefs, delusions, precepts, categorical imperatives—call them what you will) which animals, at least, never verbalize. I have dealt with these so-called Ur-defenses rather extensively elsewhere (Masserman, 1953 a & b); here I can merely name them as follows:

1. *The conviction of personal invulnerability, power and literal or vicarious immortality,* rooted in primary narcissism and never completely surrendered.

2. *The necessity of "faith in humanity,"* derived from the almost equally illogical assumption that because each child's mother presumably at one time loved and cherished him, the rest of mankind is assumed to be almost equally provident and indulgent. This expectation of survival through dependence, when combined with ancillary erotic yearnings, but seasoned with rivalries and mistrusts, determines many of our interpersonal relationships, including those in psychotherapy.

3. *The postulate of the Transcendent System and Perfect Servant,* expressed consciously in the belief that one can impose order and security on a universe of chaos and danger (a) by the invention of necessarily "anthropocentric" scientific or philosophic systems, sometimes including (b) the intercession of omnipotent and omniscient Beings who can be controlled by wheedling, bribery or command much as one once controlled one's subservient parents.

These are, of course, but bare statements that, taken alone, may sound pretentious and oracular, but strangely disturbing. However, reflection will reveal how many transference phenomena and verbal and other therapeutic maneuvers resonate with these mystic, irrational, but universally wishful and, therefore, ubiquitous beliefs, and consequently how futile or explosive are the results of any attempt to traduce or abolish them either in an individual or in a society. While it may be too cynical to propose outright that therapy consists in re-establishing these and other of man's essential delusions in proper working order, wise psychiatrists eventually learn—along with wise teachers and ministers—that truly to aid a man, one must help him rebuild his own universe of *useful* fact and fancy, and, largely on his own terms, his own faith in himself, in his fellowman and in his personally conceived social and cosmic systems.

REPLIES TO THE QUESTIONNAIRE ABOUT SHORT-TERM THERAPY

Question: Are there any special kinds of symptoms or syndromes that respond better to short-term than to long-term methods?

Dr. Masserman: Very often, the best way to deal with a question in science is to clarify it. Briefly, the true measure of therapy is not its length, but its effectiveness, and the question is rendered even more oblate by the fact that we classify "syndromes" in large part by their supposed amenability to treatment. In effect, I treat all cases that come to me, never consider any two-word diagnoses worth even a file card, and treat everyone as effectively—and therefor, as briefly as possible. I avoid long therapy because I'm not interested in being a baby sitter. So also, despite my being a card-carrying psychoanalyst, I'm interested in helping people other than through furnishing long-term medical tax deductions until "insight" is achieved. Regrettably, most "insight" is a delightful set of delusions mutually shared by patient and therapist.

Question: Since it is manifestly impossible within the confines of a short-term psychotherapy program to arrive at the definitive psychodynamics in many cases, is it possible to present a general formulation of dynamics that may be meaningful to the average patient?

Dr. Masserman: What I'm interested in—and what I try to help the patient acquire—is for him to become a relatively happy and useful member of society. This may take only one interview for an acute anxiety state over a resolvable stress, a week to a month for a "depression," six months to a year for many a person discarded by others as "schizophrenic" or a bit more time for the social parasites, dilettantes or escapists who had almost learned how to get away with it. Perhaps the greatest shortener of therapy is one bit of pragmatic insight: namely that whether the patient admits it or not, he *is* responsible for what he does—and that whether they say so or not, other people will hold him to that fact. Ergo, the temporary gains of neurotic behavior are not only evanescent, but socially adaptive patterns are more fun and preferable.

Question: Are goals in short-term therapy limited to symptom relief, or are reconstructive personality changes possible?

Dr. Masserman: The key term in that, again, is "personality," and somehow we think of personality as a thing apart from what a person does! The term "personality" is derived from the Greek per-sona: a facade or mask. As in classical Greece, players acted out the plays of Aeschylus or Euripedes and wore masks to conceal their true identities. However, not only the facade, but the inner identity should and does change under good therapy regardless of duration. True, any change can be transient, limited or sweeping—but again, it should be borne in mind that this is a measure of the effectiveness, not the length of the therapy.

Question: Methodological differences between long-term and short-term methods: Are there qualitative differences in techniques in short-term as compared to long-term treatment?

Dr. Masserman: Lucy Ozarin once defined long-term psychosis as the permanent deviation in behavior *produced by* hospitalization in a long-term hospital. So also, a "long-term treatment" can produce the very difficulty you're supposed to be treating.

Question: Treating Target Symptoms: Psychotropic drugs deal with target symptoms. Are there any special psychotherapeutic techniques that can also deal with target symptoms?

Dr. Masserman: Again, so much of the internal logic of science consists of examining the questions asked. Is there any internist or surgeon in this audience that can tell me of any single drug or operation that treats only a symptom? Even Ehrlichs "magic bullet" was aimed not at the symptoms, but at the infectious agent (partial *cause*) of syphilis. Diphtheria antitoxin does not treat the rash or the fever, but the toxicity that underlies both. All good psychotherapy resolves underlying conflicts and promotes healthier adaptations; it is, therefore, more than "symptomatic."

Question: Transference Neurosis: Is a transference neurosis desirable in short-term therapy? How may it be managed most constructively, if it does develop?

Dr. Masserman: Again, the key term is "transference neurosis." Freud, who was never an orthodox Freudian, implied in his autobiography that a "transference neurosis," when it was not simply a neurotic transference being analyzed, was nothing less than "an artifact of poor therapeutic technique!" A "transference neurosis" is thus to be distinguished from "normal" transference, which comprises the individual types of relationship, patterned on the patient's transactions with previous important persons in his life that he again plays out with his therapist. But if these patterns, instead of being revealed and corrected, are enhanced by cooingly inviting the patient to regress into an analytic crib sans sidebars, or by fostering an escape into fantasies of dreamy omnipotence, or by providing another set of unworkable delusions called "insights"—then the therapist is dealing with a transference neurosis in the sense that he is transferring one from himself to his patient. As I pointed out in my "Modern Concepts of Psychoanalysis," back in the middle ages all surgeons believed that to be a good surgeon, you had to create a wound which developed pus. This was called "laudable pus" and both patients and surgeons regarded it as essential to the cure. Then a thirteenth century surgeon named Teodorico Borgognoni wrote these memorable lines: "For it is not necessary (though modern surgeons teach it) that pus be generated in wounds. No error can be greater than this. Such a practice is indeed to hinder nature, to prolong the disease, and to prevent the conglutination of the wound." In short, if we can't help a patient, let's not, in any form of therapy, complicate his life with an added neurosis, "transference" or otherwise.

Question: Handling Resistance: Are there ways of managing resistance in short-term therapy that differ from those methods used in long-term therapy?

Dr. Masserman: The term "resistance" is an interesting one. If psychotherapy is akin to rape, resistance is a good idea. But if the patient is helped to seek psychotherapy as communication, exploration and re-education for his own benefit, there may be confusion, misunderstanding or even inertia, but little or no actual "resistance." May I venture another heresy: that "resistance" other than the above may be a good healthy rejection of pseudoanalytic indoctrination, and, therefore, also the result of poor technique.

Question: Since there are many patients who develop dependency relationships and consequently attempt to make therapy an interminable affair, how do we deal with such patients in the short-term approach?

Dr. Masserman: We've already discussed one aspect of this question in our discussion of the artifact of transference neurosis. But as a matter of fact, one can't live without dependency. I'm very dependent on my wife, on the airplane, on my secretaries, my publishers, my bankers, my university—and so are you; as a matter of fact, civilization is a maze of interdependencies. But these are interdependencies in the sense of mutual service and profit, not as cooperation spelled out in terms of "you coo, while I operate." If the therapist himself has this understanding, he can impart it to his patients.

Question: Are there ways of breaking through resistances without stirring up too great anxiety?

Dr. Masserman: Let me answer that with a clinical example. A rather talented lady was referred to me after having been treated by several analysts for quite a number of years, during which time she had acquired a huge arsenal of pornographic but supposedly intriguing symbolisms and erudite "interpretations." I could not break through this protective fog until one day, while she was working in the garden of her estate she fortunately got a rusty nail stuck in her hand. At her therapeutic session an hour later she showed me the swollen hand, and began enlightening me about it to this effect: "You see, doctor, this is actually a pregnancy fantasy with the rusty nail as a phallic symbol. It entered my hand, when I had it in a vaginal position around a rake—and my husband, like I said, was a sexual rake. Or do I identify my hand with his swollen penis? Or with my mother in a rage . . . " At which point I said, "Excuse me a moment." I went downstairs to the pharmacy and got a vial of tetanus antitoxin and a syringe. On my return, I injected the antitoxin into her upper arm and told her to interpret that any fool way she wished including symbolic rape and ejaculation, but as a physician I didn't propose to lose a patient in tetanic convulsions. This was the turning-point in her years of therapy; for the first time she found somebody who really was a physician interested in her welfare, with whom, in addition, she could get down to realities. Her detachment and her pseudopsychoanalytic double talk disappeared and we got along famously after that. Her therapy was over in two months, and she's been doing very well since for the last five years. Various forms of detached dependency can also be sponsored by poor technique, and yet be reversed by proper methods.

Question: How does one utilize dreams in short-term therapy? Does one employ them in any way other than a long-term therapy?

Dr. Masserman: May I point out that no one has ever analyzed a dream despite the old song, "Did You Ever See a Dream Walking?" What one really analyzes is a person's *communications* the day or the week after he had a "dream." These are related to his particular situation at the moment, his motivation, his "transference relationship," and what he's working through; hence, such communications are no more or less the royal road to the Unconscious than if he described the pain in his toe, or day dreamed that he'd won a Nobel prize, or married Princess Grace, or saw you sink into the floor. These would represent wishes, but *wishes contingent to the moment.* The more experience I accumulate, the fewer become my free associations to dreams, and the less I explore their "symbolic significance in the roots of infantile neurosis"; instead, I respect their description as but another communication. Nor do I as readily fall for the patient's ploy: "Let me take the whole hour to tell you what I dreamt last night. Isn't that interesting! Now you interpret it, because I want to deal with your fantasies rather than my realities."

Question: Psychotropic drugs—how valuable are drugs in short-term therapy?

Dr. Masserman: I don't need to prescribe alcohol because my patients think of that themselves. But I use other old-fashioned drugs as indicated: the barbiturates, bromides or chloral hydrate. I use antabuse as a means of communication with alcoholics when they take their morning preventive; I use anti-epileptic drugs, and so on. But there will be a separate chapter in which I'm sure the subject will be covered very well by Dr. Kalinowsky.

Question: What supportive approaches are helpful in short-term therapy?

Dr. Masserman: Well, I have a couch and a chair, with a good solid floor beneath to support the patient. And I pay rent on all of them. But support that remains useful outside the office occurs when the therapist has been a bridge to a physical and social reality in which the patient can continue to live.

Question: What are the techniques that foster reconstructive changes in the therapeutic and post-therapeutic period?

Dr. Masserman: Let me, again, illustrate very briefly with a clinical example. I had a 65 year old ex-president of a cigar factory, who was retired with great honors and a gold watch and half a million dollars. And so he had nothing to do except try to re-assert his authority over his sons and daughters and grand-children and everyone else within his crotchety, ill-tempered reach. Obviously what this old gentleman needed was to recover his status and prestige, and so my therapy once consisted of taking a stroll with him down to the cigar counter in my particular building, and waiting five minutes while he got increasingly angry about the poor merchandise and poorer service. The next time he came in, he said: "You know, Doc, I think I've been wasting a lot of time bugging my poor kids. They think I'm a has-been, but I'm going to set up a chain of cigar counters that will really give service with a smile and not charge high prices for poor tobacco." This he proceeded to do, and got so busy, and so successful and happy at it, that all talk of appointing comservator for this putative "presbyophrenic" ceased. This nice old gentleman and I are still friends, though he slyly sends me a box of fine cigars every Christmas knowing I don't smoke.

Question: Is it helpful to see related family members in short-term therapy. If so, for what purpose?

Dr. Masserman: Of course, it is helpful, especially if you help them to become aware of their own roles in the patient's problems—though that very often takes tact and courage. At a recent International Peace Conference in Athens, to which I was invited, a member of the British Cabinet half-seriously proposed that the heads of various states, who were putting the world in chaos, should be induced to seek psychiatric help. When the Chairman asked my opinion on this technical point, I told the apocryphal story of the patient who came into a psychiatrist's office dresed in a tiger skin with spinach hanging from his ears and a fried egg on his head, and said, "Doctor, I would like to consult you about my brother." Members of patients' families will come to you in the same spirit, unmindful of the fried eggs on their own heads.

Question: Do you use psychological testing and other psychological approaches in short-term treatment?

Dr. Masserman: Infrequently, except when the employer, the court or other referring agency, with the patient's consent, wants a supplementary psychological report. This is not because of lack of confidence in the tests; on the contrary, I once used them extensively and still have a long chapter on them in my "Practice of Dynamic Psychiatry." It is merely that I have developed more confidence in a thorough clinical examination than in one done only with pictures, paper and pencil, and have validated this by decades of collaboration with good clinical psychologists.

But perhaps I should now close with a story that affirms your right of immunity to any challenging or disturbing statements I may have made. One of the delights of travelling round the world, is having various people repay visits to you at the crossroads of Chicago. I had such an individual, a likeable fellow from England to dinner whose name, of course, I've conveniently forgotten. And over liqueurs, I asked him if a talk I had recently given to the British Psychoanalytic Society had had any discernible effect. To which he replied "Well really, old chap, I'm not sure. You see, in England we're really getting away from this talkie-talk, and back to scientific psychiatry, and making really definitive diagnoses. Then, if the patient has simple schizophrenia, we give him Largactil; if paranoid schizophrenia, why the thing to do is to give him insulin;

and if he has a reactive depression, we give him electroshock, and so on. So we've gotten away from the conversational approach, which is the infancy of psychiatry, back to medicine, biology, physiology, and specific therapy. But how are things in your country?"

I know I should have refused the gambit, but instead I said, "Well, we're a young country, we're not quite so certain about things as you people who've been at it longer. So we're not as adept at diagnosis; in fact, we're not quite so sure of the whole system of classification in psychiatry. Instead, we try to understand the individual in a rather more holistic way: his genetic predisposition, early environment, experiential traumata, recent and current physical and emotional stresses, and so on. Therefore, we use not only drugs and EST, but individual therapy, social readjustment, group techniques, and various other therapeutic modalities." As I went on this way for 15 or 20 minutes, he kept stroking his chin, attentively and quite politely, and when I was through, he said reflectively: "Dr. Masserman, you have given me a bit to think about. What I propose to do is to go home, sleep on it, and I'll warrant that by tomorrow morning, I shall have forgotten all about it." Well, this was a nice way of saying that each of us has to live within his own particular way of looking at things. But we also have a right to think that my British friend's so-called "specific therapy" was far less specific than he thought. The hospitalization of the patient, the self-confidence of the therapist, the communication of such confidence to the patient, the rehabilitation inherent in many of the social techniques that are used in Britain may have had as large a part in the therapy as the drugs, EST or insulin.

Question: Is it very dangerous for a patient to be treated by a neurotic therapist?

Dr. Masserman: Let us once again first focus on the two key terms in the question. "Treatment" as we have seen, has very broad connotations, and "neurotic" may mean only "somebody I don't like." For example, many observers might regard Father Divine as a "paranoid psychotic." Yet he has a group of ardent followers who actually believe he is God, has cured their ills and saved their souls by divine power, and has constituted them a heavenly host of angels on earth. Many of these people are good providers and useful citizens; would you commit them all as psychotic? Or walk around a corner to a Holy Roller meeting. You will see a preacher that goes off into trances, and a congregation that shouts and rolls in the aisles, crying out, mourning, dancing, sometimes tearing off some of their clothes and acting in a way that in the back wards of the state hospital would be diagnosed schizoaffective excitement. Yet at the end of the service, they get up, dust themselves off, straighten up their neckties, put on their hats and coats, go back home, have a good night's sleep, and go to work the next morning. Is the "psychotic" preacher subverting his congregation or has he evolved a *modus vivendi* essential to both in this anti-Dionysian age? I wonder how many of our current "scientific" treatments will be regarded fifty years from now as largely a *folie-à-dieu* between ourselves and our patients. In the event that interminable psychoanalysis does, in fact, prove to be just such a *folie*, I shall tell you an anecdote.

I once gave a lecture to the British Psychoanalytic Society which like all British societies is divided neatly down the middle by an aisle. To the right sat the conservative Anna Freud and her disciples; to the left, Melanie Klein and her cohorts. At the end of my lecture which also ended with a question period, somebody would get up from the right side of the aisle, and say: "Dr. Masserman, what you are presenting, of course, is a searching confirmation of the tenets of our great leader Anna Freud, and I am happy that the data you furnish are so compatible with her teachings." Then somebody would get up from the other side of the aisle and counter with: "On the contrary! On the contrary! What Dr. Masserman has told us, with regard to his data and his inferences, supports without any reservations, the basic understandings of our great leader Melanie Klein." Finally somebody asked me a question that I felt I could answer, to wit: "Dr. Masserman, in your country, we understand that psychoanalysis lasts only two or three years, whereas here in Britain, we think that a proper psychoanalysis should persist at least for 7, 8, or 9 years." My reply, recorded in the annals of the British Psychoanalytic Society, was simply that "I'd heard somewhere that it took the British a little longer to see a joke."

Question: At what point does one part ways with his patient in short-term psychotherapy?

Dr. Masserman: Exactly the same sort of point at which an internist parts with his patient or a surgeon thinks the patient is ready for discharge from the hospital: when I believe the patient is equipped sufficiently with broader understanding, restored skills and with adequate techniques to function well enough in his society so that he no longer needs my particular guidance. This may occur after one interview and may not occur after two or three years.

Question: Do you conceive of short-term therapy as relationship therapy, or is it a structured type of thing?

Dr. Masserman: All therapies are structured. As I said, the parameter is not short-term or long-term, but whether or not the treatment is understanding, skillful and effective.

Short-Term versus Long-Term Therapy

=============================== PAUL H. HOCH, M.D.

(Editor's Note: In this chapter, Dr. Hoch deals with many questions related to the practice of short-term therapy. He differentiates conditions that will require long-term treatment from those that can be effectively tackled on a short-term basis. Among the many technical problems discussed are the management of target symptoms, the handling of panic, modes of dealing with detached, depressed and dependent patients, and the employment of psychotropic drugs. Considered also are problems of resistance, transference, activity, and combinations of techniques that are components of an integrated short-term treatment program.)

THERE ARE SKEPTICS in the field of psychotherapy. Some psychotherapists will tell you that practically no patient can be treated on a short-term basis. Some will say that certain types of patients can and that others cannot be managed briefly. I classify myself in the second group and shall elaborate on those conditions that do respond well to short-term methods.

SELECTION OF CASES FOR SHORT-TERM THERAPY

A few years ago, some psychiatric centers introduced so-called "emergency treatment services" for persons who came to them any time of the day or night. Both non-psychotherapeutic and psychotherapeutic methods were applied. A common observation was that patients suffering from all varieties of psychotherapeutic disability could suddenly develop acute crises, especially intense anxiety and panic states. It was found that the latter conditions could be handled very effectively in short-term treatment. Moreover, some chronic patients who ordinarily would be assumed to require prolonged therapy could, in states of crises, be adequately managed with short-term methods.

Generally speaking, short-term therapy is useful in the resolution of acute conflictual problems. It is also helpful for the relief of situations where the neurotic response is immediately reactive to the environment. This contrasts with what one reads in the older literature, especially psychoanalytic literature, which denies the possi-

bility of helping acute conflictual problems since these are presumed to be deeply embedded in early childhood experiences.

A good deal of sophistication is required for short-term therapy.
The therapist must be keenly aware of what he is doing since he
does not have quantities of time available for experiment. For this
reason untrained people are not able to employ the method. Furthermore, a short form of treatment must be more active than the prolonged form. For instance, it is impossible to utilize some techniques employed in orthodox psychoanalysis where the therapist remains passive and allows the patient to work out his own problems
leisurely.

To consider for a moment the type of case where I would not
advocate short psychotherapy, we would include chronic psychiatric
disorders that have never undergone treatment. Among these are
neurotics such as obsessive-compulsives who have struggled for a
considerable time, but have not been treated. In my opinion, approaching such cases with short-term therapy cannot be vindicated
by the outcome. Anxiety states and hysterical reactions are all
amenable to short-term psychotherapy; but chronic psychosomatic
reactions and obsessive-compulsive states are not.

I do not undertake short-term therapy with certain psychotic patients such as paranoids. Paranoid patients, generally need a prolonged form of therapy. They have to be seen quite often, but not
necessarily for a full session.

PSYCHODYNAMIC FORMULATIONS

The question of whether it is possible to present a general formulation of dynamics that may be meaningful to the average patient,
since it is manifestly impossible within the confines of a short-term
psychotherapy program to arrive at the definitive psychodynamics,
is a challenging one. It is usually sufficient for the therapist to apply general dynamic formulations rather than detailed dynamics.
Actually, the very refined psychodynamic formulations are not often
picked up and utilized by the patient even in long-term therapy. The
exception to this is the patient who derives a great deal of pleasure
in intellectualizing every emotional experience and, of course, intellectualizing the attempts at emotional correction practiced by
the therapist. To such a patient, the session is primarily a form of
fencing match between himself and the therapist, an intellectual
exercise. The patient may then look for refined psychodynamic
formulations. Other patients do not.

In discussing psychodynamics, another important factor must

be brought up—namely, how short-term therapy differs from the prolonged form of therapy. Different theoretical frames of reference may be utilized here. One would be that the repetitive discussion of psychodynamic factors removes repressed material. Another theoretical point of view would focus around learning—namely, that the person acquires new abilities in the actual coping with conflictual situations. Again we may assume that due to repetition, conditioning takes place.

Whatever theoretical view one may have, the main issue is that there is less possibility of experiencing what we call a corrective emotional experience in short-term therapy than there is in a prolonged form of therapy. If it occurs, it sometimes is far more violent and, therefore, requires very astute therapeutic handling. Everything is more concentrated. Nothing is as diluted as it is in the prolonged form of therapy. However, when in speaking about resistances, we may see the counterpart—namely, that resistances are usually not as over-powering in the short form of therapy as in the prolonged. This is because the patient does not have the possibility or opportunity of building up as much hostility and, at the same time, as much of a negativistic attitude toward the therapist or the therapeutic maneuver that is possible in prolonged psychotherapy. In prolonged psychotherapy, long stretches in treatment are often devoted to overcoming the patient's resistances to the very treatment he seeks.

GOALS IN SHORT-TERM THERAPY

In considering whether short-term therapy circumscribes the attainable goals, we need to define what we mean by reconstructive changes. There are levels and degrees of reconstruction. However, our question must be delayed by another question. Does prolonged therapy achieve reconstructive goals? The statistics on this issue are not too convincing. Not important is the too commonly cherished belief that if a treatment is short, it should be regarded as bad, and because it is long it should be regarded as good. But it *is* important to know where one can obtain results only with long-term treatment, and not with the short form. For instance, in one group of patients, with the exception of one or two persons, I have never seen a good therapeutic result with short-term therapy. These involve persons who have been suffering over an extended period from marked sexual aberration. I do not believe that anyone is able to "cure" homosexuality, for instance, in six sessions. I have not seen patients with severe sado-masochistic sexual difficulties who were "cured" in a few sessions. The few cases where positive results were obtained in short or abbreviated therapy are the exceptions which confirm the rule. All in all, these cases do not lend themselves to short-term therapy and, in the light of this experience, I do not undertake to treat them.

There is one exception—homosexual panic is very common and is very amenable to short-term therapy; some of the emergency services often deal with it in one or several sessions. Obviously, this treatment will not change the homosexuality of the patient, but it will give him some possibility of overcoming his panic, and probably help him to see his whole deviational constellation in a somewhat different way.

I believe short-term therapy can do more than simply relieve symptoms. I see persons after short-term therapy adapting and adjusting themselves quite well. A much deeper change has been brought about than symptom control.

Sometimes a patient who has been under treatment with short-term psychotherapy will need psychiatric intervention at a later date, but many can go on for years without further treatment. I do not believe that long-term psychotherapy necessarily gives the guarantee that later on the patient will not show a relapse or will not need some psychiatric intervention. The relapse rate after psychotherapy is unknown simply because the patient often does not seek out the same therapist, but goes to another. If there is no communication between the present and previous therapist, it is possible that the first therapist will never know that the patient whom he "successfully" treated is again under treatment.

Relapses occur more frequently in disorders that are more deeply structured than those of the average anxiety or hysteric state. Thus, relapses are more common in persons suffering from obsessive-compulsive manifestations or in those falling into the borderline or outright schizophrenic groups. We have to accept the fact that no single form of therapy known today in psychiatry is anything but non-specific and hence is directed at symptoms. This is obvious because the etiology of most of the disorders seen today is not known, and therefore a causal therapy cannot be instituted. This should not discourage us because the removal of disabling symptoms is a most gratifying and important task. I am not too disturbed by the fact that in many individuals the underlying causal matrix is not uprooted. If some of the main symptoms are eliminated and if the person is able to function, I am satisfied with that. After many years of practice, I am probably more easily satisfied with this result than when I first began in psychiatry. I believe that removing symptoms is a very important objective and in most instances sufficient.

METHODOLOGICAL DIFFERENCES BETWEEN LONG-TERM AND SHORT-TERM METHODS

Qualitative differences in techniques in short-term as compared to long-term therapy are of some concern. Perhaps the most important methodological difference is the activity of the therapist. The therapist cannot be as passive in the short-term treatment as he may choose to be in the long-term treatment. He will have to deal aggressively with the patient's difficulties and he may have to interfere with many of the patient's actions. This is particularly true if the patient has acting-out tendencies, for instance, if he is drinking excessively. Should the patient display behavior patterns which are socially inacceptable, the therapist will have to advise him and even give him directives as to what should and should not be done. One cannot expect that the patient's behavior will change automatically because of the treatment procedure. This is actually one of the main difficulties in short-term therapy. If therapy is not executed with judgment, if it is not based on extensive experience with different types of individuals and with different kinds of psychiatric disorders, the person may fail to show change. These are some of the reasons why some therapists, after administering short-term treatment, become discouraged and disappointed with their results. They are then apt to say that they cannot do a short-term therapy. I believe that in the teaching of short-term therapy, this is one of the most important issues to be stressed. What do you do with a particular patient? What would you do if the patient suffers from an acute anxiety state? How would you handle it? What are the actual causative factors, and what are the probable consequences? In long-term therapy you have more time, more possibilities to contemplate, and you may even assume that you do not have to do anything because the patient will do the therapy for himself and for you. Otherwise, every technique which is known in the long form of treatment can be used in the short form.

TREATING TARGET SYMPTOMS

The concept of target symptoms comes from psychopharmacology. Basically it means that psychotic patients have outstanding symptoms at which we aim our therapeutic fire, for instance, the use of drugs in removing in a schizophrenic patient hallucinations, delusions, or bizarre behavior patterns. The question we must answer is whether we have such target symptoms in neurotic patients. Are the symptomatologies here so diffuse that it is not possible to identify target symptoms? I am convinced that in neurotic disturbances, just as in the psychoses, one may always find target symptoms. Actually, in any form of therapy it is essential to formulate for oneself what one considers to be the patient's main difficulty, how one wishes to handle it, and how to modify one's approach based on the patient's reaction. I do not believe—and this is especially true in short-term therapy—in a diffuse form of treatment where the patient sits and discusses matters at random, practically anything and everything without some aim.

This may be suitable for an introductory session, but after the patient's difficulties are evaluated, one has to establish some relationship between the therapeutic maneuvering and the target to be attacked. Otherwise the approach is nothing more than preliminary to a prolonged form of treatment. There is a basic difference between introductory treatment, prolonged treatment and short-term therapy. Short psychotherapy means that in a relatively short time one influences the patient's symptoms to such a degree that the patient is able to function. How this is achieved is different in each case. This brings up two fundamental issues which preoccupy therapists. The transference neurosis is one and handling of the resistance is the other.

TRANSFERENCE NEUROSIS IN SHORT-TERM THERAPY

Is a transference neurosis desirable in short-term therapy? How may it be managed most constructively, if it does develop? Not enough research experience is available today to answer either of these questions conclusively. The answers must, therefore, be tentative, and probably not fully satisfactory.

A transference neurosis, or a repetition of the patient's neurosis in relationship to the therapist, occurs in short-term therapy just as in long-term treatment. It is interesting to note, however, that some individuals in short-term therapy do not develop transference to the same degree as those undergoing a prolonged form of treatment. On the other hand, we do see patients who develop a massive transference neurosis rapidly in short-term approaches. I have not been able, based on diagnostic categories, to differentiate between these two groups. Schizophrenic patients and certain pseudoneurotic schizophrenic patients sometimes develop very intensive transference reactions. These responses, in my opinion, exceed the positive and negative transference manifestations seen in ordinary neurotic individuals.

Two types of craving in therapy may be differentiated. There is, first, a very deep dependency craving, where the individual puts himself into a helpless role and feels the therapist should resolve all of his issues quickly and his participation in therapy is minimal. He abandons himself to the therapist as a price for being helped. This is infantile in attitude and is especially common in schizophrenic or borderline patients, although we have also often observed it in neurotic patients. In the second group of patients, there is a great deal of expectation for a magic solution of their problems with or without dependency needs. Similar to the first group, the patients, themselves, do not want to contribute to the therapeutic process, but expect the solution to come completely from the therapists. These patients are usually highly ambivalent about the therapeutic process. They expect their therapists, during the course of treatment, to convince them to accept them as therapists.

Handling such transference relationships in short-term therapy is difficult because the transference manifestations can occur in a much more acute and disturbing form than in prolonged therapy. The management is especially difficult in those patients who expect magic solutions for their problems. Patients who have a hazy reality concept struggle a great deal to replace reality with these magic demands and magic desires. I may add that this group of patients is also very difficult to handle in prolonged therapy.

HANDLING RESISTANCE

The handling of resistance is an important problem in short-term therapy, but one resistance barrier does not occur, which develops frequently in the prolonged form of treatment. This resistance, based upon transference, is crystallized in the relationship with the therapist, and is far less common than in the prolonged form of treatment. I do not say that transference resistance does not occur, but usually there is no opportunity in short treatment to allow this kind of resistance to gather and harden. Where resistance develops, it must be dealt with rapidly.

DEALING WITH DEPENDENCY

The question of the dependent patient is an important one. Here it is essential that we face one issue squarely that I alluded to before. Do we really believe that the patient we are treating can become, in a relatively short time, a person who can manage his own affairs constructively, or do we believe that he will have to remain dependent for some time in order to be able to function? Actually, in many ways our whole psychotherapeutic reformulation today rests upon these considerations. Are we dealing with an individual who can be reconstructed to such a degree that he can take over on his own? Or are we dealing with an individual with a certain amount of deficiency who can only be tided over by a constructive dependency relationship? If the latter is true, this would mean the patient would have to be treated at intervals over a long period to help him carry on and to resolve his problems.

I personally differ from quite a number of my colleagues who believe that the majority of persons suffering from serious psychiatric illnesses can quickly be made to function in an independent fashion. Of course, many of these persons do function in a seemingly independent manner, but at the same time they also create a great many difficulties for themselves. I think it is far better to treat such a dependent patient for a year, seeing him once every two weeks, and later on perhaps once every four weeks, than to give him fifteen or twenty sessions, and following this let him maneuver by himself only to see him fall apart after six months. I do not really consider this form of management a type of prolonged therapy. In my opinion, this is equivalent to orthopedic maneuvering in the framework of psychiatry. There are a number of patients who need orthopedic psychiatric appliances in the same way that orthopedic patients need physical appliances.

What we must do in the future is to determine better ways of diagnosing what kind of patient needs a supportive type of treatment and what kind can tolerate and should have treatment that is more than supportive. At present treatment is applied by rote. Thus reconstructive and supportive forms of therapy are applied without distinction. Actually, we should divide patients into the two groups I have just outlined and selectively apply our reconstructive and supportive therapies.

DEALING WITH DETACHMENT

Are there ways of breaking through characterologic detachment rapidly without stirring up too great anxiety? This is a very difficult question. If one is dealing with an individual where the detachment is not of a neurotic protective origin, but is a coping mechanism to prevent a schizophrenic disintegration, it would not be advisable to break through the detachment in an ambulatory setting. On the other hand, detachment may be a sign of the individual's protective maneuvering simply to ameliorate anxiety situations. In other words, detachment here would serve as a form of self-administered anesthesia in order that anxiety situations need not be faced. In the latter case, I believe it can be handled. No doubt there will be difficulty in breaking through. Activity is essential since one cannot leave it up to the patient alone. Even in prolonged therapy detachment is not easily influenced being one of the most complicated forms of anxiety-protective mechanisms.

HANDLING DREAMS IN SHORT-TERM THERAPY

The handling of dreams is the same in short-term as in long-term therapy. There are restrictions here, of course, since one does not have the time that one has in long-term therapy to explain to the patient in detail some of the condensations, displacements, distortions, and symbolic replacements that occur in his dreams. To some extent, however, one may introduce the patient to the meanings of his dream mechanisms. This can prove difficult unless one is dealing with a very intelligent patient. I believe the salient issues in a dream should be explained, but the dream should not be necessarily used as a focal point in a therapeutic session.

PSYCHOTROPIC DRUGS

Drugs should be used in patients where they are indicated and should not be employed as a routine measure. An important issue here relates to dependency. There are drug-dependent individuals in the same way that there are therapist-dependent patients. The therapist may not be flattered at being compared with a capsule, but there are patients who really think this way. The patient has the feeling that it is the medication that relieves his symptoms; therefore, he does not need to do anything. It is unncessary, he believes, to work through any of his symptoms. Or he may imagine that the therapist will do everything for him and that it is unnecessary for him to do anything for himself. In such patients, obviously, the use of drugs is not indicated.

On the other hand, one encounters patients where the anxiety is so great, the vegetative manifestations of anxiety so diverse, the psychosomatic symptoms so disabling, that therapeutically one can accomplish nothing unless the anxiety is reduced to a manageable level. Drugs are of very great importance here, truly an important adjunct to therapy. I have published a number of papers on this subject, and I am convinced that quite a number of patients who formerly were not amenable to psychotherapy are amenable today because of the possibility of reducing their anxiety. However, I do not believe the drug necessarily eliminates the patient's conflicts. However by reducing his anxiety, it may place the patient into the position of being able to take over. In a number of patients this is not the case. Here, the anxiety is reduced, but the adaptational difficulties are still there. Many of the conflictual issues remain. These must be handled by psychotherapeutic approaches. How one blends drugs and psychotherapy depends entirely upon the patient.

USES OF VARYING TECHNIQUES

My feeling is that all techniques—counseling, supportive, reconstructive—should be used even more extensively in short-term than in long-term therapy. One wants the patient to overcome some of his major roadblocks. If one is able to achieve this through any environmental manipulations, these should be attempted. There is considerable danger, however, in stopping there. Short-term therapy should not degenerate into manipulating the patient and his environment with the assumption that this process will eliminate the patient's difficulties. Occasionally one may run into a patient who has a great deal of anxiety alleging that he feels upset because he has to work with a certain person with whom he does not get along. One may, through an acquaintance at his place of work, be able to manipulate the situation so as to enable the patient to work with another person. This may suffice to restore equilibrium. With most patients, however, the complaint factor is not the sole cause of trouble. Therefore, restricting the treatment of the patient only to a type of manipulative maneuver, without assessing his other difficulties, is not good practice. The counseling of related family members is of great importance in short-term therapy provided no counseling is done so that the relatives of the patient— especially after a short assessment of the patient's difficulties— feel themselves put in a defensive position with the patient or with the therapist assuming that he has to change the total atmosphere of the family in relation to the patient. On the other hand, in short-term therapy it is of immeasurable help if one really knows with whom he is dealing in the immediate environment of the patient, particularly if the neurotic manifestations of the patient incorporate members of his environment. They inevitably do, of course, and the patient's behavior and even his symptom formulations are influenced.

USES OF SOCIAL RESOURCES

Psychiatric treatment cannot replace social deprivation or entirely eliminate difficulties produced in the patient's socio-economic environment. The reverse is also true. In many places today there is a fundamental confusion regarding the treatment of certain patients, especially the underprivileged. One may help these patients through social therapy, but this must not be utilized with the idea that it will be able to eliminate the patient's symptomatology. The patient may have a genuine psychiatric disorder in which socio-economic environmental factors play a considerable role. These factors may be discussed with the patient and no doubt some help can be given him to improve his social and economic situation. However, for the therapist to assume that by changing the patient's socio-economic status, a complicated neurosis will vanish is a misconception. This misconception is based on certain current theories about the neuroses and the psychoses. Attempts have been made to interpret neurotic disturbances, and some psychotic disorders, as nothing other than reactions to the social environment. While it is possible that some psychotic reactions are influenced perhaps by social difficulties, I am fairly certain that in our culture the psychoses with which we deal have another etiology.

QUESTIONS AND ANSWERS

Question: In regard to the epidemic in our society of depression and suicidal tendencies how would you in a short-term approach handle these patients that come to you for therapy and how would you determine if the approach should be a short-term one? What is the best way of preparing, explaining, or defining the approach to the patient?

Dr. Hoch: I do not want to discuss depression, and especially suicidal preoccupations in over-simple terms, because this is a very extensive topic. The number of depressions and suicidal tendencies is actually rising. This is interesting because it is in conflict with those statistics that say that mental disorders, in general, are not rising. Therefore, we have to assume the incidence rate of mental disorders is probably the same, but that the depressive manifestations and suicidal preoccupations in our society are becoming more common.

As to their relatedness to short-term therapy, depressions are very difficult to treat in this way. Depressions are simply very difficult to treat!

Anyone who has tried to approach depressions psychotherapeutically knows how much time is involved and how difficult the task can be. In the end one does not know if the patient has recovered simply because the depression is over or because treatment has been administered.

Depressions are of varied duration and to discuss the relationship of the depression to therapeutic procedure is very difficult. If one uses a short-term technique and is able to demonstrate that a depression can be cured in five or six sessions, we might regard this as a sound therapeutic cure. But generally in the treatment of depression, short-term treatment, in the sense that we have discussed it, does not exist. One must treat the patient as long as the depression lasts. The best treatment for a depression is to treat it both psychotherapeutically and with drugs and to see the patient frequently. It is not necessary to see him for a full session, because a full session does not usually pay off. The patient is exhausted and the therapist can become even more exhausted. However, short sessions at frequent intervals, giving the patient every opportunity to use the therapist as a base of contact, are of great importance.

Insofar as explaining the approach to the patient is concerned, this will depend on what he expects and what he has been told about the treatment he is to receive. A patient may ask "Are you a Freudian analyst" or "Are you a Horney analyst," "Are you this or are you that?" Here one may have to answer his questions directly attempting to determine what is behind them. One may then tell the patient that a form of treatment will be used which is intended to help him. The patient must then decide whether or not to accept this form of treatment. I do not indicate to the patient, as some therapists do, from a tactical point of view, a termination date. I do not do this because I have had bad experience with it. For instance, you may tell the patient his treatment will last for ten months or ten sessions, or four weeks. I tell the patient that psychotherapy will be used to an extent that it will benefit him. I tell him how often he should come, and that I hope in a reasonable time that some of the symptoms will be ameliorated. I do this with the idea in mind that after three, four or five sessions, when the patient is better clinically evaluated, that I may decide whether or not he needs prolonged treatment. In the latter instance, I have not prejudged the case. Suggesting long-term treatment is not too difficult. Today many of these patients are conditioned for long-term treatment.

Question: In a clinical setting where a group of psychiatrists are working, wouldn't you have to make up your mind beforehand what your goal in therapy was going to be and then decide upon whether to do short or long-term therapy?

Dr. Hoch: Yes. The question actually is how soon can you make up your mind. Can you, upon seeing the patient once, immediately make a decision whether or not to use short-term therapy, or if necessary long-term therapy? As I mentioned before, when I see a patient for the first time, I know from some of the indications whether or not I shall use a short-term form of psychotherapy. However, an attempt with short-term psychotherapy can be made with most patients with the exception of some serious habit formations, like sexual deviations. Clinics operate in a strange way. They use all kinds of treatments based upon expediency, and seemingly against any theory. We have learned that many of these treatments, based on expediency, are successful. One can attempt the short-term treatment of practically all problems which are not too difficult or too deeply structuralized, so there may be a feeling that there is no sense in attempting long-term therapy. I know clinics that give short-term treatment for all kinds of difficulties because they feel the patient will derive at least some benefit from treatment. You will also find psychiatrists who argue in reverse that no treatment is better than prolonged treatment. I do not accept this statement, but there are purists. Just the other day I heard one physician making a pronouncement that there is no treatment other than full psychoanalysis.

Question: If you have a patient you have accepted for short-term therapy, when you have reached your goal and ameliorated certain target symptoms and the patient in your opinion is ready for discharge, yet still has a certain dependency, what do you do? Do you accept this patient and continue therapy as a supportive therapy, or would you try to wean the patient away from treatment?

Dr. Hoch: I would try to wean the patient away from the treatment, but I would not do this with an outright schizophrenic where I know a certain amount of dependency leaning is necessary. In the average neurotic patient, if you observe that he is clinging to you for security's sake and uses treatment for this purpose, it is advisable to diminish gradually the sessions and see him less frequently. I find this a better method than an abrupt termination because the patient may have some difficulties in self-confidence, and in his capacities for handling the situation. If he returns to treatment, some of these symptoms can be rediscussed. However, the tapering off should be such that the patient does not feel he is being dismissed while he has been only partially helped. In other words, the motto should not be

"You are not too well, but I think you can manage." I believe this is bad for the patient and it is far more feasible to tell him that you think he is now better able to function adequately and should continue to improve. This patient comes to you for a cure, but what is the cure? Should he be symptom-free and in a state of perfect bliss, or can he merely be able to handle some of his problems more constructively even though certain lesser symptoms remain? One must make this clear to the patient.

Question: I wonder if you would call a patient's deciding to discontinue treatment after a few sessions "a flight into health?"

Dr. Hoch: Yes. A flight into health is a favorite past-time of some patients. But this is not always the case. In most instances, the reverse is true in the form of "a flight back into illness" with the idea that wherever he goes or to whomever he turns, he cannot be helped. Very cleverly constructed by many patients are reasons why they cannot be helped. This is especially common in patients who have some depressive anxiety. "I tried. You couldn't help me. I tried Dr. 'X' and he couldn't help me." Therefore, he actually comes to you for two or three sessions to confirm the idea that you will not be able to help either.

Question: Do you think this is different than a patient feeling better after a few sessions?

Dr. Hoch: Yes.

Question: Are there any cases where you would feel that short-term treatment would be the treatment of choice even if you have time to provide other kinds of treatment?

Dr. Hoch: I personally feel that short-term treatment is the choice for individuals who have acute neurotic or psychosomatic disorders. This is also true where the examination discloses that the patient's ego strength is such that brief treatment is advisable. Many psychiatrists do not believe in short-term forms of treatment because they either see only a few patients or they have theoretical preconceptions regarding treatment modalities and lengths of treatment. The neurotic patient seen in general hospitals usually can be benefitted from short-term psychiatric help. This is not an expediency treatment. It is how treatment should be designed and executed.

Question: Could you comment on the usefulness of general formulations of dynamics at the beginning of therapy, the first session or second session where you would obviously describe to the patient the role his illness plays?

Dr. Hoch: This depends on the type of patient. There are many patients who come to you with preconceived ideas. This is the product of popular psychiatric literature. Many patients offer you their own dynamic explanations. I usually wait in discussing dynamics until I have seen the patient for a few sessions. I like to be fairly sure of what the main dynamics are. I do not like revisions of formulations as I go along. A great many patients put it down that you told them this and that, and then they see after a few sessions that what you told them is not so. In a prolonged form of treatment you have far more opportunity to revise and formulate. In a short-term treatment it is better to wait until you see clearly what the patient's main difficulties are so that you are able to outline them. The important issue, however, is to give the person two or three outstanding things around which his problem is structured. Otherwise he cannot see the forest for the trees. This may be extremely difficult for the patient to follow. The best thing is to try to determine the main anxiety-producing factor in his situation. This should be the target. I do not like to introduce very complicated dynamic formulations at the beginning. Later on formulations can be refined. However, there are usually only two or three main issues that should be involved.

Question: Do you consider the modern trend of psychiatric treatment that is limited to weeks as a token type of treatment? And could you comment on the day hospital?

Dr. Hoch: This is exactly short-term therapy by definition. The day hospital is a treatment modality which replaces full hospitalization. You find some patients who go to a day hospital for a considerable length of time. It is possible that the day hospital could be used for short-term therapy, but most of these set-ups are for the treatment of psychotics. You are not really using the full hospital facility, but a half facility for this purpose. Nevertheless, the treatment methods are similar to those given to hospitalized patients. There are, however, a few day hospitals devoted only to neurotic patients or only to those neurotic patients who have a marked symptomatology. I must repeat that this day hospital care is not necessarily short.

Question: Will you touch upon countering the transference and especially in short-term therapy as against the prolonged, and whether or not it can be used therapeutically in any way?

Dr. Hoch: Transference in short-term therapy does not develop as massively as is usual in prolonged therapy. The reasons for this are, of course, obvious. In short-term therapy strong emotional attachments do not develop in the same way as in prolonged therapy. However, this does not mean that in certain cases strong transference and counter-transference reactions will not develop. A danger exists in cases where the therapist feels that he has to reward the strong transference feelings of the patient. In such an instance, he may attempt to manipulate the patient or his environment too drastically and more than is indicated. In addition, the therapist may step out of the usual patient-doctor relationship by engaging in social activities with the patient. In my opinion, this may be cautiously done in a group therapy framework, but I do not believe it is a good technique in individual treatment.

Question: Could you comment on the technique of dealing with acute homosexual panic?

Dr. Hoch: An acute homosexual panic usually quiets down if the patient has a therapist to whom he can ventilate his particular panic. The treatment of homosexual panic is really a very simple affair. The panic usually develops if the person is suddenly made aware of his homosexual deviation and feels that it is ostracized. It also occurs when the patient is in a social situation of temptation and either succumbs or is very ambivalent about whether to succumb or not. When these situations are ventilated to a sympathetic therapist, the panic usually subsides. In some of these cases medication may also be advisable for a day or two. The medication to be used is usually one of the tranquilizers in moderate dosages. However, the therapist must be aware that sometimes the use of barbiturates causes the homosexual panic to terminate into a suicidal attempt. The most difficult thing encountered in some panics is that they are not short-lived, but continue to be sustained. In such cases, one must be prepared to see the patient more extensively. Short-term therapy is most effective here, but the patient should be seen for short periods of time, such as every day for the first week, for say fifteen or twenty minutes, and then until the panic subsides at frequencies. As it is known, some homosexual panics are in reality schizophrenic episodes and this most important factor should not be overlooked. The treatment procedure then takes on an entirely different form.

IV

Relationship of Short-Term Psychotherapy to Developmental Stages of Maturation and Stages of Treatment Behavior

════════ SANDOR RADO, M.D., D. POL. SCI.

(Editor's note: A psychodynamic formulation is presented in this chapter which views the transactions in psychotherapy through the lens of motivation, and provides guide-lines for short-term treatment. Dr. Rado points out that there are a number of motivational forms existent which are identical in all human beings. These correlate with stages in personality development. Four categories of motivation may be identified: (1) magical craving, (2) parental invocation, (3) cooperative striving, and (4) realistic self-reliance. Illness or forces that stimulate helplessness foster activation of, or regression to lower levels of adaptation; productive experiences encourage higher levels. We are unable to approach the varied problems in psychotherapy unless we understand the operative motivations which condition how patients will respond to therapeutic tactics.

Technical processes employed in psychotherapy may effectively be fashioned to the existing level of motivation. Thus, suggestive technics are efficacious where levels of motivation are geared to the craving for magic or for parental invocation. It is possible, however, to help patients to achieve a higher level of motivation and thus to utilize technics effective for emotional learning and permanent change. No matter how short therapy may be, if proper motivation is induced and adequate learning technics are employed, significant results may be obtained. This is important for the future era of psychiatric therapy, which will have to be geared to the needs of millions of people. The development of short-term methods, a social necessity, must be related to more research that shifts the focus from clinical empiricism to scientific discipline. It is essential, as an objective, that we correlate psychological aspects of experience with brain physiology. Interesting practical suggestions for the conduct of short-term therapy are given by Dr. Rado, in the question and answer section of the chapter, that emphasize the importance of flexibility in approach in short-term treatment.)

PSYCHOTHERAPY IS AS OLD AS the human race. Unquestionably it is one of the earliest activities of man ever since he appeared on the evolutionary scene. In this sense, innumerable variations of psychotherapy have been used, and I think we are entitled to the generalization that no psychotherapeutic method of whatever kind has ever been invented which, given the right circumstances, in one case or the other, would not have been successful.

From this, however, it does not follow that the ideas of our inventive colleagues concerning how their inventions work are correct. "Theories" proposed for these many hundreds of types of procedures have all been based on speculation, and speculation is a self-serving business.

It was only about one hundred years ago that modern scientific psychotherapy began. The story is well-known—the appearance in medicine of hypnosis, encouraged by Charcot and other pioneers. But psychotherapy was in no hurry to follow the example of other procedures in clinical medicine which had gradually improved their scientific status by building on the so-called basic sciences of medicine like anatomy and physiology. The difficulty was that the then known basic sciences were felt to be almost completely useless when one attempted to describe and organize experiences gained not by looking at things but by listening to patients. If we had at our disposal, a basic science related to introspective observational data, we might be able to develop a better understanding and, therefore, an explanation of the ways in which various therapeutic methods work.

Freud made a magnificent beginning. But, unfortunately, he became a victim of the times in which he worked. There was very little methodological understanding of investigative procedures in existence—indeed, very little interest in them. Inadvertently, Freud turned to concepts and ideas which were altogether vitalistic if not animistic, drifting further and further from most of what we know about the brain in particular, and about the scientific method in general. He brought forward such concepts as *instinct*, which obscured his most important realization—that in building a theory about behavior, the number one consideration is the understanding of *motivation*. The general public, including many psychiatrists, still confuse instinct with motivation. Motivation can and must be stated in terms of clinically observable phenomena, as are the motivated actions. Otherwise, the clinician fishes in the troubled waters of clouds. Historically, instincts are the derivatives of what were once called "vital forces" supposedly dwelling in the ventricles of the brain. In physiology this assumption was abandoned about a century and a half ago.

Some of us, including myself, made efforts to work out a conceptual system of behavior, its description and interpretation, which was based on motivation and control. And, lo and behold, it was discovered that we could dispense with the huge number of words used in the theory and practice of psychotherapy which as a rule hardly express more than empty abstractions. One cannot argue against clinical observation, but in order to make it scientifically valuable, clinical observation must be described unambiguously and interpreted in scientific terms accessible to verification. The tragedy of many of Freud's theories is that they are based on concepts that cannot be verified by any known method.

What does the total field of psychotherapy look like when we dare to make an attempt to describe essential phenomena in terms of motivations? (Rado, 1962a) If we can answer this question, only then do we have the basis upon which clinical procedures can be understood and developed for therapy or any other purpose.

The greatest surprise came when it was seen, in pursuit of this goal, that there are only a limited number of motivational forms, and that basically they are identical in every human being. These are easily understood if one examines the developmental stages of maturation, and the various forms of growing up. Then one can see that the same individual is capable of different therapeutic motivations, and thus can go from one motivation to the other. One also can see, when this change in motivation occurs, with the patient progressing forward or regressing to a more primitive level (as fostered by a specific motivation) that this underlying motivational force is the fundamental dynamic—no matter whose therapeutic method we study and how or when it was invented.

For the sake of simplicity, I have classified these fundamental forms of motivation into four categories of levels of motivation in treatment behavior. Note the term "treatment behavior." (Rado, 1956c) In psychiatry, it has become common to call all treatment behavior "transference," which is patent nonsense, because that would exclude realistic behavior. Treatment behavior is *everything* the patient does in the treatment situation, that is, his mode of cooperation with the therapist. Treatment behavior is contrasted with life performance that embraces all the work-a-day motivations and activities of daily life.

Now the lowest level of motivation to be found in every human being occurs in infancy, and every human being—including professors of philosophy and psychiatry—can regress to it under certain circumstances. In psychotherapy, I propose that this treatment behavior be called "magic craving." A completely discouraged and helpless adult patient retreats to the hope that the parentified physician will do miracles for him. *"The doctor must not only cure me, he must do everything for me, by magic."* If a human being's situation becomes desperate enough, eventually he will find himself on this rung of the ladder. His motivation, thinking, hoping, and craving will be along these lines. In effect, he will implore or dragoon the therapist, or try to win him over by expiation, to get the therapist to fulfill this desire. (Rado, 1956 c, d) Let me repeat: he can hold all the degrees of science that have ever been distributed, or he can be a simple, illiterate person. The intelligence and educational level make no difference. This reaching backward is triggered by distress and helplessness of the patient.

If we go a little higher up the motivational ladder we discover a child-like regressive tendency which corresponds to that somewhat higher rung of individual development and maturation—the period of infantile reliance upon the parents. This is the first really adaptive pattern in every human being's life. The child is not kept alive by his own adaptive abilities, by what he can do for himself; but he is sustained by means of what the mother or mother substitute can do for him. We all started out in this way, in a world in which a wonderful, admirable, almost magic-like person did everything or almost everything we wanted. The patient who regresses to this level sees in the therapist an idealized reincarnation of the parental images under whose auspices his life began.

This, then, is the model: When an adult patient feels like a helpless child, he seeks parental help and, therefore, parentifies the physician: *"I don't know what the doctor expects of me. I couldn't do it anyway. He should cure me by his efforts."* Whenever the patient is on that level of motivation (and again it makes no difference as to the kind of treatment, or brand of technique), his real interest is: *"What can the doctor do for me? He should do everything for me. I want to be his favorite child."*

This is, of course, also a regressive level of adaptation. When we go higher up, we then arrive at the self-reliant level of cooperation, that of the average adult person who has been capable of learning the simple adaptive patterns of daily life. *"I am ready to cooperate with the doctor. I must learn how to help myself and do this for myself."*

A consideration of these levels of motivation is fundamental for the understanding of any kind of psychotherapy. An adult realistic attitude of self-reliance culminates in the question: *"What can I do for myself: How can I best use the help of the doctor?"* This sponsors a constructive use of psychotherapy. The moment the realistic cooperative attitude is lost, and the patient regresses to the level of reaching out for a parent, and, beyond that for a magician, we are dealing with an entirely different situation. There is no more any desire, any interest for learning or for maturation. *"I just want to be your favorite and you must show me what a magician you are."*

Patients always feel and respond in either a dependent or a self-reliant manner, even when unable to observe and express these feelings.

The first self-reliant stage is, however, not the highest level of adaptation. Intelligent patients with a good educational background and a certain degree of aspiration can get further up the ladder. But this is usually available to only the adult patient who is desirous and capable of self-advancement, and it necessitates extensive learning. *"I am delighted to cooperate with the doctor. This is my opportunity to learn how to make full use of all my potential resources for adaptive growth."*

It gradually became clear to me that in the scheme I have presented, we have a foundation for a simplification of our description and understanding of what is going on inside of therapy, a simplification with a gain in, rather than loss of purpose.

In this connection, the unfortunate thing about trying to understand therapy in terms of such concepts as transference is that the word "transference" does not happen to be a *motivational* statement. It is a purely *descriptive* statement. The patient behaves in the way he used to behave in childhood toward his parent. But this is not all we are interested in. We are interested in *why* he does this, and *when* and *how*. After introducing the concept of transference it took Freud ten years before he raised the question, "What brings transference into play?" (Freud, 1924(a, b) & 1935) The answer he gave was a super-speculative one. He did not relate the appearance of transference to instinct as he had related almost everything else. What he said was that there was an even more elementary bio-psychic force: a "compulsion to repeat." Suddenly the patient's compulsion to repeat comes into play. But why does this compulsion appear at a given time? How is it associated with what is going on in the patient's life outside or inside the treatment situation? This was never asked and never answered. And the answer is simple enough. So long as the patient is capable of operat-

ing like an adult, he looks upon his treatment as he looks upon
any other enterprise: he wants to learn about himself and improve
his controls. He is capable of moving on a realistic level. Yet the
transference theory does not even have a category for the description of realistic behavior. Transference is childish behavior. When
the patient loses hope and self-confidence and becomes helpless,
then what does he do? The natural thing we would expect him to
do: he resorts to the behavior of those who are helpless because
they are undeveloped—children. It is natural to reach out for help.
The adult person, in a state of helplessness does the same thing.
He reaches out again for help in much the same way the child does,
and for much the same ends.

With the scheme I have presented, we have the fundamental facts
governing the requirements of all kinds of psychotherapy.

The question arises: which one of these levels of motivation can
we use for psychotherapy? The answer is, *every one of them,* depending on the circumstances. Of course, the attainable goals of
treatment differ from level to level. The higher the level, the closer
it approximates the most extensive degree of maturation, and the
more ambitious can the therapist be toward effecting change. The
less mature the motivation, the more the craving for magic, then
the more limited will be the goals. The goals, of course, must be
considered in terms of the time that is required or available for
treatment, and this consideration fits well into our approach for the
classification of the diverse forms of psychotherapy.

In considering short-term psychotherapy, I must first affirm that
I am employing a language somewhat different from the one customarily used, but one which I have tried to define. I should like
to begin by considering one treatment process which corresponds
to the lowest level of motivation, the level where the patient seeks
the magical help of his parents. This is hypnotherapy. Hypnotherapy
may fit into and bring about a materialization of the patient's hope
for magic. As a child, the patient knew that the "magic" help of his
parents was contingent on his own obedience. When the physician
tells him to go to sleep, whether he is sleepy or not, he senses that
again he will gain security through obedience; and so by the
action of his own secret desire, he enters into a hypnotic state in
which uncritical obedience to the parentified physician is automatic.
Surprisingly, beneath his complete surrender to the hypnotist he
feels triumphant because his own dream is coming true; he is receiving the magical help he craves. It comes true because he feels,
deep down in his mind, that he is a magician himself. The hypnotist

is but a deputy of his secret powers. The success of hypotherapy is indeed produced by the patient himself, who uses the hypnotist for the almost mechanical execution of his own innermost desire. (Rado, 1956c) Although hypnotherapy does not give lasting results, it is an excellent method of tiding the patient over an emergency, a situation which does not call for lasting results.

There are other treatment procedures at the lowest level of motivation, procedures which are based on "medical suggestion" or "waking suggestion." These are more or less counterparts of hypnosis, but are executed in the waking state. While many phenomena present in hypnosis cannot be produced in the waking state, nevertheless, the dynamic essentials remain the same.

Many patients approach treatment by maintaining the self-reliant attitude expected of an adult patient. Or, even if they are temporarily down to the level of dependence, they can be helped to move back to the level of self-reliance. Contrary to general pronouncements, this is often enough possible even in short-term psychotherapy. The consequences of working at the self-reliant level are of great importance, for only at this level can the therapist help the patient to acquire *new emotional skills* which are prone to be self-perpetuating, that is, no longer dependent on the ups and downs of the patient's feeling toward the therapist. This then is the mechanism through which short-term therapy can produce lasting results. Engaged in this type of work one finds that while some types of inhibitions can be broken up so that the patient becomes capable of acquiring new emotional skills, some other inhibitions have become rigid and apparently irreversible. In my opinion this is the most crucial area for systematic investigation. (Rado, 1962d)

We have found it convenient to refer to the procedures I have discussed so far as *reparative psychotherapy*. This term is used in contrast to the term *reconstructive psychoanalytic therapy*, which refers to the procedure developed in adaptational psychodynamics through the revision of Freud's early psychoanalytic technique. (Breuer & Freud, 1957), (Freud, 1924(a, b), 1925, 1935, 1950) The essence of the revision is this: Freud insisted that the patient should remain in "positive transference," which means in a state of infantile dependence on, and uncritical obedience to the physician, in his eyes the *ersatz-parent*, throughout the entire treatment procedure. The adaptational techninque requires that the therapist carry out the treatment as much as possible on the patient's self-reliant level of cooperation. (Rado, 1956 a, b, c, 1958, 1962 a, c) This move was probably impossible in an authoritarian European country such as Austria was in Freud's time, but it is certainly an essential requirement in a democracy such as this country.

At present, thanks to the initiative of the federal government, we are at the threshold of new mental health developments on a nation-wide scale. We are looking forward to the establishment of community mental health clinics by the thousands. While these clinics-to-come will have many responsibilities, the ministration of psycho-therapeutic help will be one of their foremost tasks. These clinics will expose the need for therapeutic techniques which we do not yet possess. But I am an optimist and firmly believe that we will be able to develop them, perhaps after a transitional period of uncertainty. The few remarks I have been able to make about the learning of new emotional skills and the struggle with petrified inhibitions indicates an important direction in which this development will take place.

These efforts will be aided from the outside by the change in our entire educational system. (Rado, 1962d) The country is learning fast: children have to be educated not to obedience but to self-reliance. The more this educational change advances, the smaller will be the number of patients who are not only suffering from disorders, but quickly come to feel utterly helpless and dependent. I refer, of course, to the so-called psychoneuroses, that is, over-reactive disorders, and in some respect to schizophrenia.

At the dawn of civilization, psychotherapy began with the mother's emotional ministrations to the child. Today it is still in the process of becoming scientific, and the time is not so far away when it may become at least as scientific as the other branches of medicine already are.

QUESTIONS AND ANSWERS

Question: Are there any special kinds of symptoms or syndromes that respond better to short-term than to long-term methods?

Dr. Rado: In general, nothing responds better to short-term therapy than to longer treatment, but brief therapy may be available in cases where long-term therapy is not. The most important criterion is emergency, where an important but temporary change is needed. The method of choice here is hypnosis. Criteria for other methods, organized according to types of cases, symptoms or syndromes, are not at the present time objectively available. They are available in what is known as the "feel" of the experienced therapist. After he has seen fifty cases, or a hundred cases, a therapist when he sees a patient gets a feeling that not much can be hoped for, that he had better limit his goals, that certain methods will work best, and so on.

Question: What about psychodynamic formulations as an aid to short-term therapy?

Dr. Rado: Without knowing the dynamics of the therapeutic process, the patient's own motivations and the dynamics of the patient's symptoms, we cannot do scientific work. What we know is surely only a fraction of what we expect to learn in the coming decade.

Question: How do we handle the problem of transference neurosis in short-term therapy?

Dr. Rado: Since we have, lovingly but definitely, challenged the concept of transference, we must question the concept of transference neurosis. Freud thought that the central dynamics could be copied in a neurosis focused through the relationship of the patient to the physician. Once I took the liberty of asking Freud, "Here is an impotent man, here is a frigid woman, now they develop a transference neurosis. In what way does this transference change his impotence; in what way does it change her frigidity?" I must confess that he was somewhat embarrassed, because he said to me, others being present at the time, "You are taking the statement too seriously, too verbatim. These are approximations." He did not know that the approximations would develop into full-fledged dogma in ten, twenty or thirty years.

Question: How do we deal with dependency?

Dr. Rado: This is a crucial item in short-term therapy. Since a patient tends to go down in his adaptational level, we must employ the reward principle, and with all our skill, bring him back to reality and make him behave in a manner we expect of an adult person.

Question: Should we deal with dreams in short-term therapy?

Dr. Rado: The idea that dealing with dreams is limited to long-term reconstructive therapy is an undefendable proposition. We may approach dreams somewhat differently, if we know that we will see a patient only a very limited number of times. But to say, "Please you have first to go into a psychoanalytic treatment of a conservative type before anybody can interpret or misinterpret your dreams"—that is not quite in order.

Question: Should one handle another member of the family other than the patient?

Dr. Rado: Talking to a husband, wife, parent or child, whoever is available and halfway rational, may help avoid impending breakdowns. There are many completely legitimate methods of psychotherapy that somehow are held suspect. To an extent this is due to the setting of rules of orthodox treatment. What the therapist needs is sound judgment, not knowledge of a rulebook, because none exists. Freud never dreamed of making all these rules that are attributed to him. In the very beginning, when people thought that he must be a charlatan because he was only "talking" to patients, he was happy if he did not see a relative of a patient. Today, when you cannot pick up a newspaper without reference to psychoanalysis, it is inexcusable for the therapist not to get all of the outside information he can possibly accumulate. When I talk to the husband or wife of a patient, I surely know that I will get a biased picture; but I do find out many things about a patient which I can utilize in my treatment. Not to do this is in my opinion a violation of elementary medical responsibility. Fifteen or twenty years ago, I listened to a speaker who said that he who invites relatives to appear in the doctor's office is not a psychoanalyst. This just doesn't make sense.

Question: What about using outside resources?

Dr. Rado: Utilizing whatever social and environmental resources that may be available is legally and morally permissible. It should not be up to the therapist on the grounds of who-knows-what theoretical considerations to deny the patient the help of useful resources.

Question: In the great wealth of your experience, can you describe what happens in treatment with relatively few sessions, the specific kinds of approaches you have used and what you believe was accomplished?

Dr. Rado: I have seen people benefit from as little as two sessions. What goes on in such cases, or in which types of cases these things can happen, is difficult to say. First, in a patient who manages to isolate himself from the human environment, the opportunity to reestablish contact with the world, even briefly, via the therapist, can have a very beneficial effect. Second, just to pour out, to use this relationship to talk about one's problems, to expose one's miseries, and to listen to a friendly human being respond (he should be friendly and not sit there like a Buddha), can have a very great influence in people who have long since lost that ability to turn to a friend, or to open up and reveal their agonies and troubles and fears so as to get some reassuring words. By reassurance, I don't mean that one needs to sell the patient the Brooklyn Bridge. Reassurance can be given on a realistic basis. You reassure by emphasizing, or, if you wish, overemphasizing the value of accomplishments achieved by the patient. Now, don't underestimate the value of this kind of help in some patients, for instance the patient who has isolated himself in a big city. Nowhere is it easier for a person to isolate himself than in a metropolis like New York. It would be impossible to hide this way in any suburban or country place. There are, I do not know how many people, in this position. The other day a patient came to see me. She gets some little money which saves her from starvation. Once or twice a week she goes to the supermarket to supply herself with food. The rest of the time she sits at home indulging in the elaboration of an imaginary love affair. She phantasies that a certain man is in love with her and she wants to be around when the telephone rings. She does not see a living creature, sometimes for one week, sometimes for two weeks. If she is sick somebody whom she knows may come in. Have you an idea how many people of this description exist in this city? Now, if a person of this kind comes in, the very breaking of her isolation, bringing her back to a human contact, encouraging her, attempting to help her regain the friendship of people whom she has dropped one by one until she has nobody, may in one or two sessions start a completely new trend in her well-being.

Question: In connection with this particular illustration, would you make some comments on the educational activity of the therapist? Can one devise a general formulation of dynamics that may be meaningful to the average patient?

Dr. Rado: If I understand the question, you wish me to elucidate by some example what is meant by helping the patient to learn. What is he to learn? First, he is not expected to learn intellectual formulas. If that would have any therapeutic value, he could sit down and read any number of books. Many people do try to read books, and after finishing them they find themselves precisely where they were in the beginning, if not more confused. Factual information in certain areas may be essential to communicate. For instance, many people have no idea as to the parts played in their lives by sex or competition. They may have struggled competitively all their lives without having an inkling of what they were doing. There is ordinary psychological information which has to be given the patient because he will never find it in books. But this is not *the* essential. All intellectual insight becomes therapeutically effective only when it percolates so that the patient begins to change his emotional reactions. In this emotional learning, intellectual formulas are a means to an end. For example, I can cite the case of a grown-up person who in matters sexual remained completely illiterate. Sex made her panicky. The very moment anybody began to talk about sex, her mind wandered off and there was no possibility of reaching her. You wouldn't have known that beforehand, because in our society, everything under the sun, from shoe-shine to farm implements to perfume, is advertised with reference to sex. How a person can remain so ignorant in matters of sex is puzzling. The answer lies in the fact that, because of fear, no information can penetrate the mind. And until in some way you manage to get hold of this fear, reduce it in some part, so that the intelligence again has an opportunity to operate, you can achieve nothing. In short-term or long-term therapy, the idea that insight alone has therapeutic influence is a fallacy. At the first real emotional upheaval, the whole effect of insight is over. The target of all psychotherapy is emotional change.

Question: In the patient in your illustration who poured out his heart to a friendly human being and after once or twice doing this was benefitted, which motivational level was operating?

Dr. Rado: This is difficult tc decide on the basis of the few days interrogation. In effect, it is the realistic level to which you appeal. You convey to her the idea that she should try to live again instead of existing in a death-like state. Now this is an appeal to reason. At the same time, her enjoyment of the physician's interest, the fact that this "learned man" has spent so much time listening to her story with such respect, naturally gives her a good deal of emotional satisfaction. So, probably an accurate description of this type of treatment would be a bit more complicated than the very schematized design which I have presented to you. But the realistic element evoked may be the germ, the basis on which further improvements can be built. The emotional satisfaction gained from a phantasied friendship with a man who knows nothing about it, may be amply substituted for by her feeling, much more realistic, that her doctor is her friend. There is, of course, no real telling what she will do with this experience, but one germ of realistic orientation has been planted, and perhaps that germ will give her an opportunity to grow. If you plant no germ for realistic adaptation, then her thinking can never be revised.

Question: I was a little bit concerned with your statement about emotional learning. Learning, of course, has a primary root in the soil of instruction. Well, would it then not be the function of the therapist to instruct the patient in a realistic meaning of normal and abnormal theory?

Dr. Rado: We may understand more about emotional learning by observing it taking place spontaneously without the benefit of a psychiatrist's efforts. For example, almost all children cry, because crying is a wonderful method for discharging tension. However, whereas one little boy would be ashamed to cry because he is told that he is four years old, another four year old girl would not dream of being ashamed of crying. What happened in the boy which did not happen in the girl or vice versa? This is all a matter of emotional control. The boy has learned self-control. He perhaps began to practice putting on a false facade. The girl is miles away from this hypocritical maneuver. A few years later, it may be different. The girl may be ahead of the boy. In other words, it is impossible in one or two words to describe what goes on except to emphasize that at all times, and at any age, we are all capable of changing our emotional responses. Emotional reactions are accessible to change through human influence. Psychotherapy is a form of human influence. Again, emotional reactions in people change decade after decade. If you do nothing more than observe what goes on in the daily life of people who never consulted a psychiatrist, who do not even know that there is such a thing as psychiatry, then there will be no doubt in your mind that emotional response may be altered.

Question: Do you think it is possible, or are you optimistic about the possibility, that a patient's commitment to treatment might change this patient's willingness to utilize the learnings of psychotherapy?

Dr. Rado: Yes, and the very moment that happens, you can bring him to a realistic level, and you can change your whole program of therapy. The very moment that he is willing to learn, you can say, "Well, this is a promising case. I can reach out for more than I originally thought possible." But the opposite happens, frequently, too. You have high hopes for the patient, but as time goes on, you begin to lower your goals. You are satisfied if you achieve even these minimal goals. A virtue in the psychotherapist is to have a realistic appraisal of how much he can constructively do for the patient. You know, in the old days, when the teaching was permeated with conservative analytic folklore, which soon infected all of psychiatry, the therapist was not supposed to be too much concerned with therapeutic results. That is like saying that a baker should not be too much concerned with whether the rolls he bakes are bad or good. Now, this was a tragedy. It is equally dangerous for the therapist to overshoot his mark, to find his own self, his therapeutic ambitions, his pride hurt if he is not achieving the impossible with his limited patient. How far one can go with therapeutic ambition depends on the circumstances. One should neither neglect the patient nor be over-ambitious for him since results will be self-defeating.

Question: Do you interpret the lower level of emotional operation in order to bring the patient to a more realistic level?

Dr. Rado: Certainly, but not in terms of levels. Let us assume you have a female patient who is operating on lower emotional levels. You do it somewhat like this. You tell the patient, "Now, let us just discuss for a moment what you are actually doing here." And then you describe to her that she is really not interested in anything you are trying to tell her, because she imagines that little good can come out of this by contrast with her grandiose phantasies of what must be done, and will be done for her by you. And then in such language as the patient's background and educational level prescribes, you explain that this is a dream, an illusion, that she cannot go along in life carrying the therapist in her pocket. You explain to her that she is not powerless and as hopeless as she makes herself out to be. You may say, "Now, you went to school, you were graduated, you finished that class, you went into a higher class, and so forth." Then you may give her a list of her achievements. "You must know that you are capable of doing things for yourself. You have to recapture your own self-confidence. You just throw away all the opportunities of an adult existence by behaving the way you do." You do not blame her for her defections. You know her responses are automatic. But they can be brought under control when she discovers that she is being victimized by a tendency to run away from everything. And, you explain to her that she cannot run away, because when she runs, all her problems run with her. There is no alternative but to try to do things for herself. And you explain to her that she should not mistake this for an invitation to bite into the bitter apple. This is really a magnificent opportunity to live. She has an opportunity to live like anybody else, and every day that she misses that opportunity is a day missed forever. She should be glad that she has an opportunity to recapture life *for herself.* In other words, you do not allow her to distort what you are telling her, thinking that she is going to the opera "on doctor's orders," or having intercourse with her husband "on doctor's orders." The idea is to redevelop hope and realistic desire and measures of self-confidence, which dictated her need and made it possible for her to come to your office in the first place. If she had been consistent in her parent-seeking and magic-craving attitudes, she would never have sought therapy. Even the most dependent patients can be shown little realistic activities—activities on which they can build. But it is important not to allow the patient to indulge in the illusion that the changes the doctor is talking about can be brought about in a few days. You have to say that progress may be inch-wise at first; then it will be a little faster, and so on. In other words the entire procedure must be imbued with the spirit of realism and common sense. And, I can assure you from years of experience, that many people, even sick people, have more common sense than one ordinarily realizes. A large percentage of humanity considers it a particular achievement to bury their common sense. Almighty God alone knows what slogans and fashions may have to be used to dig out the common sense and use it. But we do what is pos-sible in brief psychotherapy. The emotion that has to be changed is fear and resentment against fate.

Question: Do you have a concept of the unconscious in your sys-tem?

Dr. Rado: Even more than before, but under a different name. But I will first tell you what is wrong with the term "unconscious." This term was invented not by Freud, but by a German philosopher long before Freud was born. Freud reluctantly went along, step by step, using this term. The word "unconscious" then became one of the shibboleths of psychoanalysis. But the word refers to nowhere. How can we talk about such a thing, for instance, as unconscious consciousness of guilt—we have to replace the word with something more meaningful. Brain activity, in part, is self-reporting; these are your conscious phenomena. In part, it is non-reporting. But through certain efforts, you can discover that this non-reporting brain activ-ity can indirectly have a motivating influence. So we simply say the motivational significance of non-reporting brain activity discerned by a method like free association can be expressed in terms quali-fied by the word "non-reporting." You talk about "non-reporting" fear. In other words, the patient behaves as if he were afraid, and he is; but he is unaware of his state of fear. So when you talk about non-reporting fear, the word non-reporting refers to the brain. We are now well out of mysticism. The discovery of non-reporting motivational inner influences plays a tremendous role in long-term reconstructive therapy, and to some extent even in short-term ther-apy. This exploration is not a privilege that is confined to long-term psychoanalytic therapy.

Question: A little while ago, you remarked about how you would talk to patients, explaining that they had abilities, could develop themselves, could take advantage of potentials, and so forth and so on. Supposing this were an intelligent patient who had come to the same conclusion for herself previously. Why would your say-ing the same thing make any difference to her?

Dr. Rado: People very often talk to other people, in order to have other people tell them the same things that they tell to themselves, because thereby it becomes a verified reality, a fact. Many times people say these things to themselves, but something is missing. Something escapes them. Once this deep cleavage is breached through a relationship with the environment, as represented in the person of the therapist, activity is reopened; new opportunities, new developments may occur. Without the therapist, there would be little action. Also, we should not forget how many people improve from serious neuroses without any treatment. There is such a thing as a spontaneous recovery, which we very poorly understand except that there is no free association involved, nor a couch. Just ordinary living, perhaps fortunate changes in the life circumstances. She makes a good marriage; he gets a good job. Something happens, and then they pull themselves out of the hole by their own boot-straps. One criticism I feel I am justified in making is that too little attention is given to the study of spontaneous recovery. The reason, in part, is technical. You cannot single out in advance the people who will recover spontaneously. You can only say in retrospect, "My God, I used to know this man ten years ago—I can hardly recognize him for his change." Still, a retrospective study would be very challenging. I tried to do that once or twice, and I got a very curious response. "I feel so much better. Why in heaven's name do you suggest that I should go and trace back this whole development? Do you want to destroy what I built up for myself?" Still there are opportunities which may present themselves, which should be grasped so that we can learn about the mechanisms of spontaneous recovery.

Question: You said that if at a certain point we will know the motivations of human beings, we can establish a science of psychotherapy. Is that correct?

Dr. Rado: We can establish a scientifically refined form of psychotherapy. In other words, we can lift psychotherapy from the present level of a clinical science to a scientifically founded science.

Question: Now comes my question. With the enormous number of motivations and feelings that exist in any one human being, do you think it will ever be possible to know the real essence of what makes people do what they do?

Dr. Rado: We may take a lesson from the science of physics, and study how they succeeded in finding a few fundamental abstractions by ignoring countless variables. I have made an attempt to simplify the understanding of treatment behavior by elaborating a hierarchical scheme of four levels of motivation, a scheme that applies to every human being in western civilization. If we begin to collect the information which applies to everyone, not to certain groups of people, that is the type of inquiry in which psychiatry can invest its future. And, I am convinced that this will come about. It is only a question of time. An enormous amount of time is wasted discussing alternatives in the crude terms of clinical empiricism which do not permit such distinction. Let us consider, for a moment, physics and technology. I do not remember what the degree of precision is in measuring a milli-angstrom. It involves a fraction of a fraction of a millimeter. And if you make an error in one or two grades, which is an unspeakably tiny fraction of a millimeter, your whole project may be ruined in physics. Now ask yourself what is the degree of precision for a bricklayer? About a half an inch or an inch. For a man who makes a roof? Still more. There are crafts where the allowable precision is no more than about a variation of several inches. Thus, the very nature of the subject determines the degree of precision. You cannot, today at least, expect precision in introspectional data that exceeds the precision of the available methods. One can make oneself unpopular in the eyes of his colleagues if he says that in all psychologies, the means of validation should be a correlation with corresponding brain physiology, something demonstrable. But as long as psychological observations are to be validated only by psychological observation, the range of impression is so tremendous that it is unlikely that we will ever have a theory that is universally accepted.

V

Psychoanalytic Contributions to
Short-Term Psychotherapy

================================ FRANZ ALEXANDER, M.D.

(Editor's note: Dr. Alexander points out that psychoanalysis has supplied us with a model which enables us to study the dynamics of psychotherapy. It can help us in formulating practical principles about short-term therapy. Psychotherapy acts basically as a corrective emotional experience in which the therapist actively participates in creating a climate which does not repeat the traumatizing experiences of childhood. This rule must be followed no matter how provocative the patient may be. Discerning the nature of hurtful experiences with parental figures, the therapist may by design act in ways completely opposed to what the patient expects from authority. The key to shorter therapy lies in this ability to control transference. Another modification of technique is the changing of the number of interviews at certain phases in treatment to make the patient conscious of his dependency needs by frustrating them. Experimental temporary interruptions of treatment are also useful. Reminding the patient that treatment must be as short as possible discourages procrastination in facing up to important issues. There is a general trend toward over-treatment which caters to a universal regressive dependency trend. Much time may also be wasted in therapy in a fruitless search for early experiences. These, in recall, often constitute for the patient regressions that serve the purpose of avoiding handling later pathogenic conflicts. Dealing with the present and with the immediate life circumstances should supercede a concern with the past. What prolongs therapy, also needlessly, is counter-transference reactions, which are of a quality similar to parental attitudes that were traumatizing. On the contrary, what shortens therapy are reactions that are diametrically opposed to these parental attitudes. Urgent is the avoidance of a "parentifying" transference to enable the patient to take over his own life management. Improvement of existing techniques presupposes sophisticated research in the therapeutic process itself. The traditional modes of studying psychotherapy are now outmoded and new approaches are needed to deal with the countless variables in therapy. The model best suited for study of the psychotherapeutic transactional process is that of learning theory. In the "Question and Answer" section, Dr. Alexander covers many practical as-

84

pects of short-term treatment. An interview with a patient who was randomly selected illustrates some of the points stressed in the technical part of the paper).

BRIEF PSYCHOTHERAPY CALLS FOR MODIFICATIONS in technique. These modifications can best be understood if we examine the precepts on which psychoanalytic treatment is based. For psychoanalysis has provided us with fundamental insights into the underlying principles of all psychotherapies. I shall make some general statements about psychoanalysis and particularly comment on what psychoanalysis strives to do in treatment. I shall then consider modifications in analytic method that may be helpful in shortening treatment. I shall, finally, discuss some theoretical ideas about psychoanalysis in the light of learning theory. The case interview that terminates my contribution will hopefully illustrate some practical points.

There seems to be little doubt that the essential psychodynamic principles on which psychoanalytic treatment rests have solid observational foundations. I shall treat this subject briefly because these basic psychodynamic principles do not differ with different techniques. Technique is the application of sound psychodynamic principles, of psychodynamic knowledge and the understanding of psychological processes. The areas of agreement among psychoanalysts of different theoretical persuasions consist in the following observations and evaluations:

1). During treatment, unconscious material becomes conscious. Now this is true whether you do uncovering or supportive therapy. The patient's awareness about himself increases. He acquires insight, not because of interpretations, but because his ego faculties, one of which is perception of internal processes, increase. So during treatment, unconscious material becomes conscious in different degrees. That is true for all psychotherapy, including short-term therapy. Now this process increases the action radius of the conscious ego. The patient becomes cognizant of unconscious impulses and thus is able to coordinate the latter with the rest of the conscious content.

2). The mobilization of unconscious material is achieved mainly by two basic therapeutic factors. Interpretation of material emerging during free association and the patient's emotional interpersonal experiences in the therapeutic situation, the transference. The therapist's relatively objective—I emphasize and will come back to this—his relatively objective, non-evaluating, impersonal attitude is the principal factor in mobilizing unconscious material. Now I mentioned free association. Now free association is a word, a term, and it does not need to take place only on the psycho-analytic couch. If you sit with the patient during an interview, and you listen to the patient and let him spontaneously tell his story—that is also free association.

3). The patient shows resistance against recognizing unconscious content. Overcoming this resistance is one of the primary technical problems of psychoanalytic treatment to be sure.

4). It is only natural that the neurotic patient will sooner or later direct his typical neurotic attitude towards his therapist. He develops transference which is the repetition of interpersonal attitudes, mostly the feelings of the child to his parent. Now that is again not restricted to psychoanalytic treatment. There are psychotherapeutic situations in which this develops if one does not interfere with the development. This process is favored by the therapist's encouraging the patient to be himself as much as he can during therapy. The therapist's objective, non-evaluative attitude is the main factor, not only in mobilizing unconscious material during the process of free association but also in facilitating the manifestation of transference. Now why is that? The child learns that certain things are not done, or not thought, or not acted. Certain values are introduced in every child. He gradually eliminates those "bad things" from his consciousness because they have caused trouble for him in the past, such as rejection, punishment and so on. Freud emphasized this, namely that the child's ego is weak, and does not have adequate controls. What appears in consciousness is carried out right away. The child cannot resist temptation. I speak here of the small child. If the child wants to protect himself from trouble, the only way for him to do so is to exclude dangerous things from consciousness, because once they are conscious they are carried out. That is the basis of repression, which is a defense of the weak ego against impulses which are not accepted.

Now what happens in the psychotherapeutic situation? It defies the values which have caused the child to repress. No such values are expressed. The patient gradually learns that anything goes. So what caused the repression originally is more or less eliminated, namely a restricted value system. And that allows those things which were the cause of these early values to be introduced into consciousness. Not only does the therapist not condemn such thoughts, but there is a prize for expressing those things which once were forbidden.

I saw a wonderful cartoon the other day in the New Yorker Magazine. A bearded therapist is sitting behind the couch, on which there is a little girl, completely lost in the pillows. The admonishing therapist is saying, "Naughty, naughty, today you again have had a few nice thoughts." This is a caricature of the therapist's encouraging the patient not only to have forbidden thoughts, but to express them in relationship to the therapist who welcomes them. Not only is he not angry when the patient says, "Why you are an ass!" He says, "Bravo. That is what I want to hear."

The original neurosis of the patient which is based on his childhood experience is just transformed into an artificial transference which is encouraged to appear and which is a less intensive repetition of the patient's infantile neurosis. The resolution of these revived feelings and behavior patterns, the resolution of the transference neurosis, becomes the aim of the treatment. Now this applies primarily to the psychoanalytic process, or to any uncovering type of process.

There is little disagreement concerning these fundamentals of the treatment. Controversies which sporadically occur pertain primarily to the technical means by which the transference neurosis can be resolved. The optimum intensity of the transference neurosis is one of the points of contention. How long, how strong it should be, how intensely should the patient get involved?

Now here, if one could control transference, this could become a very important means of differentiating between more prolonged, more profound and shorter, briefer therapy. How long you allow this transference neurosis to go on, how intensive you let it become, how much you encourage it, and what you do about it, we shall talk about these matters a little later.

Now this is not the place to detail the various therapeutic suggestions which arose in recent years. Most of the modifications consisted in particular emphasis given to certain aspects of treatment. There are those who stress interpretation of resistance, others focus on the interpretation of repressed content. Fenichel stated that resistance cannot be analyzed without making the patient understand what he is resisting. (Fenichel, 1945) This is a very good remark. I often listen to discussions that state that one should focus on the resistance and minimize content. When I listen to these things I always ask myself, "Now how can you analyze resistance without calling attention to what is repressed, what the patient is resisting?"

It is most difficult to evaluate modifications in method because it is generally suspected—and I have repeatedly convinced myself of this—that authors' accounts about their theoretical views, do not precisely reflect what they are actually doing while treating patients. The reason for this discrepancy lies in the fact that the therapist is a participant observer who is called upon constantly to make decisions on the spot. The actual interactional process between therapist and patient is much more complex than the theoretical accounts about it.

In general, there are two main trends: (1) Emphasis on cognitive insight as a means of breaking up neurotic patterns. The patient understands it; he knows that it belongs to the past; he sees what he is doing. (2) The other places emphasis upon the emotional experience the patient undergoes during treatment. These are, of course, not mutually exclusive principles—insight and experience, yet most controversies center around emphasis on one or the other: cognitive versus experiential.

While mostly similarity between the transference attitude and the original pathogenic childhood situation has been stressed, I emphasize the therapeutic significance of the difference between the old family conflicts and the actual doctor-patient relationship. This difference is what allows a corrective emotional experience to occur which I consider as the central therapeutic factor both in psychoanalysis proper and also in analytically oriented psychotherapy. When I say "analytically oriented" I mean therapy that uses psychoanalytic principles.

The new settlement of an old unresolved conflict in the transference situation becomes possible not only because the intensity of the transference conflict is less than that of the original conflict, but also because the therapist's actual response to the patient's emotional expressions is quite different from the original treatment of the child by the parents. This difference is the crucial point. The therapist does not react to the patient's expressions of hostility either by retaliation, reproach or signs of being hurt. The fact that the patient continues, however, to act and feel according to outdated earlier patterns, while the therapist's reactions conform to the actual therapeutic situation, makes the transference behavior a kind of one-sided shadow box. The patient has the opportunity not only to understand his neurotic background, but what is the most important thing, at the same time, to experience intensely, the irrationality of his own emotional reactions. He sees that they do not fit the present situation. The fact that the therapist's reaction differs from that of the parent to whose behavior the child adjusted himself as well as he could with his neurotic reactions, makes it necessary for the patient to abandon and correct these old emotional patterns. After all, that is precisely the ego's basic function: adjustment to the existing external conditions. As soon as the old neurotic patterns are revived and brought into the realm of consciousness, the ego has the opportunity to readjust them to the changed external and internal conditions. This is the essence of the corrective influence of these series of experiences which occur during treatment. (Alexander & French, 1946) (Alexander, 1956, 1958) However, one must consider that the emotional detachment of the therapist often turns out, under observational scrutiny, to be less complete than this idealized model postulates. The ideal is not achieved, but he is objective and detached.

Since the difference between the patient-therapist and the original child-parent relationship appeared to me a cardinal therapeutic agent, I made technical suggestions derived from these considerations. But these are again technical suggestions applicable to any form of psychotherapy, and especially to short-term or brief therapy. The therapist, in order to increase the effectiveness of the corrective emotional experiences, should attempt to create an interpersonal climate which is suited to highlight the discrepancy between the patient's transference attitude and the actual situation as it exists between patient and therapist. For example, if the original childhood situation which the patient repeats in the transference was between a strict punitive father and a frightened son, the therapist should behave in a calculated permissive manner. If the father had a doting, all-forgiving attitude towards his son, the therapist should take a more impersonal and reserved attitude. This suggestion was criticized by some authors, in that these consciously and purposely adopted attitudes are artificial and will be recognized as such by the patient. Experience showed me that that is not the case. If it were the case, then we could not handle people at all. Every nurse, given instructions, behaves kindly, but firmly with one patient, permissive and understanding with another. Every teacher does it. He knows which boy needs a strong hand and which a permissive hand. And we therapists, we can and should correct and adjust our behavior to the existing situation. I maintain that the therapists's objective emotionally non-participating attitude is itself artificial, inasmuch as it does not exist between human beings in actual life. Neither is it as complete as has been assumed. This controversy will have to wait, however, to be decided by further experiences of practitioners.

I made still other controversial technical suggestions aimed at intensifying the emotional experiences of the patient. I mean that unintentionally they really lead to an influence of the time factor which we are so much interested in for good reasons. One of these suggestions was changing the number of interviews in appropriate phases of the treatment in order to make the patient more vividly conscious of his dependency needs by frustrating them.

Another of my suggestions pertains to the ever-puzzling question of termination of treatment which is a problem in any form of psychiatry. How long should we ask a patient to come? You know that volumes have been written about this. And I do not believe there is still any consensus. The traditional belief is, however, that the longer the analysis lasts, the greater is the probability of recovery. Experienced analysts more and more came to doubt the validity of this generalization. If anything, this is the exception. Very long treatments lasting over many years do not seem to be the most successful ones. On the other hand, many so-called "transference cures" after very brief contact have been observed to be lasting. A clear correlation between duration of treatment and its results has not been established. There are not any reliable criteria for the proper time of termination according to my experience.

We tried to formulate at the Chicago Institute certain ideas about this behavior in the therapist's office, in his family, in his feeling about himself, in his dreams, in the character of the dream change during therapy, and so on. I did not find any one of these criteria, or all of them taken together as reliable. Improvement in therapy often proved to be conditioned by the fact that the patient was still in the treatment situation. Again and again, I thought that all these supposed criteria had been fulfilled. The patient behaved wonderfully at home and elsewhere. He was really a different man, *as long as he was in treatment*. His changes were conditional to his having his pound of flesh every day—his dependent gratification. He could be mature if he were fed, so to speak, at the same time. The patient's own inclination to terminate or to continue the treatment is not always a reliable indication of how well he is either. The complexity of the whole procedure and our inability to precisely estimate the proper time of termination induced me to employ the method of experimental temporary interruptions, a method which in my experience is the most satisfactory procedure—at least for me. At the same time it often reduces the total number of interviews substantially. The technique of tentative interruptions is based on trusting the natural recuperative powers of the human

personality, which are largely under-estimated by many psychoanalysts and psychotherapists and psychiatrists in general. There
is a normal general trend towards over-treatment. A universal regressive trend in human beings has been generally proclaimed by
psychoanalysts and others. Under sufficient stress everyone tends
to regress to the helpless state of infancy and seek help from others.
The psychoanalytic treatment situation caters to this regressive attitude. As Freud stated, treatments often reach a point where the
patient's will to be cured is outweighed by his wish to be treated.
This was a very early statement of Freud. He said it but I have
never seen a reference to it. I believe I may be the only living psychoanalyst who has called attention to this very momentous statement. It is true that Freud did not follow up on this thesis.

In order to counteract this universal regressive trend, continuous
pressure on the patient is needed to make him ready to take over
his own management as soon as possible. During temporary interruptions, patients often discover that they can live without their
analyst. When they return, those emotional problems which are
still unresolved come clearly to the fore. This, I think, was used
very early in Berlin, at the Berlin Psychoanalytic Institute—frac-
tioned analysis, they called it. But that also went into oblivion.

But if I can pick out the most erroneous thing which I learned—
fortunately, I did learn non-erroneous things, for the most part—
but one of the most erroneous things I learned, and this from my
own analyst, a very experienced man, who explained to me in
portraying analysis, and particularly how to handle a patient, that
when a patient comes to the analyst, he is to be told that it will
be a long process. He is asked not to bother about time or worry
about the duration of treatment. Analysis will last, we do not know,
a year, two years, three years or indefinitely. I believe that is the
worst kind of attitude that one can convey to a patient. A patient
who comes to you with an acute anxiety state wants immediate
help, but he wants to procrastinate getting well too. Every human
being, but neurotics even more so, has a desire not to face the
actual issues. If one starts out treatment by saying to the patient
that one can forget about time—that is the wrong emphasis. You
encourage procrastination by this. Instead, one should say that we
wish to complete treatment as fast as possible. Of course, we are
not magicians, but our intention is to make therapy as brief as we
can. It may last longer than we hope, but at least we make an attempt at shortening treatment.

In this connection, I want also to discuss another point. I called attention not long ago to Freud's distinction between two forms of regression. That is very pertinent at this time. Freud first described regression to a period of ego development in which the patient was still happy, in which he functioned well. Later, Freud described regression to traumatic experiences which he explained as attempts to subsequently master an overwhelming situation of the past. In traumatic neurosis, we see patients dream again and again of the combat situation in which they were traumatized. They conjure up most unpleasant experiences.

During psychoanalytic treatment, and in all psychotherapies too, both kinds of regression occur. Regressions to pre-traumatic or pre-conflictual periods, and regression to unresolved traumatic situations. The regression to these pre-traumatic fixation points, these satisfactory modes of instinctual behavior, may offer excellent research opportunities for the study of personality development. But therapeutically they are not relative. Often we find that the patient regresses in his free associations to conflictual early infantile material as a maneuver to evade the essential pathogenic conflicts which occurred later. This material appears as "deep material" and both patient and therapist in mutual self-deception spend a great deal of time and effort in analyzing this essentially evasive material. The recent trend to always look for very early emotional conflict between mother and infant as the most common source of neurotic disturbance is the result of overlooking this frequent regressive evasion of later essentially pathogenic conflicts. Serious disturbances in the earlier symbiotic mother-child relation occur only with exceptionally disturbed mothers. The most common conflicts begin when the child already has a distinct feeling of being a person, has an awareness of himself, and relates to his human environment, to his parents and his siblings, as to individual persons. The oedipus complex and sibling rivalries are accordingly the common early sources of neurotic patterns. There are many exceptions, of course, where the personality growth is disturbed in very early infancy. These are still the minority of cases.

Another issue which gained attention in the post-Freudian era is the therapist's neglect of the actual present life situation in favor of preoccupation with the patient's past history. This is based on the tenet that the present life circumstances are merely precipitating factors mobilizing the patient's infantile neurosis. In general, of course, the present is always determined by the past. That is true for both neurotic and nonneurotic persons. Freud, in a rather early writing, proposed the theory of complementary etiology.

A person with severe ego defects acquired in the past will react to slight stress situations in his present life with severe reactions. A person with a relatively healthy past history will require more severe blows of life to regress into a neurotic state. These latter, are the cases where the briefer treatment approach is most successful.

Some other authors like French, Rado and myself feel that there is an unwarranted neglect of the actual life circumstances. The patient comes to the therapist when he is at the end of his rope; he is entangled in emotional problems which have reached the point where he feels he must have help. These authors feel that the therapist should never allow the patient to forget that he came to him to resolve his *present* problems. The understanding of the past should always be subordinated to the problems of the present. Therapy is not the same as genetic research. Freud's early emphasis upon the reconstruction of past history was the result of his primary interest in research. At first, he felt that he must know the nature of the disease he proposes to cure. The interest in past history at the expense of the present is the residue of the historical period when research in personality dynamics was of necessity a prerequisite to developing a rational treatment method. Some of the so-called neo-Freudians, of course, went to the opposite extreme, insisting that they did not believe in the necessity for the therapist to delve into the infantile history of the patient. This is also not a good policy, because the past is important. Not to a degree though that it eliminates the present.

These controversial issues will have to wait for the verdict of history. Their significance cannot yet be evaluated with finality. Do not be mistaken, however, that there is no growing inclination to question the universal validity of some habitual practices handed down by tradition over several generations of psychoanalysts. There is a trend toward greater flexibility with the patient and his problems. This principle of flexibility was explicitly expressed by Edith Weigert (1954), Thomas French, myself (Alexander & French, 1946) and still others.

While there is considerable controversy concerning frequency of interviews, interruptions, termination, the mutual relationship between intellectual and emotional factors in treatment, there seems to be a universal consensus about the significance of the therapist's individual personality for the results of the treatment. That is still an unexplored area—really an extremely rich field in which to make new discoveries. The interest in the therapist's personality first manifested itself in several contributions dealing with the therapist's own emotional involvement with the patient, the so-called "counter-transference phenomenon." Freud first used the expression "counter-transference" in 1910. It took, however, about thirty years before the therapist's unconscious, spontaneous reactions toward the patient were explored as to their significance for the course of the treatment. The reasons for this neglect were both theoretical and practical. Originally Freud conceived of the analyst's role in the treatment as a blank screen, a mirror, which carefully preserves the analyst's incognito, and upon which the patient can project any role, be it that of the image of his father, mother or any significant person in his past. In this way the patient can re-experience the important interpersonal events of his past undisturbed by the specific idiosyncratic qualities of the therapist. The phenomenon called counter-transference, however, sharply contradicts the "blank screen" theory.

It is now generally recognized that in reality the analyst does not remain a blank screen, an uninvolved intellect, but is perceived by the patient as a concrete person. There is, however, a great deal of difference among present day authors in the evaluation of the significance of the therapist's personality in general and in his counter-transference reactions in particular, and I will not go into the different opinions. Mostly the therapist's involvements are considered an impurity, a disturbing factor. Some of us mentioned certain assets in the counter-transference, like Fromm-Reichmann (1957), Benedek (1953), Weigert (1954), who are, by the way, all women. This is really not an accident. Women are specialists in counter-transference through their predestination to become mothers and to interact with and counter-transfer to their children. They considered that counter-transference has important, helpful connotations. They point out that the analyst's understanding of his counter-transference attitudes may give him a particularly valuable tool for the understanding of the patient's transference reactions. There is, however, general agreement that too intense emotional involvement on the therapist's part is a seriously disturbing factor.

I myself believe that the counter-transference may be helpful or harmful. It is helpful when it differs from that of the parental attitude towards the child which contributed to the patient's emotional difficulties. The patient's neurotic attitudes, as I mentioned before, develop not in a vacuum, but as a reaction to parental attitudes. If the therapist's reactions are different from these parental attitudes, the patient's emotional involvement with the therapist is not realistic. This challenges the patient to alter his reaction patterns. If, however, and this is very important, if the specific counter-transference of the therapist happens to be similar to the parental attitudes toward the child, the patient's neurotic reaction patterns will persist and an interminable analysis may result.

That is one of the things I discovered. If I had feelings towards the patient which resembled his father's attitude, I might just as well discontinue treatment because the patient's neurotic reactions were developed directly in relation to this type of a parent figure. If I am the same, the reactions are applicable. The patient knows how to deal with such a parent, neurotically to be sure, but still as an adaptation. I see this also in supervising treatment. Very recently, I worked with a candidate who could not get anywhere with a specific patient. Finally, we discovered that his attitude towards the patient was exactly the same as that of the patient's father. When he recognized this and consciously worked against his own inclination, he started to change the whole tenor of the treatment. The treatment then began to move.

One of the most systematic revisions of the standard psychoanalytic procedure was undertaken by Sandor Rado. His critical evaluation of psychoanalytic treatment and his suggested modifications deserve a particular attention because for many years Rado has been known as one of the most thorough students of Freud's writings. As years went on, Rado became more dissatisfied with the prevailing practice of psychoanalysis, and proposed his adaptational technique. As is the case with many innovators, some of Rado's formulations consist of new terminology. Some of his new emphases, however, are highly significant. He is most concerned, as I am, with those features of the standard technique which foster regression without supplying a counter-force toward the patient's progression, that is to say, to his successful adaptation to the actual life situation. Rado raises the crucial question: Is the patient's understanding of his past sufficient to induce a change? He said, "To overcome repressions and thus be able to recall the past is one thing; to learn from it and be able to act on the new knowledge, another." Rado recommends, as a means to promote the goal of therapy, raising the patient from his earlier child-like adaptations to an appropriate adult level which will "hold the patient as much as possible at the adult level of cooperation with the physician." The patient following his regressive trend, parentifies the therapist, but the therapist should counteract this role and not allow himself to be pushed into the parental role. Rado criticizes orthodox psychoanalytic treatment as furthering the regressive urge of the patient by emphasizing the "punitive parentifying" transference upon the parentalized image of the parent. Rado points out that losing self-confidence is the main reason for the patient to build up the therapist into a powerful parent figure. This is because he needs one. Rado's main principle, therefore, is to bolster up the patient's self-confidence on realistic grounds. He stresses the importance of dealing with the patient's actual present life conditions in all possible detail. Interpretations must also embrace the conscious as well as unconscious motivations. In concordance with French's and my similar emphasis, Rado simply states: "Even when the biographical material on hand reaches far into the past, interpretation must always begin and end with the patient's present life performance, his present adaptive task. The significance of this rule cannot be overstated." I agree.

Rado considers his adaptation technique but a further development of the current psychoanalytic technique, not something basically contradictory to it. It should be pointed out that while criticizing the standard psychoanalytic procedure, Rado in reality criticizes current practice, but not theory. According to accepted theory, the patient's dependent, or in Rado's terms, "parentifying" transference should be resolved. The patient during treatment learns to understand his motivations. This enables him to take over his own management. He assimilates the therapist's interpretations and gradually he can dispense with the therapist, from whom he has received all he needs. The therapeutic process recapitulates the process of emotional maturation. The child learns from the parents, incorporates their attitudes and eventually will no longer need them for guidance. Rado's point becomes relevant when one points out that the current procedure does not always achieve this goal, and I may add, it unnecessarily prolongs the procedure. The reason is that the exploration of the past became an aim in itself, indeed the goal of the treatment. The past should be subordinated to a total grasp of the present life situation and serve as the basis for future adaptive accomplishments.

At this point my emphasis is pertinent, that it is imperative for the therapist to estimate correctly the time when his guidance not only becomes unnecessary but detrimental, inasmuch as it unnecessarily fosters the very dependency of the patient on the therapist which the latter tries to combat. I stated that deeds are stronger than words. The treatment should be interrupted at the right time in order to give the patient the experience that he can now function on his own and thus gain that self-confidence which Rado tries to instill into the patient by positive interpretations. No matter, however, what technical devices they emphasize, the goal of these reformers is the same: to minimize the danger implicit in the psychotherapeutic situation, namely encouraging undue regression and evasion of the current adaptive tasks. It is quite true that regression is necessary in order to give the patient opportunity to re-experience his early maladaptive patterns and grapple with them anew to find other more appropriate levels of feeling and behavior. The key to successful psychotherapy is, however, not to allow regression in the transference to become an aim in itself. It is necessary to control it.

In view of these controversies, there is a feeling that it is necessary to study the therapeutic process much more precisely than was done before. All that we knew came from the therapist's own account. A therapist who does not record the analysis, permits words to fly away. He reconstructs from memory sometimes six or seven hours of therapy, often after seeing many other patients. There is error in this reconstruction. If he does it right after the hour, he will still forget and repress many things. In every science on which theoretical conclusions are based, observations must be preserved and re-examined. In our field this is not yet the case. Therefore, the urge to study therapeutic process by objective means, by direct observation, by records and films, is understandable. Finally, the Ford Foundation gave out large grants to several research centers. I received such a grant and we studied over five years the therapeutic process by several trained observers, watching every move through the one-way-mirror, listening to every interview from the first to the last. The interviews are recorded. Some of them are photographed. And these records have been restudied innumerable times. In one case which consisted of ninety-eight interviews, I practically know each interview by heart. I use this material for teaching. This is an entirely different approach than what we were accustomed to. It is much more controlled. The material which was collected is, as was expected, really most overbearing and voluminous. It took several years of collaborative work to process it. Yet, even at the present stage, several important conclusions emerge, the most important of which is the fact that the traditional descriptions of the therapeutic process do not adequately reflect the tremendous complex interaction between therapist and patient. The patient's reactions cannot be described fully as transference reactions. The patient reacts to the therapist as to a concrete person and not only as a representative of parental figures. The therapist's reactions also far exceed what is usually called counter-transference. They include in addition to this, interventions based on conscious deliberations and also his spontaneous idiosyncratic attitudes. Moreover, his own values are conveyed to the patient even if he consistently tries to protect his incognito. The patient reacts to the therapist's overt but also to his non-verbal hidden intentions, and the therapist reacts to the patient's reaction to him. It is a truly transactional process.

In studying this transactional material, I came to the conviction that the process can be best understood in the terms of learning theory. For the tremendous problem of how to study and the parameters to be chosen, I have finally arrived at the conviction that if you apply the basic principles of what we know about the learning process, that can give us the best leads, particularly the principle of reward and punishment and also the influence of repetitive experience. I almost do not dare to say principle of reward and punishment because that is so contradictory with the original psychoanalytic concept. Learning is defined as a change resulting from previous experience. In every learning process one can distinguish two components. First, the motivational factor, namely the subjective needs which activate the learning process, such as the hunger of the rat that drives him to run the maze. Otherwise he would not be hungry and he would not run. And, second, certain performances by which a new behavior or pattern suitable to fill the motivational need is actually acquired, such as the rat turning left, right and so on in the maze. In most general terms, unfulfilled needs, no matter what their nature may be—hunger for food, hunger for love, curiosity, the urge for mastery—all of these initiate groping trial and error efforts, which cease when an adequate behavioral response is found. After the rat satisfies his hunger, he lies down. He does not try to learn anything more immediately. And when he knows the maze, he does not need to learn it anymore. When he is hungry this triggers off behavior that rewards him. Adequate responses lead to need satisfaction which is the reward for the effort. Rewarding responses are repeated until they become automatic and their repetition no longer requires effort or further experimentation. This is identical to the feedback mechanism described in cybernetics. Every change of total situation requires learning new adequate responses. Old learned patterns which were adequate in a previous situation must be unlearned. They are impediments to acquiring new adequate patterns.

I am not particularly concerned at this time with the controversy between the more mechanistic concepts of the older behaviorist theory and the newer Gestalt theory of learning. The controversy pertains to the nature of the process by which satisfactory behavior patterns are acquired. This controversy can be reduced to two suppositions. The older Thorndike and Pavlov models operate with the principle of contiguity or connectionism. Whenever a behavioral pattern becomes associated with both a specific motivating need and a need satisfaction, the organism will automatically repeat the satisfactory performance whenever the same need arises. So hunger, satiation and the specific pattern which was found, no matter how—these three things are connected with each other. And Thorndike and Pavlov had an idea that they are imprinted, so to say. Because they are not connected spatially and temporally with each other, they are imprinted in the brain and become functional like reflexes. The organism's own active organizing function in creating these connections is neglected. The finding of the satisfactory pattern, according to the classical theory, takes place through blind trial and error. So that one tries and finally an effort is successful. This effort is then repeated. But the finding of the solution is based on luck. One tries many things until one finally fits by accident and that becomes set.

In contrast, the Gestalt theoretical model operates with the supposition that the trials by which the organism finds satisfactory behavioral responses are not blind, but are aided by cognitive processes. The memory of previous experiences helps. I am not concerned with the essential difference between the connectionist and the Gestalt theories of learning. Probably both types of learning exist. From our point of view it makes no difference if one learns through intelligent trials which are based on partial previous experiences and generalizations, or whether one simply shoots a machine gun so to speak, in the dark, and knows that somewhere there is the target at which he will shoot with as many bullets as he has. No matter how one finds the solution, once found, it becomes connected. And that is the basis of new learned patterns, a forging of a connection between three variables: a specific motivating impulse, a specific behavioral response, and a gratifying experience which is the reward.

Accepting Freud's definition of thinking as a substitute for acting, that is to say, as acting in fantasy, the reward principle can be well applied to intellectual solutions of problems. Groping trials and errors in thought, whether blind or guided by cognitive processes, lead eventually to a solution which clicks. Finding a solution which satisfies all the observations without contradictions, is accompanied by a feeling of satisfaction. After a solution is found—occasionally it may be found accidentally—the problem solving urge, as everyone knows who has tried to solve a mathematical equation or a chess puzzle, ceases and a feeling of satisfaction ensues. The tension state which prevails as long as the problem is not solved yields to a feeling of rest and fulfillment. This is the reward for the effort, whether it consists of blind or intelligent trials. The principle of reward can be applied not only to a rat learning to run a maze, but to the most complex thought processes as well.

The therapeutic process can be well described in these terms of learning theory. The specific problem in therapy consists in finding an adequate interpersonal relation between therapist and patient. Initially this is distorted because the patient applies to this specific human interaction feeling and behavior patterns which were formed in the patient's past and do not apply either to the actual therapeutic situation or to his actual life situation. During treatment the patient unlearns the old patterns and learns new ones; that is, if the therapy is successful. This complex process of relearning follows the same principles as the more simple relearning process hitherto studied by experimental psychologists. It contains cognitive elements as well as learning from actual interpersonal experiences which occur during the therapeutic interaction. These two components are intricately interwoven. They have been described in psychoanalytic literature with the undefined, rather vague term "emotional insight." This is a magic word. The word "emotional" refers to the interpersonal experiences; the word "insight" refers to the cognitive element. The expression does not mean more than the recognition of the presence of both components. The psychological process to which the term refers is not yet spelled out in detail. Our present observational study is focussed on a better understanding of this complex psychological phenomenon—emotional insight—which appears to us as the central factor in every learning process including psychoanalytic treatment or psychotherapy. Every intellectual grasp, even when it concerns entirely non-utilitarian preoccupations, such as playful puzzle-solving effort, is motivated by some kind of urge for mastery and is accompanied with tension resolution as its reward. In psychotherapy the reward consists in less conflictful, and more harmonious interpersonal relations, which the patient achieves first by adequately relating to his therapist, then to his environment, and eventually to his own ego ideal. At first he tries to gain the therapist's approval by living up to the supreme therapeutic principle—to the basic rule of frank self-expression. At the same time, the patient tries to gain acceptance by living up to the therapist's expectations of him, which he senses in spite of the therapist's overt non-evaluating attitudes. And, finally, he tries to live up to his own genuine values, to his cherished image of himself. Far-reaching discrepancy between the therapist's and the patient's values is a common source of therapeutic impasse.

This gradually evolving dynamic process can be followed and described step by step in studies made by non-participant observers. Current studies give encouragement and hope that we shall eventually be able to understand more adequately this intricate interpersonal process and to account for therapeutic successes and failures. As in every field of science, general assumptions gradually yield to more specific ones which are obtained by meticulous controlled observations. The history of sciences teaches us that new and more adequate technical devices of observation and reasoning are responsible for advancements. In the field of psychotherapy, the long overdue observation of the therapeutic process by non-participant observers is turning out to be the required methodological tool. This in itself, however, is not sufficient. The evaluation of the rich and new observational material calls for new theoretical perspectives. Learning theory appears to be, at present, the most satisfactory framework for the evaluation of observational data and for making valid generalizations. As it continually happens at certain phases of thought, development in all fields of science, different independent approaches merge and become integrated with each other. At present, we are witnessing the beginnings of a most promising integration of personality theory with learning theory, which may lead to unpredictable advances in the theory and practices of the psychotherapies. It should lead to a shortening of our psychotherapeutic techniques.

QUESTIONS AND ANSWERS

Question: How do you handle the complex problem of the emotional experience when the psychological relationship with the mother and father has been very different? What are some of the things that you do in working with this all too common kind of situation?

Dr. Alexander: You see, the whole theory is obviously over-simplified. Assuming that in the patient's adaptational history, there was one important parent whom the patient learned to react to with a certain attitude, that is what we will be repeating in the transference. That is what we try to avoid in the therapist's reactions—the repetition—the repetition of the parent's reaction. Obviously, this is an over-simplification because as you correctly say, sometimes the patient has two equally important interpersonal dilemmas, so to speak. What do you do then? How can you relieve both? Well, I do not have the answer. This is still an experimental question. Peculiarly, however, the original neurotic adaptation of the person is already an integration of these different genetic factors, so to speak. It makes very little difference which angle is acted in the parent. There is only one Gestalt, so to say. The reaction to the mother or father is partially determined also by the other parent's attitude. And in the present the whole complex situation, the pattern is then directed towards the therapist. We do not find it difficult to discern what is the real issue today. Usually there is a leitmotif in every patient's neurosis which has different facets. It makes no difference which facet you attack. When one facet is changed, the whole Gestalt is dissolved. That might sound a bit too theroretical, but I cannot answer it with a more tangible answer.

Question: Are there any special kinds of symptoms or syndromes that respond better to short-term than to long-term?

Dr. Alexander: My first reaction would be that symptoms or syndromes are not the best way of trying to categorize between indications for long or short-term therapy. What counts, if I may again use a theoretical concept, is the patient's integrative capacity or ego strength. The important thing is that the cure never takes place entirely in the psychotherapeutic situation. What happens in therapy is that one puts the patient on the right track, and then the ego takes hold. Eliminating one emotional block sometimes suffices to allow ego development. Now to take one hurdle, eliminate this hurdle and others follow. So to say, the organism does it for itself. You know not even a surgeon can accomplish a cure. What can a surgeon do? He can cut and then put together the surfaces of the wound and wait for nature to heal. The ends must grow together. The surgeon cannot grow them together. He can protect the patient from infection, create conditions which are good for healing. And that is exactly the same in a mental problem. We cannot do the integrative work, but we can create conditions for the work. We can create an interpersonal situation which the patient can handle because it is less intensive and because it does not repeat, so to say, the neurotic pattern. But that is all. So whether the therapy will be short or long

really depends in the ultimate analysis on the ego's integrative capacity, not what kind of symptoms or syndromes the patient has. I
have seen ulcer patients who reacted after ten interviews. One case
which I saw, in one interview reacted beautifully. Others, two,
three, four years went on and with not much having been achieved.
So the question is not what kind of syndromes and symptoms but
what type of patients we are dealing with.

Question: Since it is manifestly impossible within the confines of
a short term psychotherapy program to arrive at the definite psychodynamics in many cases, is it possible to present a general formulation of dynamics that may be meaningful to the average patient?

Dr. Alexander: You know again, here, the individualist comes out
of me. Because my idea is that every patient—to a good psychotherapist—every case is a problem in itself. Of course, you can say crossword puzzles are different, but there are certain general principles
which you can apply to all crossword puzzles. But human beings—
with human beings we are a little bit more particular. Each case
has its own solution. Everybody has his own number. And I do not
think we can achieve very much if we try to treat the patient according to a roughly correct formula. Now you know when the sociological approach became very popular, these avant garde psychoanalysts begin to ask such questions. Here is a patient of a middle
class Jewish family, or a mountaineer family, or a strict Catholic
background. Here is what interested him, that satisfied him. Now
I know the patient's sociological background, so I understand the
patient better. And they came to the conclusion that for sociology
that is a magnificent thing. If we are interested in groups and group
attitudes, and want to understand, say the typical middle class
person in the fifties, we can then come to some generalizations. The
differences are not important. But when you are a therapist, you
do not care whether the patient became neurotic because his father
belongs to the middle class. The sociological influences in each
concrete case were through interpersonal reactions between parent
and child. Now you can be a typical middle class parent, but have
a very peculiar individual neurosis. Your influence upon the child
will be entirely different from another middle class person. Again
we are interested in the individual case. And I do not think, as
strong as we cherish psychotherapy in our Western civilization, that
we should forget that psychotherapy is a highly individualistic
procedure. We are interested in each individual person. We want
differences, and we do not want to come to some great generalization which fit a little bit, but not entirely. In our society, we believe

that these individual differences are good. If you take a totalitarian state where individual differences are only disturbing because there is one formula and everybody must behave accordingly, and feel as he is expected to feel, in such a civilization individual psychotherapy is not what it is here. You try to understand why the patient feels as he does. Psychotherapy does not try to adjust the patient to one formula, but to find a compromise between his idiosyncratic qualities and the existing milieu in which the patient lives. There is no general formula for everything. In other words, the sacrifice of individual creativeness, the differences and so on, that is a different world, and in such a world maybe psychotherapy can be practiced this way. But not in our civilization. As long as we believe in the sanctity of individual differences, the dignity of the individual, which Renaissance humanism introduced, this is the principle which still animates us in Western civilization.

Question: Are goals in short-term therapy limited to symptom relief or are reconstructive personality changes possible?

Dr. Alexander: My answer is definitely yes, definitely yes for reconstructive change. Again, the time element is not what would determine whether personality changes occur or not. Everybody knows Les Miserables of Victor Hugo, in which one experience changes Jean Valjean from a hardened criminal into a law abiding citizen. It is, of course, a novel, and this probably happens very seldomly in a dramatic way. But the principle is very correct. You remember the story when that hardened criminal faces the Bishop. All the silverware is there, and he says, "Well, what are you doing here? I give you all that as a present. Now go home." That cured him. But his whole personality was geared to the fact that the world was bad and hard, that it had mistreated him, and made him want to mistreat the world. And now here was an exception to this principle which undermined his whole philosophy of life—his emotional philosophy, not intellectual. This lesson is still the most important one in psychotherapy. Now this does not happen so dramatically in psychotherapy as in literature. It happens with small reactions, small experiences that repeat themselves. One of our cases, for example, explained to me at the very end of a follow-up study. He came in and announced that something bothered him. And we talked about the results, and so on. He said, "Yes, doctor, but I must tell you now that I am still embittered that you used me as an experimental animal. You treated me, not to help me, but to get benefits for yourself or for your colleagues." And I looked at him and said, "Yes, of course, I thought you knew that. Nobody said I didn't.

But that is quite natural. Does it mean that I was less interested in you, in helping you because I also wanted to learn? Are these mutually exclusive? Of course, I wanted to learn. And that was only one of my motives. So I had, in treating you, two motives. To help you and to learn. That meant my interest was only greater." And he said then a strange thing. He said: "You know this is something so incredible that I hear now. You are the first person who has told me the truth. My mother and my brother always pretended that they did everything for me even when they exploited me for their own purposes. And you admit it." This was a corrective emotional experience for the patient. During therapy several such corrective emotional experiences had happened. For example, the first time he showed hostility, and knowing the family background, I was anything but retaliatory. He said, "But that is so peculiar. I expected that you would throw me out. And nothing like that happened." Well these are the things that change a patient. Now, whether it will take place in one session or twenty sessions or two hundred sessions, I think will depend on many factors. In short-term therapy, the same thing can happen. The intensity of the emotional experience can be strong if the two personalities, therapist and patient, fit to create a corrective experience. That same patient with one kind of doctor will need only a few sessions; with others, five years could not be enough. The range is so tremendous, the variables are so numerous, and the combination of them so enormous that you cannot generalize. There is a tremendous chance element in therapy. In every treatment situation, I feel, that it is a great chance whether the two personalities will click. And such things determine whether therapy is short or long.

Question: Are there any methodological differences between long-term and short-term methods, and qualitative differences in techniques in short-term compared to long?

Dr. Alexander: Not as I practice therapy.

Question: Are there any special psychotherapeutic techniques that can deal with target symptoms, like obsessional states, or phobias, or depressions?

Dr. Alexander: Well I think one probably could formulate a few rule of the thumb statements. For example, I learned that phobias cannot be treated successfully on the couch with daily interviews over long periods of time. It is much more important to pressure the patient from the beginning, not to follow the strong regressive tendency which fear and anxiety cause. So I do not put those patients through long treatments or even make regular appointments.

I say: "You come when you have fear again. Call me up and we'll try to fit you in." Now this may be very complicated for your schedule. But no reliance should be given the patient on you. After I know the patient's history and have seen the patient for let us say two weeks or so, then I begin to be completely irregular. I use the same technique with obsessive compulsive cases who make out of treatment the essence of life. I do not anymore use any structured therapy with this type of case.

Question: Is a transference neurosis desirable in short-term therapy? How may we manage it most constructively if it does develop?

Dr. Alexander: I think a transference neurosis develops in every case. The doctor is an authority person and the patient begins to behave toward the authority person, like a child does to the parent. This is always there, and you must use it and work with it. It is the essence in every therapy. How much you call attention to it; how much you allow it to develop by too intensive contact; how much you encourage the patient to transfer outside of therapy—those are problems which you must decide from case to case. But you cannot simply eliminate transference because it is a natural phenomenon. How can you prevent water from flowing downwards and not upwards? Transference develops because, essentially, that is the nature of the beast.

Question: Are there ways of managing resistance in short-term therapy that differ from long-term therapy?

Dr. Alexander: Yes, I think there are, but whether you can always apply the rules, is another question. I would think that if you trust the patient's ego strengths, you can analyze resistance and what is resisted much more directly. If you are not sure how much the patient's ego can take, and if you try to eliminate resistances too fast, the patient then will react with increased regression. Those are things which we must find out by groping experimentation. I consider that every psychotherapy is a rule in itself, since there are few general rules one can follow. I like to use the technique of trial interpretations which I give very early only to decide how the patient will react. If used too drastically, this may not turn out too well. This happened to me once and I lost the patient after the second interview. This was a retired businessman who had a phobia. He lived in the suburbs and the phobia consisted in his not being able to go farther away than the sight of his house. Turning around the corner and not seeing the house created panic. His wife had to accompany him in going downtown. Now this man had several partners. In fact he had made a very clever arrangement. Since he was the senior originally, he had arranged that no matter what happened to him, whether he retired or worked, he would indefinitely have same share of the business profits. He came to me with his phobia, and he said: "Doctor, you must help me, because I can't let them alone, I mean they can't—they'll ruin the business." The more he talked, the clearer it became to me that the opposite was true. He was beginning to be a little senile and apparently they did not want him around. They were glad to pay him only so that he would not come near the office, since his presence created only trouble. This was such a denial technique, that the situation became obvious to me in the first half hour. Anybody would have seen it. So I thought "What shall I do with him? He is a little senile. His theory is that he got his phobia from a sunstroke in his garden. He believes that it is an organic thing and nothing can be done for it. But everybody says he should come to me. So listening to him at the second interview when he gave me more details, I gave him a trial interpretation. What I had in mind was this: If I let him face the facts, what would he do? Would he run out? Or would he consider what I told him and then want to continue in treatment? This was for me an acid test, a criterion of whether I should bother with him at all. So I told him that sunstrokes never cause phobias. Let us forget about the sunstroke for the time being. I said: "I think that you have a nice financial arrangement and don't need to go to the office. You feel that they don't like you anymore. You bother them, and that hurts your pride. So you develop a phobia. You regress; you react like a child; you are afraid; you want a good excuse now not to go to work. You do not want to base it on a lack of usefulness, but rather, because sunstroke created a phobia within you, you are unable to appear at work. I think the only thing is to face these facts. That is the situation and you see how you can adjust yourself to this. You are financially secure. Maybe you should draw the conclusion to stay home, and then you won't need the phobia." He looked at me, got up, called to his wife who was sitting in the waiting room, and, in an extremely childish voice, he exclaimed, "Mama, let us go home." Whereupon the wife came in, took him by the hand and they walked out. The next day she called me back and said that her husband told her what my ideas were. She exclaimed: "You hit the nail on the head. I know that. I don't need a psychiatrist for that. What you said I knew all the time. But I'm very glad you told him. Now he will either be cured and give up this phobia, or I don't know what will happen. But that was the only thing you could have done."

I said to myself then, that either the patient would come back and I could then work with him toward the best solution or he would stay away with his phobia. The solution he evolved to save his face, and to believe that sunstroke gave him a phobia that justified his not needing to face the situation, and that because of this his partners would run the business into the ground, was the only solution he wanted for his problem. So sometimes a neurosis is the best solution for a person. Therefore, I would say that the handling of the interpretations should not be too drastic. This should not stop you from experimenting boldly. Trial interpretations, not quite so drastic, but you know, ambiguous interpretations will tell you, give you clues as to how much the patient can take now. That will determine how slowly or rapidly you have to work.

Question: How does one utilize dreams in short-term therapy? Does one employ them in any way other than that in long-term therapy?

Dr. Alexander: You use dreams exactly the same way as in long-term therapy.

Question: Since there are many patients who develop intensive dependency relationships and, consequently, tend to make therapy an interminable affair, how can we deal with such patients in a short-term approach? Are there ways of by-passing dependency or resolving it, or directing it at therapeutically corrective foci other than a never-ending therapeutic situation?

Dr. Alexander: You can't deal with such patients in a short-term approach. The extremely dependent person can probably never get along without symptoms, some kind of crutch. It depends again on the resiliency of the ego. Interruptions are probably the best way to convince the patient that he does not need he therapist as much as he believes. Let him become dependent and then at the last moment interrupt therapy and see what he does.

Question: Is that why vacations help the patient often more than not?

Dr. Alexander: That's right. Absolutely.

They were all very difficult and catchy questions, but I hope I was able to answer some of them.

CASE INTERVIEW

(*Editor's Note:* The following history of the patient interviewed by Dr. Alexander is from the case record: The patient is a twenty-three year old, single man who came to the Postgraduate Center for Mental Health for an intake interview. He is tall, thin, wears horn-rimmed glasses, has unruly long brown hair, and is dressed in rumpled, casual clothes. At first, he seems diffident and frightened, rolling his eyes and appearing mildly disorganized. In the course of the interview he becomes more composed, abstracted and sarcastically contemptuous of himself and others. His complaints are that he cannot study as well as he wanted to; he is afraid to date girls; he is tense all the time; he has attacks of asthma. He had been in psychotherapy for a year at the age of seventeen with a social worker at the Jewish Board of Guardians who saw him once weekly; following that he was seen by a psychiatrist once a week. He entered therapy then for essentially the same difficulties that brought him to the Center, but his asthmatic and allergic attacks were infrequent and he was able to look at a girl "without throwing up." He had considerable feeling about the psychiatrist he had seen, complaining that he was never interested in him and even fell asleep in one session. However, he was never able to express any resentment towards the doctor for fear "he wouldn't help me."

The patient's family consisted of father, mother, a sister five years older than the patient, and the mother's mother. His father was a factory foreman, a very nervous, strict man who easily became angry with his son and hit him for talking too much when the father came home from work or when he exhibited enuresis, which continued until the patient was seven years old. The patient felt that the father preferred his sister, who was very pretty and bright, giving her a much larger allowance while being a "miser" with him, explaining that men should work for their money and that he should begin to learn this as soon as possible. Other recollections of the father are negative ones also. The father teased him at the dinner table about his enuresis, saying that he would have to "put a rubber band around it" if he did not control himself. He felt bitterly resentful and embarrassed over this and over many other instances when his father rejected or humiliated him.

The death of his father when he was eleven years old came as a severe trauma. Death was sudden. The father had been in mildly poor health for some time; the patient returned from school one day to be told that his father was dead. His response to this news was to cry constantly for several days; he still remembers this event as "the worst time in my life." A tic-like habit of pulling hair dated from this time. He recalls having wished his father dead as a child, but he was also faced with the fact that his father's death had left him as the only man in a household with three women, a position he did not like or feel able to deal with. At one point he said that even though he had disliked his father, he felt he "had a soul" and he really loved him.

The patient's mother is described as a "fool, stupid but sweet, dull." She worked as a secretary. He remembers her as affectionate when he was a little boy, although he felt her seductive intentions toward him. He feels that she was "too interested" in his penis and fondled it when washing him. He felt also that she was really a very "non-giving" and impersonal woman who did not want to know about his school work or other interests. He felt that she had been very dependent on his father, but he professed being unable to see how they got along with each other. When the father died, he felt that the mother tried to make him the head of the house, which frightened him. He became very aloof, teasing, sardonic and provocative with her and they soon settled into a distant relationship. He became very concerned that she might see him nude at this time, and he remembers locking the door carefully to exclude her and his sister and grandmother. Recently the patient's mother remarried, of which he approved. He moved from her house shortly before this marriage.

The mother's mother also lived with them, but she was a rather passive woman whom the patient always remembers with contempt, as an ignorant and superstitious person.

The patient's sister was fairly close to the patient after the father's death, although they had been competitors prior to that. He remembers being a deliberately bothersome little brother to her. He felt that she was a sadistic, aloof person and he always identified himself with the boy friends that she rejected. She was, he avowed, like his father, irritable and nervous. However, she settled down after her marriage to a successful lawyer. She now has two children and seems happy.

His asthma attacks began at the age of sixteen when he was spending the night with relatives in the country. He awoke during the night and he was terrified to the point where he "passed out." He awoke the next morning without symptoms, and he did not experience a return of symptoms for several months. At that time he had been discussing leaving the city to go to college, and he was told by his first therapist that this was the reason for the asthma. He has been told by his mother that he had asthma when he was two or three because of an "allergy to a cereal" she fed him. His attacks increased in frequency and severity, complicated by a severe "hay-fever type of allergy almost every morning." At one point he left the city to attend camp. This was his first absence from home. He was free of asthma symptoms, but he was so lonely and unhappy that he returned after a short time. He remembers many childhood nightmares prior to the asthma attacks, but he feels that they stopped after the asthma began. At times he has awakened with the "asthma feeling," a "fear of death" and acute anxiety, but no physical symptoms.

Another major symptom, his difficulty in studying, began to be apparent after the father's death. He remembers his father's "fencing him in" to learn the multiplication table. His scholastic difficulties began, he feels, with a teacher ridiculing him in algebra class when he was twelve years old. In spite of feeling very inferior academically, he was in a special progress class through high school. He achieved very high scores on various tests of scholastic aptitude and currently he has a scholarship for full-time graduate study. He has sexual fantasies or obsessive thoughts whenever he studies; he cannot write a paper because he finds his efforts not up to the self-imposed high standards he must reach. He demands of himself that he aspire to great things in life, but he is dissatisfied with every goal he has achieved, immediately setting another and blaming himself for not having grasped it immediately.

Although as a child he was very easily frightened, awkward and not athletic, he found friends attracted to him by his ready wit and his skill at clowning. He tended to be the class jokester who "baited" the teachers. He demands of his friends that they be very intelligent, and he tends to have only male friends, most of whom are socially awkward and afraid of dating. With his own recent experience in dating, he has found for himself the role of "man about town." He has been aware of how he can make another person feel uncomfortable without knowing why by his joking and his sarcastic comments.

A fear of girls started when he was twelve years of age, soon after the father's death. Prior to that time he remembers carrying girl's books home from school and feeling relaxed with them. Later he mastered his fear and recently he has begun to date an intelligent, attractive college student, having an affair with her, almost getting engaged but backing out at the last minute for fear that she was not the right girl. Not long ago he had involvements with two girls, roommates, who live in the next apartment. In all these relationships he has found himself unable to be affectionate and tender, automatically reverting to his usual sardonic and teasing manner as soon as "sex-in-itself" is over. He has also been very critical of the girls next door for their low intelligence and lack of beauty, wondering anxiously how his friends and others would feel about him for dating them since they are not perfect. Women he does not know he assumes to be like his sister, i.e., aloof and contemptuous of him. Those women he *does* involve himself with and who care for him are, he believes, like his mother; they are "stupid" and he teases them in the same way he teases his mother. He has a markedly sadistic conception of sex as "sticking" the girl and achieving pleasure only for himself. He also feels that he needs a woman who is stronger than he is, to push him towards a career; and he complains that the girls he dates are "not motherly enough."

He is very critical of himself and expects himself to live up to extremely high standards. If he fails to experience himself according to these demands, he feels very angry with himself and complains that he "cannot do anything" and that there is "nothing good" about him. He fears his emotions as "animal" or as "sentimental" and not in accord with his demand of himself that he be witty, urbane, composed and brilliant.

Toward the interviewer he manifests an ambivalent attitude, and he is much too free to express the negative side of these feelings, complaining that "all this psychology is bullshit." He is afraid of getting a therapist who is not old or experienced enough to help him, *"tres gauche,"* and not "stern enough to stop me from clowning."

He revealed a recurrent anxiety dream in childhood of coming home and finding the house gone. This dream is similar in emotional tone to his many dreams of traveling, of being alone and feeling anxious about it. On several occasions his dreams have been frankly sexual, involving sexual relations with a younger woman who was in some way associated with his sister or a younger cousin who was close with him during childhood.

When approached about having an interview with Dr. Alexander, he was at first flattered and enthusiastic in his acceptance. Later he expressed anxiety and concern about it, but was willing to be interviewed. The interview was conducted in a one way mirror room into which the patient walked diffidently and greeted Dr. Alexander.)

Pt: Hello.
Dr: Hello. (pause) .... If you can, give me as much detail about yourself as you can.
Pt: I suppose you want to know how the attacks of asthma started. I left my home for a weekend to stay with some friends of the family. They were rebuilding their house at the time. There was paint and sawdust, and building tools around. I felt that the time may have contributed to the attack. The attack came during the middle of the night.

It woke me up very suddenly. I remember no dreams. I remember being awake. The image is all very clear. It was a very severe attack, with, I almost felt the time—well, it was very frightening. Well I felt I wouldn't survive it, and I fell asleep. I think the attack itself brought on sleep. My breathing was very troubled, and I fell asleep and I woke up; my breathing was unimpaired when I woke. I felt very frightened.

Dr: Frightened?

Pt.: Yes. I was sent home immediately.

Dr: Oh, you were in the country.

Pt: Yes. This was I think in the month of August. Well, I was going to a general practitioner who recommended that I not go swimming for the balance of the summer. (Pause).

Dr: Swimming?

Pt: And I don't think he recommended anything else, but he may have given me some little pills.

Dr: But no skin tests?

Pt: No skin test.

Dr: Allergy tests?

Pt: No.

Dr: You never had that at any time in your life?

Pt: Yes, I think several years after; probably the end of my fifteenth year or seventeenth, at any rate, my last year or two in high school. Then I had regular trouble. It began with asthma, which probably occurred infrequently, but almost continually my nose was clogged, painfully so. Very distressing. And then it occurred to me that I had asthmatic difficulties, which would come several times during the week, all the time at night. I was not aware of any medication at the time, any effective medication.

Dr: You woke up with an asthma attack. That was the regular disturbance?

Pt: Yes. Yes.

Dr: You woke up from sleep?

Pt: Yes.

Dr: You mentioned before that sometimes you dreamt.

Pt: Well, yes, but not much. (Pause).

Dr: You don't remember any at all?

Pt: Well, I was not at the time particularly impressed with the content. Though I felt at the time, well, the dream, when there was asthma, I felt that the asthma precipitated the dreams, more than the other way around. I never felt that the dreams were so terrible that they could bring on an asthmatic attack.

Dr: Did it impress you that they were nightmares or anything like that?

Pt: Not that I recall. My first dreams were dreams as a child.

Dr: Oh, as a child you had dreams?

Pt: Yes, I probably had occasional nightmares, as an adolescent, but I can't remember them.

Dr: You don't recollect, you don't know whether they were upsetting or not?

Pt: My memory is not too good, but I don't think, even then, that I thought they were connected. (Pause).

Dr: Now, you say that it was in the month of August.

Pt: I think so.

Dr: You were there only for one night?

Pt: I may have been there several nights before the attack. In any event, I had visited the place before.

Dr: Oh, you did. That is the first time that you slept there though?

Pt: Probably not the first time I slept there either. I had until that age, and even beyond that, very rarely left my home. This had been one of the first times that I was scheduled to be away from home for perhaps a week.

Dr: But that's of interest, the first time you were scheduled to be away? (*Often in asthma the anxiety of separation from mother is a basic etiological factor.*)

Pt: It may have been. I certainly had never otherwise, I think, been away from home for more than a few days.

Dr: Now, why was it that you never were away from home?

Pt: Oh, I was afraid to go away, but I don't think the opportunity presented itself.

Dr: You were afraid?

Pt: Yes, but I think, if I felt that these were the people, ... that these people ...... I don't think I could have been too frightened. I think it's more out of circumstances than calculations. (*This is probably a denial mechanism to mask his fear of separation.*)

Dr: Than what?

Pt: Than calculation. I don't think it was calculated by myself or my parents that I shouldn't go away. It just worked out that way.

Dr. It just happened. I see. Yes, but there is the spirit that the family was close.

Pt: I don't understand.

Dr: It was a close family.

Pt: Very true.

Dr: What do you think of that?

Pt: By close, do you mean continuous contact?

Dr: Was it continuous contact?

Pt: It was.

Dr: There was your family, and a grandmother?

Pt: My grandmother came to live with us only when my father died.

Dr: Your father died much before that?

Pt: Oh yes, so there were just the four of us. At this point there is my grandmother, my mother and my sister and myself.

Dr: Did you exclude anybody? Somebody you did not think of?

Pt: There were never more than four. Unless I'm missing something. There were never five. There were always four.

Dr: Your father died.

Pt: He sort, of—my grandmother sort of substituted.

Dr: Yes. Would you tell me a little bit about your family.

Pt: Well, my father, I probably think of him as a severe person, not especially open; often irritable. Well usually irritable. Usually his moods were not predictable. (Pause).

Dr: Not predictable?

Pt: Yes.

Dr: You were not free with him?

Pt: Not especially, and he worked I think six days a week, and I went to sleep very early and he came home late.

Dr: You were on your guard, when you saw him?

Pt: I guess that would be so.

Dr: He was irrascible?

Pt: I may be painting too bleak a picture, but I mean my feelings were such that it was like that.

Dr: Well that's the important thing, how he lived in your memory, not how he was exactly.

Pt: Yeah, my memory tends to sympathize with him.

Dr: Well, yes, that is what is important for us.

Pt: I mean, I've repeated this to doctors so often now, that I'm, I'm making, that's what I feel really.

Dr: But you have felt that he was not an easy person?

Pt: No, not an easy person to live with.

Dr: And your mother?

Pt: My mother was always under his shadow. He respected her very much, I mean. He was always very considerate of her, as he was by and large with the whole family. He was a very good family man. Uh, my mother, was a pretty simple soul. She tries to purge all thoughts from her mind. She doesn't, doesn't think too much even now. I suppose I got along well with her till I was thirteen or fourteen, when I was increasingly disappointed and very disillusioned by her extreme simple mindedness, or what seemed to me at the time to be extreme simple mindedness.

Dr: Now, how did she treat you? Was she a demonstrative person?

Pt: I always thought she treated me well, but looking back, it was extremely reserved. (Pause).

Dr: She was very reserved.

Pt: Yes. And I don't think so, in the early years so much. But certainly as an adolescent. She was very reserved. We didn't have too much communication.

Dr: Not much communication.

Pt: I mean that the social situation was good, you know. It was a nice family and everything; but looking beneath the surface, there was no rapport.

Dr: Did you confide in her?

Pt: No, no, no. I did very little. I had no confidence.

Dr: Why not?

Pt: Mostly because she did not present the opportunity. I guess I should have wanted to.

Dr: Were her reactions—well how were her reactions?

Pt: Mostly, I didn't have the opportunity to get any reactions, because she didn't present herself. Even afterwards, like I tried to communicate with her, her reactions were mostly, "You're thinking too much."

Dr: She didn't encourage you?

Pt: No. Very little, very little.

Dr: Were you an unhappy baby?

Pt: I don't think so. I was a very timid child. I don't think I cried too much. I do not think I didn't cry enough either, I mean I think I didn't.

Dr. Why didn't you cry? (*These questions are related to what may be the source of his asthma, the substitutive cry for mother.*)

Pt: I mean I think I cried when it was necessary to cry, I *think* I cried. I probably cried, but I don't think I was a cry-baby.

Dr: Well, wait a second, you said you didn't cry and now you say you cried. (*His confusion and denial are perhaps resistance mechanisms.*)

Pt: I, I, I, cried, maybe a little more than most kids, but I don't think I was a cry-baby, I mean.

Dr: It all depends.

Pt: One who cries more than a non-cry-baby. I guess, I don't know what a cry-baby is.

Dr: A baby who cries a great deal.

Pt: No, I didn't cry too much.

Dr: And what was mother's attitude? Try to reconstruct that.

Pt: I guess that she wasn't very noticing of my crying.

Dr: Yes.

Pt: I find it hard, I can't get any particular image of it. I just have a feeling.

Dr: Would you say she was impatient?

Pt: If I had to pick one feeling, I would say impatient, if I had to pick one attitude.

Dr: But not so that she directly punished you when you were crying.

Pt: No, no. (Pause).

Dr: She would say—well you are a big boy, are you not ashamed, and that type of thing?

Pt: She probably would say just that.

Dr: Well, how was she towards your sister?

Pt: Well, uh, my feelings occurring, I guess now, was that a greater relationship existed between them. But I think I always wrote that off to their being of the same sex. My sister was very bright, and so at a pretty age she was able to, you know. She was close to my mother. And that made for a greater relationship.

Dr: How did you react to this?

Pt: I don't think it concerned me that much. I had a better relationship with my sister; I had a stronger relationship with my sister than my mother. But I don't think, well, my sister at this point, when my father died, and my sister was maturing at this point, she was an adult, and the rivalry was lessened.

Dr: When I read your history, it appeared that not only you were feeling rejected, but you had not much confidence in yourself. Is that correct?

Pt: That's true, I had very little confidence.

Dr: Yes.

Pt: Definitely true.

Dr: In what respect?

Pt: Probably any respect at all. I feared everything. I feared everything. I had confidence in nothing. No, I had no confidence in anything at all. As much fear as I could possibly have.

Dr: Physically and emotionally?

Pt: I don't think there's anything I wasn't afraid of.

Dr: Have you ever thought of what made you so fearful, what kind of experiences?

Pt: I think I was born to it.

Dr: Yes? Well, why do you think that?

Pt: It's the logical thing. I started off timid, and I've come to live with my timidity somewhat, and I—(Pause).

Dr: And you know that the timidity can be diminished and encouraged by experiences with the people who are living with you,—your parents, peers and all that, teachers.

Pt: Yes.

Dr: Now, one incident in your history. The teacher, when you were twelve years old, came at you when you were in front of the class, and you couldn't solve that mathematical problem or something?

Pt: There were any number of incidents, where the kids used to make fun of me. But they were, they made no more fun of me than they made of the other kids in the class. I remember incidents that now, you know, are completely ordinary. But yet they offended me even as a six-year-old or five-year-old. I was hurt by the slightest discouragement from a teacher.

Dr: So you were very sensitive. Well, you know, that is too easy an explanation to say, "Well, I was born that way." A person becomes sensitive to criticism. There is a history and reasons why one becomes sensitive to criticism. The logical assumption is that maybe you were much criticized early and you couldn't do much about it.

Pt: Yes.

Dr: That would be logical. But what do we know about it from your recollections?

Pt: I remember being criticized and I remember being extremely dismayed by the criticism.

Dr: Well, who criticized you?

Pt: Well, it doesn't seem to make a difference.

Dr: But who did?

Pt: Everybody. Any criticism just meant that the criticism was of such a nature, as to, I mean, my objective recollection of it, little things, like "stop making noise," or "why don't you go play elsewhere?" or— these things.

Dr: I am very interested to hear about this. Snatches of memory, for it gives us an idea about the atmosphere which prevailed, you know.

Pt: Yeah, but the, I mean, I can't have any hard feelings for being criticized, because the criticism was very routine.

Dr: But you only grow up in one family, not in two. You can't compare what happens and what is routine.

Pt: Well, I went to moving pictures. I know what other families are. I got ideas of how I would talk to a child. Even with extreme benevolence, I would probably criticize the child, as I was criticized, and the child would not be disturbed, as I was disturbed. (*This again seems like a denial mechanism.*)

Dr: So it's really a very deeply ingrained characteristic of yours.

Pt: Yes.

Dr: Well, you told me your father was unpredictable, you never could know how he would react.

Pt: He was not too predictable.

Dr: Yes.

Pt: He was moody.

Dr: Never warm?

Pt: Never warm.

Dr: And mother was the same?

Pt: My mother was not as moody. My mother was predictable. She was always pretty reserved. My mother's attitude was pretty passive. My mother was pretty much always the same.

Dr: Yes. But after your father died, you must have had a rather difficult situation there.

Pt: Yes, yes, I must say. I don't think I realized the full impact at the time. I knew it was increasingly awful. But I don't think I added up the figures, you know.

Dr: One doesn't add up the figures, but the feelings about it remain.

Pt: Well, I never attributed anything to it, I didn't know at the time that it was because there were three women and one male.

Dr: Would you think that they expected of you,—your mother maybe —a great deal?

Pt: Respected?

Dr: No, expected. Expectation.

Pt: They expected of me? No, no, they expected very little of me, my mother was very permissive. I mean, from the age of thirteen or fourteen, I had to account to her for extremely little.

Dr: No, not accounting to her, and expecting things from you.

Pt: I know, yeah, she also expected very little of me, she expected little. Whatever I did was alright with her. Even being a slob.

Dr: You were not pushed in any direction?

Pt: No.

Dr: But you did push yourself. Were you a very perfectionist type of person, never satisfied with your own performances?

Pt: This is a new revelation, I mean, I don't, I wasn't aware of this. I mean, now, looking back, I would say it could be attributed to perfectionism, my behavior at the time, but then I wouldn't have thought beyond that.

Dr: Yes, but you must feel badly about being a slob.

Pt: No, not always, sometimes I was comfortable with myself.

Dr: But you changed your idea about that sometimes?

Pt: Well, now, it's been suggested to me, I see it myself, but I am, tend towards, if something isn't as it should be, I guess I just kind of disassociate myself from it.

Dr: Would you enlarge upon that.

Pt: If my school work is not,—it's hard for me to enlarge upon it. This is not, it's not a conscious process. I don't think this is, I mean, an inflexible thing. Where, uh, I write things off to perfectionism, uh, my school work is poor perhaps just because I'm inept. I just can't do well.

Dr: And you worry about it.

Pt: Yeah.

Dr: You try hard.

Pt: I don't always try hard. I frequently do give in.

Dr: Give in?

Pt: More often give in, yeah, I don't try very hard. I try hard, but, you know, I'll just say to myself: "I'll stay home and study for the evening. But my studying does not come off."

Dr: But you give the impression as if you have accepted the fact that you are ineffective, or can't live up to certain expectations, your own expectations. You give in, more or less, compromise or accept things. That's the impression which you are giving me.

Pt: I don't accept it on a large view, the over-view. I accept it at the moment, but I mean, I'd like to do something successfully. But when it comes to studying for it, and opening a book, my concentration is weak, and I discourage easily and would just as soon close the book as not.

Dr: How old are you now.

Pt: I am going to be twenty-three.

Dr: When did you start going out with girls?

Pt: I was eighteen.

Dr: And there you were also timid?

Pt: Oh, extremely.

Dr: Ineffective?

Pt: Well, as with books, I like them as an idea, but with them, I was frightened.

Dr: You didn't touch a girl even if you were attracted?

Pt: That's true.

Dr: Kissing?

Pt: Not so easily, perhaps a good night kiss.

Dr: Oh, a good night, not a so-called sensual kiss.

Pt: No.

Dr: You wanted to, but—.

Pt: I wanted it as a general idea, at the moment.

Dr: Well, you felt attracted.

Pt: Oh, yes.

Dr: Excited?

Pt: Not when I was with the girl.

Dr: Oh?

Pt: Well, in the nineteenth year, I was more frightened, more than before. When I was home, I may have felt excitement.

Dr: The idea, but then the presence of the girl; you were so frightened that your excitement disappeared, vanished, so to say, is that about it?

Pt: Yes.

Dr: You went to bed with girls, no? When you were eighteen or nineteen?

Pt: No. Well, I went to bed with a girl at twenty-one.

Dr: And you knew this girl already before?

Pt: Yes.

Dr: You were in love with her or it was only a physical thing?

Pt: Yes, it was love.

Dr: What do you call love?

Pt: I'm not quite sure.

Dr: Tender feeling, or only sexual feeling?

Pt: No tender feeling always; it was tender feelings sometimes.

Dr: And also sexual. You had no difficulties?

Pt: No.

Dr: Did anybody know that you were having an affair at home?

Pt: Yes, I suppose so. I, uh, I guess so.

Dr: Who?

Pt: Well, I didn't come home to sleep every so often.

Dr: Oh, they concluded things. But you didn't tell them you had a girl friend.

Pt: Oh they knew I had a girl friend.

Dr: But when you stayed out with her, you wouldn't say that anything happened at all.

Pt: Uh, I never described anything sexual to them.

Dr: Not describe, but did you make any direct reference?

Pt: Perhaps indirectly, but not direct, no, not direct.

Dr: And if so, then to whom would you say that indirectly.

Pt: Oh, indirectly they would say—like my mother would advise against spending a night with this girl whom I was seeing. My mother advised against it. She would say, "It's not a very good idea. Spending a night with this girl. Doesn't look nice. Especially if you're thinking of marrying her, or if you are at all serious with her." And they would perhaps make a comment, not a full sentence, but just a comment, as a matter of fact. It would never be certain that I was sleeping with her, or something. Well, the certainty, I conveyed not openly, but she was certain I was sleeping with her.

Dr: You mean mother.

Pt: She wasn't too expressive about it. She mentioned it two times, maybe three times, twice as a matter of fact. It was ill-advised, if I was serious with the girl.

Dr: Well, how would she feel now if you would go home and say, "I want to marry the girl."

Pt: Oh, it would be alright with her. Yeah.

Dr: How do you know?

Pt: I've never been given reason to think otherwise, at this point, well, she's always been, whatever I did, was overtly all right with her.

Dr: Overtly, yes, but how does she feel?

Pt: My guess is that she would, she probably, at my age of twenty-three, she wouldn't, I mean, that wouldn't seem to her a reasonable age. She would probably think I couldn't get married until I was more mature. Uh, this would just be a sociological value. She just feels that boys should have a business or something before marriage.

Dr: How do you feel about it? You want to marry soon?

Pt: Yes.

Dr: Have you somebody in mind?

Pt: No.

Dr: You have now a girl friend don't you? At present?

Pt: No.

Dr: No?

Pt: Oh, I have a neighbor, I have a girl who I go out with, I went out. I may have called her a girl friend, but probably facetiously.

Dr: You are not too excited by her?

Pt: Not too excited.

Dr: And you don't sleep with her?

Pt: I've slept with her, but never wanted to—I mean, we've slept and almost.

Dr: Almost? But with others you did, or was it always only almost?

Pt: The first girl I mentioned it was real. And several times after that.

Dr: Nothing since.

Pt: I haven't looked at it quite that pessimistically, but that's true, nothing since.

Dr: And that doesn't bother you?

Pt: Doesn't bother me as long as there's something almost as good. It doesn't bother me.

Dr: Now what is almost as good?

Pt: Well, sleeping with a girl, and doing everything but.

Dr: But—I see.

Pt: Uhum.

Dr: You think it is the wrong thing to do, or something like that?

Pt: No, no, I don't think it's the wrong thing to do. (Pause).

Dr: Now it is not fear, or is it?

Pt: No.

Dr: So what do you think, what holds you back?

Pt. Oh, with that, fear of sex per se, no. Only social fear.

Dr: Social fear.

Pt: It's very real. You see I still find it very difficult meeting girls. Each of the three girls that I have been intimate with, I've spent whole nights with; it was not as if I introduced myself to them. They were girls that I was living in very close proximity with, so they could just as readily introduce themselves to me.

Dr: You don't pick up a girl?

Pt: No.

Dr: Not able to do it?

Pt: I should live and be well and maybe someday I will do it. I can't see it though in the offing.

Dr: You told the doctor that your mother was quite interested in you physically when you were a little boy and played around with your private organs, and so on. Is that conscious memory?

Pt: Yes, that's a conscious memory.

Dr: How do you square that with her being a rather cold and undemonstrative person?

Pt: I suppose that I should say that early, as a child, perhaps she was more demonstrative.

Dr: But this was conspicuous so it stuck in your memory. Possibly because it excited you?

Pt: It didn't excite me.

Dr: What is it that you actually remember?

Pt: Well, the image I have now conjured up is one of having been given a bath, and my mother fondled my penis.

Dr: Yes.

Pt: Most mothers do that I suppose. Well, my mother, I mean, I was not upset at my mother's intentions at all, I'm sure of that, and as she dried me off, she sort of loved the privates or admired them. And I recall that, for whatever reasons, she admired and had great affection for my privates.

Dr: There was no two ways about it, no doubt about it?

Pt: In my memory, no. I should imagine, perhaps, so far as reality may have had it, that perhaps she was just as fond of my ears.

Dr: Yes. But that attracted your attention more.

Pt: Not at the time, only the memory stayed in my mind.

Dr: Does it impress you now?

Pt: I probably remember things that don't impress me too.

Dr: Oh, well, why are you so defensive about it? Is that true that it aroused your interest too.

Pt: Well, I don't think I'm defensive, I mean, I am. But I don't think I am as defensive as—about that, I mean.

Dr: Noncommittal, let us say.

Pt: Yeah, well, I mean, I don't know.

Dr: When did that stop with your mother?

Pt: Well, I guess, it was just, I would rather wash myself rather than be washed.

Dr: And you didn't notice anymore that she was seductive, let us say.

Pt: Well, if you want to say that. But I guess, as a child, early adolescence, I suppose, I don't know if she was, I suppose I felt that she was.

Dr: You don't know whether she was, but you felt it.

Pt: Yeah, I don't know at all that she was.

Dr: Now you had a fear perhaps that mother will enter the bathroom when you are naked?

Pt: Yeah, that's right, that's right. I would have been extremely shy appearing before most, anybody naked, but I imagine more so with her.

Dr: You don't think you are developed, or what?

Pt: Well, I was very skinny as a child.

Dr: Very skinny, that bothered you?

Pt: Yeah, that bothered me, but I don't think that was the issue.

Dr: That is still a somewhat strange idea, that mother would enter when you are naked.

Pt: I'm not, I'm not, convinced that mother would enter so much as that anybody would enter. I, I imagine more with mother than other people.

Dr: Your sister for example?

Pt: I imagine I'd be more disturbed by my mother entering than by my father entering. Uh, I'm sure I would be.

Dr: But that was later, then since your father didn't live anymore.

Pt: Oh, oh, later? Yeah. It was probably directed at my mother. No, I mean, anyone. (*The patient continues to display denial mechanisms. How he responds to interpretations will determine the speed one could proceed with therapy.*)

Dr: What about sister?

Pt: Well, my sister would be less inclined, would have less interest in me.

Dr: Oh, now, that may be important. Obviously, then, if you thought of mother, it was because you assumed that she was more interested in you.

Pt: Yeah, that my mother would be more in a position to enter.

Dr: That she might intentionally enter the bathroom when you were there naked.

Pt: Yes, she might have, not intentionally, but, yeah, intentionally consciously, whereas my sister would do it you know, inadvertently.

Dr: That is not like mother.

Pt: Whereas my mother, if she wants something in the medicine cabinet, she would enter.

Dr: Did it bother you?

Pt: I think it did.

Dr: What age are we talking about?

Pt: No, I think we're talking about a lot of ages. I would say, let's say, eight, nine, ten.

Dr: Oh, not twelve, fourteen, fifteen?

Pt: No, not anymore. I was very sensitive and I saw to it, that, you know, any dressing I did, was in the room.

Dr: What was the sleeping arrangement?

Pt: Till I was fourteen, I was sleeping in the same room, till I was fourteen, I was sleeping in, between the ages of say twelve and fourteen, I was sleeping in the same room as my grandmother.

Dr: Did you like it?

Pt: No, it was awful, I disliked it.

Dr: Between twelve and fourteen, and how was it before and after?

Pt: After fourteen, I had my own room. Before it varied from sleeping in the same room with my parents until I was probably seven or eight.

Dr: The same room with your parents? And what about sister?

Pt: My sister would have had a studio couch in the, another room.

Dr: She had always her own. You never slept with her?

Pt: Not for any extended period, I'm sure it may have occurred that way.

Dr: Were you attracted to your sister as a girl?

Pt: My sister is a very attractive girl.

Dr: Yes, and you were attracted to her. There's nothing wrong with that.

Pt: No, I mean, it's hard for me to judge, I guess, I, yeah.

Dr: Are you aware of how non-committal you are?

Pt: I guess, I guess I am non-committal.

Dr: Now tell me something about what happened, something I didn't ask you, something you think is important. We couldn't cover everything in this one interview.

Pt: Yes, that's, I, I had a lot of trouble. But if I'm noncommittal, I'm noncommittal only because I, uh, I want to be sure not to say the wrong thing.

Dr: Oh.

Pt: I guess I also don't want to believe things inadvertently. I don't want, I guess I'm afraid . . . afraid that academic material will focus to my mind, and it's hard to take it up literally.

Dr: Now what do you think I should know to understand you better? Whatever you think is necessary. The purpose of this interview is to get an idea of what your problems, your feelings are. What type of person you are. What bothers you, and all that. So, what is it that I should know to get a correct picture? (*This question is given to test his comprehension, his resistance, his trust of me and his demands of me.*)

Pt: If I had any, if I could have volunteered something, I would. But every second that passes, it becomes more difficult. At this point, my mind feels stuffed with cotton or newspaper, and I really have trouble thinking. (*We have here resistance which may come from his having anxiety about my too aggressive probing, or because I have not fulfilled his expectations of doing something for him.*)

Dr: Well, you give the impression of a person who from childhood on always lacked confidence, and that you accepted this as a fact.

Pt: Yes, at college, I already tried seizing on different points to greater or lesser effect, and made, and tried making myself more viable.

Dr: And the other impression which you gave me is that you have not had much rapport with other members of the family, certainly not with your mother and not with your father.

Pt: That's right, any rapport is with my sister. She was not like my father in moodiness. The same stimulation from me would get any variety of responses from her.

Dr: One last question is whether you can recall a recent dream, any one dream?

Pt: Well, I would have some exciting dreams, where I'd be unable to get to where I'd want to be going; where I'd be unable to get where I wanted to go.

Dr: You can't reach something.

Pt: Can't reach something geographically. Either late for class, or either late to the doctor. Just can't make any progress at all.

Dr: Do you feel that way, that you don't reach what you want in life?

Pt: I guess you can say that. I mean it's just an interpretation. It makes you want to cry.

Dr: Do you cry sometimes as an adult?

Pt: Very rarely, if I'm moved to tears, usually it's not for serious things.

Dr: What moves you?

Pt: Oh, it may be watching some Grade C moving picture or something.

Dr: What kind of scene?

Pt: Any kind of scene, any kind of sad scene.

Dr: Give me a concrete example.

Pt: Oh, well, any, if an animal be hurt, or something, I feel very sad about it.

Dr: Or a little child?

Pt: Animals more, dogs and cats.

Dr: That is particularly the dreams you have?

Pt: Yeah, and political things too.

Dr: What, for example.

Pt: Seeing some revolution crushed in some impoverished country, and people suffering.

Dr: So you identify yourself with the underdog.

Pt: Well, it's not hard to feel sorry. Well, if I were, if I were moved to tears, it would be because I identify myself with the underdog. If I'm moved to gloat, it doesn't mean I'm identifying myself with the top guy.

Dr: In truth what do you do?

Pt: Well, I do both. If it's in a, say a film where the good guys are very, very good and they're winning, I feel little.

Dr: But then you don't feel good.

Pt: If the protagonists are suffering.

Dr: Then you cry.

Pt: Well my eyes well with tears.

Dr: Do you try to express such situations with sobbing or something?

Pt: I probably do.

Dr: Successfully?

Pt: Usually, yeah.

Dr: If you sit in a movie, it doesn't happen that sobbing comes out.

Pt: No, it doesn't come that far. I can control it.

Dr: Well I believe our time is up now. Thank you.

Pt: Thank you, doctor.

(If I were to have continued treating this man, I would have conducted the interview less hurriedly and with not so much pressure. I tried to get as much material from him as I could. He brought out some typical dynamic material found in asthma. Also from the history and this interview we would suppose that the patient considered his father tyrannical, rejecting and humiliating. We would, therefore, attempt to counteract these feelings by assuming a warm and accepting attitude in therapy. This would best serve as the basis for a corrective emotional experience and would avoid a long negative period which would prolong therapy or make it unsuccessful. As the patient would realize that he was not rejected and that the therapist was interested in him, he would begin to feel differently about authority and this would make him feel differently about himself. By playing an accepting role we would, therefore, make his treatment shorter. We would, of course, have to deal with his dependency, which is strong in such conditions, and this would necessitate the kinds of interruptions in therapy to which I alluded previously.)

VI

The Technic of
Short-Term Psychotherapy

================================ LEWIS R. WOLBERG, M.D.

(Editor's Note: Guidelines for the organization of a methodology of short-term therapy are detailed in this chapter that may be coordinated by a therapist with his training and special style of working.)

IN HIS LAST, AND WHAT is considered by some to be his greatest clinical paper, Sigmund Freud (1937) soberly reflected on the futility of shortening psychoanalysis. He admitted that such endeavors required no justification prompted as they were by considerations of reason and expediency. But, commenting on Otto Rank's attempts to overcome in a few months what Rank considered the core of neurosis, the birth trauma, Freud compared his efforts to that of a fireman, summoned to deal with a house set on fire by an upset oil lamp, who merely removed the lamp from the room and neglected to deal with the conflagration itself.

That Freud did not believe his strictures on short-term therapy as vigorously as he expressed them is evident in the same paper from the account of his referral of one of his patients to a pupil, Dr. Ruth Mack Brunswick. Recurrences of a severe neurosis were, claimed Freud, successfully resolved by "a short course of treatment." Ernest Jones tells of an incident in Freud's practice in which the originator of psychoanalysis treated Gustav Mahler, the famous composer, for a total period of four hours, analyzing and interpreting the sources of the latter's impotence with a resulting complete resolution of the problem. (Jones, 1955) Most experienced psychotherapists can attest to how effective a few sessions can be with certain patients, and there are those who believe that some day we may be able to refine our methodology sufficiently to make short-term approaches the treatment of choice in most emotional problems.

There are, however, obvious limitations to short-term psychotherapy as we practice it today. There are certain problems that do not respond to short-term psychotherapy as it is now done. But, on the whole, the virtues of short-term treatment, even at its present stage of development, have not been fully appreciated. Published surveys reflect the general belief that the longer patients continue in treatment, the greater the potential improvement. This is not true for all patients. For a considerable number, beyond a certain point benefits diminish because a crippling dependency relationship develops which breeds discouragement, inner resentment, and a shattering of self-confidence. So long as such persons remain in therapy, they hobble around on the crutches of dependency, expecting the therapist to bring about change and making themselves helpless to provoke supportive bounties. Surveys do not reveal the catastrophe of these patients who go on year after year in a vainless search for emotional health that is being debilitated by the prolonged therapeutic relationship itself. Nor do surveys inform that short-term treatment done well can, even in a few sessions, create sparks that years later kindle the flames of inner change, and even incubate substantial personality alterations that may lead to greater self-fulfillment.

The most pressing problem that confronts us today in short-term therapy is that we do not yet possess an adequate methodology. We apply the same tactics that we find useful in prolonged treatment, namely relaxed listening, permitting the relationship to build up and move into zones of transference, waiting expectantly for the patient to acquire motivations for self-direction, and peeling off layers of resistance to reach the treasures of the unconscious. The effect of such operations within a short span of treatment is dubious. Actually, the application of traditional methods of long-term therapy will usually leave the patient in the middle of nowhere. An evaluation of what has been done for him at the time of termination will reflect all the frustrations and disappointments that invest an interrupted task.

A common misconception is that short-term therapy involves haphazard maneuvers that can be implemented by beginners and relatively unskilled therapists. The truth is worlds away. Short-term treatment requires a sophistication borne of the wisdom of experience. Only a therapist schooled in the widest varieties of technic and seasoned through treatment of the broadest spectrum of emotional problems, can move the patient beyond the comforts of support into areas that hold promise of personality change. The tolerances in short-term therapy are fine; there is place for only the barest margin of error.

Almost every therapist has had the experience of treating a patient with severe symptoms who after a few sessions quieted down to move in the direction of a better total adjustment. The end of treatment need not halt the metamorphosis which may continue the remainder of the individual's life. This circumstance is not fortuitous: the therapist through his activity has succeeded in liberating constructive forces within the person that have both resolved the immediate stress situation and promoted personality transformation in depth. It is difficult to define in retrospect what has occurred. It is even more arduous to structure from this experience exact precepts that may apply to other cases. Nevertheless, the fact remains that important changes may be brought about through propitious handling even in a few sessions.

The burning question is what constitutes "propitious handling." Prior to discussing technical approaches, it may be expedient at this point to consider the essential compromises one will have to make in order to function with greatest effectiveness in short-term therapy.

ESSENTIAL COMPROMISES IN SHORT-TERM THERAPY

1. *Acceptance of Abbreviated Goals.* Deep personality problems are registered indelibly in the substance of the individual. They express themselves repetitively and with little regard for reality or reasonableness. Dating back to earliest conditionings, they involve the person as a totality, and they may persist in spite of the understanding that they are useless and destructive. It requires a great deal of time to extinguish such embedded personality traits, and we may have to content ourselves with the immediate objective of symptom relief.

The interesting thing is that once a basic modification has been accomplished, irrespective of how tiny, the adaptive equation becomes unbalanced and more substantial alterations can continue. Even short intervals in therapy may cause the individual to challenge certain assumptions, and this may serve as the nucleus for other and more profound transformations involving all facets of adjustment and influencing modulations in the environment, in interpersonal relations and even in the intrapsychic structure itself. Nor will it be necessary for the individual to remain in therapy during these permutations. There are those who once introduced to a new way of thinking about themselves, and recognizing that their current upset is rooted in their past history, challenge the fundamental conceptions which have ruled their existence. Having achieved a start in this new logic during a few sessions of psychotherapy, improvement then becomes self-perpetuating. Sometimes through forces that we cannot divine, a chain reaction occurs in the absence of any apparent conscious deliberation. Follow-up studies may reveal extensive shifts that were scarcely discernible at the time of termination, and that justify the most optimistic pronouncement of successful achievement equivalent to what we might have expected had the patient remained in therapy over a period of years.

Reasonable expectations of what short-term treatment should accomplish in the average person are the following: (a) relief of symptoms, (b) restoration to the optimal level of functioning that existed prior to the present illness, (c) an understanding of some of the forces that initiated the immediate upset, (d) recognition of some pervasive personality problems that prevent a better life adjustment, (e) at least partial cognizance of their origin in past experiences and childhood conditionings, (f) recognition of the relationship between prevailing personality problems and the current illness, and (g) an identification of remediable measures that can be applied to environmental difficulties and perhaps to aspects of personality distortions as a whole.

No further change may be apparent in the patient at the end of treatment than the reconstitution of homeostasis. However, if therapy has been conducted properly (which means that more than supportive tactics have been employed) we may anticipate greater developments as time goes on and as the patient applies himself to the essential tasks he has learned during his treatment experience.

2. *Acceptance of Intercurrent Healing Agencies.* In every interviewing situation a number of adventitious influences operate to promote improvement, conditioned by the individual's faith in the agency to whom he has applied for help. The most important elements are the placebo effect, the impact of the relationship situation and the calming power of emotional catharsis. Other factors come into the picture of an apparently "spontaneous" nature which foster relearning and a recasting of values. Among these is the influence of suggestion.

The placebo influence is rooted in the individual's expectations that the person whom he consults has the knowledge, the means and the magic to bring his difficulties to a halt. It is operative in every authority-subject, counselor-client, therapist-patient relationship. The particular prescriptions owe a good deal of their efficacy to the notion that they *must* help in the specific ways suggested by the expert. Astonishing changes may be brought about through suggestion. In drug administration, for instance, a suggested response may be accepted that is diametrically opposite to the expected and true chemical reaction. In psychotherapy the particular technics utilized are tinctured with placebo. This represents on a primitive level the warrants of sorcery, at least at the start of therapy before resistance counterattacks. Treatment is often influenced in a definitive way.

Since the aura of placebo will permeate the therapeutic situation irrespective of the wishes of the therapist, it is important that he neither exaggerate nor crush it, but rather gratefully accept it as an ally. If the therapist flamboyantly parades the virtues of his system, or promises a cure, he will be handicapped in dealing with resistance which, when it stirs, may disillusion the patient and thwart the therapist's ability to help. On the other hand, if the therapist minimizes his capacity to cure the patient, a negative placebo effect may vitiate the treatment effort. The best tactic is an unostentatious display of confidence in what one does, expressing the conviction that if the patient has a desire to resolve his problem, he can receive help to the degree that he cooperates.

Unlike the quack or shaman, the therapist is unable to kindle hope by exposing his bag of magical tricks. Witch doctors and medicine men appreciate the need to impress their clients by demonstrating presumably supernormal powers. They touch a piece of wood and it bursts into flame; they walk on glass that would cut ordinary feet. Thus proven is their God-given accreditation. Implied is the promise that healing wizardry will be made available to the sufferer. Once a proper impression is scored, a diagnosis through a system of mysterious maneuvers is made of the malevolent forces responsible for the prevailing mischief. Having finally confirmed his diagnosis through divine consultation, the shaman proceeds to convince the victim of its authenticity. If depression in a member of a primitive tribe is diagnosed as the product of a demon introduced into the body by an offended spirit, the shaman may implement reparative ceremonials, utter incantations, and finally, as evidence of his effectiveness, pluck a bloody feather from the forehead of the sufferer thus removing the diabolical remains of the invader. The therapist is unable to conscript the patient through invocations and legerdemain, but by manifesting confidence in what he is doing he also tries to inspire trust in his methods thus bringing favorable winds to the therapeutic climate.

The relationship situation is a second significant healing force that serves as a positive auxiliary. A person who experiences anxiety or any of its somatic equivalents, or who is caught in the web of defenses against anxiety that snare his adaptive capacities, suffers from a loss of mastery. This robs him of faith in himself, and spurs him to seek out an idealized parental figure who can lift him from the morass of his suffering to the sunny fields of health and self-fulfillment. The sicker the individual the more desperately he will reach for any strong hand that will disentangle him from his twisted fate. And he will project his need for omnipotence onto his therapist, since he cannot countenance in him weakness or ineffectuality.

On the basis of hope, then, he may experience a surcease of symptoms. In the relationship he finds asylum, a refuge from the devils that stir him up from within. His tension resolves as he puts himself into the protective sweep of the therapeutic alliance. This amalgamation, powered by his dependency, may divert him sufficiently to foster a more realistic adjustment. This may enable him to take advantage of provident environmental opportunities. If his experiences prove rewarding, he may consolidate a better adjustment. He may even discard coping mechanisms that, though mollifying anxiety, disrupt his well-being. Under such circumstances a transference "cure" may come about, generally temporary, but occasionally solidified into something more permanent.

There are some patients who, taking advantage of the lessening of tension that follows in the wake of a reassuring relationship, pull themselves together sufficiently to strike out on their own. On the other hand, where ego strength is poor, the patient may seek to continue indefinitely in the comfortable confines of therapy. This is where the skill of a therapist counts. If he recognizes dependency forces that operate in the relationship, he will be in a better position to divert the patient before he can establish a permanent beach-head in treatment. This presupposes that the therapist himself does not have needs for domination and control.

The aspect of the relationship embodying expectant trust operates automatically at first, but soon this is reinforced or neutralized by activities of the therapist and by transference, which in short-term therapy is less of a hazard than in prolonged treatment due to the time limitation.

At work in all helping situations are the effects of verbal unburdening with a consequent *emotional catharsis*. The mere process of talking to an interested person tends to bring relief. Many individuals sit on charges of emotional conflict that are so upsetting that they scarcely dare acknowledge their inner feelings, let alone verbalize them. If they can be encouraged to open up to an interested, accepting and non-punitive listener who does not respond to their revelations with conventional commentaries and condemnations, they will, first, experience relief, and, second, tend to revalue that which they have been cherishing as a dreadful secret. In a way this is like a confessional in which guilt is assuaged by recognizing, in the attitude of the listener, his reassuring comments and perhaps his pointed interpretations, that one is neither as sinning nor errant as he imagines himself to be. Unfortunately, a kind of conflict-generating machine inside the patient makes mandatory repeated purgings, though he seemingly has expurgated himself thoroughly before. Nevertheless, at last temporarily, the individual may relieve himself sufficiently to approach his daily tasks without a sense of doom. By putting amorphous feelings into words, he may gain some control over himself; things of dread acquire a different signification. He may realize that his transgressions violate no divine law and that he is neither morally depraved nor irretrievably degraded. Since ventilation is particularly helpful when it occurs in the presence of an authority the individual respects, the therapist may encourage the patient to talk about things that bother him most, adopting toward these revelations a sympathetic and understanding bearing.

Reinforcing the above three agencies that operate in the average interviewing situation and serve to reinforce the therapeutic effect, are other prodigious *spontaneous forces.* Much as the body has reparative devices that are constantly working to overcome disruptive pathological states, so the mind possesses defensive maneuvers, balances and counterbalances, which persist in adapting the person to old conflicts and new challenges. People incessantly strive to heal themselves psychologically, and sometimes these efforts are successful. We are still uncertain of the premises of such "spontaneous cures" where modifications of personality warpings are mediated without benefit of conventional therapy. Such recoveries surely do not occur in isolation, but are predicated on constructive relearning which takes place in the informal classroom of life experience.

We tend to minimize the importance of spontaneous relearning because we observe in our patients the repetition compulsion which dragoons them to act out their neurotic conflicts no matter how bountiful the environment may be. While the neurotic individual constantly twists reality to conform with the misconceptions of his past, he coordinately is being pressured by healthy reconditioning forces in his milieu. Which elements will win out in this tug-of-war depends upon how deeply repressed are his conflicts, their affiliation with basic drives, and whether or not life circumstances repeat the depriving or hurtful experiences of his past. Where favorable conditions reverse the individual's expectations of hurt and where, because of a fortunate human relationship, he realizes that he has been misconstruing reality, true personality growth may ensue.

Can one take advantage of these "spontaneous " elements during psychotherapy? By alerting oneself to the distortions that the patient seeks to impose on his environment, encouraging him to challenge these; by urging him to exploit every opportunity in his life situation that promises ablation of old and the relearning of new patterns, the therapist may be able to help the patient consolidate his therapeutic gains.

Another auxiliary is *suggestion*, which is activated by the propensity on the part of people to accept the formulations of authorities they respect. In the communication field the suggestibility of the populace is well-known, how easily swayed it is by editorials, "public opinion," and statements from "experts" in the press and over the air. The therapist avails himself of this expediency by drafting for the patient an outline of his operative dynamics. These proffered "insights" obviously reflect theoretical biases, mirroring the school of the therapist. But if the outline is accepted by the patient, it may provide him with a different and hopefully more salubrious way of looking at himself. Accepting the fact that wide divergencies exist in our contemporary ideas of human nature, we know enough about personality development and psychopathology to compose reasonable hypotheses about our patients' problems. Though "insight" may serve primarily as a placebo force, a pin-pointing of possible sources of vexation may enable the patient to take steps to rectify remediable trouble spots in his life.

By the same token, serving as a guiding authority, inadvertently or by design, the therapist through suggestion may serve to alter some of the patient's values, realigning his modes of looking at reality. One of the essentials of good mental health is an adequate life philosophy. Successful psychotherapy embodies a recasting of the patient's value systems, which permits him to approach his past by way of a more enlightened route, his present from a more practical perspective, and his future without recriminations or forebodings.

In prolonged therapy, patients are presumed to arrive at new values on their own. Even though the therapist's interpretations embody definite value directives, the therapist does not insist that the patient accept them. This is not a correct assumption, since the patient will, irrespective of how passive and tolerant the therapist may seem, incorporate many of the values of the therapist through pure suggestion. In education, we deliberately depend on this process. The student is expected to take over the ideas of the teacher whose knowledge and experience qualifies him to instruct and indoctrinate. In psychotherapy, we are prone to minimize this educational role which nonetheless exists. Many therapists are coming to the viewpoint that a bold presentation of wholesome values is not only helpful, but essential in educating the patient toward a healthier life orientation.

3. *Encouragement of Therapist Activity.* Anathema to short-term therapy is passivity in the therapist. Where time is of no object, the therapist can settle back comfortably and let the patient pick his way through the lush jungles of his psyche. To apply the same tactics in the few sessions that are available in short-term therapy will usually bring meagre rewards. Treatment failures are often the product of lack of proper activity. It is for this reason that the conventional non-directive, detached attitude is unwise, as are free-association and the use of the couch. Focused interviewing in the sitting up position is almost mandatory.

There are some therapists, of course, whose personalities support a passive role. Such practitioners may still be able to make an effort at involving themselves more actively, assuming as their objective a rapid assay of the central problem, dealing with its most obvious aspects. If one concentrates his fire, he will be able to hit the target with greater certainty. At least he will prevent the patient from steering the course of treatment into unproductive channels.

In short-term therapy, one cannot afford the luxury as in prolonged treatment of permitting the patient to wallow in resistance until he somehow muddles through. Resistance will, of course, occur, but it must be dealt with rapidly through an active frontal attack before it paralyzes progress.

One of the most difficult things to teach a student aspiring to become a short-term therapist is that activity in the relationship, with an involvement of oneself as a real person, and open expressions of interest, sympathy and encouragement, are permissible. Somehow passivity has become synonymous with doing good psychotherapy, with the result that when fifteen or twenty sessions have gone by, the patient is no further advanced toward resolution of his problem than when he first started. Often the therapist is not aware of how uninvolved he is, until he is observed working behind a one-way-mirror and his passivity is pointed out to him by a supervisor. Whether he can do anything about his impassiveness is another matter, but, in my experience, encouragement to express a more open interest, to engage himself more vigorously in the interview, to give his facial expressions a free release, to offer advice where needed, and to make interpretations when necessary may vitalize the therapeutic situation sufficiently to convince the therapist that a stoic bearing, a blankness of countenance and an unresourceful adherence to a phlegmatic role are not necessarily the "scientific" way of giving therapy. This does not mean that the therapist will have to revolutionize his personality in order to do short-term therapy. Individuals are constituted differently. Some therapists by nature are quiet and reserved; forcefulness is not within their behavioral range. But they will still be able to exercise the essential activity through a communicative and reassuring relationship. Activity means being interested in the patient and his immediate life problems; it does not mean being controlling of him. Neither does it give the therapist license to cuddle the patient, make his decisions and otherwise rob him of the responsibility of doing things for himself.

4. *Acceptance of Eclecticism in Method.* Psychoanalysts are particularly fearful of therapeutic contaminants. Mindful of the long struggle for acceptance of analytic covenants, they are reluctant to take what they consider to be a backward step by dignifying non-analytic technics. In this attitude they attempt to delay Freud's prediction that it eventually may be necessary to blend the "gold" of psychoanalysis with the "copper" of other therapies.

Short-term therapy requires a combination of procedures from psychiatric, psychoanalytic, psychological and sociological fields. Often utilized in the same patient are psychoanalytic technics, casework, drugs, hypnosis, group therapy, psychodrama, desensitization and reconditioning procedures. This fusion of methods, in which there are extracted from the different approaches tactics of proven merit, promise the most productive results. To implement such an eclectic regimen, a degree of flexibility in the therapist is required which enables him to step outside the bounds of his training biases and to experiment with methods from fields other than his own.

Here we run headlong into prejudices about what will happen to a personally cherished system of psychotherapy if one introduces into it foreign elements. It may reassure the therapist to keep reminding himself that there is nothing sacred about any of our present-day modes of doing psychotherapy. They all work in some cases and fail in others. We actually owe it to our patients, as well as to ourselves, to experiment with as many technics as we can in order to learn which of these will be effective and which do not yield good results.

Certain rigidities in the therapist will interfere with the proper experimentation, for instance, with hypnosis. Having worked with hypnotherapy for many years, I have found it to be remarkably effective in certain patients. And yet it has been difficult to persuade some of my colleagues to utilize hypnosis. Prejudice has deep roots, which are sustained by fear of entering into forbidden zones. There is a peculiar notion that hypnosis may open psychic pockets that once exposed will bring therapy to an ill-fated end. When I have succeeded in convincing prudent practitioners to try hypnosis in selected patients, they generally discover that hypnosis is no wanton tactic, and that it may tilt the scales toward a favorable outcome in instances that had seemed doomed to failure. Surprisingly, some of these over-cautious colleagues swing over to an enthusiasm for hypnosis that knows no bounds simply because it has proven successful in one of their cases, thus exercising their prejudice in an opposite direction.

Eclecticism does not sanction wild therapy. It presupposes a scrupulous empirical attitude, assaying the values of the different methods for the great variety of conditions that challenge the therapist in his daily practice.

5. *Overcoming Prejudices of "Depth."* Before a therapist is capable of doing effective short-term therapy, he will need to abandon value judgments about "superficial" versus "deep" therapy. There is a tendency on the part of psychotherapists to put varying significances on levels of depth as they apply to the content of the therapeutic interviews. Material that relates to the past, from the dredgings of the unconscious and from transferential interactions become emblazoned with special virtue. All else is labeled "superficial" from which little may be expected insofar as real personality change is concerned. Such notions are the product of a misuse of psychoanalytic wisdom that purports that the only true road to cure is through the alleys of the unconscious. This in spite of the fact that clinical experience persuades that the divulgence of unconscious content carries no guarantee that a patient will get well.

Psychotherapy is no mining operation that depends for its yield exclusively on excavated psychic ore. It is human interaction that embraces a variety of dimensions, psychological and social, verbal and non-verbal. Some of these elements are so complex that we can scarcely express them in words. How can we, for example, describe such things as "faith," "hope," "trust," "acquisition of insight," "meaning," "restoration of mastery," "self-realization," and "development of capacity to love." These are aspects of therapy fluctuating within the matrix of change. In the architecture of personality building, no one tissue or girder stands alone. They are all inter-related. Revelation of the unconscious blends into the total thera-peutic gestalt. It does not constitute it.

Even though in short-term therapy we can only deal with the immediate and manifest, we may ultimately influence the total personality in depth, including the unconscious. Human warmth and feeling, experienced by a patient in one session with an em-pathic therapist, may achieve more profound alterations than years with a probing, detached therapist intent on wearing out resistance. This does not mean that one should be neglectful of the uncon-scious. For within a short span of therapy, repressed psychic aspects may still be elicited and handled.

SELECTION OF CASES

It may be argued that if a few sessions can potentially induce cor-rective change, would not prolonged treatment do the job even more effectively, enabling the individual to apply to his current life situation the kinds of discipline that sponsor a healthy perspective? There is no question that an extended time period permits the therapist to handle resistance that some patients mobilize toward the giving up of their neurosis. There is no question, too, that some patients—for instance, those that are masochistically inclined—gain a subversive gratification out of their neurotic misery and are loathe to yield it too readily. Here the therapist functions as a senti-nel, alerting the patient to the presence and to the particular mani-festations of his resistance. Such patients would probably do better in prolonged treatment if we could avoid the trap of dependency and could successfully deal with transference elements that un-leashed tend to enmesh the patient in the tangled folds of his past.

On the other hand, we may over-emphasize the need for long-term treatment in many patients. We may assume that all persons pos-sess healthy and resilient elements in their personality, which given half a chance, will burgeon forth. A brief period of treatment may be all that is required to set into motion a process of growth.

The question of the superiority of long-term over short-term therapy is therefore a rhetorical one. Experience persuades that some patients get nowhere with long-term therapy and do remark-ably well with short-term approaches. There are others in whom short-term treatment does not succeed in denting the surface of their problem and who require a prolonged period of therapy before the slightest penetration is made. The problem of selection of cases is as poignant a one as is the utilization of proper technics. It is doubtful that we can define syndromes that best will respond to either approach. Factors other than symptomatology determine how the patient will progress. Nor is it possible to delineate precisely special tactics that can expedite treatment in all cases. What works with one therapist and one patient may not work with others. Each therapist will need to experiment with methods that he eventually will find are best suited to his style and personality.

At the present stage of our knowledge, long-term treatment is not always an indulgence. If the patient is so constituted that he can take advantage of explorations into his psyche, and if the therapist is equipped to work on a depth level, extended therapy may be a rewarding adventure. Without question the "working-through" of psychological blocks, and the resolution of the manifold facades and obstructions the mind concocts to defeat itself, can best be accomplished in a prolonged professional relationship. Here the therapist concentratedly and continuously observes the patient, dealing with resistances as they develop, and bringing him to an awareness of the basic conflicts that power his defensive operations. Given the proper patient with a personality problem of long-standing, who possesses an adequate motivation for change, with an ego structure sufficiently plastic, an environment that is malleable, a social milieu which will accept his new-found freedoms, who can afford luxuries of time and finances, and who relates himself constructively in a treatment experience with a well-trained psychotherapist, long-term therapy will offer him the best opportunity for the most extensive personality change.

Morover, there are conditions that respond to no other instrumentality than continuous psychotherapy, no matter how assiduously the therapist applies himself toward releasing forces of assertiveness within the patient. The situation is akin to diabetes in which the patient survives solely because he receives life-giving insulin. In certain problems, dependency is so deep-rooted that the patient can exist only in the medium of a protective relationship in which he can receive his dosages of support. The patient appears to thrive in therapy and seemingly may be utilizing his insights toward a better integration. But this improvement is illusory; the patient constantly needs to maintain a life-line to the helping authority to whom he clings with a desperation that defies all efforts at treatment termination. Such patients obviously will not do well with short-term methods, although long-term approaches may be inadequate also.

From the foregoing one may get the impression that long-term therapy is the preferred treatment where the patient has a chronic personality disorder. This is not always the case. There are some risks in employing prolonged treatment in many patients. Dependent individuals who have been managing to get along on their own, albeit on a tenuous independency level, may become more and more helpless, and importune for increasing demonstrations of support with an exaggeration rather than a relief of their symptoms. Individuals with fragile ego structures will tend to develop frightening transference reactions in prolonged treatment, or they may go to pieces in the process of releasing repressions.

Patients who have been found to respond best to short-term therapy are those who possess a resilient repertoire of coping mechanisms, and who prior to their immediate upset were functioning with some degree of satisfaction. Acute anxiety reactions, with and without a diversity of defenses, may often be brought to a rapid equilibrium, particularly where symptoms serve a minimal protective purpose. This does not imply that the change wrought through short-term treatment need be merely palliative. With appropriate technics permanent personality modifications may be accomplished which will permit of greater stress tolerance.

It is essential here to qualify the finding that acute problems are best suited for short-term approaches. Our frame of reference is the conventional body of technics that we utilize today. There is no reason to assume that with the refinement of our methodology even chronic personality difficulties may not be significantly improved on a short-term basis. I have personally treated chronic cases with short-term methods, including obsessive-compulsive neurosis and borderline schizophrenia, and I have observed in many gratifying results. Indeed, had I permitted these patients to continue in therapy, I am certain that some would have marooned themselves in permanent treatment waters which would have swamped their tiny surviving islands of independence.

The best strategy, in my opinion, is to assume that every patient, irrespective of diagnosis, will respond to short-term treatment unless he proves himself to be refractory to it. If the therapist approaches each patient with the idea of doing as much as he can for him, within the span of say up to twenty treatment sessions, he will give the patient an opportunity to take advantage of short-term treatment to the limit of his potential. If this expediency fails, he can always then resort to prolonged therapy.

Were we, in summary, to list conditions suited for long-term treatment, we might classify them as follows:

1. *Where extensive personality reconstruction is the prime objective.* Included here are patients of all diagnostic categories for whom we strive to bring about widespread alterations in personality, who possess proper motivation, sufficient ego strength, and the ability to afford the time and financing of prolonged treatment. The prognosis and the duration of therapy will vary with such factors as the severity of the problem and the skill of the therapist.

2. *Where dependency is so entrenched that prolonged support is essential.* In this category are patients whose problems are of such severity, whose immaturity and dependency are so great, that they will, the rest of their lives, need some dependency prop to prevent them from decompensating. Here the long-term approach is sustentative in nature irrespective of what kinds of technics are employed. The patient utilizes therapy for purposes of support and reassurance though the tactics may be of a reconstructive nature.

3. *Where there are persistent and uncontrollable acting-out tendencies.* Some patients are unable to subjugate impulsive drives except when they feel themselves to be under the aegis of an authority figure who, they insist, must save them from themselves. Homosexuals, psychopathic personalities, drug addicts and alcoholics are among such persons, as are individuals driven by repressed infantile needs to involve themselves in self-destructive and dangerous activities.

4. *Where there is constant and irrestrainable anxiety.* Among these patients are severe neurotics whose drives and values cause them to distort reality often to their consternation, and borderline and psychotic individuals who trust the intelligence and integrity of the therapist to help them distinguish fact from fantasy.

Conditions that might best respond to short-term treatment are these:

1. *Where the goal is a rapid restoration of homeostasis in an acute neurotic disorder.* Included are patients in whom the adaptive breakdown is of recent origin, and whose personality structures and defenses have enabled them to function satisfactorily prior to the present illness. Here the objective is the resolution of the immediate homeostatic imbalance by whatever technics may be indicated —drugs, support, environmental manipulation, insight into dynamics, etc.

2. *Where the goal is a resolution of an acute upset in a chronic personality disorder.* Patients here are those with long-standing neurotic problems who have functioned marginally or who may have become disturbed and threatened with decompensation by an im-

mediate precipitating factor. The object is the reconstituting of habitual defenses that have enabled the individual to function optimally.

3. *Where the goal is reconstruction of personality in cases unsuited for or who are unable to avail themselves of long-term therapy.* In this group are individuals with acute neurotic reactions and chronic personality disorders who aspire to greater self-development, and who should be given an opportunity, after a short period of treatment, to see how far they can go by themselves. There are also those who are unable to enter into long-term therapy because of limited finances or inability to make sufficient time available for treatment. Included, furthermore, are (a) persons who possess strong dependency drives, but are managing to operate with some degree of independence and who may become infantilized by prolonged therapy, and (b) persons with fragile ego structures which may shatter through the use of probing technics or because of violent transference reactions.

INGREDIENTS OF A SHORT-TERM SYSTEM

A flexible system of short-term psychotherapy may be schematized as follows:

1. Establishment of a rapid working relationship.
   a. Sympathetic listening to the patient's story.
   b. Communicating understanding.
   c. Communicating confidence in one's approach.
   d. Reassuring the patient that he is not hopeless.
   e. Structuring the therapeutic situation.
2. Arriving at a tentative diagnosis.
3. Evolving with the patient a working hypothesis of his psychodynamics.
4. Circumscribing the problem area as a focus for exploration. Elucidating neurotic patterns and encouraging the patient to observe himself for these.
5. Employing dream interpretation where the therapist is analytically trained.
6. Alerting oneself to resistances and resolving these as rapidly as possible.
7. Searching for and managing transference to avoid a transference neurosis.
8. Dealing with destructive elements in the environment expeditiously before they build up to explode the relationship.
9. Dealing with "target symptoms," like excessive tension, anxiety and depression.

10. Teaching the patient how to employ insight as a corrective force, how to relate symptoms to inner conflict, and how to recognize self-defeating defensive mechanisms.
11. Outlining with the patient a definite plan of action by which he may utilize his insight in the direction of change.
12. Encouraging the development of a proper life philosophy.
13. Terminating therapy.
14. Follow-up visits.

THE INITIAL INTERVIEW IN SHORT-TERM THERAPY

Since time is of the essence, the initial interview should point at a number of objectives which may or may not be completely fulfilled. Among these are the following: (1) to establish a relationship with the patient; (2) to gather essential information for diagnosis, prognosis and treatment planning; (3) to arrive at a tentative diagnosis; (4) to give the patient a broad idea of the nature of his problem (tentative dynamics); (5) to explain in general terms what will be done in therapy; (6) to arrange for future visits or for referral; (7) to terminate the interview.

Roughly the first objective, the establishment of rapport, is accomplished, as has been indicated, by communicating interest and empathy, and by building hopeful expectations through the therapist's behavior that reflects confidence in his methods and a conviction that the patient may be helped. Essential data is obtained by exploring the immediate complaint factor. The patient is encouraged to see if he can relate his current difficulties to previous episodes of the same or an allied nature as far back as his early childhood. The making of a diagnosis usually poses no problem where the therapist possesses reasonably good diagnostic skills. If the therapist is experienced, he will be able to structure the tentative dynamics, presenting the patient with a kind of blueprint of the problem. The formulations must be in terms the patient can understand and must indicate that the therapist has an intelligent grasp of the existing basic difficulties. The therapist may then, in general terms, talk about the conditions of therapy, the fact that as much as possible will be accomplished in as short a period of time as is feasible. If the patient insists on knowing how many sessions will be required, the therapist may tell him that this is difficult to estimate, since the time required will depend on how rapidly the patient moves in treatment. The patient may be informed, however, that therapy will be as short as is consistent with his needs. After a few sessions a better estimate may be possible. No promises of cure are made, but the patient is assured that if he works at his problem, his symptoms can be brought under control. He will also have an idea of what he can do in line with working on himself after the treatment period is over in order to continue his improvement. Fees are discussed and appointment times are set. The interview is then terminated.

The specific technics utilized will be conditioned by the skills of the interviewer and by his special ways of working. In the conduct of my own initial interviews, I try to get the patient to talk about those symptoms that concern him most. After he walks into the room and is seated, I smile at him, nod my head and wait expectantly for him to talk. If he hesitates, I say: "Would you like to tell me about your problem, then we will see what we can do about it; or would you rather I asked you questions?" Generally, the patient is bursting with feelings he would like to express so there is little need to urge him on. However, if the patient states that he would rather I ask him questions, I inquire: "What is the thing that bothers you most?" I then encourage him to expand on this and to detail associated complaints, probing their origin, his reactions, and his theories concerning them. When the patient has finished, I get the essential statistical material—his age, marital status, address, telephone number, education, occupation and statistical facts about his mate and children. I then specifically inquire about symptoms other than those mentioned by the patient, like tension, anxiety, depression, physical complaints, phobias and obsessions. I casually ask: "Do you have any sexual problems?" I do not probe this, since it may be a painful area. I then inquire about what medications the patient is taking and whether alcohol has an effect on his symptoms. I gather from this whether or not the patient is drinking too much. I also learn the reaction he has to the specific tranquilizing, energizing and hypnotic drugs he is taking or has taken, jotting down notes for future reference. Finally, I ask him about insomnia, whether he dreams a great deal or a little, whether he has repetitive dreams or nightmares. If he recalls it, I encourage him to tell me a dream that he remembers vividly, which I record and later try to correlate with other data in order to formulate in my mind a general picture of the dynamics.

Next, I ask the patient to tell me a little about his relationship with his mother and father, the kinds of people they were when he was growing up, his particular relationship with each, and how he feels about his parents now. Siblings and other significant adults in his early childhood are covered in the same way. Earliest memories he can recall, the nature of his upbringing, problems he had in growing up are rapidly reviewed. Naturally, the patient's accounts are colored by his guilt feelings, his defensiveness, his anger and his amnesia; but I usually get an idea about his early conditionings and the kinds of formative experiences that have molded his personality structure. At some point, I will ask him to inform me briefly about the personalities and problems of his mate and children.

A tactic that I employ, having studied the Rorschach test, is showing the patient the cards successively, encouraging him to tell me what he sees or what comes to his mind. I am afraid that clinical psychologists will be horrified by what I do, since I am not at all perfectionistic, the entire process taking only a few minutes. I know enough about the Rorschach to spot gross pathology from the responses, which incidentally are recorded, but not scored. What interests me is the character of the sequential responses, and the light they may shed on the dynamics and the prevailing ego resources. What I derive from the test (if one can call it a test) is a general *feeling* about undercurrent pathology, incomplete and rough as it may be. But what is perhaps more important than this from the standpoint of the patient is that some objective measure is being employed. This may impress him with my interest. I am also in a better position to reassure the patient that there are no indications from what I can see that he is about to become insane, and that there is no reason for him to feel that he cannot get better. Much as a patient often benefits from the reassuring effects of a physical examination, so he may respond with relief to the curious instrument of the Rorschach, particularly when, in the broad phrasing of the dynamics, executed at the end of the interview, I say something that strikes home, which I have gleaned from his reaction to the cards.

What I do then is to tell the patient that I now have a general picture of his problem, and I sketch out some broad formulations, fitting his current complaint factor into this design. I reassure him that he can be helped if he really wants help, and that together we may be able to arrive at some solution for his difficulty. I answer briefly any pertinent questions that he may spontaneously bring up. We arrange fees and time. Finally, I terminate the interview.

A great deal goes on during a productive initial interview, but the most that should be expected is that rapport will be established, tension relieved, hope built, and a conviction implanted that the therapist has a grasp of the problem, is skilled and confident in his being able to help.

Elsewhere there is detailed more information about the conduct of an initial interview and about interviewing technics in general. (Wolberg, 1954)

ESTABLISHING A RAPID WORKING RELATIONSHIP

It is not too difficult to develop a working relationship with a patient within the first few sessions, perhaps even at the initial interview. If one tries to put oneself in the patient's position, attempting to empathize with his feelings, and to divine and reflect what must immediately be on his mind, one has made an important beginning.

When the average patient gets to the point where he is willing to see a psychotherapist, he is usually so entangled in the reverberating circuits of his neuroses that he is unable to extricate himself from its effects. Though his customary defenses are no longer capable of maintaining him in a state of homeostasis, he has been unable to elaborate new and more serviceable ones. He is either experiencing or is threatened with an imminent breakdown in his adaptation, one sign of which is disagreeable symptoms, such as tension, depression, anxiety and psychophysiological manifestations. He feels bewildered, perhaps frightened and hopeless at having lost his sense of mastery. Generally he harbors a destructive attitude toward himself, a disrespect for his own weaknesses, failures, and ineffectualities—products of a devalued self-image. His self-esteem, self-confidence and assertiveness are at low ebb and he may feel himself to be out of control. Face-saving compensations may be present; for example, he may manifest a defiant attitude as a defense, or he may indulge in expressions of bitterness and even braggadocio.

In practically every case, one may expect an enhancement of dependency as a result of a shattered sense of mastery. This takes the form of a regressive seeking for succor and support. The more intense the anxiety, the greater the dependency impulse. Reactions to his dependent yearnings will follow his customary defenses. There may be an obsequious pleading for help; self-punitive and masochistic maneuvers; detachment; or a denial of his helplessness with compensatory competitiveness and power strivings. A distrust of authority may be registered in terms of resentment, which may be further enhanced by the feeling that he has finally come to a bad end: he must put himself at the mercy of a "head shrinker" with the sacrifice of time, money and self-respect that such a destiny entails. What may be going on through his mind at the first interview is a fear of revealing the reprehensible secrets of his past, as well as impulses and yearnings of which he is ashamed. He may dread opening up torrential forces within himself, since he is not sure he can keep the floodgates from collapsing. Perhaps he will find out that he is insane or homosexual or a murderer at heart. Nor does he know how the therapist will react to his divulgences. With condemnation? With contempt? With indifference? Undoubtedly he will be considered weak or hopeless. Added to these fears are complications stimulated by misconceptions he nourishes about psychiatry and psychotherapy, gleaned from distortions in the press, over the air, and from friends who know of people who have been in psychotherapy and psychoanalysis for years and are now worse off than when they started.

The therapist, if he is perceptive, will be able to sensitize himself to these expressed and unexpressed fears, misgivings and resistances that the patient brings to the interview, and, by dealing with them in a non-condemnatory and reassuring way, he may be able to initiate a good relationship. Among the resistances one must handle in the first interview is disappointment that the therapist does not satisfy the stereotype of a psychiatrist. This may be a kindly, oracular, middle-aged Viennese who strokes his beard in great wisdom, or it may be a pundit of television fame. The patient may believe that the therapist is too old, or too young, or not of the right stature, or physiognomy, or race or religion.

An immediate handling of these feelings is mandatory. If the therapist senses that the patient is uncomfortable with him, he may ask one or more of the following questions: "How do you feel about coming here?" "What has been on your mind just before coming here?" "Have you been a little worried about coming here?" "Do you feel disappointed in coming to talk to me?" A section of an interview follows the last query made by a therapist upon discerning that the patient was fidgeting in his chair.

Dr: Are you disappointed in coming here?

Pt: I had expected to see an older man.

Dr: Well, how do you feel about talking to me?

Pt: I don't know that I am going to be able to work at this thing or have confidence in you. I thought I would have an older person, can you—I don't see how you're going to be able to help me.

Dr: Apparently you have some doubts about my ability to work with you.

Pt: (pause) Well, yes. I wanted someone older.

Dr: Perhaps you are afraid I do not have enough experience. But supposing you tell me something about yourself. I can then help you, if you wish, find an older person who would be suited to deal with your particular problem.

A statement such as the latter serves to lessen tension, since it indicates that the therapist is not on the defensive. A similar approach may be adopted with proper substitutions if a patient is disappointed that the therapist is a woman instead of a man, a non-Catholic instead of a Catholic, and so forth. In a properly conducted interview the chances are overwhelming that the patient will want to continue with the interviewer who has demonstrated his perceptiveness by pointed questions, his sensitivity by reflecting the patient's feelings, and his empathy through appropriate facial expressions and verbal utterances.

The building of a relationship implies an unqualified acceptance of the patient. During the first few sessions the patient is generally chary of being accepted. A detached, "deadpan" attitude is fatal. It will kill the therapeutic situation almost immediately. Responding with proper facial expressions, like smiling or concern, being attentive in manner, showing an interest in what is being said, and asking appropriate questions will give the patient an idea that the therapist is really interested in helping him. An understanding of the plight and suffering of this human being in trouble is revealed non-verbally, although the therapist may, when he senses turmoil in the patient, make such statements as: "This must be difficult for you." "This must upset you a great deal." "It is understandable that you would be discouraged by what has gone on." "You must be very concerned about all of this." A non-punitive manner must be displayed irrespective of the revelations of the patient or the intensity of his emotional catharsis. If, for instance, the patient blurts out. "I'm a homosexual!" the therapist may say, "So?" or "You sound as if you feel ashamed of this."

Important in setting up a working relationship is the communication by the therapist to the patient *through his attitude* of enthusiasm with his work, a confidence in his methods, and a feeling that he can help the patient get better. Many patients will ask the therapist directly if he can cure them. What the therapist may say prior to his having completed an assay of the problem is: "Supposing we complete our interview and then I will give you an idea of what I can do for you." Once the therapist has gathered sufficient data to evaluate the problem, he may indicate that a good deal can be done to help the situation. He must not promise miracles or a cure. Instead he should concentrate on building a hopeful expectation. He may say: "From what I can see, there is no reason, if you work at this problem in therapy, why you cannot get yourself to feel better. If you have a desire to get well, this is nine-tenths of the battle. How fast you move will depend on how you apply yourself." Actually no matter how sick the patient may be, some improvement may be anticipated.

THE TENTATIVE DIAGNOSIS

At the present time our nosological systems are insufficiently refined to tell us much about how the patient will respond to treatment. Psychotherapy is so dependent on indefinable nuances in the therapist-patient relationship, that few diagnostic yardsticks can be set up to prognosticate results. Suffice it to say that every patient, irrespective of diagnosis, potentially may be helped in removing or reducing tension, anxiety and other symptoms, and perhaps even to achieve a better life adjustment.

Despite extensive residual psychopathology, an individual may be capable of functioning provided he has elaborated adequate mechanisms of defense and his environment does not impose on him undue burdens. He may have to circumscribe his needs, narrow his interpersonal and social orbits, and limit some of his activities, but if he stays within bounds of his restricted environment, and the demands on him are not taxed too harshly, he may be able to get along in a relatively normal way. Problems occur when external stress is greater than his coping capacities, or when inner needs and conflicts no longer can be mediated through his customary resources.

In our diagnostic survey, we assay the degree of disturbance and estimate the recuperative potential of the individual. Helpful here are four factors which complement the particular label of syndrome. These are: (1) the degree of homeostatic imbalance as indicated by tension, anxiety and its equivalents, (2) the kinds of mechanisms of defense that are being elaborated to deal with anxiety and to gratify existing needs, (3) the personality structure in terms of the dependence-independence continuum, self-esteem, and character of interpersonal relationships, and (4) the disintegrative potential. There is little relationship between the diagnosis, phrased according to our conventional terminology, and the ability of the individual to return to his optimal level of functioning, utilizing the therapeutic relationship as a supportive prop. There is some relationship between diagnosis and the capacity for reconstructive change. Thus organic brain disorders, schizophrenia, manic-depressive reactions, involutional psychosis, chronic anxiety reactions, sexual deviations, alcoholism, psychopathic personality, chronic obsessive-compulsive disorders, and borderline cases will tend to resist reconstruction of personality. This does not mean that they will not respond to the proper therapeutic handling, ultimately to achieve some strengthening of personality, even after a relatively short period of treatment. But one may anticipate more resistance, a stormier course during therapy and greater tendencies to relapse.

So many things can happen for the good and bad during psychotherapy that all efforts at prediction are at best tentative. What is most essential in determining the outcome of a psychotherapeutic effort, more important than diagnosis, is the way transference and counter-transference are managed, the therapist's skill in resolving resistance, and his astuteness at interpretation. After a therapist has practiced for a number of years and has evaluated his successes and failures with a variety of patients and problems, he may be able to set up prognostic criteria for the different diagnostic categories that apply exclusively to himself, and that are conditioned by his personality strengths and weaknesses, his theoretical biases, his technical virtuosities and lacks, and his particular preferences in working with different syndromes and special individuals.

PSYCHODYNAMIC FORMULATIONS

Helpful in short-term therapy is the formulation of a hypothesis about the operative dynamics that can act as a structure around which the therapeutic program is organized. In making such a formulation we must remember that human behavior is so capricious that it cannot be explained by an existing psychodynamic system. Current theories are applicable to some aspects of adaptation, but they each possess great gaps in interpreting the totality of behavior. These lacunae are constantly being filled in by new hypotheses as fresh observations bring challenging perspectives and potentialities. But we are still far from the day where we can point with certainty to an exacting picture of what goes on in the human mind.

Unfortunately, there is a great tendency on the part of some therapists to consider our present-day psychodynamic conceptualizations as inviolable, in spite of the fact that our structures have been built upon the wreckage of sacred theories of human behavior that were cherished by past generations of scientists and philosophers. There is no reason for us to assume smugly that our present constructs will not some day crumble and become part of the rubble on which more enlightened theories of tomorrow will be erected, which in turn will undergo alterations as our knowledge of the universe expands.

Nevertheless, there are some concepts of behavior derived from psychoanalysis, sociology, psychology and anthropology which have gained reasonable verification. An assumption that we make is that the original endowment is modified significantly if not decisively by early formative experiences. If these have been satisfying, the child's physical and emotional needs having been adequately fulfilled, a personality structure will evolve capable of mediating a good adjustment and of enduring at least average vicissitudes and stresses of living. If, on the other hand, experiences have been depriving or destructive to his needs, the individual is apt to evolve a personality riddled with insecurity, a devalued self-esteem, an inability to relate himself well to people or of expressing his inner impulses in conformity with the mores of the group.

Patterns of behavior will generally follow the chains of conditionings that date back to childhood. Many of the patterns have become firmly fixed, operate automatically, and, while the circumstances that initiated them no longer exist, and the memory traces are firmly embedded in the unconscious, they continue to display themselves often to the dismay of the individual and the consternation of those around him. Thus, where defiance in childhood was a prerequisite to expressing assertiveness in relation to overly restrictive and moralistic parents, defiant, recalcitrant, aggressive, or hostile outbursts may be essential before assertiveness can be released. Where self-worth was measured in terms of vanquishing a sibling or parent and proving oneself better than these adversaries, compulsive competitive activities may preoccupy the individual to an extraordinary degree. Where sexual feelings were mobilized by parental provocations, strokings, spankings, enemas, observation of adult sexual activities, or precocious stimulation in varied kinds of sex play, engagement in similar activities, or the exploitation of phantasies about such activities, may be requirements for the release of sexual feeling. These impulses may become organized into perversions. Recrudescence into adult life of unusual behavior is often explicable on the basis of the linkage of adult needs with outmoded anachronistic patterns. Such behavior is usually rationalized when it is manifestly out of keeping with the reality situation.

The individual is, more or less, at the mercy of personality distortions, since the experiences that produced them are sealed off from his awareness by repression and are thus not easily available to his conscious deliberation or control. He is driven by needs, drives and defenses that clash with the demands of society on the one hand and with his personal values on the other.

Since he carries the burdens of conflict, which impose extraordinary pressures on him, he will be prone to over-react to stressful circumstances in his environment particularly when these create insecurity or undermine his self-esteem. If his coping mechanisms falter, he may become overwhelmed by a catastrophic sense of helplessness and by shattering of his feelings of mastery. This contingency may bring upon him the frightening experience of anxiety with which he will have to deal with whatever mechanisms of defense he can muster. Often these revive early defenses, which at one time were employed in his childhood, but which are now worthless, since though temporarily allaying anxiety, they foster complications that further tend to disorganize the individual in his dealings with life.

One must not underestimate the importance of promptings developed in childhood which have been relegated by repression to the dubious oblivion of the unconscious. These underpinnings of personality—the drives and defenses of childhood—assert themselves throughout the life of the individual.

Thus a man, undermined by an overprotective mother who crushed his autonomy and emerging feelings of masculinity, may have sufficient ego strength to rise as an adult above his devalued self-image, by pushing himself into positions of power and achieving monetary success. To all outward appearances he may appear masterful, strong and accomplished. Yet his feeble inner promptings to make himself dependent register themselves in passive impulses with homosexual phantasies. He will drive himself into compromising relationships with men, promoting fierce competitiveness, needs for identification with their strength, paranoidal outbursts and perhaps desires for sexual contact when under the influence of alcohol. Understandably, the individual will function under a great hardship being in almost constant conflict, with little awareness of what is going on inside of himself.

APPLICATIONS OF DYNAMIC FORMULATIONS TO THERAPY

"The special merit of psychoanalysis is that from the painstaking, long-continued treatment of some individuals so much has been learned that is helpful in the shorter treatment of other individuals." (Menninger, 1963) These words of Karl Menninger echo the feelings of many therapists that we can adapt analytic concepts to the special conditions of short-term approaches.

Essentially the process of therapy that is rooted in the dynamic theoretical model consists of utilizing the relationship situation with the therapist as a means of helping the patient to gain an understanding of himself in regard to how his current reactions and interpersonal involvements are related to formative experiences in his past. He is brought to an awareness of unconscious needs, drives and value systems, their origin, signifiance and contemporary manifestations through special technics, such as free association and dream interpretation. The resistances to unveiling these repressed ingredients are dealt with by interpretation. In the course of working with the patient, the therapist will observe the development of attitudes toward him that reflect early disturbed feelings toward authority (transference). Repeated in the medium of the therapeutic relationship ultimately will be some important incidents that resemble traumatic experiences in the past (transference neurosis).

It goes without saying that the therapist must have the education, understanding and the personality stability to cope with the patient's projections in order to help the patient gain an awareness of his unconscious maneuvers. The therapist may tend to become frustrated by some patients. He may feel enervated by the acting-out, demandingness, hostility, critical attitudes, and unreasonableness of the patient who will watch carefully for the therapist's reactions. Should the therapist respond in ways similar to actions of the parents, the therapeutic process will probably stop. Actually, the patient will probably engineer the situation so that he can re-enact certain traumatizing experiences with the therapist. If the therapist acts in a therapeutically positive manner and in contrast to the past actions of the parents, he may help the patient gain a different conception of what rational authority is like. The hope is that eventually the patient will, because of his understanding, begin to relate to the therapist in a way different from his habitual responses to authority. Thus, he will utilize the therapeutic situation as a vehicle for the evolution of constructive attitudes towards himself and others. He will develop new capacities as a person, lessened severity of conscience, greater assertiveness and independence, and an ability to express his basic drives in relation to the standards of his group.

The taming of irrational impulses in the direction of social control, the expansion of the repertoire of adaptive defenses toward greater flexibility and balance, and the reduction of the severity of the conscience with a more wholesome adjustment to inner promptings and reality demands are a formidable task. This is because the various components of personality are forged into a conditioned system that is almost impervious to outside influence. Homeostatic balances are maintained to safeguard neurotic interactions. Reaction formations absorb energy investing intolerable impulses. Resistances block attempts to interfere with coping mechanisms and defenses. Acting-out temporarily drains off accumulating tensions.

To cut into this elaborate structure of forces and counterforces is not only a heroic task, but it is usually an unsuccessful one unless one possesses the persistence to engage an enemy that has successfully, throughout the life of the individual, defied both detection and restraint. How then, if this task is so difficult and even unsuccessful with long-term therapy, can one hope to effect any reconstructive change whatsoever with a short-term approach? The answer to this question is contained in the experience of many therapists who have noted that once the individual has gained an awareness of the relation of even a few facets of his current personality distortions to his past conditionings, and has then challenged some defenses, a chain reaction has developed, slowly to be sure, but ultimately with a reconstructive influencing of the personality in depth. In a ten year follow-up of several hundred patients treated from two to twenty sessions, I have been gratified at the extent of change in many individuals which, scarcely discernible at termination, had apparently, over the ensuing years, continued progressively as the patient applied himself to the tasks of reconditioning. Understandably, the patient will need to have something to work with; whatever insights he may have retained after his brief treatment, must have touched on a significant area in his life.

The particular way of working will depend on the experience and skill of the therapist. One cannot, as a rule, due to lack of time, employ the time-honored devices of free-association, passivity and anonymity. Nor should the couch be the preferred position. Transference reactions are dealt with rapidly with the object of avoiding a transference neurosis. While the latter may release the deepest conflicts, there is no time available for the essential working-through. If a transference neurosis develops without intention, this must be dissipated as soon as possible. Resistance is managed by active interpretations.

To help the patient gain a better understanding of himself, the therapist utilizes focused interviewing, structures a broad picture of the existing dynamics, and encourages the patient to fill in the details through concentrated self-observation. If he knows how to employ them, he can advantageously utilize dreams. For example, a patient in the early part of therapy experienced an unaccountable recrudescence of symptoms which discouraged him greatly. Productions were relatively sterile, and, since there was currently no concentration on depth material, and no explanation for the relapse on the basis of unusual environmental difficulties, I assumed that he was resisting talking about matters that bothered him. He denied having any particular feelings toward me, but, when I specifically inquired about dreams, he recalled the following:

"I'm in a room where there is a performance going on, like a theatre. But I'm not paying attention to it. A quite heavy, unattractive, chunky man is there carrying a large gun, like a machine gun. This man—he and I are emotionally involved, but there is no connotation of physical sex. He gets up and leaves, and I follow. He said he was told by his doctor that day—I don't know how he put it—that he had a heart attack. He began to cry. It meant the end of everything between us. Life was not absolutely desolate for me. He was losing everything, but I was detached and unconcerned. The heart attack meant I would be free of him. Then later in the night I had a second dream involving you. A law suit is going on, something like a trial. You are the lawyer. You are cross examining people. I am disappointed in your performance, the way you handle the cross examination—jumping around, no logic. (Patient laughs) You make a reference to making money. I feel let down. All you want is to make money—calculating."

The portion of the session that follows brings out what was bothering the patient—a transference response in which he was equating me with his inadequate greedy father from whom he desired escape.

Dr: You must have had some feelings about me that upset you.
(Pause. Patient laughs.)
Pt: That day you took off on ethics. I felt you were taking off on something I had no desire to talk about. Also when I talked about the law suit I had contemplated and the lawyer handling the case, (The patient was involved in a minor civil suit) you said: "You act precipitiously." I felt you misunderstood me because I don't act precipitiously. I nullify action by indecision. You spoke strongly.
Dr: Yes.

Pt: I guess I seek perfection from you, like I do from my girl friend. When you make a grammatical error, I dwell on it all day.

Dr: You seem to have a need for a powerful, accepting, perfect person in whom you can put your trust, and you get infuriated when that person shows any weakness. *(Interpreting the patient's feeling as a response to not finding the idealized authority figure.)*

Pt: I see that, but this doesn't have to be that way.

Dr: Why do you think it *is* that way?

Pt: I don't know. *(pause)*

Dr: What about your ever having had a perfect person around? Have you?

Pt: Jesus, no. I wish I had. My father was cruel and weak. I couldn't depend on him. He left my mother and me. I felt helpless and dependent on my mother. *(The patient's father had abandoned his mother when the patient was a boy.)*

Dr: Maybe you hoped that a strong man would come into your life some day?

Pt: I always wanted one. Even now I get excited when I see such a person.

Dr: Perhaps you felt I was going to be such a person? *(Patient laughs.)*

Pt: This is a false outlook on life. I'm not in bondage. I'm not a slave. This is all a lot of crap.

Dr: What about bondage to me? In the dream you escape when the man claims to be sick.

Pt: I do feel I need you, but seeing you puts me in bondage. But I don't dare let myself feel angry toward you. Only toward my girl friend.

Dr: Perhaps that's why you had a return of your symptoms. The feelings of being trapped with me, in a dependency, with an inadequate father figure at that. *(Interpreting the patient's symptoms as a product of conflict.)*

Pt: Yes, yes, I am sure of it.

It is quite possible that the patient may have been able to work through his transference without the use of dreams. However, I felt that handling his dream short-circuited this process.

There is no substitute for experience. The seasoned therapist will be able to attune himself sensitively to what is going on, gauging how boldly he may make an interpretation, and moving from challenge to support in response to the immediate reactions of the patient. It is difficult to outline specific rules that apply to every case since no two therapists will develop the same relationships with any one patient. And a patient will play different roles with different therapists, depending upon where in his characterologic scheme he happens to fit the therapist. Almost anything can happen in a therapeutic situation, but if the therapist is flexible, sensitive, empathic and understands the basic processes of psychotherapy, and if he is aware of his neurotic impulses as they are mobilized in his relationship with his patient, he should be able to bring the average patient to a sufficient understanding of his basic problems within the span of a short-term approach.

SELECTING THE PROBLEM AREA FOR FOCUS

A man entering a woods with a shotgun which he explodes blindly in all directions, may over a stretch, eventually hit some animal target at random. Adventitiously, a foolish rabbit may come to a bad end in the path of buckshot. If we spend a long enough period in the woods, we may gain our reward. On the contrary, if we have a limited time to hunt, and do not have too many shots at our disposal, we must be very careful about stalking our game, aiming our rifle and firing at the target with precision.

Analogically, if we settle back to work with a patient in a long-term program, it does not matter so much how vague our focus may be. Eventually we will be able to score. Sooner or later, the patient's symptoms, the current precipitating factor, the immediate conflicts activated in the present disorder, the underlying personality structure, deeply repressed conflicts originating in childhood, the relationship with parental agencies, and the defensive mechanisms will become defined and correlated. The working-through process proceeds on all levels of the psychic organization, and no aspect of personality or environment is considered unimportant in the investigative design.

In short-term therapy, we cannot afford the leisurely pace which so extensive a proceeding requires. It is essential to focus on areas that will yield the highest dividends. Generally these deal with problems of immediate concern to the patient. While aspects which trouble the patient topically may not actually be the most important elements of his disorder, they do engulf his attention. Skill as a therapist is revealed in the ability to establish bridges from the complaint factor to more basic difficulties. Only when a continuity has been affirmed between the immediate stresses and the conflictual reservoirs within the personality, will the patient be able to proceed working on more substantial issues. To focus on what the patient considers to be mere corollaries to his pain, before one has shown him that they are actually the responsible mischief makers, will usually turn out to be an unproductive exercise. It would be as if in a business faced with bankruptcy we were to advise delay in regulating office expenditures in favor of studying the economic picture of the world at large. The perturbations of management could scarcely be allayed with remote objectives when what immediately occupies them is the anxiety of meeting the weekly payroll. Were one to consider the day-to-day survival needs, and tangentially relate current operations to more comprehensive, and ultimately more important, general business factors, greater cooperation would be secured.

The particular problem area to be attacked is, therefore, more or less of the patient's own choosing. Often this deals with the *precipitating stress situation* an exploration of which may alleviate tension and serve to restore the individual to an adaptive balance. Here an attempt is negotiated to identify the immediate trouble source, and to relate it to the patient's subjective distress. An endeavor is made at working-through, at least partially, of the conflicts liberated by the stress situation. These, derivatives of and related to fixed underlying core conflicts, are handled as autonomous sources of anxiety. Historical material is considered only when it is bracketed to the current problems. Not only may the patient be brought back to emotional homeostasis rapidly, particularly when he is seen immediately after the stress situation has set in, but inroads on his deeper conflicts may be engendered.

A bright young man of eighteen applied for therapy on the basis that he was about to fail his last year of hgh school. What worried him was that he would not receive a certificate and could, therefore, not enter college. His parents were no less disturbed than the patient at his impending educational debacle. While his first three years of high school work had yielded passable grades, these were far below his potential as revealed by an intelligence test. What was even more provoking was that in his college entrance examinations he had scored lowest in his class. He had also been unable to secure a passing grade in his mid-term examinations. Embarrassed and manifestly upset, he expressed a futile attitude during the initial interview toward his inability to study. What kept happening to him was that his mind wandered. When he forced himself to read his assignments, he could not retain what he read. The prospect of repeating his last year at school was a severe blow to his pride. He envisaged accepting a position as a general helper at a local gasoline service station.

No comment was made to discourage him from stopping school. Instead my retort dealt with the wisdom of adjusting one's career to one's intellectual capacity. If it were true that he was unable to keep up with his class because of his inferior mental ability, it might be very appropriate to accept a less ambitious career status. Why burden oneself with impossibilities? The patient then spent the remainder of the session trying to convince me that his intelligence quotient was in the upper ten percentile. This was most extraordinary, I admitted. Perhaps there were emotional reasons why he had to fail.

During the next few sessions we feverishly explored his fears of competitiveness, his desire to remain the favorite child in his family, his dependency on his mother, his impulse to frustrate and punish his father for pushing him to satisfy a personal selfish ambitiousness, and his dread to leave home and to pursue an independent life. The meaning of his need to fail soon crystallized in his mind. He realized that it required an effort to avoid educational success, that he was actually trying to fail in order to retain the pleasures of irresponsible childhood.

No moral judgments were expressed as to the virtues of these aims. If he really wanted to be a child, if he desired to hurt himself in order to get back at his parents, if he had the wish to retreat from being as good as any of his colleagues, this was within his rights as a person. However, he had to realize that he was doing this to himself. Angrily he protested that such was not at all the case. He was convinced that his parents did not want him to grow up; they lamented losing their older children when they went to college. They wanted him to be dependent. Why then should he go along with their designs and nefarious intentions; why should he be the "fall guy"? The rage he vented at his parents was followed shortly by a clearing of his mind and a greater dedication to his studies. His successful final examinations were a fitting climax to his fifteen sessions of therapy. Letters that I have received from the patient from an out-of-town college, and a follow-up visit one year later, have revealed measures of personality growth hardly consistent with the relatively short period that he stayed in treatment.

Another focus in therapy is on *distressing symptoms*. The patient is only too eager to talk about these. Their exploration may lead to a discovery of provocative anxieties and conflicts that initiate and sustain them. The importance of giving some meaning to disturbing or mysterious complaints cannot be overemphasized. So long as a symptom remains unidentified, it is like an autonomous and frightening foreign body. To label it, to explain its significance, gives the individual a measure of control, helping him to restore his sense of mastery. This enables him to function better, since, in finding out some reasons for his symptoms, he can utilize his energies to correct their source.

Generally, the presenting symptom is explored thoroughly in the context of the question: "How is the symptom related to the individual's personality structure as a whole?" For example, a man comes to therapy undermined by uncontrollable bouts of anxiety. The history reveals that the first attack followed a quarrel with his wife. From the character of his relationship with his mother, his Rorschach responses and his dreams it is apparent that he basically is a dependent individual who is relating dependently to his wife. The symptom of anxiety is explicable on the basis of his releasing hostility toward the parental substitute and fearing abandonment and counter-hostility. Our focus shifts then from his symptom to his personality structure in operation.

Other areas of focus may present themselves, for instance transference and resistance manifestations which, when they appear, will occupy the therapist's attention to the exclusion of any other concern. But here, too, when such reactions arise, they should be integrated with the general theme of the patient's personality functioning.

The principal tools for inculcation of insight are clarification and interpretation.

CLARIFYING AND INTERPRETIVE ACTIVITIES

All persons possess blind spots in understanding. Many of these are due to gaps in education; some are distortions promoted by parents and friends; some are perversions of factual data; some are misrepresentations initiated and sustained by misguided resources. During therapy some of these falsifications will require greater clarification.

In assuming a role geared toward clarification, the therapist must make it clear that he is no oracle of wisdom, but that there are some facts of which he is confident. If the therapist is not sure of his stand, he may offer his ideas with some reasonable reservations, since it may turn out that he is wrong. For example, if a patient is in dread of injuring himself physically by masturbation on the basis that he has heard somewhere that masturbation drains off one's strength and makes one liable to disease, the therapist may firmly state that there is no evidence that masturbation can physically undermine a person. However, one's attitudes about masturbation, and one's obsessive worries about it, can be anxiety provoking. The important thing is to find out why masturbation, and the concern with masturbation, have become so over-valued and important to the patient.

On the other hand, if a patient has been having fainting spells and credits these to a brain tumor, the therapist should not categorically dismiss the patient's fears as foolish. He may assure the patient that anxiety and insecurity may have physiological effects that sometimes take the form of fainting spells. However, a good physical and neurological examination are necessary, so that even on the odd chance that his problem is organic, something corrective can be done about it.

A woman consulted me about her inability to have an orgasm. This preoccupied her to an unreasonable degree. She resented the fact that other women were able to experience "the great moment," and that she was destined to miss the experience that her friends considered a heavenly gift. Even though her husband had tried various ways of stimulating her, she had never succeeded in achieving a climax. My response was that under customary conditions of sexual repression in our civilization, the proper release mechanisms are sometimes never established. Her condition was certainly not a unique one, since many persons in our society never achieve an orgasm. This does not mean that they cannot enjoy sex. Feelings of love and closeness, and the joy of givingness to one's mate could make the experience a rewarding one. She could certainly find herself savoring sex more if she stopped worrying about being inadequate. The very contamination of sexual participation with feelings of inadequacy robbed the act of its potential meaning. If she changed her approach to sex, if she ceased hating herself and the world for an imagined blight providence had foisted on her, she would give herself the best opportunity to relish the marital act. The realization that she was not suffering from a private predicament, and that there was nothing seriously wrong with her, put to an end a good deal of her bitterness and tension and enabled her to love her husband more tenderly. Three years later at a follow-up visit the patient proudly announced that, starting a few months back, she had been experiencing occasional orgasms. What was equally important was that she was very much better adjusted to life in general, having stopped resenting her "deprivation."

In short-term therapy, the interpretation of deep unconscious motives prior to their eruption into awareness is generally avoided. This is because the therapist may not in a brief contact feel sure of his ground, and because he does not wish to stir up powerful resistances which will negate his therapeutic efforts. Interpretations deal with immediately discernible feelings and personality reactions. However, it is sometimes possible for an extremely experienced psychoanalytically trained therapist, who has established good rapport with a patient, to interpret in depth, albeit in a reassuring way. This may have a dramatic impact on the patient. For example, a young man in a state of anxiety with uncomfortable somatic accompaniments reveals great fear of standing next to strong looking men in the subway. His dreams repetitively picture him fleeing from men with destructive weapons. The therapist, on the basis of his experience, and his intuitive feelings about the patient's problem, concludes that the patient is concerned about homosexual impulses. The therapist has, in the first few interviews, won the confidence of the patient. He decides to interpret the patient's inner conflict. The following is from a recording of the interview:

Dr: You know it is very common for a person who has lost confidence in himself to assume he isn't masculine. The next thing that happens is that he gets frightened of being beat up, hurt, attacked and even sexually assaulted by strong men. He begins to feel that he is more feminine than masculine. The next thing he begins to assume is that he is homosexual and this scares the devil out of him. *(pause.)*

Pt: Yes, yes. Isn't he? I mean how does one know?

Dr: I get the impression this is something that is bothering you.

Pt: I get caught in this terrible fear. I feel I'm not a man and that I'll do something terrible.

Dr: You mean like letting yourself get involved sexually with a man?

Pt: Not exactly, but when I have a few drinks, I find myself looking at the men with muscles and it scares the hell out of me.

Dr: When you have a few drinks, you *might* get sexually aroused. This is not uncommon. But what makes you think you are a homosexual?

Pt: I know I'm attracted to women and I enjoy being with women. But I constantly compare myself to other men and I come out the low man on the totem pole.

Dr: So the problem is your position in relation to other men, and your feelings about yourself. This seems to me to be your real problem. You've probably had a low opinion of yourself as far back as you can remember. (*In this interchange the patient has been given an opportunity to face his inner phantasies and to give them another interpretation than that he is a hopeless homosexual. The emotional relief to the patient was manifest even in one interview.*)

Unless the therapist is on firm ground psychodynamically, and has developed a good working relationship, probings in depth are apt to pose a hazard. They may create great anxiety, or they may provoke resentment and resistance. The best rule is to preserve a good relationship with the patient by testing the patient's reactions to a few interpretations in depth which are presented in a casual and tentative manner.

A patient with an obsessive fear of being hurt, injured and cut, and thus of coming to an untimely death, had so gentle and obsequious a manner with people that I was convinced he was concealing profoundly destructive tendencies. On one occasion when he was discussing his fear of death, I said: "A problem like yours may be touched off by a number of things. I had one patient who imagined himself to be a killer. This scared him so that he had to push the idea out of his mind. Instead he substituted fears of being hurt or killed. This happens over and over again. Whether or not the same thing is happening to you, I don't know. But if so there may be reasons for it. In the case of the man I treated, he confused being assertive with being aggressive and murderous."

This initiated an exploration into the patient's childhood. There was little question that he had felt over-protected and thwarted in various ways, particularly in exploratory activities. Quarreling, fighting and even disagreeing with others were considered to be evil and "against God's will." My indirect interpretation was accepted and utilized. Where an interpretation is premature or wrong, or where the patient's ego resources are unable to sustain its implications, he may on the other hand, react badly. The therapist then will have to retrieve the situation, working toward the reestablishment of a positive relationship.

The interpretation of a transference reaction is especially helpful when correct. An adolescent boy treated his visits with me as a casual incident in his routine, refusing to talk about himself and waiting for me to do something dramatic to remove his facial tic. At one visit I remarked, "You just won't say anything about yourself and your feelings. I get the impression that you don't trust me." The patient's reaction was a startled one. He blushingly revealed that he was embarrassed at his thoughts. He never was able to be frank with his family. Whenever he divulged any secrets to his brothers or his parents, they were immediately revealed to the whole family to his great embarrassment. When I retorted that there must be something about coming to see me that made him feel sheepish, he admitted wanting to ask me for some "sex books" to explain masturbation and sex. Perhaps, I replied, he felt I might get the idea he wanted to stimulate himself pornographically with this literature. He blushed furiously at this, whereupon I reassured him that there was nothing to be ashamed of, that a strong sexual interest at his age was normal, and that I certainly would reveal nothing about our conversations to his parents. After all, what we talked about was beween ourselves. This maneuver had the effect of releasing a flood of memories of incidents in which his confidence had been betrayed. Our sessions thereafter took a new direction with the patient participating actively. I repeatedly reassured him that his parents or family would never know about the content of our talks.

In some cases, it may be expedient to present the patient with a general outline of personality development inviting him to see which elements apply to him. I have found that this is occasionally helpful where insufficient time is available in therapy to pin-point the precise pathology. Patients are usually enthusiastic at first at having received some clarification, and they may even acknowledge that segments of the presented outline relate to themselves. They then seem to lose the significance of what has been revealed to them. However, years later on follow-up many have brought up pertinent details of the outline and have confided that it stimulated thinking about themselves.

For instance, a man whose depression was set off by his losing face at work when a younger colleague was advanced ahead of him, came to therapy in an extremely discouraged state and with little motivation to inquire into his patterns of adjustment. Deep resentments were apparent from the violent responses to the Rorschach cards, and from his dreams which centered around destruction and killing. When I commented that it would be natural for him to feel angry under the circumstances, he countered with the remark that he had written advancement off years ago, that he bore no resentment toward his victorious colleague, and that he was resigned to getting the "short end of the stick." From childhood on he was the underdog in the family, and he was accustomed to this role. Apparently, I retorted, he was not as resigned as he imagined himself to be, otherwise he would not have reacted to the present situation with such despair. Maybe he had not written himself off as a permanent underdog. Then I sketched an outline that followed along lines which I have used on other patients with minor variations.

"I believe I have a fair idea of what is going on with you, but I'd like to start from the beginning. I should like to give you a picture of what happens to the average person in the growing up process. From this picture you may be able to see where you fit and what has happened to you. You see, a child at birth comes into the world helpless and dependent. He needs a great deal of affection, care and stimulation. He also needs to receive the proper discipline to protect him. In this medium of loving and understanding care and discipline, where he is given an opportunity to grow, to develop, to explore, and to express himself, his independence gradually increases and his dependence gradually decreases, so that at adulthood there is a healthy balance between factors of dependence and independence. Let us say they are equally balanced in the average adult; a certain amount of dependence being quite normal, but not so much that it cripples the person. Normally the dependence level may temporarily go up when a person gets sick or insecure, and his independence will temporarily recede. But this shift is only within a narrow range. However, as a result of bad or depriving experiences in childhood, and from your history this seems to have happened to you to some extent (*the patient's father, a salesman was away a good deal of the time and his older brother brutally intimidated him*), the dependence level never goes down sufficiently and the independence level stays low. Now what happens when a person in adult life has excessive dependency and a low level of independence? Mind you, you may not show all of the things that I shall point out to you, but try to figure out which of these do apply to you.

"Now most people with strong feelings of dependence will attempt to find persons who are stronger than they are, who can do for them what they feel they cannot do for themselves. It is almost as if they are searching for idealized parents, not the same kind of parents they had, but much better ones. What does this do to the individual? First, usually he becomes disappointed in the people he picks out as idealized parental figures, because they never come up to his expectations. He feels cheated. For instance, if a man weds a woman who he expects will be a kind, giving, protective, mother figure, he will become infuriated when she fails him on any count. Second, he finds that when he does relate himself to a person onto whom he projects parental qualities, he begins to feel helpless within himself; he feels trapped; he has a desire to escape from the relationship. Third, the feeling of being dependent, makes him feel passive like a child. This is often associated in his mind with being non-masculine; it creates fears of his becoming homosexual and relating himself passively to other men. This role, in our culture, is more acceptable to women, but they too fear excessive passivity, and they may, in relation to mother figures, feel as if they are breast-seeking and homosexual.

"So here he has a dependency motor that is constantly operating, making him forage around for a parental image who will inevitably disappoint him. (*At this point, the patient interrupted and described how disappointed he was in his wife, how ineffective she was, how unable she proved herself to be in taking care of him. We discussed this for a minute and then I continued.*) In addition to the dependency motor, the person has a second motor running, a resentment motor, which operates constantly on the basis that he is either trapped in dependency, or cannot find an idealized parental figure, or because he feels or acts passive and helpless. This resentment promotes tremendous guilt feelings. After all, in our culture one is not supposed to hate. But the hate feelings sometimes do trickle out in spite of this, and on special occasions they gush out, like when the person drinks a little too much. (*The patient laughs here and says this is exactly what happens to him.*) If the hate feelings do come out, the person may get frightened on the basis that he is losing control. The very idea of hating may be so upsetting to him that he pushes this impulse out of his mind, with resulting tension, depression, physical symptoms of various kinds, and self-hate. The hate impulse having been blocked is turned back on the self. This is what we call masochism, the wearing of a hair shirt, the constant self-punishment as a result of the feedback of resentment. The resentment machine goes on a good deal of the time running alongside the dependency motor.

"As if this weren't enough, a third motor gets going along with the other two. High dependence means low independence. A person with low feelings of independence suffers terribly because he does not feel sufficient unto himself; he does not feel competent. He feels non-masculine, passive, helpless, dependent. It is hard to live with such feelings, so he tries to compensate by being overly aggressive, overly competitive and overly masculine. This may create much trouble for the person because he may try to make up for his feelings of loss of masculinity. He may have phantasies of becoming a strong, handsome, overly active sexual male, and, when he sees such a figure, he wants to identify with him. This may create in him desires for and fears of homosexuality which may terrify him because he does not really want to be homosexual. Interestingly, in women a low independence level is compensated for by her competing with men, wanting to be like a man, acting like a man, and resenting being a woman. Homosexual impulses and fears also may sometimes emerge as a result of repudiation of femininity.

"A consequence of low feelings of independence is a devalued self-image which starts the fourth motor going. The person begins to despise himself, to feel he is weak, ugly and contemptible. He will pick out any personal evidence for this that he can find, like stature, complexion, physiognomy, and so on. If he happens to have a slight handicap, like a physical deformity or a small penis, he will focus on this as evidence that he is irretrievably damaged. Feelings of self-devaluation give rise to a host of compensatory drives, like being perfectionistic, overly ambitious and power driven. So long as one can do things perfectly and operate without flaw, he will respect himself. Or, if he is bright enough, and his environment favorable, he may boost himself into a successful position of power, operate like a strong authority and gather around himself a group of sycophants who will worship him as the idealized authority, whom in turn the individual may resent and envy while accepting their plaudits. He will feel exploited by those who elevate him to the position of a high priest. "Why," he may ask himself, "can't I find somebody strong I can depend on?" What he seeks actually is a dependent relationship, but this role entails such conflict for him that he goes into fierce competitiveness with any authority on whom he might want to be dependent.

"So here we have our dependency operating first; second, resentment, aggression, guilt, and masochism; third, drives for independence; and, fourth, self-devaluation and maneuvers to overcome this through such technics as perfectionism, over-ambitiousness and power strivings, in phantasy or in reality.

"To complicate matters some of these drives get sexualized. In dependency, for instance, when one relates to a person the way a child or infant relates to a parent, there may be experienced a powerful suffusion of good feeling which may bubble over into sexual feeling. There is probably a great deal of sexuality in all infants in a very diffuse form, precursors of adult sexuality. And when a person reverts emotionally back to the dependency of infancy, he may re-experience diffuse sexual feelings toward the parental figure. If a man relates dependently to a woman, he may sustain toward her a kind of incestuous feeling. The sexuality will be not as an adult to an adult, but as an infant to a mother, and the feelings for her may be accompanied by tremendous guilt, fear and perhaps an inability to function sexually. If the parental figure happens to be a man instead of a woman, the person may still relate to him like toward a mother, and emerging sexual feelings will stimulate fears of homosexuality. (*If the patient is a woman with sexual problems, the parallel situation of a female child with a parental substitute may be brought up: A woman may repeat her emotions of childhood when she sought to be loved and protected by a mother. In body closeness she may experience a desire to fondle and be fondled, which will stir up sexual feelings and homosexual fears.*) In sexualizing drives for independence and aggressiveness, one may identify with and seek out powerful masculine figures with whom to fraternize and affiliate. This may again whip up homosexual impulses. Where aggressive-sadistic and self-punitive masochistic impulses exist, these may, for complicated reasons, also be fused with sexual impulses, masochism becoming a condition for sexual release. So here we have the dependence motor, and the resentment-aggression-guilt-masochism motor, and the independence motor, and the self-devaluation motor, with the various compensations and sexualizations. We have a very busy person on our hands. (*At this point the patient revealed that he had become impotent with his wife and had experienced homosexual feelings and fears which were upsetting him because they were so foreign to his morals. What I said was making sense to him.*)

"In the face of all this trouble, how do some people gain peace? By a fifth motor, that of detachment. Detachment is a defense one may try to use as a way of escaping life's messy problems. Here one withdraws

from relationships, isolates himself, runs away from things. By removing himself from people, the individual tries to heal himself. But this
does not usually work because after a while a person gets terrified by
his isolation and inability to feel. People cannot function without people.
They may succeed for a short time, but then they realize they are drifting away from things; they are depriving themselves of life's prime satisfactions. Compulsively, then, the detached person may try to reenter
the living atmosphere by becoming gregarious. He may, in desperation,
push himself into a dependency situation with a parental figure as a way
out of his dilemma. And this will start the whole neurotic cycle all
over again.

"You can see that the person keeps getting caught in a web from
which there is no escape. So long as he has enough fuel available to
feed his various motors and keep them running, he can go on for a
period. But if opportunities are not available to him to satisfy his different drives, and if he cannot readily switch from one to the other, he may
become excessively tense and upset. If his tension builds up too much,
or if he experiences great trouble in his life situation, or if his self-esteem
gets crushed for any reason, he may develop a catastrophic feeling of
helplessness and expectations of being hurt. (*The patient here excitedly
blurted out that he felt so shamed by his defeat at work that he wanted
to atom bomb the world. He became angry and weak and frightened. He
wanted to get away from everything and everyone. Yet he felt so helpless
he wanted to be taken care of like a child. He then felt hopeless and
depressed. I commented that his motors had been thrown out of gear by
the incident at work and this had precipitated excessive tension and
anxiety.*)

"When tension gets too great, and there seems to be no hope, anxiety
may hit. And the person will build up defenses to cope with his anxiety,
some of which may succeed and some may not. For instance, excessive
drinking may be one way of managing anxiety. Fears, compulsions,
physical symptoms are other ways. These defenses often do not work.
Some, like phobias, may complicate the person's life and make it more
difficult than before. Even though ways are sought to deal with anxiety,
these prove to be self-defeating.

"Now we are not sure yet how this general outline applies to you. I
am sure some of it does, as you yourself have commented. Some of it
may not. What I want you to do is to think about it, observe yourself in
your actions and relations to people and see where you fit. While knowing where you fit will not stop the motors from running, at least we will
have some idea as to with what we are dealing. Then we'll better be able
to figure out a plan concerning what to do."

Sometimes I draw a sketch on a blank paper showing "high dependence," "low independence," "devalued self-image," "resent-
ment-guilt-masochism," and "detachment," and repeat the story of

their inter-relationship that I have detailed above. I then ask the patient to study which drives apply to him. If a general description of dynamics is given the patient, and his responses are observed, a little insight may be inculcated which may serve as a focus for greater self-understanding. The insight may be temporarily reassuring at first; then it seemingly is forgotten with a resurgence of symptoms. A review of what has occurred to stimulate anxiety may consolidate the insight and solidify better control. An important tool here is self-observation which the therapist should try to encourage and which will help the "working-through" process without which insight can have little effect.

ENCOURAGING SELF-UNDERSTANDING

It is important even though a patient can spend limited time in treatment that he gain some insight into the nature of his problems. This ideally should establish his complaint factor as a parcel of a much broader design, and should point to the fact that self-defeating patterns are operating that are outcroppings of elements rooted in past experiences. Once the patient gets the idea that his troubles are not fortuitous, but are events related to definite causes —perhaps carry-overs of childish needs and fears—he will be more apt to utilize his energies toward resolving his difficulties rather than expending them in useless resentment and self-recriminations. Insight may operate primarily as a placebo force at first, but if it enables the individual to relate significant forces in his development to his day-to-day contemporary functioning, this may enable him to establish inhibitory controls, and even to structure his life along more meaningful and productive lines.

The degree of insight that can be inculcated in the patient in a short period of therapy is understandably limited. Additionally, resistances will tend to sabotage self-understanding. Though the patient may seek to rid himself of anxiety and disturbing symptoms, though he possesses incentives to be assertive and independent, though he wishes to fulfill himself happily and creatively, he is a prisoner of his conditionings that tend compulsively and confoundingly to repeat. Moreover, there are virtues derived from a perpetuation of neurotic drives: symptoms do tend to give the patient temporary protection from anxiety; secondary gains operate which supply the individual with spurious dividends for his illness; normality poses dangers more disagreeable than being well. To work-through resistances toward complete understanding, and to put insight into practice with corrective personality change, is a prolonged procedure that will have to go on outside of therapy, perhaps the remainder of the individual's life.

What will be needed is a form of discipline that will permit the patient to apply himself to the task of self-understanding and to the use of his understanding to achieve liberation from his destructive patterns. In order to get well the patient will have to acquire the strength to renounce patterns that have values for him. When he becomes aware of the fact in therapy that he may have to give up certain ways of behaving, he may prefer to hang on to his particular way of life even though it involves neurotic suffering. What he desires are the fruits of victory without bothering to till the soil and plant the seed. He wants to retain his neurotic patterns, but to avoid the accompanying pain; and he may become resentful to the therapist for not reconciling his irreconcilable objectives.

For example, a female patient seeks love from men at the same time that she is extremely competitive with them. To outdo and outshine them has intense values for her. When she fails to vanquish them, she becomes infuriated; when they stop short of giving her the proper affection, she goes into despair. Her lack of insight into her ambivalence toward men is startling in view of the fact that she is capable of advising her friends in *their* affairs of the heart. From her history it is suspected that her problem stems in part from her competitiveness with an older brother against whom she was pitted by her mother, who herself was in rivalry with her passive husband. Yet the patient loved and admired her brother. What bothers the patient is that she can never hold on to a strong male; only weak and passive men seek her out, for whom she has only contempt.

Within six sessions of therapy the patient became aware of her two antagonistic drives—to give affection and to defeat. An inkling of her strong penis envy also filtered through. She acknowledged how contradictory her motives were, but this had no effect whatsoever on her behavior. Indeed, she became embittered with and repudiated my suggestion that until a change occurred in her rivalrous attitudes toward men, she could not expect that they would respond to her, nor would she be able to realize the love she desired. She countered with the statement that she was looking for a man with "guts" who could fight back and make her feel like a woman.

Ordinarily, one would anticipate that a problem of this severity could be resolved only in prolonged treatment, preferably with the setting-up and working-through of a transference neurosis. For many reasons long-term therapy was not feasible, and after eighteen sessions treatment was terminated with symptomatic relief, but with no alteration of her patterns with men. What I enjoined her to do was to practice principles of self-observation, which I encourage in all patients who have a desire to achieve more than symptomatic change. Follow-up visits over a ten year period have revealed deep and continuing changes with a successful marriage to a man she respects with whom she has enjoyed raising two children.

Among the areas around which self-observation is organized are the following:

1. *Relating outbursts of tension, anxiety and symptom exaggeration to provocative incidents in the environment and to insecurities within the self*. The patient may be told: "Whenever you get upset, tense or anxious, or whenever your symptoms get disturbing, ask yourself: 'What is going on? What has upset me?' Keep working at it, thinking about matters until you make a connection between your symptoms and what has provoked them." If the patient has gotten clues about the operative dynamics from his treatment experience, he will be in a position to pin-point many of his current upsets. Even if the assigned determinants are not entirely complete, the fact that he attempts to identify the sources of his trouble will help to overcome his helplessness and to alleviate much of his tension.

2. *Observing circumstances that boost or lower feelings about oneself*. The patient is instructed to watch for incidents and situations that make him feel good about himself and those that demoralize him. He may then attempt to relate these circumstances to what he knows about his special personality assets and liabilities. For instance, if he achieves a feeling of peace and contentment only when he first forms a relationship with a person, he may recognize that he feels well because he assumes that the relationship will magically resolve his problems. He may then realize that such inordinate expectations must precipitate a parade of troubles for him later on, and that every relationship merely satisfies his neurotic dependency. If, on the other hand, he experiences greater self-esteem on the basis of doing something constructive through his own efforts, he may become aware that working toward increasing independence and self-growth justifies further efforts in this direction.

3. *Observing one's relationship with people*. The patient is encouraged to ask himself: "What tensions do I get with people? What kind of people do I like or dislike? Are these tensions with all people or only with certain kinds of people? What do people do to

upset me and in what ways do I get upset? What do I do to upset them or to upset myself when I am with them? What do I do and what do they do that tends to make me angry? What problems do I have with my parents, my mate, my childern, my boss, associates at work, authorities, people in general?" Whatever clues are gathered about habitual reaction patterns will serve to consolidate an understanding of one's general personality operations.

4. *Observing daydreams or dreams during sleep.* The patient may be reminded, if during therapy he has learned that his dreams have a meaning, that he may be able to get some valuable data about himself from his phantasies or dreams. He may be instructed: "Make a note of any daydreams or night dreams especially those that repeat themselves. Try to remember them and to figure out what they mean." How valuable this exercise may be is illustrated by the case of a young man with fears about his masculinity who developed stomach pains the evening of a blind date that forced him to cancel his appointment. Unable to understand why his pains disappeared immediately after the cancellation, he asked himself to remember any dreams that night. The dream he recalled was this: "My father had his arm around my mother and kept me from her. I felt guilty." He was so enthusiastic that he had made a connection between the incident of the blind date and his oedipal problem that he telephoned me to say that he was going to challenge his putting women into the role of his mother by seeing his date through another evening. This he was able to do. Obviously not all patients will be able to utilize their dreams in self-observational practices.

5. *Observing resistances to putting one's insights into action.* The patient is advised that every time he applies his understanding to the challenging of a neurotic pattern, this will tend to strengthen him. "You will eventually get to a point where you will be able to block destructive or self-defeating actions before they get you into trouble. But expect some resistance, tension and fear. When you stall in doing what you are supposed to do, ask yourself why? What are you afraid of? Then deliberately challenge your fear and see if you can overcome it."

By a studied application of the above principles of self-observation, the patient may be able to achieve considerable personality growth after his treatment has stopped. Gradually he may become aware of patterns that have to be revised before he can expand his interpersonal horizons. Understandably, this process is slow. First, the individual realizes that his symptoms do not occur at random, but rather are related to life situations and relationships with people which stir up tensions, hostilities and anxieties. This leads to a questioning of the types of relationships he has been establishing. Yet it seems incredible to him that he can be any other way than he is. A suspicion that he can be different spurs him on to inquire into the origins of his attitudes toward people and toward himself. He establishes a continuity between present personality traits and his past conditionings, applying the understanding he has gained during therapy. The "blueprint" of his personality that was tentatively sketched while in treatment becomes more solidly outlined, and he makes essential revisions in it. He sees more clearly the conditions under which his early fears and conflicts originated to paralyze his functioning. In the course of this investigation he may recover memories long forgotten, or he may revive feelings associated with early recollections that have been repressed. There is an increasing facility to master the anxiety associated with his past. He begins to doubt that life need be a repetition of past happenings and he becomes increasingly convinced that it is unnecessary to inject past attitudes into present situations. He then tenuously, against resistance, tests new responses which in their reward help gradually to extinguish old reactions. Throughout this reconstructive process, the old patterns keep coming back, particularly when the individual feels insecure or his self-esteem becomes undermined. The recognition that he is trying to regress as a security measure assists in reversing his retreat. More and more he expresses his claim to a new life, his right to be more self-expressive. His ego expands; his conscience gets less tyrannical; his inner promptings find a more healthy release; his relationships with people undergo a marked change for the better.

There is, of course, no guarantee that these productive developments will take place in all cases. Nor can any estimate be made as to how long a period change will require. But persistence in the practice of self-observation, and active challenging of neurotic patterns, are prime means of achieving reconstructive results. Where the patient has been taught self-relaxation or self-hypnosis, he may advantageously employ these technics to catalyze self-observation.

ENVIRONMENTAL MANIPULATION

In practically every emotional problem an improvement in wellbeing is accompanied by an alteration in living circumstances. This comes about as the patient recognizes that he does not have to exist under conditions of stress and deprivation. Demoralized by his inner turmoil, he may have hopelessly accepted a bad environmental plight as inevitable. In desperation he may seek surcease from his troubles by involving himself in situations that offer asylum, but he then gets himself into predicaments which turn out to be a greater blight than boon. He may even masochistically arrange matters so that he can suffer as if he has to pay penance for pervasive guilt feelings. Over and over we observe the phenomenon of people, distraught with inner conflict, deliberately attempting to give this objectivity by immersing themselves in outside vexations that consume their attention and concern.

In the course of therapy, it is essential to help the patient break the grip of forces that are hurtful or depriving by identifying them and pointing out their effects. Unless the patient has a basic understanding of the role he plays in supporting difficulties of which he bitterly complains, wresting him from one jam will only result in his arranging for another in a very short time.

Generally, it is better for the patient to figure out for himself what he can do to straighten out his life. However, active suggestions may have to be given him if he cannot devise a plan of action by himself, and, toward this end, the therapist may suggest available resources that can aid the patient in his particular need. For instance, a patient who has withdrawn from activities may be encouraged to participate in sports, hobbies and social recreations, the therapist guiding him to groups where such diversions may be found. The patient's economic situation may have to be supplemented through opportune expediencies to supply funds for medical and dental care. A husband, wife or child may be ill, and the pressures on the patient will require alleviation through referral to appropriate clinics or agencies. Better housing may be essential to remedy overcrowding or to remove the patient from neighborhoods where he is exposed to prejudice, threats to his life and crime. A handicapped child may require assignment to a special rehabilitative clinic. A child failing at school may need psychological testing. An aging parent with nothing else to do to occupy his time may rule a household with an iron fist and be responsible for an impending break-up of a family. Appropriate outlets may have to be found to consume the oldster's energies. Adoption of a child may be the best solution for a childless couple who are anxious to rear a boy or girl. A patient who has moved from another town may feel alone and estranged and need information about recreational and social facilities in his community. These and countless other situations may require handling in the course of psychotherapy.

The therapist, may, of course, be as puzzled as the patient regarding how to fill an existing need. He may not know the suitable resources. The chances are, however, that resources do exist if a proper search is launched. A voluntary family agency, or the family agency of the religious faith of the patient, may be able to act as the initial information source, as may a Council of Social Agencies, Welfare Council, Community Council, Community Chest, local or State health or welfare department or children's agency like, a Children's Aid Society. Public health nurses and social workers are often cognizant of immediate instrumentalities in the community, and it may be appropriate to call in a social worker to work adjunctively with the therapist as a consultant.

Perhaps the most pressing problems will concern the patient's relationships with members of his immediate family. Pathological interactions of the various family members are the rule, and the patient may be imprisoned by his family role. Indeed, the patient may not be the person in the family who needs the most help; he may be the scapegoat or the member with the weakest defenses. Active assistance may have to be given the patient in resolving family crises. For example, a woman sought help for depressive spells accompanied by sporadic lower abdominal spasms. Although she rationalized her reasons for it, it soon became apparent that she resented deeply a situation that she had brought upon herself. Her sister's son who was getting a Master's degree at college needed his thesis typed. The patient casually offered to help and soon found herself working steadily against a deadline, typing several drafts of a two hundred page manuscript. This she did without compensation and with only minimal acknowledgement from her sister and nephew. Yet the patient felt obligated to continue since she had promised to complete the thesis. Periodically she would abandon her typewriter when her abdominal cramps became too severe; but her guilt feelings soon drove her back to work. Encouraged by the therapist's appraisal of the unfairness of the situation, the patient was able to discuss with her nephew, with reasonable calmness, her inability to complete his manuscript. This precipitated a crisis with her sister who credited the patient's defection to ill-will. After several sessions were focused on the role she had always played with her exploitative sister, the patient was able to handle her guilt feeling sufficiently to desist from retreating from her stand. A temporary break with her sister was terminated by the latter who apologetically sought to restore the relationship which assumed a much more wholesome tenor.

It may at times be necessary to see other family members to enlist their cooperation. Patients rarely object to this. For instance, a patient though married was being victimized by an over-concerned and dominating mother who visited her daily and assumed control over the patient's household. It was obvious that the patient's protests masked a desire to maintain a dependent relationship with her mother. She refused to get into a fight with her mother or to offend her by requesting that she stay away. Mother would never understand her protest to be left alone; she was greatly concerned over the patient's depression and helplessness. This was why she commandeered the role of housekeeper in her daughter's home. The patient was urged to discuss with mother her need to become more independent and to take over increasing responsibility. It was pointed out that some of her depression and helplessness were products of her refusal to accept a mature status. The more she depended on her mother, the more inadequate she felt. This sponsored a retreat from self-reliance. It was important to urge her mother to stay away from her apartment. I then suggested to the patient that I have a talk with mother. The presumed purpose was to get as much historical data as possible. Her parent readily acquiesced and the interview centered around the patient's great sensitivity as a child and her lack of confidence in herself. Feeling myself to be in rapport with the woman, I pointed out to her how urgent it was to help her daughter grow up. I suggested that it might be difficult to resist her daughter's pleas for help, but that it was vital that she do so in order to stimulate her daughter's independent growth. Nor should she come to her child's rescue when the latter made mistakes. It was important for her daughter to make her own decisions and to take the consequences of her blunders. As a matter of fact the more mistakes she made, the more she would learn. The mother agreed to assist me in helping her daughter, and her cooperation in restricting visits to weekly intervals, as a guest not as a housekeeper, was a principal factor in my being able to bring the patient to a much more self-confident adjustment.

Psychotherapy may have to be prescribed for one or more members of the patient's family in order to alter a family constellation that is creating difficulties for all. In our search for pathology we are apt to overlook the fact that every family unit contains healthy elements which if released can aid each of its constituent members. Instead of or in addition to individual therapy "family therapy" may be employed. (Ackerman, 1958) If family therapy is decided on, sessions may be held with as many of the family group as possible.

Each person must be made to see how he is deprived and depriving, punished and punishing, and exploited and exploiting. Even a few sessions with this intimate group may serve to release feelings and attitudes that may rejuggle the family equation sufficiently to permit the emergence of healthy trends.

DEALING WITH TARGET SYMPTOMS

While symptoms are the product of emotional conflicts and often disappear when these are resolved, we may not in short-term therapy be able to wait for this millennium. We may have to alleviate the existing distress as expeditiously as we can, hopeful that the patient will not cease working on his inner problems simply because he manages to feel better. Handling disturbing symptoms is particularly important where these debilitate the individual and force him to adopt emergency corrective measures that divert him from more permanently harmonious aims.

The symptoms that are most disturbing to the individual are manifestations of a breakdown in homeostasis, namely tension, anxiety and their somatic and depressive by-products and equivalents. In recent years a significant break-through has been registered through the introduction of tranquilizers, energizers and the anti-psychotic drugs. These substances are very valuable as adjuncts, but they must be prescribed cautiously and for definite purposes mindful of their side effects, and, in the case of tranquilizers, of the dangers of habituation. While tranquilizers are valuable when tension and anxiety become overwhelming, or when the patient reaches a point in therapy where he wishes to challenge a neurotic pattern by exposing himself to a new situation for purposes of reconditioning, their prescription must be temporary. Otherwise, the patient may find it difficult to avoid making tranquilizers a way of life. Withdrawal symptoms, similar to those with barbiturates, may precipitate where an abrupt interruption of medication occurs after large doses have been taken over a long period of time.

The therapist, on the basis of his own experience, will usually confine himself to a few favorite drugs of which there are many on the market. The most useful tranquilizers in my experience are meprobamate (Miltown, Equanil,—400 mg. 1-4 times daily; chlordiazepoxide (Librium, 10 mg. 1-4 times daily) and diazepam (Valium, 5 mg. 1-3 times daily). These minor tranquilizers tend to suppress anxiety, tension and their somatic and depressive residues. Generally, in recommended doses (the amounts above or below average dosages must be adjusted to individual patients and situations) there are few adverse reactions, but sensitivity to any drugs may occur in some patients, causing drowsiness, fatigue, ataxia, dizziness, excitement, depression and other untoward symptoms. Such complications are rare, however, and disappear with discontinuance of the drug. Patients will respond uniquely to the various medicaments. For instance, some do better with Miltown than with Librium and vice versa. Valium is probably the most potent of the tranquilizing agents and should be used with caution where psychotic tendencies are suspected which underly the anxiety. In acute panic states, intramuscular or intravenous Librium (50-100 mg), repeated if necessary in 4—6 hours, may bring about the necessary calming.

There has been too great a tendency to abandon barbiturates with the advent of tranquilizers. Barbiturates, such as phenobarbitol, are still of value particularly where anxiety is strong. The daytime use of non-barbiturate hypnotics like glutethimide (Doriden) in small doses (125-250 mg.) has also proven of value. Again caution must be exerted against continued use of hypnotics to avoid habituation.

Parenthetically it may be appropriate to mention that in any problem where tension is strong, one may be able to avoid tranquilizers, or reduce their dosage, by encouraging the patient to attempt some motor release. Physical exercises, sports, dancing and walking may provide an avenue for tension disposal.

The phenothiazine derivatives are indispensable for the symptomatic relief of schizophrenic symptoms and play an important role in any psychotherapeutic program for these conditions, short or long-term. Since habituation is unknown and withdrawal symptoms are rare, they may constitute a means of prolonged maintenance for patients who otherwise could not make an appropriate adjustment. In my own practice, I utilize chlorpromazine (Thorazine, 25 mg. 3 times daily, increased in two days by 25-50 mg., and then semi-weekly to 800 mg., if necessary, until a desired effect has been obtained) only in severely excited manic and schizophrenic episodes; and thioridazine (Mellaril, 25 mg., 3 times daily, slowly increased, if necessary, to 400 mg. daily) in less severe overactive and excited reactions. Trifluoperazine (Stelazine, 2 mg., 3 times daily) has proven valuable in borderline patients and in schizophrenic persons who are depressed or withdrawn. The few side reactions which have occurred with any of these phenothiazines have been easily controlled with antispasmodic, anticholinergic and antihistaminic drugs. For example, trihexyphenidyl (Artane, 1 mg., the first day, increased by 2 mg. daily until a total of 6-10 mgs. is given daily, in individual doses near meal times) may be used to control side effects when they develop. Since sensitivity generally shows up in the early stages of drug administration, persons who are intolerant of phenothiazines can soon be identified and the dosage more rigorously controlled. The phenothiazines should not be employed for neurotic anxiety reactions for which the milder tranquilizers are better suited.

Hypnosis and self-hypnosis are also valuable in lessening tension and anxiety. During hypnosis the patient is encouraged not only to feel his tension resolving, but to observe himself for its sources. More detailed technics are contained in another chapter in this book.

In depressions, the treatment of choice will depend on the depth of depression and its nature. Mild transitory depression and situational depressions associated with discouragement, apathy and lethargy often yield to dextro-amphetamine and amobarbital (Dexamyl, in spansule form, 10 or 15 mg., taken in the morning; or in tablet form of 5 mg. when indicated). In endogenous depressions, affective depressions (manic-depressive, depressed psychosis), involutional depressions, depressions associated with somatic disorders, and neurotic depressions associated with anxiety, imipramine (Tofranil) may prove useful provided there is no sign of glaucoma. Adequate dosage is essential, since small doses are ineffective. Up to 200 to 250 mg. may have to be given daily in gradual steps at the start, with maintenance doses of from 50 to 150 mg. Amitriptyline (Elavil) is also a useful drug and similarly must be given in good dosage (two 25 mg. tablets, increased to six tablets daily until an effect is registered). The monoamine oxidase inhibitors, like phenelzine (Nardil), are sometimes helpful where other drugs fail. Three tablets daily until the depression lifts are followed by a maintenance dose of 1-2 tablets daily. As is well known the monooxidase inhibitors are not compatible with imipramine. Tranylcypromine (Parnate, one tablet of 10 mg. in the morning and afternoon, increased by another tablet if necessary) may be helpful with due caution observed, such as avoiding other medicaments (except Stelazine which is useful in combination treatment) and eliminating cheeses from the diet which tend to raise the blood pressure.

New antidepressants include desipramine (Norpramin) 150 mg. daily and Aventyl, 20 mg. increased gradually to 100 mg. daily. Mellaril also appears to possess an antidepressant influence in some patients. While the placebo effect cannot be eliminated, there is evidence that "energizers" may possess values that justify their use.

Because of the dangers of suicide, electro-convulsive therapy (ECT) continues to be a most important measure in any depression in which there is even the slightest possibility of the patient taking his life. The results can be dramatic and life-saving. Patients with recurrent depressions may often be kept symptom free by periodic maintenance ECT. Electro-convulsive therapy is also useful in schizophrenic excitements, as well as in the intense anxiety episodes often seen in borderline cases and obsessional neurosis.

In early schizophrenia, where insulin shock therapy is available, a full course of treatment should be prescribed as a measure that can potentially interrupt a process which, if prolonged, may become irreversible. Psychotherapy following insulin may then be possible.

Insomnia may call for the cautious prescription of hypnotics, particularly the non-barbiturates, like the piperidine derivative, Noludar (300 mg.), glutethimide (Doriden, 500 mg.) or ethchlorvynol (Placidyl, 500 mg.) Barbiturate products may also have to be prescribed on occasion, like pentobarbital sodium and carbromal (Carbrital, full strength), Seconal sodium (1½ grains) or Tuinal (1½ grains). The habituating effects of the prolonged use of hypnotics should be kept in mind, their administration being halted as soon as possible. Relief of insomnia may also be possible through the use of hypnosis.

In alcoholism it may be necessary to manage tremors, agitation and beginning or actual delirium tremens and hallucinosis as rapidly as possible. Librium, intramuscularly or intravenously, in 50-100 mg. doses, repeated in three hours, may be valuable. Where the patient is unable to control his drinking, disulfiram (Antabuse) may be necessary. It need scarcely be mentioned that some group approach, such as Alcoholics Anonymous, can advantageously supplement psychotherapy.

Phobias may require special handling. Where phobic states are so intense that a panic state impends, intramuscular or intravenous Librium (50-100 mg. repeated, if necessary, in four hours) may bring the patient out of his immediate upset. In severe phobic disorders, there is a danger of the patient getting dependent on the therapist, and treatment should be periodically interrupted even though the patient insists on continuing. The patient must also be encouraged to challenge his phobia once he understands some aspects of the dynamics. Tranquilizers may be employed to lessen his anxieties sufficiently to encourage a process of reconditioning. Desensitization technics are often helpful in phobias, particularly with hypnosis, the patient exposing himself gradually to increasing increments of anxiety through the phantasying of progressively more fear inspiring situations, and, finally, actually exposing himself to his phobic predicament. (Wolpe 1958) Sometimes hypno-analysis, with induced regression, may help dissipate a phobia by tracing its source. (Wolberg 1964a)

Conversion and dissociative reactions of an hysterical nature can disable the individual so that immediate relief is necessary. Here a strong authoritarian approach utilizing suggestion, with or without hypnosis, may correct the symptom in relatively few sessions. A light barbiturate narcosis may be useful where great resistance is encountered.

In obsessive-compulsive reactions, what often helps is an authoritative persuasive approach in which the patient is enjoined to push his mind away from his preoccupations whenever he tortures himself with them. Such suggestions may be reinforced through hypnosis. The patient's dependency will have to be managed so that therapy does not become interminable; this is always a danger in obsessive-compulsive problems. Where bouts of anxiety become overwhelming, tranquilizing drugs, temporarily prescribed, may help restore equilibrium. If a psychotic break impends, a few electroconvulsive treatments may restore the psychic equilibrium.

EVOLVING A CONSTRUCTIVE LIFE PHILOSOPHY

So far we have considered in our short-term program the need for (1) rapid establishing of a working relationship, taking advantage of intercurrent healing forces, (2) formulating a working hypothesis of the existing emotional problem, (3) alerting ourselves to resistance and transference, and dissipating these as quickly as possible, (4) applying dynamic formulations to clarifying and interpretive activities, (5) teaching the patient how to utilize self-observation to validate or alter hypothetical assumptions regarding the prevailing mechanisms, (6) dealing with disturbing factors in his environment, (7) encouraging the utilization of insight to foster corrective actions, and (8) handling target symptoms that require immediate resolution. We now come to an aspect in therapy that is usually neglected even though it may be primarily responsible for the enhancement of well-being. This is the development of the proper life philosophy and of more constructive values. The spontaneous evolution of more wholesome ways of looking at things, often occurs subtly as a result of the cogent application of principles the patient has learned in therapy. Life is approached from an altered perspective. What was at one time frightening or guilt inspiring is no longer disturbing; what brings insecurity and undermines self-esteem ceases to register such effects. This revolution takes time. Value change may not be discernible until years have passed beyond the formal treatment period. Only then may one hear such comments as these which were recorded during follow-up studies:

"What I got out of treatment was the feeling that it was senseless to act as if I were a child using the world as a family. The minute I stopped carrying over my silly childish ideas into my life I started getting better."

"I learned that I was not as bad and ugly and stupid as I imagined. I realized that if I felt this way about myself, I must assume everybody else felt that way about me. What I learned in my treatment was that even with my mistakes I wasn't as bad as I imagined. Then I noticed that people did like me; and I liked my self better."

"The real thing that happened to me was the realization that it wasn't necessary to feel guilty about everything. Nobody was going to kill me if I enjoyed myself. So I began to enjoy myself."

"I realized that everybody had good and bad parts of them. So one day I said to myself, 'Why not see the good in people and minimize the bad.' That included my husband and children. This was a fantastic idea, but it was really quite simple. I should have thought of it before."

"I began to feel that I was the one responsible for making life a bouquet of pleasure or a living hell. I said to myself, 'Stop wearing a hair shirt all the time!' I'd keep catching myself doing this and I knew why, and I'd stop myself and things would clear up."

These comments, succinct and oversimplified as they may seem, are condensations of months and years of the working-through of insights.

While it is true that new philosophical ideas may be incorporated by the individual sometimes overnight; for instance as a result of authoritative mandates of secular and religious leaders, unless the individual subjects such edicts to his critical reasoning, and establishes their essential soundness in his mind, they are apt to be evanescent. They are replaced over and over again by new doctrines to which the person clings hopefully for a while in quest of bringing some meaning to his existence. The history of the majority of patients, prior to their seeking therapy, attests to futile gropings for some kind of philosophical answer to their dilemmas. The search may proceed from Christian to Oriental philosophies, from prurience to moralism, from self-centeredness to community mindedness. But what at first seems firmly established soon becomes dubious as new ideas and concepts are proffered by different authorities.

It is far better to evolve philosophies that are anchored in some realistic conception of one's personal universe than to accept fleeting cosmic sentiments and suppositions no matter how sound their source may seem. Even a brief period of psychotherapy may till the soil for the growth of a healthier sense of values. We may be able during this span to inculcate in the person a philosophy predicated on science rather than cultism.

The question that naturally follows in a short-term program is this: can we as therapists expedite matters by acting in an educational capacity, pointing out faulty values and indicating healthy ones that the patient may advantageously adopt? If so what are the viewpoints to be stressed?

Actually, no matter how non-directive a therapist may imagine himself to be, the patient will soon pick up from explicit or implicit cues the tenor of the therapist's philosophies and values. The kinds of questions the therapist asks, the focus of his interpretative activities, his confrontations and acquiescences, his silences and expressions of interest, all designate points of view contagious to the patient, which he tends to incorporate, consciously and unconsciously, ultimately espousing the very conceptual commodities that are prized by the therapist. Why not then openly present new precepts that can serve the patient better? Superficial as they sound, the few precepts that can be tendered may be instrumental in accelerating recovery. Among possible propositions are the following:

1. *Isolating the past from the present.* All persons are victimized by their past which may operate as a mischief monger in the present. A good adjustment presupposes modulating one's activities to present-day considerations rather than to resigning to promptings inspired by childish needs and misinterpretations. In therapy the patient may become aware of what early patterns are repeating themselves in his adult life. This may provide him with an incentive for change. On the other hand, it may give the patient an excuse to rationalize his defections on the basis that unalterable damage has been done to him by his parents who are responsible for all of his trouble. The therapist may remind the patient that he, like anyone else, has a tendency to project outmoded feelings, fears and attitudes into the present. His early hurtful experiences undoubtedly contributed to his insecurity and to his devalued self-esteem. They continue to contaminate his adjustment *now* and he, therefore, must try to overcome them. "Ruminating on your unfortunate childhood and bitter past experiences are indulgences you cannot afford. These can poison your present life if you let them do this. It is a credit to

you as a person to rise above your early misfortunes. Attempt to restrain yourself when you fall back into thinking about past events
you no longer can control, or when you find yourself behaving child-
ishly. Remember, you may not have been responsible for what happened to you when you were a child, but you *are* responsible for perpetuating these patterns in the present. Say to yourself: 'I'm going
to release myself from the bonds of the past!' And work at it."

2. *Handling tension and anxiety.* The patient may be reminded
that tension and anxiety may appear, but that he can do something
positive about them. "Everytime you experience tension, or any
other symptoms for that matter, ask yourself why? Is it the immediate situation you are in? Is it something which happened before that
is stirring you up? Is it something you believe will happen in the
future? Once you have identified the source of your tension or
trouble, you will be in a better position to handle it. The least that
will occur is that you will not feel so helpless since you know a little
about its origins. You will then be in a better position to do things to
correct your trouble." The idea that one need not be a helpless victim of symptoms tends to restore feelings of mastery. A patient who
was given this suggestion went to a new class. While listening to
the lecturer, she began to experience tension and anxiety. Asking
herself why, she realized she was reacting to the presence of a classmate who came from her own neighborhood and knew her family.
She then recognized that she felt guilty about her interest in one of
the men in the class. This happened to be the real reason why she
registered for the course. She realized that she feared the neighbor's
revealing her interest in the man to her parents if she sat near him
or was friendly to him. She then thought about her mother who was
a repressive, punitive person who had warned her about sexual
activities. With this understanding, she suddenly became angry at
her classmate. When she asked herself why she was so furious, it
dawned on her that she was actually embittered at her own mother.
Her tension and hostility disappeared when she resolved to follow
her impulses on the basis that she was now old enough to do what
she wished.

3. *Tolerating a certain amount of tension and anxiety.* Some
tension and anxiety are inherent parts of living. There is no escape
from them. The patient must be brought around to accept the fact
that he will have to tolerate and handle a certain amount of anxiety.
"Even when you are finished with therapy, a certain amount of tension and anxiety are to be expected. All persons have to live with
some anxiety and tension, and these may precipitate various symp-

toms from time to time. If you do get some anxiety now and then, ride it and try to figure out what is stirring it up. But remember you are no worse off than anyone else simply because you have some anxiety. If you are unable to resolve your tensions entirely through self-observation, try to involve yourself in any outside activities that will get your mind off your tensions."

4. *Tolerating a certain amount of hostility.* If the patient can be made to understand that he will occasionally get resentful, and that if he explores the reason for this, he may be able to avoid projecting his anger or converting it into symptoms. "If you feel tense and upset, ask yourself if you are angry at anything. See if you can figure out what is causing your resentment. Permit yourself to feel angry if the occasion justifies it; but express your anger in proportion to what the situation will tolerate. You do not have to do anything that will result in trouble for you; nevertheless, see if you can release some of your anger. If you can do nothing more, talk out loud about it when you are alone, or engage in muscular exercise to provide an outlet for aggression. In spite of these activities you may still feel angry to a certain degree. So long as you keep it in hand while recognizing that it exists, it need not hurt you. All people have to live with a certain amount of anger."

5. *Tolerating a certain amount of frustration and deprivation.* No person can ever obtain a full gratification of all of his needs, and the patient must come to this realization. "It is important to remember that you still can derive a great deal of joy out of eighty per cent rather than one hundred per cent. Expect to be frustrated to some extent and learn to live with it."

6. *Correcting remediable elements in one's environment.* The patient may be reminded of his responsibility to remedy any alterable factors in his life situation. "Once you have identified any area of trouble, try to figure out what can be done about it. Lay out a plan of action. You may not be able to implement this entirely, but do as much of it as you can immediately, and then routinely keep working at it. No matter how hopeless things seem, if you apply yourself, you can do much to rectify matters. Do not get discouraged. Just keep working away."

7. *Adjusting to irremediable elements in one's life situation.* No matter how much we may wish to correct certain conditions, practical considerations may prevent our doing much about them. For example, one may have to learn to live with a handicapped child or a sick husband or wife. One's financial situation may be irreparably marginal. There are certain things all people have to cope with, cer-

tain situations from which they cannot escape. If the patient lives in the hope of extricating himself from an unfortunate plight by magic, he will be in constant frustration. "There are certain things every person has to learn to accept. Try your best to alter them as much as you can. And then if some troubles continue, just tell yourself you must live with them, and resolve not to let them tear you down. It takes a good deal of courage and character to live with your troubles, but you do have a responsibility to carry them. If you start feeling sorry for yourself, you are bound to be upset. So just plug away at it and build up insulation to help you carry on. Say to yourself: 'I am not going to respond to trouble like a weathervane. I will remedy the trouble if I can. If I cannot, I will adjust to it. I will concentrate on the good things in my life and minimize the bad.'"

8. *Utilizing will power to stop engaging in destructive activities.* One of the unfortunate consequences of a dynamic approach is that it gives the patient the idea that he is under the influence of unconscious monsters he cannot control. He will, therefore, justify acting-out on the basis of his "automatic repetition-compulsions." Actually once he has a glimmer of what is happening to him, there is no reason why he cannot enlist the cooperation of his will power to help inhibit himself. "If you know a situation will be bad for you, try to divert yourself from acting it out even if you have to use your will power. There is no reason why you can't work out substitute solutions that are less destructive to you even though they may not immediately be so gratifying. Remember a certain amount of deprivation and frustration is normal, and it is a complement to you as a person to be able to give up gratifications that are ultimately hurtful to you. Remember too that some of the chief benefits you get out of your symptoms are masochistic, a kind of need to punish yourself. You can learn to overcome this too. When you observe yourself acting neurotically, stop in your tracks and figure out what you are doing."

A woman, living a conventional life as a housewife, was involving herself sexually with two of her friend's husbands. She found herself unable to resist their advances, even though the sexual experiences were not particularly fulfilling. She felt ashamed and was guilt-ridden by her actions. There were obviously some deeper motives that prompted the patient to act out sexually, but the threat to her marriage and relationship with her husband required an immediate halting of her activity. My remark to her was: "Until you figure out some of your underlying feelings, it is best for you to stop your affairs right now. How would you feel about stopping right now? Let's give ourselves a couple of months to figure out this thing. Frankly, I don't see how we can make progress unless you do." The patient reluctantly acquiesced; but soon she was relieved that somebody was supporting her inner resolution to resist. The interval enabled us to explore her disappointment with her husband, her resentment toward him, and to find outlets for her desires for freedom and self-expression in more appropriate channels than sexual acting-out.

9. *Stopping unreasonable demands on oneself.* If the patient is pushing himself beyond the limits of his capacities, or setting too high standards for himself, it will be essential for him to assess his actions. Are they to satisfy his ambitions or those of his parents? Are they to do things perfectionistically? If so does he feel he can achieve greater independence or stature as a person when he succeeds? "All people have their assets and liabilities. You may never be able to accomplish what some persons can do; and there are some things you can do that others will find impossible. Of course, if you try hard enough you can probably do the impossible, but you'll be worn down so it won't mean much to you. You can still live up to your creative potentials without going to extremes. You can really wear yourself out if you push yourself too hard. So just try to relax and to enjoy what you have, making the most out of yourself without tearing yourself to pieces. Just do the best you can, avoiding using perfectionism as a standard for yourself."

10. *Challenging a devalued self-image.* Often an individual retires on the investment of his conviction of self-devaluation. What need is there for him to make any effort if he is so constitutionally inferior that all of his best intentions and well-directed activities will lead to naught? It is expedient to show the patient that he is utilizing his self-devaluation as a destructive implement to bolster his helplessness and perhaps to sponsor dependency. In this way he makes capital out of a handicap. Pointing out realistic assets the patient possesses may not succeed in destroying the vitiated image of himself, but it does help him to reevaluate his potentialities and to avoid the despair of considering himself completely hopeless. One may point out to the patient instances of his successes. In this respect encouraging the patient to adopt the idea that he can succeed in an activity in which he is interested, and to expand a present asset may prove to be a saving grace. A woman with a deep sense of inferiority and lack of self-confidence was exhorted to add to her knowledge of horticulture with which she was fascinated. At

gatherings she was emboldened to talk about her speciality when an appropriate occasion presented itself. She found herself the center of attention among a group of suburbanites who were eager to acquire expert information. This provided her with a means of social contact and with a way of doing things for others which built up a more estimable feeling about herself.

Logic obviously cannot convince a person with devalued self-esteem that he has merit. But unless a proper assessment is made of his existing virtues, the person will be retarded in correcting his distorted self-image. "You do have a tendency to devalue yourself as a result of everything that has happened to you. From what I can observe, there is no real reason why you should. If you do, you may be using self-devaluation as a way of punishing yourself because of guilt, or of making people feel sorry for you, or of rendering yourself helpless and dependent. You know, all people are different; every person has a uniqueness, like every thumbprint is unique. The fact that you do not possess some qualities other people have does not make you inferior."

11. *Derive the utmost enjoyment from life.* Focusing on troubles and displeasures in one's existence can deprive a person of joys that are his right as a human being. The need to develop a sense of humor and to get the grimness out of one's daily life may be stressed. "Try to minimize the bad or hurtful elements and concentrate on the good and constructive things about yourself and your situation. It is important for every person to reap out of each twenty-four hours the maximum of pleasures possible. Try not to live in recriminations of the past and in forebodings about the future. Just concentrate on achieving happiness in the here and now."

12. *Accepting one's social role.* Every adult has a responsibility in assuming a variety of social roles: as male or female; as husband or wife; as a parent; as a person who must relate to authority and on occasions act as authority; as a community member with obligations to society. Though he may feel immature, dependent, hostile and hypocritical, he still must try to fill these roles as completely as he can. If the patient is destructively involved with another individual with whom he must carry on a relationship, like an employer, for example, he must attempt to understand the forces that serve to disturb the relationship. But at the same time he must try to keep the relationship going in a way that convention dictates so that he will not do anything destructive to his security. "One way of trying to get along with people is to attempt to put yourself in their position and to see things from their point of view. If your husband

(wife, child, employer, etc.) is doing something that is upsetting, ask yourself: 'What is he (she) feeling at this time; what is going on in his (her) mind? How would I feel if I were in his (her) position?' At any rate, if you can recognize what is going on, correcting matters that can be resolved, adjusting to those that cannot be changed; if you are able to relate to the good rather than to the bad in people, you should be able to get along with them without too much difficulty."

TERMINATING THERAPY

The termination of short-term therapy is predicated on the principle that while immediate accomplishments may be modest (symptom relief, for example) the constant application by the patient of the lessons he has learned will probably bring further substantial changes. Deep personality alterations may require years of reconditioning which may go on outside of a formal treatment situation.

If the patient has been appraised of and has accepted the fact that he will be in therapy just as long as is deemed necessary, that he will be helped in understanding some of the sources of his difficulty, and shown ways to proceed to rectify these, he should accept termination without great protest.

What goals may we reasonably expect with the average patient in sessions that have averaged, let us say, once weekly and have extended over no more than a five month period? From the standpoint of the therapist, the following objectives may be considered: (1) establishment of good rapport with the patient, (2) identification of the precipitating factors in the patient's illness, (3) delineation of important elements in personality development that have sensitized the patient to his difficulty, (4) a fairly good idea of the patient's personality structure and the most important coping mechanisms that keep him in homeostasis, (5) designation of the most important conflicts that burden the patient, (6) appraisal of the existing anxiety and recognition of its symptomatic manifestations, (7) outlining to the patient some of the causes of the present illness, (8) teaching the patient the process of self-observation, (9) helping him to translate some aspect of his insight into action, (10) instructing the patient how to employ self-relaxation or self-hypnosis if this is necessary, (11) discusisng with him some constructive philosophical ideas which can help the patient adjust himself.

From the standpoint of the patient, the following objectives should have been achieved: (1) diminution or resolution of tension and anxiety, (2) relief or recovery from other disturbing symptoms, (3) some insight into the sources of his difficulty, including factors in his development, existing conflicts, faulty personality patterns and inappropriate coping mechanisms, (4) understanding of what is essential in making a better adjustment and a willingness to try to establish new patterns, (5) a greater capacity to handle frustration, deprivation and difficult life situations, (6) better mastery of some aspects of the environment, and a facing up to the demands on him he must accept, (7) cognizance of a somewhat different outlook on life, (8) understanding of how to employ self-observation, and, if it has been taught him, self-relaxation or self-hypnosis, and (9) ability to terminate treatment.

Not all of these objectives may have been accomplished at the time termination is contemplated for a number of reasons, such as lack of motivation and diminutive ego strength. Patients who are non-motivated for anything other than symptom relief will usually want to discontinue therapy on their own once they have achieved this goal. Those with weak ego structures will not be able to work with a reconstructive approach, and they may go to pieces when the therapeutic relationship gets too intense or when resistances are analyzed. In such sicker patients one may have to halt probing for conflicts or the attempt to inculcate insight into unconscious processes. Here what starts out as a short-term project may have to be stretched out into prolonged supportive treatment, controlling the dangers of dependency by shorter sessions (15 or 20 minutes), by adequate spacing of visits (once in two weeks if possible), and by periodic interruptions of therapy. Experience persuades, however, that persistency can steer patients with the most fragile personalities toward a better life adaptation, provided the therapeutic climate remains warm. Where the relationship is a good one, the patient will readily accept interpretations even of unconscious content. If the patient begins detaching and his anxiety becomes extreme with ensuing disintegrative symptoms, one may halt working in depth. Drug therapy may be employed. If anxiety gets out of hand, electric convulsive therapy may be considered to bring the patient back rapidly to some kind of equilibrium. And, when homeostasis is restored, the therapist may again carefully start working with reconstructive therapy, employing supportive approaches as they are required.

There are some patients who are disposed to continue in prolonged treatment following a short-term program for reasons other than as a prop for support and a need to propitiate dependency.

They genuinely seek to work-through their inner conflicts in a dis-
ciplined way. In instances where the motivation for therapy is good
and the patient's ego is basically sound, long-term therapy may enable the patient to arrive at reconstructive goals more expeditiously
than if he were to try this on his own. Long-term therapy should also
be prescribed for indications mentioned in an earlier part of this
chapter.

In certain cases, the therapist may decide to put the patient into
a therapeutic group following a period of short-term therapy. Group
therapy may help the patient, particularly if a relationship disorder
exists, to understand better the dynamics of his problem by watching his multiple transference reactions with the various group members. Resistances can in this way more readily be broken and the
working-through process enhanced. Group therapy may also be
helpful for sicker patients who need support to enable them to
function, but who would get locked in a crippling hostile-masochis-
tic dependency relationship in individual therapy. Group therapy
may furthermore act as a bridge to the world for isolated souls who
have drifted away from people.

Where treatment is to be terminated, I find it helpful to warn the
patient that, while he may feel better, there will be required of him
a consistent application of what he has learned in therapy to insure a more permanent resolution of his deeper problems. I stress
the need for self-observation and for the active challenging of neurotic patterns. I also tell the patient not to get upset if he experiences a set-back. "Set-backs are normal in the course of development. After all some of these patterns are as old as you are. They
will try to repeat themselves even when you have an understanding
of their nature. But what will happen is that the set-backs will get
shorter and shorter as you apply your understanding to what produced the set-back. Gradually you will restructure yourself. In a
way it is good if a set-back occurs, because you will have an opportunity to come to grips again with your basic problems to see how
they work. This can build up your stamina. It is like taking a vac-
cine. Repeated doses produce a temporary physical upset, but complete immunization eventually results. In other words, if your symptoms come back, don't panic. It doesn't mean anything more than
that something has stirred up powerful tensions. Ask yourself what
has created your tensions. Is there anything in your immediate situation that triggered things off? Relate this to what you know about
yourself, about your personality in general. Eventually, you will be
able to stop your reaction. But be patient and keep working at it."

In many cases, it may be wise to terminate therapy by telling the patient to return in two weeks and then in a month. If a setback occurs thereafter that the patient cannot handle himself, he is invited to come back for a "brush-up" session. Such instances, in my experience, are not common, but when they occur the patient may readily be brought to an awareness of how his old problems have been repeating themselves. This tends to reinforce his insight and to give him better control of himself.

FOLLOW-UP

A neglected aspect of therapy are follow-up sessions. Prior to his discharge the patient may be told that it is customary to have a follow-up session one year following treatment, then yearly thereafter for a while. Patients do not object to this; indeed they are flattered by the therapist's interest. An appointment for a session is best made by a personal telephone call. Where the patient, for any reason, finds it impossible to keep the appointment, a friendly letter may be sent asking him to write the therapist, detailing his feelings and progress if any. How readily patients will respond to this invitation is indicated in a follow-up study at the Postgraduate Center for Mental Health on patients terminated at least two years, in which there was a seventy-six per cent return of questionnaires. (Sager, Riess & Gundlach, 1964)

A burning question deals with the evaluation of our results. While our present propositions in psychotherapy do not lend themselves readily to scientific testing or measurement, we have sufficient information as of today to be able to make a reasonable assessment of results. It is beyond the purposes of this chapter to delineate a methodology, but some suggestions along this line have been made elsewhere. (Wolberg, 1964b)

STAGES IN THE SHORT-TERM RESOLUTION OF AN EMOTIONAL PROBLEM

A number of stages may roughly be observed in the short-term mastery of an emotional difficulty.

1. *The patient becomes reassured that he is not hopeless and that there is nothing so drastically wrong with him to prevent a resolution of his suffering.* First it is achieved on the basis of faith in the therapist prompted by the confidence and authority that he exudes. Next it follows the decompression inspired by emotional catharsis, and, if drugs are employed, such as tranquilizers or energizers, the relief they effectuate through their chemical and/or

placebo action. Later it depends upon resolution of difficulties through positive efforts made by the patient himself.

2. *He develops some understanding of reasons for his emotional break-down and he becomes aware of the fact that he has had problems within himself that have sensitized him to his current upset.* His insight, irrespective of its correctness, serves to lower his tension level and to mobilize constructive forces within himself geared toward facilitating a realistic adjustment. Efforts at insight may or may not deal with unconscious forces, depending on the therapeutic direction and the patient's motivation to perceive himself in depth.

3. *On the basis of his understanding, he recognizes that there are things he can do about his current environmental situation, as well as about his attitudes toward people and toward himself.* He may also become aware of the fact that he can, if he wishes, re-organize some of his habitual patterns. Reconditioning is first executed on the basis of the expressed or implied suggestions of the therapist. Later the patient makes constructive efforts through his own incentives, particularly after therapy has ended. Reconditioning will go on for years; perhaps for the remainder of the individual's life.

4. *He accepts the fact that there are and probably always will be limitations in his environment and in himself which he may be unable to change.* He scales down his ambitions and goals to realistic levels, or he elevates them if they are below his creative capacities. This is in line with the development of a more rational life philosophy.

5. *He fulfills himself as completely as possible in spite of handicaps in his environment and in himself, at the same time that he promotes himself to as great degrees of maturity and responsibility as are within his potential.*

WHO CAN DO SHORT-TERM PSYCHOTHERAPY?

A system of psychotherapy is no better than the professional who practices that system. If the operator is untrained, or has no skill, or possesses personality traits that are anti-therapeutic, he will not do too well with any system, other than perhaps to release some spontaneous forces that stimulate well-being through the instrumentalities of the placebo influence and emotional catharsis. Unfortunately, we have some incompetent operators in psychotherapy (as there are incompetents in any other field) who bring ill-repute to the practice as a whole.

A certain ingredient exists in some people that disposes them to become good therapists. It is probably the same constituent that one may find in successful practitioners of other disciplines, like good lawyers or social workers or psychologists. Attempts have been made to break this component down into a number of categories, like the capacity for empathy, preceptivity and sensitivity. These capacities are probably not inborn, but whether they can be taught to all people is another matter. By and large most qualified practitioners possess sufficient quantities of this important therapeutic x - factor to be able to do satisfactory short-term psychotherapy.

If we were to delineate more formally the essential qualifications of a good short-term therapist, we might classify them as follows:

(1) *Extensive Training*. Astuteness in making a rapid diagnosis, skillfullness at arriving at the essential dynamics, and sophistication in a wide spectrum of technics can be rewarding especially if these are executed in a dynamic framework. Whether formal training in a psychoanalytic institute is essential or not will depend on a number of factors including what blocks the individual possesses in working with some of the more repressed and unconscious components of personality. Since goals are abbreviated, and a transference neurosis is not considered essential, extensive psychoanalytic training may not be sought as readily as when depth analysis is envisaged. The fact that the therapist does not expose himself to the discipline of formal analytic training does not imply that he will do an inferior kind of therapy, even though he restricts himself to the more conscious psychic components. Nevertheless where the therapist does relate himself to a structured analytic program, this will probably remit rewarding subsidies, if solely to bring him to an awareness of his own intrapsychic and interpersonal conflicts that interfere with an effective therapeutic relationship.

Irrespective of training, there is no substitute for experience. Having managed a wide variety of problems and patients, the therapist can recognize his strong and weak points with the various syndromes and with different individuals. No matter how well adjusted the therapist may feel himself to be, there are some conditions he will not handle as well as others. The therapist may, when he recognizes which problems give him the greatest difficulties, experiment with modes of buttressing his defects.

(2) *Flexibility in Personality*. The therapist must possess the kind of personality that enables him to set up a working-relationship in a few sessions. Since the patient requires rapid stabilization, the therapist's manner must convey confidence, stability and under-

standing of the patient's turmoil and what is behind it. The patient will discern these integrants and react to them. It is important that the therapist be able to control himself sufficiently so that he can avoid the pitfall of his neurosis interlocking with that of the patient. Particularly, he will need to sensitize himself to the irrational projections of the patient at the very beginnings of a transference neurosis, before it is activated beyond control. Effective as a transference neurosis may be in eliciting dynamics and working-through unconscious conflicts, there is no time for such a luxury in short-term treatment. The therapist must consequently be able to handle the contingency of a transferential eruption.

(3) *Flexibility in approach.* A lack of personal investment in any one technic is of great value in short-term therapy. This necessitates an understanding of the values and limitations of various procedures, such as insight technics, ego building maneuvers, educational tactics, casework, counseling, somatic therapies, hypnosis and group therapy. It requires experience in utilizing selected technics as a preferred method, or in blending a variety of approaches for their special combined effect. Not only is knowledge of and experience with different procedures important, but their application to particular situations, and to the needs of patients at certain times, will require inventiveness and willingness to utilize the contributions of all schools of psychiatry, psychology and the social sciences toward the enhancement of therapeutic progress.

QUESTIONS AND ANSWERS

Question: Can a therapist trained in long-term methods teach himself short-term therapy?

Dr. Wolberg: Of course, but he must manifest a willingness to experiment with methods other than those he has customarily been employing.

Question: Why do so many therapists assume that short-term therapy is inferior to long-term treatment?

Dr. Wolberg: That this assumption is untrue is indicated by studies pursued over a period of years. In long-term therapy, the patient is in treatment for a sufficiently extended period for the therapist to witness personality change. In short-term therapy, the patient is generally discharged with symptom relief, but his personality patterns, unaltered at termination, may continue changing with time. However, the therapist does not see the change, hence he assumes nothing further has happened. But, most importantly, if a therapist applies the same technics in short-term treatment that he ultilizes in long-term therapy, his results will not be too productive in the brief period that is available.

Question: Can a non-analyst do good short-term therapy with reconstructive goals?

Dr. Wolberg: There is no reason why a non-analyst cannot employ methods that are derived from psychoanalysis in a short-term approach. For instance, he may be aware of transference and resistance and deal with these effectively. And he may utilize dreams, provided he has an understanding of dreams, in discerning the conflicts operating on an unconscious level. The most important factor is his understanding of his own personality difficulties as these extend themselves toward the patient in counter-transference. We assume that the therapist is sufficiently free of neurotic burdens so that he will not project his problems onto the patient, confusing him more than before. If he can control his anti-therapeutic impulses during treatment, the therapist will probably be able to do satisfactory reconstructive work, provided, of course, that he is trained to do this work.

Question: Can you succinctly and in general terms describe the most important tactic in a reconstructive short-term approach?

Dr. Wolberg: The basic tactic is to catalyze a different attitude in the patient toward himself and his problems. No better way exists than by showing him that his difficulties are not fortuitous, nor entirely fashioned by environmental agencies, but rather that they have a relationship to provocative forces in his background which have become firmly registered in consistently operative personality drives and needs.

Question: How can this be brought about in the therapeutic session?

Dr. Wolberg: In the course of working on his problems, the patient will bring into the therapeutic situation his claims on authority patterned after archaic demands on his parents. He will express convictions of his own ineffectuality as well as blocks to creativity and productivity. He will expose some of the hindering influences in his early growth process. The therapeutic situation ideally should provide him with a means through which he can work through crippling obstructions and proceed to greater emotional maturity. The most important components in the therapeutic situation, therefore, will consist of the therapist's attitudes toward the patient, and his ability to provide a situation for the patient in which the patient can grow. This will involve the handling of the patient's projections in such a manner as to avoid repetition of those situations that originally necessitated neurotic defenses in the patient. We must expect that the patient will attempt to force the therapist into positions where the therapist will be enticed to react to him after the manner of his parents. The ability of the therapist to maintain his objectivity, and to interpret to the patient the nature of his projections, may eventually force the patient to see how he is attempting to distort the therapeutic relationship in terms of his own early experiences.

Question: What characteristics in the therapist will most likely block reconstructive therapy?

Dr. Wolberg: Unresolved hostilities, needs to maintain too dominant and authoritarian a status in the relationship, and detachment will definitely impede reconstructive therapy. This is not to say that certain characteristics in the therapist that are hostile or authoritarian in nature may not expedite specific forms of psychotherapy. As a matter of fact, in various supportive therapies, an authoritarian, pompous therapist may create for the patient an atmosphere of an omnipotent parent, and bring the patient back to an emotional equilibrium on the basis of this sham security. Furthermore, where a patient manifests anxiety and insecurity on the basis of his impulse to revolt against the restraints of authority, the pressure of a powerful, hostile personage, if the therapist is such, may cause the patient to feel that he cannot cope with this new authority and had better yield to him. He will, therefore, make peace with his super-ego, or adapt it to the hostile image of the new therapist against whom he dares not revolt. He will then rapidly be brought back to an emotional equilibrium. We see this in delinquents and psychopaths. Actually nothing basic changes within the psyche of the patient. He is merely restored to his previous equilibrium, which is acceptable and perhaps even preferable in certain types of problems that cannot be handled with a reconstructive goal in mind.

Question: How does the personality of the therapist influence his doing short-term therapy?

Dr. Wolberg: The therapist will be limited by his own personality and ways of working, and will have to function within these bounds. One cannot get around some personality limitations employing all the "gimmicks," tricks, manipulations, and technics that one hears and reads about. Where one's technics blend with his personality, the patient generally will recognize the therapist's sincerity and will most likely respond to him. All therapists, in experimenting with methods, will find those that work for their particular personalities. I believe that it is silly to deify and glamorize technics, because, while they may work for one therapist, they may not work for another. And while they may be successful with one kind of patient they may fail with the next. One has to devise and improvise as one goes along with each patient. General principles are, of course, important and technical modifications are interesting and vital to know. But they must be employed in the medium of an experimental attitude.

Question: Can psychodrama be used as part of a short-term program?

Dr. Wolberg: Yes, if the therapist is conversant with it and is comfortable in employing it. It may be particularly useful in helping a patient apply his insights toward the challenging of a phobia or the resolution of certain other neurotic patterns. By verbalizing his doubts and recriminations toward another individual who becomes the symbolic representation of a person he dreads or resents, the patient may begin to establish controls and be able to follow through in real life.

Question: Shouldn't a short-term therapist be acquainted with good interviewing technics? Also would you comment on the essential elements of good interviewing?

Dr. Wolberg: A good therapist is a good interviewer. Communication is the channel of interchange between the patient and therapist. A good interviewer is able to subject the patient's communications to selective scrutiny. He can pick out from what the patient say, certain aspects that are important. He paces his comments to the elicited material. This involves an ability to use language constructions that are understandable to the patient. It includes an awareness of non-verbal behavior as a mirror of some of the most important conflicts of the patient. It entails a knowledge of how to maintain the flow of significant verbalizations, and how selectively to focus on pertinent feelings. It embraces methods of inculcating insight by interpretation, and it encompasses an understanding of how to terminate an interview. These formalities are often left to chance during training. It is only through experience that the practitioner gains the interviewing skills that are helpful to him in his practice.

Question: I take it that the relationship is the core of short-term therapy? How do you go about establishing it?

Dr. Wolberg: Yes, a relationship has to exist on some level. Unless a cooperative contact is established with the patient, the therapeutic effort may come to naught. A good psychotherapeutic system has a relationship as a prime objective, at least in the first part of therapy. The technics of achieving a working relationship are rarely formalized, but they involve a gaining of the patient's confidence, an arousal of his expectations of being helped, a mobilization in him of the conviction that the therapist wishes to work with him, and a motivating of the patient to accept the conditions of therapy. Without a working relationship there can be no movement in the exploratory and working-through phases of therapy. Unless it exists, the patient will be unable to handle anxiety associated with the recognition and facing of inner conflicts. How soon the therapist will be able to establish rapport is an individual matter. The personality structure of the therapist will determine this. Some therapists are able to establish a relationship almost immediately with any patient. Other therapists cannot do this, except with certain kinds of patients. The traditional "dead-pan" attitude of acting like a blank mirror, and expecting the patient to relate to this detachment is passé. It just does not work in short-term therapy. It may be indicated in long-term psychoanalytic treatment, but in short-term approaches we simply do not have the time to deal with the resistances and resentments that the patient will manifest at what he considers disinterest and rudeness. An immediate transference neurosis may be precipitated in relation to the detached "phantom therapist" which we cannot handle readily within the few sessions we have available.

Question: Doesn't short-term therapy make a patient content to accept a partial solution for his problems?

Dr. Wolberg: To the argument that short-term therapy plays into the patient's design to be content with a partial solution of his conflicts, one may reply that a partial solution is usually better than none, and that it may be more practical in some patients than the striving for a complete solution through years of treatment which so often end in failure. Moreover, partial solutions pave the way for more complete solutions both through a better use of self-observation and a more ready capacity to seek further therapy if more is needed later on.

Question: Shouldn't a therapist who practices short-term therapy be better trained than a person who does long-term therapy?

Dr. Wolberg: Short-term therapy is much more difficult to do well than prolonged treatment where one has ample time to make mistakes and to correct them. I believe a therapist needs to have had a great deal of experience in long-term methods before he can effectively introduce modifications in technic that will be helpful in his doing good brief therapy which has as its goal more than symptom relief. Insofar as symptom relief alone is concerned, even untrained housewives can accomplish this by letting a disturbed person talk at them, which will permit certain spontaneous reparative processes to evolve. But this is not psychotherapy, though some persons deceive themselves that it is.

Question: Aren't all neurotic persons dependent and how do you know when they are getting better?

Dr. Wolberg: All persons in trouble feel helpless and want to lean on an idealized parental agency. Being permitted to do so relieves their fear and lessens their anxiety. Whether the therapist realizes it or not he will be a target for the patient's dependency yearnings, no matter if he tries to be detached and passive, or actively supportive, reassuring or persuasive. Gratification of dependency needs is hopefully a temporary measure which is ideally followed by developing independence. This is accompanied by such signs as a decrease in sensitivity, diminished tendencies to over-react to stimuli, a greater ability to handle criticism, a channeling off into more constructive channels of rage, a better management of feelings of rejection, an avoidance of destructive competition, a reduction of personal over-ambitiousness, and a correction of distorted perceptions of the world, products of early conditionings. There are no miracles regarding such developments. They come about as the patient is helped to master his automatic repetitive neurotic patterns and to evaluate more rationally his immediate environmental situation which will then enable him to make better and less neurotic decisions.

VII

The Use of Somatic Treatments in Short-Term Therapy

=============== LOTHAR B. KALINOWSKY, M.D.

(Editor's Note: In this chapter Dr. Kalinowsky brings out the fact that somatic treatments can, where indicated, definitely shorten the duration of psychotherapy and even make possible psychotherapy where it was not applicable before. In the major psychoses somatic treatments constitute the principal therapy and expedite rehabilitative approaches. In neuroses somatic treatments may be helpful under certain conditions. The uses and dangers of electroconvulsive therapy, insulin therapy, neuroleptic drugs, the milder tranquilizers, energizers, and psychotomimetic substances in the course of psychotherapy are elaborated in the text as well as in the question and answer section.)

SOMATIC TREATMENTS IN psychiatry have been described frequently as an adjunct to psychotherapy, and there is no doubt that those psychotherapists who are willing to use somatic treatments, might shorten the duration of psychotherapy in many patients. The problem of psychotherapy and the somatic treatments had already been discussed in the 1920's. When Klaesi in Switzerland introduced the first somatic treatment in the psychoses by applying so-called prolonged sleep treatment by means of barbituates and other sedatives, he saw the value of this treatment in preparing the patient for psychotherapy. While most psychiatrists regarded prolonged narcosis as a purely organic treatment, Klaesi himself, as time went on, placed more and more emphasis on the psychotherapeutic aspects of this type of treatment. When insulin coma treatment was introduced, Max Mueller, greatest Swiss expert in insulin therapy, made extensive use of psychotherapy, both during the waking-up period after each individual hypoglycemic coma, and in the afternoon of treatment days, when group therapy as well as individual psychotherapy were given to the insulin patients.

These experiences suggest a combination of entirely different treatments in order to shorten the total treatment time. Yet, there is undoubtedly a large group of psychotic patients in whom psychotherapy is not necessarily needed to achieve a satisfactory result.

If we take the example of a severe case of involutional melancholia in a patient without any history of emotional difficulties prior to the involutional age, a short series of electroconvulsive therapy (ECT) will remove the psychotic syndrome without any attempt at psychotherapy. And there is a good chance that such a patient will not have another episode of depression in his life even though no psychotherapy, or other therapy for that matter, is applied after the removal of his depression by ECT. This undoubtedly is also "short therapy" even though not "short psychotherapy." This fact should be acknowledged because it is wrong to assume that psychotherapy, as important as it is, is the only therapeutic approach in psychiatry, a belief which is frequently held in spite of much progress in the field of somatic treatments during the last thirty years.

In this presentation I propose to discuss the various somatic treatments primarily in their relation to psychotherapy. In order to do this I shall make some remarks about the somatic treatments as such and follow this with a discussion of their combination with psychotherapy. I shall try to clarify in what way the somatic treatments may help to shorten the course of psychotherapy or make a patient accessible to psychotherapy which without previous somatic treatment might not even be applicable.

I will discuss first the question of drugs in psychotherapy. It is amazing how few studies are available to judge the value of the drugs in combination with psychotherapy. The principal and, no doubt, most successful application of the new drugs, primarily the phenothiazines and Rauwolfia drugs, was, of course, in the major psychoses. It may be questioned to what extent the major psychoses are suitable for psychotherapy in the usual sense of the word. It was immediately recognized that the drugs had their main application in the chronic mental patient in our State Hospitals. In this group psychotherapy has been applied only to a negligible degree, and mostly in some specially equipped private hospitals. A recent annual report from one of our larger mental institutions demonstrated that only a small fraction of patients received group psychotherapy, and hardly any had individual psychotherapy.

In the following section the indications for modern drugs will be discussed in the light of their value for psychotherapeutic or socio-psychological measures. The neuroleptic drugs, led by Chlorpromazine (Thorazine), have their main importance in chronic schizophrenics, a group of patients in whom psychotherapy in the usual sense has limited indications. However, the great advances made in social psychiatry with open wards, work therapy and other measures, and with early discharge of patients for treatment outside the hospital were greatly supported by the introduction of these neuroleptic drugs. There exists an argument between psychiatrists here and in other countries, such as England, whether the drugs are solely responsible for this progress in hospital psychiatry. Most of these advances in England came prior to the introduction of the drugs on the basis of the older treatments, such as shock therapy and psychosurgery. Also the work by Maxwell Jones preceded the drug era. In our under-staffed hospitals they undoubtedly have a great value, and those patients who are willing to continue on medication after their discharge from the hospital are definitely aided in their rehabilitation and possible psychotherapy by these drugs.

Pharmacotherapy of acute schizophrenia has less clear-cut indications than pharmacotherapy of chronic schizophrenia. The drugs are able to remove psychomotor excitement and acute delusional and hallucinatory syndromes. This effect is often only temporary as long as the patient is under the medication. It is our strong belief that such patients should be withdrawn from the drug while still in the hospital. An attempt with shock treatments should be made because it is in this group of acute patients where shock therapy leads most frequently to more or less lasting remissions. This statement applies to both ECT and insulin coma treatment. It is regrettable that insulin treatment is given only in very few hospitals at the present time. This is partly explained by the lack of personnel in our hospitals. Although convulsive therapy, including its newer modification of Indoklon inhalation treatment, is effective in many schizophrenics, there are ECT failures which still respond extremely well to a long course of insulin coma treatment. It may be mentioned here that insulin offers itself especially well to simultaneous psychotherapy. Most experts in insulin treatment stress the importance of group therapy as well as some individual psychotherapy in the afternoons of treatment days. It appears that insulin not only increases the rate of remissions, but also the quality of remissions appears to be better after insulin than it does after ECT.

If schizophrenic patients are cooperative enough to continue on medication after their discharge from the hospital, the drugs might be helpful in maintaining only partially improved patients on psychotherapy. This is also true for the group of pseudoneurotic schizophrenics, where neuroleptic drugs may reduce a pain-anxiety and other symptoms, although as a whole, results in this group as well as in severe neurotics turned out to be quite disappointing.

As to depressions, the so-called endogenous or psychotic depressions will be primarily subjected to somatic treatments. Of the two groups of drugs, the MAO-inhibitors are losing ground and are largely replaced by such drugs as Tofranil and Elavil. The danger of suicide in endogenous depressions is the main reason why ECT is again more and more the first choice of treatment in this group of depressions. Neurotic or reactive depressions which respond less well to ECT are more often subjected to pharmacotherapy. Here the MAO-inhibitors had their best results. This was especially the case with Marsalid which was very effective in those depressions mixed with neurotic and often also with schizophrenic features little responsive to ECT. Unfortunately, Marsalid as well as Catron and Monase had to be given up because of their toxic complications. The still available MAO-inhibitors as well as Tofranil and Elavil have definite indications in these patients whose main treatment usually consists of psychotherapy. Even though they might not clear up the psychiatric symptoms, they make a depressed patient more amenable to psychotherapy. This is one of the best indications for a combination of pharmacotherapy and psychotherapy.

In patients who have frequent episodes of depression, drugs can be used as a preventive measure together with psychotherapy, although it must be admitted that psychotherapy as a preventive for future depressive episodes in manic-depressive patients is not very effective.

The combination of psychotherapy with drug treatment or occasional ECT, while of limited value in depressions, is of greater importance in those schizophrenics who can be treated in out-patient set-ups or in the psychiatrist's office. As Hoch pointed out, many of these schizophrenics are over-anxious, over-whelmed by their conflicts and often unable to establish contact with the psychotherapist. It is in these patients that drugs have a very definite indication. Reduction of anxiety improves the transference situation, and often makes psychotherapy effective for the first time in patients treated without any progress for long periods of time. If depressive elements or severe guilt feelings make the patient inaccessible, one or a few ECT will help to remove the depressive overlay and make the patient more accessible to psychotherapy. It is obvious that in such cases organic reactions with memory impairment and confusion should be avoided, and usually they can be avoided by limiting the number of ECT's to two or three or one occasional maintenance treatment, and, where more treatments are necessary, by spacing them further apart. Also panic states can be removed by drugs, and in those frequent cases, where they become too severe to be handled by psychotherapy, again one or two ECT's are often helpful. It is obvious that in a schizophrenic patient whose delusions and hallucinations interfere with psychotherapy, again the drugs or shock treatment of a purely symptomatic nature are in order.

The question has been brought up whether the same physician should use somatic and psychological treatments. While from a practical standpoint a psychotherapist might not be equipped to use these treatments, there is no objection in principle to such a combination. It is the psychotherapist who is in the best position to decide when drugs are indicated, in what dosage they should be given without interference with the patient's functioning and accessibility, and to modify the dosage according to his observations of the patient. There is no doubt in my mind that the ability of many patients to benefit from psychotherapy is enhanced, when drugs are simultaneously and judiciously used.

The same is undoubtedly true in the larger and more important field of psychotherapy in neurotic patients. It is here that more objections have been raised by psychotherapists regarding the simultaneous use of drugs. These are objections for reasons of principle which will depend largely on the belief of the psychiatrist or his school.

It is particularly in the neuroses that psychotherapy remains the treatment of choice. Nevertheless, it can be well supported by drugs, but rarely by shock treatments. We must strongly object to the view that patients under psychotherapy should not be subjected to any somatic therapy at all, not even to pharmacotherapy. We are supported in this view by the psychoanalytical writings of Mortimer Ostow (1962) who says that some psychoanalysts fear that drug administration may interfere with the transference relation. He denies this and concludes that "the patient's motivation to work in the analysis and to struggle against his resistance, derives not only from his wish to overcome his discomfort but also in a large measure from the positive features of the transference relation. This often will seek powerful reinforcement, and the physician effects almost magical relief from the horrors of the psychosis with drugs." This, in the opinion of many, is equally true for the neurotic patient in psychoanalysis.

A more practical viewpoint limiting the use of drugs in the neuroses is the fact that it has been recognized quite early that the drugs have proven to be less useful in psychoneurotics than had been anticipated. Anxiety being the most frequent symptom in neurotics, it was disappointing, therefore, to find that the drugs, though undoubtedly reducing anxiety, turned out to be of rather limited help in the treatment of neurotic patients. I am referring here primarily to drugs like the phenothiazines and Rauwolfia drugs. They do indeed reduce anxiety and tension, but they also have many side-effects which are probably the reason why particularly neurotic patients object to their use and in many instances feel more uncomfortable with the drugs than without them. The physical complaints of drowsiness or outright dizziness, head pressure, dryness of the mouth and similar symptoms are a great inconvenience in the handling of these patients. A frequent feeling of depersonalization which patients under phenothiazine describe is a further handicap and can easily lead to panic-like states and aggravation of the whole picture. It is this observation that, while state hospital psychiatrists were enthusiastic after the introduction of the drugs, the practicing psychiatrists were highly skeptical and unable to share the enthusiasm of the state hospital people. The different type of case material accounts for these differences of opinion.

In the neurotic patient another group of drugs is far more effective, namely those like the meprobamate Miltown and Equanil, and more recent, Librium, all of which are entirely ineffective in the psychotic patient. The new era of psychopharmacology is actually characterized by those drugs which for the first time were able to remove such psychotic symptoms as delusions and hallucinations, namely the phenothiazines and Rauwolfia drugs. The group represented first by the meprobamates and often called "minor tranquilizers" should not be confused with the antipsychotic phenothiazines mentioned before. Miltown and Equanil are much more like the barbiturates. They have in common with the barbiturates, the feature of habituation contrary to the neuroleptic drugs, and their withdrawal can be accompanied by withdrawal symptoms identical with those of barbiturates. These symptoms might consist of both convulsions and delirium-like psychosis which occur two or three days after withdrawal in patients who have been using Miltown or Equanil over an extended period of time, and who are then withdrawn suddenly.

Psychiatrists should also be reminded of the fact that the old barbiturates still have not been replaced. The great propaganda for the meprobamates and Librium tend to make one overlook that they have no different indications than the older barbiturates. In severely disturbed patients, barbiturates are still preferable and also less dangerous than the neuroleptic drugs with their hypotensive effect. The barbiturates are also useful in less disturbed psychotics and in neurotics, and, in patients who need sedatives frequently, barbiturates are often preferable to Miltown; the reason being that Miltown gives the patient less of a hangover and, therefore, he will be more apt to take it more easily, and thus will become more easily addicted to it. It seems that Librium, which is also quite useful, is less apt to lead to addiction. However, it has been in use for a shorter period of time, and maybe its disadvantages are less well known at the present time. If Librium is given in larger amounts, ataxia is an unpleasant complication, and many of the claims made for it as, for instance, its specific usefulness in alcoholism, are quite unfounded. However, it appears that these mild tranquilizers are quite effective in selected cases and may enhance the effect of psychotherapy. Judicious use of drugs might help in many instances to shorten psychotherapy if the right type of drug is given to the right type of patient.

A few remarks should be made regarding the objections by some psychotherapists on the grounds that the fast removal of symptoms reduces the patient's motivation to continue with psychotherapy. To those of us who still feel that we are primarily physicians with the task of helping our patients, such considerations appear far fetched. I remember patients with recurrent depressions who were definitely suicidal, and for whom more psychodynamically oriented psychiatrists objected to the use of ECT on the grounds that if the patient's suffering were removed by it, he would lose the motivation for psychotherapy which was considered necessary to prevent the next depressive episode. Aside from the danger of suicide which should very definitely eliminate any such considerations, I have accumulated a wealth of experience in recurrent depressions over the last twenty-five years, which convinced me deeply that in the endogenous type of recurrent depression, psychotherapy in the intervals does not prevent the next depressive episode if it is bound to come. I believe that we psychiatrists invite criticism if we go so far as as to deny our patients the comfort of feeling well because it reduces their motivation to use our services. In the larger group of neurotic patients under psychotherapy it should improve the transference situation, when the patient with the help of a drug suffers less and, therefore, is better able to discuss his problems with the therapist. In my experience there are hardly any neurotic patients in whom drugs alone enable them to function. In these patients psychotherapy is necessary to work out their problems and enable them to maintain the effect of the psychotherapeutic work.

Yet, the drugs undoubtedly are serving an extremely useful purpose if, by making psychotherapy more successful they also help to shorten the total time of treatment needed.

The new era of psychopharmacology gave many psychiatrists the feeling that they could do away with all other treatments. It has been recognized by now that this is not so, and even the most maligned therapeutic approach in psychiatry, namely psychosurgery, still has its indications. It is true that the neuroleptic drugs have replaced lobotomies and other forms of psychosurgery in chronic disturbed schizophrenics, particularly in those, where the personality changes after the operation add to the schizophrenic deterioration. On the other hand, modified lobotomies, with smaller cuts as they are done today, still have very definite indications in obsessive-compulsive neuroses who failed under psychotherapy of many years' duration. The operation can be equally beneficial in pseudo-neurotic schizophrenics of long standing, some paranoid schizophrenics without deterioration and some chronic depressions unresponsive to ECT and antidepressant drugs. It is particularly in severe neurotics that psychosurgery makes patients for the first time accessible to psychotherapy. Here I refer primarily to several papers by Cattell who discussed the psychotherapeutic approach possible in patients who had such operations. He as well as Hoch mention the interesting fact that this group showed for the first time that by reducing tension and fears by means of surgery, we can achieve great improvement with psychotherapy in these patients, although we do not eliminate their conflicts. The patient only learns to live with his problems.

Pharmacotherapy also helps in many instances to reduce the impact of the patient's symptoms even if the patient is not able to work out his problems. A few remarks may be made to help in the selection of neuroleptic drugs for a given patient. In office patients under long-term psychotherapy, Thorazine, most effective in severe psychotics, often interferes with the patient's drive and initiative. Stelazine is quite useful because, contrary to other phenothiazines, it has a stimulating effect. Another useful drug in ambulatory patients, especially those with paranoid symptoms or some degree of agitation, is Mellaril. On the other hand, there is a tendency to keep patients, particularly those discharged from a hospital, under phenothiazines even when the indication for such medication has ceased to exist. In consultation work we often see patients in whom lack of drive is the most disturbing symptom. This can sometimes be eliminated by simply discontinuing the drug. Such indiscriminate use of pharmacotherapy, however, should not be used to question its great value.

The main conclusion I should like to draw from this survey is the need for equal acceptance of all treatment procedures in psychiatry. It appears to me that the greatest shortcoming in our therapeutic endeavors is that various groups of psychiatrists are partial to one particular method of treatment. This is true not only for those who limit themselves to psychotherapy, but also to some who use one singular somatic treatment in preference to others. I hope to have shown that judicious selection of a treatment method and its combination with others is the best way to benefit a vast number of psychiatric patients, and I have tried to delineate the many different ways by which psychotherapy and somatic treatments can be and should be combined.

QUESTIONS AND ANSWERS

Question: You mentioned that the phenothiazines are not indicated in the neuroses, yet the manufacturer advertises Stelazine as helpful in severe anxiety and neurotic anxiety. Is this true?

Dr. Kalinowsky: The advertising on Stelazine contends that it is a good drug for neurotics. This is right if you are talking only about phenothiazines. It is better than some other phenothiazines because Stelazine has a stimulating effect and that helps the patient feel better. There is no doubt that Thorazine is by far the best phenothiazine we have and we come back to it more and more. Yet it makes the patient groggy, and, in office practice, in ambulatory patients, where the patient is working, the grogginess is a very disturbing factor.

Question: What is the best drug in catatonia?

Dr. Kalinowsky: Stelazine is the only drug which has any value because it has a stimulating effect.

Question: Why are there so many varieties of phenothiazines sold?

Dr. Kalinowsky: I believe the fact that there are so many phenothiazines is only because each company likes to get into the act. There is no question that there are drugs that have certain advantages, but many of the names we see are there because we have many drug companies. In most other countries, so many drugs are not available. This is particularly true in Russia where they do have an interest in pharmacotherapy even more than we have here because they do not employ psychotherapy as much as we do. But it is wrong to say that they do not use psychotherapy at all because they certainly do. But they do have theoretical objections against dynamic psychotherapy. They utilize primarily insulin treatment and drug therapy. In spite of the emphasis on drug therapy, there was only one single phenothiazine in use, chlorpromazine, when I visited there a few years ago.

Question: Is Stelazine better for neurotic anxiety than meprobamate (Miltown)?

Dr. Kalinowsky: The question of whether Stelazine is better than Miltown is difficult to answer. I mean, there are different indications for the two. Stelazine is more useful in psychotic patients, while in neurotic persons I believe Miltown is better. The disadvantage of Miltown is that it leads to addiction in neurotic patients if you have to prescribe it for a long period of time. Once you give a neurotic patient a drug, you know how difficult it is to get him to give it up. There is no habituation in the sense of having to increase the dosage in phenothiazines, like Stelazine, as there is in Miltown. You do not get addicted to the phenothiazines and you do not get withdrawal symptoms from their discontinuance. You can withdraw an enormous amount of phenothiazines from one day to the next and you don't have much trouble. If you do the same thing with a barbiturate or with Miltown, you may get convulsions or delirium. You might get certain physical symptoms which are not of psychiatric interest, in withdrawing a patient suddenly from massive doses of phenothiazines taken over a long period of time. The patient may get nausea and begin to vomit because of the antiemetic effect which the phenothiazines exert. So it should be withdrawn gradually.

Question: Which phenothiazines are most useful in office practice?

Dr. Kalinowsky: I would say two are most useful. First, Stelazine which will make a patient less groggy and even have a stimulating effect. The second drug which is extremely useful in office practice, in my opinion, is Mellaril. This is an extremely important drug because it is primarily directed against hallucinations and delusions. I have quite a number of patients whom I have treated with shock in the past with some success to the point where they are able to lead perfectly normal lives. If they hallucinate again, I now give these patients Mellaril and I can keep them going for a long period of time. There are few or no side effects. Mellaril does not usually make the patient groggy. It removes the voices and delusions and I find it an extremely useful drug in office patients. Paranoid schizophrenics who are not sick enough to be hospitalized and who suffer from chronic paranoid syndromes are very well maintained on Mellaril, and I never take them off of it when there are hallucinations. But if the hallucinations are not too severe or Mellaril does not work anymore, I give them a few more electric shock treatments. Then I place these patients again on Mellaril for an unlimited period of time.

Question: Are phenothiazines dangerous given over a long period?

Dr. Kalinowsky: I believe one can make the statement that these drugs are quite harmless. Even for long-term users. With the phenothiazines you may get some fairly harmless liver complications. You get a swelling of the bile ducts, which is a kind of obstructive jaundice. This obstructive jaundice occurs only at the beginning of the medication. If the patient is under Thorazine for a month or two without complications, you do not have to be afraid that you will get liver disturbances, and you can go on with the drug. The same is true for the other serious complications which you really do not see after a certain period of time, although the time limit here is a bit longer than for the liver complications. So the question as to whether one has to make liver tests in these patients all the time can be answered with "no." In the large public hospitals they keep these patients under drugs for years. The complications are allergic reactions and if they come at all they come pretty much in the beginning.

Question: Should phenothiazines routinely be employed over a long-term period with schizophrenics?

Dr. Kalinowsky: There are certain patients in whom it is necessary to continue medication, for instance those with acute hallucinations, or patients who are constantly disturbed; but many of the patients in our State Hospitals who are under drug therapy on a continuing basis are under the drugs because the Hospital feels that this way something is being done for the patient. There is really little sense to this indiscriminate use of drugs. Once I got into some trouble with one of the protagonists of drug therapy when I made a remark that I sometimes get excellent results in my consultation work by simply withdrawing drugs. In general, however, aftercare with drugs is important. Unfortunately many patients who are discharged from a mental hospital on drug therapy do *not* continue to take their prescribed drugs. Most of the chronic schizophrenics do not realize that they are sick, and as long as they do not suffer acutely from their symptoms, they do not see the need for taking drugs. If you take these patients, who are constantly slightly groggy from drugs consumed year after year, off drugs they suddenly feel much better because the drugs do give them side effects. You eliminate these side effects, and if the patient's symptoms are not bothersome, they get along. Many of the patients whom the hospitals now discharge are "burned out" schizophrenics. They get Thorazine, but there was never any real indication for it. When these patients are withdrawn from Thorazine, they feel much more comfortable and they and their relatives are very grateful to you for what you have done.

Question: You mentioned that barbiturates are still valuable. Could you enlarge on this?

Dr. Kalinowsky: I should like to mention one case which will illustrate what I mean. This was a patient I had seen twelve years ago with a rather acute anxiety state. I gave the patient phenobarbital and asked him to call me in a week and tell me how he felt. The patient did call me a week later and said that he was feeling fine. The case did not impress me too much at the time. Twelve years later, which was recently, I saw the same patient again in an acute anxiety state, and this time I thought I would give him our best phenothiazine. So I prescribed Thorazine and told him to call me a week later. When he called he said that he felt terrible and he described new symptoms which I would classify as depersonalization. He really had experienced no benefit whatsoever. And then he said: "Doctor, couldn't you give me the same thing you gave me twelve years ago, when I was sick?" And so over the telephone I asked the druggist to give this man phenobarbital. When the patient called me again the next week, he remarked: "Doctor, it worked exactly the same as twelve years ago. I'm perfectly free from this thing." I replied: "Please do me a favor. Could you call me once more in a month's time, and then again in two months." He called me twice more and each time he told me that he *was* feeling very well. Now this, I think, is a valuable lesson.

Question: Can ECT be given while the patient is under drug therapy?

Dr. Kalinowsky: I'm opposed to electric shock with phenothiazines. We have some very clear cut cases where patients have died from electric shock treatment when placed under Thorazine. I know of a young man, in whom there were no contraindications against electric shock in any way, who was given electric shock treatments for a long period of time. When Thorazine was introduced, the doctor gave him one dose of fifty milligrams in the evening. The next morning the patient took another fifty milligrams of Thorazine. At twelve o'clock the doctor gave him a shock treatment and the patient died. We make it a rule that if a patient is under phenothiazine, we do not give any medication either for twenty-four hours before ECT treatment, or at least in the morning of the treatment. However, by now many psychiatrists have combined ECT with drugs without untoward results.

Question: What about Librium and electric shock therapy?

Dr. Kalinowsky: Librium is, I believe, entirely harmless as are meprobamates.

Question: What about anti-depressant drugs. Can one give ECT while the patient is under their influence?

Dr. Kalinowsky: I cannot see any need for this. It has been claimed that when you give electric shock treatment in combination with anti-depressant drugs, you can reduce the number of electric shock treatments. I listened to a paper once where somebody said that he could reduce the number of electric shock treatments in his depressed patients from ten to five, that is fifty per cent less when he combined ECT with drugs. Now I never give more than five or six electric shock treatments to a depressed patient. Giving more than this is often unnecessary.

Question: You mentioned that you believe ECT better for depression than drugs. Do you give ECT in all depressions?

Dr. Kalinowsky: If the patient has a severe depressive thought content, and still enough initiative left to do something about it and kill himself, ECT is very necessary. This especially occurs in the patient who goes into a depression and the patient who comes out of a depression. Suicides occurred in patients under drug therapy when they felt better, but had not lost their suicidal impulse. When at some moment things got too much for them, they now had the initiative to kill themselves. An earlier question alluded to the frequency with which electric shock treatments are given nowadays. For quite a number of years, since anti-depressant drugs, ECT was given much less in depressed patients, but now I believe it is given more and more. The danger of suicide, the time factor, and the financial problem where patients can stay in the hospital only for a limited period, explain why electric shock treatment in depression is again coming back into popularity. The drugs are losing out because of their side effects and their inferiority to ECT.

Question: Is barbiturate anaesthesia prior to ECT safe?

Dr. Kalinowsky: We should realize that we add to the danger of electric shock treatment with these anesthesia techniques. We all know that there are deaths from the simple induction of barbiturate anesthesia. We all know of cases where some small operation is performed under anesthesia and the patient dies. Since the electric shock has a hypotensive effect, and the barbiturates also, there is no question that there is a greater danger especially in cardiac cases. In cardiac cases I do use electric shock treatment with muscle relaxation, but I avoid the barbiturate. I give the patient a subconvulsive stimulus so that he will not experience a suffocating feeling from the muscle relaxation.

Question: Why isn't insulin therapy given more frequently if it is as good as you say it is?

Dr. Kalinowsky: Insulin treatment is still given in some cases. As you know, we have here in New York an excellent unit at the Creedmore Hospital, and there is one unit in the Boston State Hospital. There are a few other State Hospital systems that utilize insulin. Otherwise it is given very little. The reason for this is that it is expensive. With new methods of administration, insulin is less dangerous than it was. As far as results are concerned, although I am frequently identified with electric shock, I feel that insulin is still the most effective treatment for schizophrenia. I have seen cases respond to insulin where everything else had been done for them with no effect. The results obtained with insulin are surprising, when deep comas and enough comas are given. Both here at Creedmore and at a European center for insulin treatment in Vienna, they came to the conclusion that you need actually more comas than were given in the past. You need eighty, a hundred and sometimes more hypoglycemic comas in order to get results. Now in practice, of course, only a small number of patients can be admitted to this type of treatment. Therefore, for practical reasons, insulin is neglected, but this does not say anything about its actual value. Not only the number of remissions, but what is also of greatest importance, the quality of remissions of schizophrenic patients is best with insulin treatment. But this is all theoretical because it will be very difficult to revive insulin in view of the great practical difficulties that it embraces, and this is regrettable. Now the target symptoms of schizophrenia can be influenced well by drug therapy. It is easy for the State Hospitals to quiet the patient down and even to get the patient out of the hospital. But most of the patients come back. As is generally known, the increasing admission and particularly the readmission rate of all of our mental hospitals rather upsets all the predictions which were made a few years ago. The unfortunate thing is that the acute schizophrenic does not get the chance to be treated with all available methods, because he soon with drugs becomes symptom free, more or less. And so everybody is happy and the hospital discharges the patient. The patient then relapses or discontinues the medicine and comes back to the hospital. What is overlooked is that the older treatments like electric shock and insulin treatment in schizophrenia are effective only when they are applied during the first six months or at maximum the first year of the illness. An extremely important point brought out at the Paris clinic, and which I incorporated in my work with patients when the drugs came over here, was that after two or three months of satisfactory medication with the drugs in acute schizophrenics, the medications were discontinued. If then the patient remains symptom free, fine. If the patient does not remain well, he should be given electric shock or insulin treatment, at a time when it can still be effective, rather than continuing to drug the patient beyond the point where he can respond to the other treatments.

Question: Do you use drugs in combination?

Dr. Kalinowsky: The effect of combinations of drugs is something that is very difficult to judge. I do not combine too much, perhaps because of scientific curiosity. If four or five drugs are given at a time, I do not know how one can find out what really works. There are very few indications for a combination of drugs. If Tofranil does not work and you want to give another drug of the MAO group, then you have to wait several days before giving the new drug. But one sometimes can combine tranquilizers and energizers if patients are depressed and tense at the same time. If you have two different target symptoms for which you have to give two different types of drugs, it is justified to combine them.

Question: If during psychotherapy you need to introduce a drug, how do you explain this to the patient?

Dr. Kalinowsky: I just tell them that a certain drug will make them less depressed and so on.

Question: Do you find Tofranil helpful in depression?

Dr. Kalinowsky: Yes, but the dosage of Tofranil I think is important. Many patients who come to me for consultation, for electric shock treatment after Tofranil was given up, were on three tablets a day. That is ineffective. You must give a patient at least 150 to 250 milligrams daily. I start the first day on two or three tablets in order to avoid sensitivity reactions in some patients. If the patient isn't so depressed that you must be afraid that something will happen to him, you can do this. The greatest shortcoming of these drugs—all the anti-depressant drugs—is that they work very slowly.

Question: What would you recommend as to the number and frequency of electric shock treatments?

Dr. Kalinowsky: I give my patients three electric shock treatments in the first week, because I know that practically every depressed patient in whom I find an indication for electric shock treatment is out of the actual depression and thereby out of suicidal danger after three treatments. Thereafter, I avoid making the patient more confused than necessary because you certainly do not need the organic reaction or confusion to complicate matters. I wait usually five days between the third and the fourth treatment, and a week between the fourth and fifth treatment. If the patient does not relapse during that week, I discontinue treatments, or I give a sixth treatment. As far as "regressive treatment" in schizophrenics is concerned, which means several electric shock treatments daily, I can answer that question briefly. Several psychiatrists claim that they get better results with intensive treatment. I found that this is not superior to the ordinary run of treatment. The only effect of this is that when you give a schizophrenic patient three or four treatments closely together, he is usually symptom free, and you are inclined to discontinue treatment at that point. The patients invariably relapse. If you give the patient regressive treatment, you must decide ahead of time up to what point you want to bring the patient. Since you give him three or four treatments a day, in a week or a little longer he has had twenty or thirty treatments. If you compare two groups, as I have done at one State Hospital, one group of schizophrenics treated with twenty electric shock treatments given as regressive treatment to the point where the patient gets incontinent within a period of a week or so, or a second group where you give these twenty treatments over a long period of time, you see that the results are not really different.

Question: What about electro-stimulation as an aid to psychotherapy?

Dr. Kalinowsky: I was never able to see any particular value for nonconvulsive electro-stimulation. I can look back to the time when we did not have any somatic treatments. At that time some electric stimulation was customary particularly in Germany. Nerve specialists in private practice would give their patients some kind of stimulation. It did not matter where they applied it, it had some psychotherapeutic effect. There is no doubt about it. But this is not different from anything impressive that you do with the patient. When you combine electro-stimulation—as you have to do to avoid the painful electric stimulus—with barbiturates, then you get a narcocathartic treatment rather than electro-stimulation.

Question: How do you feel about carbon dioxide treatment?

Dr. Kalinowsky: Carbon dioxide treatment is, I believe, recognized as a failure. I had treated two groups of cases with it, one of private patients, and another group at the Psychiatric Institute. I could not see any results with this treatment in either group. I suppose it is equal to some other inhalents. You can use ether, which has been used by Sargant of England, and you can use nitrogen and several other gases. You get the patient elated somewhat, but there is nothing specific about the treatments, and they are slightly dangrous. I think everybody has given them up as far as I know.

Question: Can you use electroconvulsive therapy in pregnant women? How about insulin and drugs in pregnancy?

Dr. Kalinowsky: I can answer this question very authoritatively because we have all the possible tests on this. As far as electric shock treatment is concerned, we definitely know that there is no effect either on the pregnant woman or on the fetus. This never surprised us because when you remember the fact that epileptic women never have any trouble in their pregnancies, even when they have their epileptic attacks, we couldn't expect anything other from electric shock treatment which is actually not more than the induction of an epileptic convulsion. That it does not even precipitate labor in any way was demonstrated to me by a patient admitted to a hospital because labor had started. Then labor stopped again, and it turned out that the patient was pschotic. They could not keep her so they sent her to us at the Psychiatric Institute and I gave her two or three electric shock treatments. She became quiet and was returned to the maternity hospital. A few days later labor started again and she bore a normal child. There are many followups in patients treated with electric shock treatments in all types of pregnancy and no trouble of any kind is recorded. Incidentally, there is some evidence that insulin given at the beginning of pregnancy might have an effect on the fetus. The evidence is not very convincing, but it should be mentioned. There is no evidence of any untoward effects of drug therapy, at least not with those drugs which we use in psychiatry. I do not talk about those cases which we all know about, treated in Germany, with Thalidamide. But the usual tranquilizers we use produce no damage to the child as far as I know. If a rare case of malformation has occurred, we should remember that malformations in children occurred before in many cases who had never taken any particular drug. There is no evidence that the drugs we use in psychiatry really have any bad effect on the child and certainly not the mother.

Question: What is your opinion of LSD?

Dr. Kalinowsky: I do consider all these experimental drugs somewhat dangerous, because we do not know what we are producing. I cannot convince myself that these drugs are of any particular value in psychotherapy. I would not expect much from them because I think we all had the experience when narco-cathartic methods were used in the last World War of getting very good results in acute neurotic symptoms, but not getting such good results in the chronic peace time neuroses. I do not know why we would expect more from psychomimetic drugs which produce symptoms which are often frightening. We do not know what is going on in the patient. I wouldn't know exactly how to conduct treatment like this with an ambulatory patient, because I do not know when the psychotic symptomatology would really clear up, or if it did clear up and you sent the patient home whether the symptoms might not come back after the patient got home. This can lead to trouble. I feel very strongly that what you cannot get in psychotherapy with the direct approach to a patient who is more or less accessible to psychotherapy, you would not get with drugs like lysergic acid except perhaps in certain acute situations.

VIII

Short-Term Group Psychotherapy

============ ALEXANDER WOLF, M.D.

(Editor's Note: Reviewing the abundant literature on short-term group therapy, which he prefers to call "accelerated group therapy," Dr. Wolf stresses the social contribution of this therapeutic resource and the avenues of possible approach in shortening what traditionally has been regarded as a long-term method. Dr. Wolf believes it is necessary to explore these avenues if therapists are to meet the ever-growing demand for therapy and the equally increasing number of health and insurance plans which provide for a specific number of paid treatments. In the type of group therapy that includes the alternate meeting, this limited number of sessions may extend as long as two years. Among the technics discussed are those of simplified diagnosis, classification of patients, limitations of goals and an ego-building technic which may be used in one form or another in all types of treatment. The chapter concludes that if this urgent challenge is met successfully, there will be not less, but more demand for deeper treatment in the future.)

IN 1944, THE ARMY issued a training bulletin which contained the following terse statement: "The favorable response of patients to comparatively brief treatment in groups warrants widespread adoption of this method of therapy. When patients are treated properly, a majority can be salvaged." (Training Bull., 1944)

To some psychotherapists familiar with the group analysis of Trigant Burrow in the 1920's and the attempts of Louis Wender and Paul Schilder in the 'thirties to introduce psychoanalytic methods in groups, this army bulletin was a clarion call, not only for short-term group psychotherapy, but also for group psychotherapy in deeper reconstructive work with patients.

Between 1947 and 1962, over a hundred papers on short-term group psychotherapy were published. At the same time the ranks of long-term group therapists swelled year by year. The majority of psychiatrists and psychoanalysts, however, remained aloof, claiming that only lesser forms of therapy could be accomplished in groups. They chose to disregard, as many still do, the fact that too many people needed treatment when there were too few analysts to render that treatment; and that it is part of the responsibility of the therapist to find new methods as new social needs arise.

Psychotherapy and psychoanalysis are, like education, no longer a special privilege for the elite. They have been and should be made increasingly available to as many people who need and want them. There are many who cannot afford and indeed do not actually need long-term group therapy; there are many who, for one reason or another, cannot proceed with an individual analysis; for these patients, I believe, we should turn our attention to the practical and technical possibilities of short-term group therapy.

The recently published research project report by Group Health Insurance, Inc. on the feasibility of psychiatric insurance to finance short-term ambulatory treatment (Avnet, 1962), makes the social demand clear, as well as the necessity to try to answer it in some way.

"The project," says the report, "resulted from this combination of circumstances:

Increased attention to mental illness as a serious social and economic problem of national proportions;

Promising developments in the treatment of mental illness—greater emphasis on early ambulatory treatment at the local community level, new hopes for the potentialities of short-term therapy;

Unavailability of the benefits of modern psychiatry to many of the mentally ill;

Phenomenal growth of the voluntary insurance movement;

Increasing resentment toward medical insurance discrimination against mental illness;

Uncertainties as to the definition of mental illness, the probable demand for insured treatment, the sufficiency of psychiatric and insurance resources to cope with these unknowns;

The desire of GHI (Group Health Insurance, Inc.), the American Psychiatric Association, and the National Association for Mental Health to lessen some of these uncertainties."

Insurance companies have well-developed techniques for gauging the direction of social and economic trends. But any thoughtful person, observing the world around him, could have come to the same conclusion. It is no secret that there are hundreds of doctors, psychologists and self-appointed advisors to the troubled, dispensing panaceas through the columns of newspapers and magazines. Advertising today is providing more medical advice than overworked doctors can possibly take care of. Headaches, colds, coughs, constipation, diarrhea, hemorrhoids, hernias, that tired, listless feeling, anxiety, depression, impotence—you name it and you'll find a TV commercial or TV show with an instant and ready answer. If your trouble seems to be general, there is Dr. Kildare, while Dr. Casey is available for neurosurgical disorders. And if you want a quick solution to emotional conflicts, you will find Drs. Bassett or Graham standing by at the Eleventh Hour. And whatever the specific problem, each of these fictional gentlemen can and do straighten out some major life conflict in the space of an hour.

In real-life, professional therapists cannot claim such spectacular results. But we should take seriously, the implication of the popularity of the mass media and its approaches to medical and emotional problems: a headache, constipation, or what have you, must all be relieved one way or another; people want this relief, and they will latch on to anything which gives it to them even if it is not of the best or does not last more than a while. It seems to them far better to plug the hole in a leaky boat than to have the boat sink.

It would be most unrealistic for group therapists to emulate the tolerant condescension toward short-term group therapy displayed by some individual analysts toward group therapy in general. Condescension on their part did not stop the progress of therapy in groups, analytic or otherwise. The social need did not disappear because certain practitioners decided it was not for them. What happened instead was that other therapists stepped into the breach. Group workers, social workers, psychologists and more flexible psychiatrists began, in the late 'thirties and early 'forties, to experiment with group methods, with the specific intent of meeting the social demand as well as expanding their own knowledge. With the passing years, these more adventurous therapists gradually developed analytic and other therapeutic skills to a point where, today, increasing numbers of younger therapists are exploring the possibilities of group therapy in their early training.

There is no doubt that if the analyst continues to evade the larger social responsibility and to confine himself to the treatment of fifty to a hundred patients in a lifetime, he will leave the way open to the growing number of inexperienced therapists—even to charlatans. Abdication will not erase the problem or the demand. It will only permit the untrained to take over the job of therapy.

The same thing holds true for the group therapist. He also cannot maintain the position that his method of treatment is the only one he will practice, no matter how long it takes. Nor can he afford the danger of becoming a member of still another elite "in-group." If he does, he will also find others, well-trained or not so well-trained, stepping in to fill the treatment gap.

This brief history makes it clear that if trained analysts, who are the most able therapists, do not try to meet the current need for short-term therapy, others will. Those of us who are trained and experienced should be in the vanguard, forging new forms and new methods, not trying, in Emerson's words, "to open the portals to the future with the blood-rusted keys of the past."

In the GHI report I mentioned earlier, it was considered significant that of the 923 patients studied, 96 per cent used their benefits for individual psychotherapy, and only a total of 22 of the 923 used group therapy. Of these 22, 10 were in hospitals where the insurance benefits went for per diem care with no additional fee for the group therapy treatment. Of the remaining 12 who had group therapy in the psychiatrist's office, only 2 used all their benefits for group therapy exclusively. This figure is especially interesting since one of the two practical suggestions made for improving the GHI coverage plan, was that in the future more extensive use be made of group therapy in the treatment of subscribers.

There are no clues in the report as to why group therapy ranked so low as a treatment method of choice. But one can guess that prejudice still exists among the psychiatrists participating in the panel and in the organizations that drew up that panel. Clues do exist, however, as to certain inadequacies in short-term methods, and these clues can be profitably pursued by others who are studying the problems of short-term therapy.

For example, it was found that when a patient changed psychiatrists, for one reason or another, no two diagnoses of that patient's disturbance were ever the same. It was also noted that, although the project allotted forty-five dollars for psychological testing, the psychiatrists availed themselves of this tool in only 66 of the 923 cases, and then, mostly with patients under nineteen years of age. One might draw the conclusion that very little pre-planning of treatment was felt to be required or done, except to apprise patient and psychiatrist that treatment would be limited to fifteen office visits. It is no wonder that the report should find that though there is "increasing emphasis on the benefits of early care and ambulatory treatment in the community involving all types of mental illness, including the neuroses and the personality and behavioral disorders—yet in these areas the greatest vagueness was found. In addition to the absence of guidelines demarcating the zones between mental illness and mental health, there was no standardized treatment technique and no criteria of successful treatment."

The report then adds rather plaintively, "In these respects, at least, it was impossible to apply the aphorism that 'mental illness is an illness just like any other illness.' Medical insurers were accustomed to dealing with facts, with 'norms,' with generally accepted standards in the community. For ambulatory psychiatry there were none."

This conclusion is certainly no news to psychotherapists. We all know we are split into many schools espousing varying theories. We know we have no standardized "norms" for sickness or treatment or cure. We have no centralized base for pooled experimentation or follow up studies. And though we may never achieve the specificity of the exact sciences, nor do we necessarily want to, short-term therapy may be just the challenge we need to orient ourselves toward these goals.

My first suggestion toward that end would be that group therapists, at least, reexamine their position on the subject of psychological testing. Clearly there is widespread resentment against testing. Why? Is it because testing techniques have failed as aids to diagnosis or is it because they have been used for sometimes frightening reasons by large commercial and governmental organizations? Or are the testers themselves considered inadequate? If so, it would be well to remind those who are anti-testing, that the misuse of testing methods does not invalidate them. Misuse indicts the user and not the instrument he uses.

But perhaps the therapist has a deeper reason for resenting tests which he rationalizes as wishing to do his own therapy his own way. Granted that the nature of psychotherapy makes it difficult to standardize practice, it would still seem that we could be secure enough to accept the use of testing techniques as a help to our diagnosis and planning of treatment for our patients, without regarding it as inadequate diversion or controlling invasion of our privacy. On the contrary, if we are to undertake short-term group therapy, on an organized scale, a clearing house for the testing and screening of patients is a practical necessity. In short-term group therapy proper classification of patients becomes especially important, since it will certainly be necessary to do a great deal of pre-planning in order to get results in the allotted time. Not only will we have to find methods of grouping the proper types of patients together, we will also have to find ways of getting the right patient to the therapist best suited by talent and experience, to treating the particular problems involved.

Some of us have always subscribed to the formation of heterogeneous groups in the practice of analytic therapy in groups. Now, since this wider demand for treatment needs to be met, it may be necessary to reexamine this position. It may well be that in short-term group therapy, patients should be homogeneously grouped. In that case we shall have to consider which kinds of homogeneity we can work with best and find ways to get *to* that type of patient and him to us. In all likelihood each therapist will be called on to treat several different kinds of homogeneous or heterogeneous groups at the same time as he is conducting deep, long-term analytic therapy with other groups and individual patients.

This will make the technique of referrals much more complicated, but a necessary complication. It is just as impractical to assume that every therapist can treat every type of homogeneous group with equally good results in an equally prescribed time, as it would be to introduce every short-term patient to a heterogeneous group which has been previously formed with long-term analytic therapy in mind.

The selection of patients for short term group therapy becomes, therefore, a sharply pointed question that had better not be left to chance, theoretical bias or even to the "school" to whose theories we happen to subscribe. Some of us may use projective testing to help us in our evaluations, others may continue to prefer one or more clinical interviews, and still others might desire an evaluating group where the patient could be studied for several sessions. But whatever the choice, it eventually must come through some gathering field larger than our personal selves and our personal circle. In trying to solve this problem, we may eventually be forced to that centralization of therapist activity many of us have long been advocating but which is, so far, still only on the dim horizon.

Such a clearing house would help patient, community and therapist alike. There testing could be done to clarify levels of homogeneity: according to symptoms, perhaps; diagnosis; psychosomatic disturbances; psychodynamics; psychopathology; sex; education; social status; background; character structure; etc. There we could discover whether the patient would best be helped by individual therapy, group therapy or combined therapy. Would he do better in a homogeneous or a heterogeneous group? Should that group be analytically oriented, affect-stimulating, repressive-inspirational or supportive? Does this particular patient need guidance, counseling, reality orientation or ego-building? Once we have decided on his most immediate or urgent need, he might be placed in a group that meets his requirments for ten, twenty, or thirty sessions. If he is able to go on after this on his own, he may be discharged. If it seems as if he then needs to develop more long-term objectives, he might be transferred to another group where such aims are the goal.

Having even partial answers to these questions can be of enormous help to the therapist. It can help him not only in treatment but also in finding more easily those patients who are best suited to his particular skills. A clearing house would also be a basis for experimentation, clinical research and experience, which would be of enormous help to all our work in groups. And it also could be a resource for follow-up studies, so badly needed today, so that we do not have to depend solely on one-man surveys or hit and miss guesses to gauge our results.

None of us, individual or group therapists, has had very much practical experience with brief group psychotherapy. My own clinical practice has emphasized *psychoanalysis* in groups and I have found, in most instances, treatment by this method to be as long and arduous as individual analysis.

There have been exceptions, of course. One could call my experience in a Rehabilitation Center, an Evacuation Hospital, and the Ninth Army Combat Exhaustion Center during World War II such an exception. It is true that these soldier patients were acutely disturbed in very special environmental stress situations, and an experience with them might not be considered applicable to our present dilemma. But the fact that the majority of them were under hospital treatment for from seven to ten days and were, on the whole, more responsive to sedation, reassurance, mutual support and ego building than to any other kind of intervention, might be taken into account when we begin to speculate about techniques we could try in an experimental program of short-term group therapy.

There have also been instances in my private practice when patients have responded to therapy in from three to eight months. But, I repeat, these have been rare and the exception rather than the rule.

How then, to approach the whole topic of short-term group thertherapy without seeming presumptuous or making too great excursions into fantasy? I did what most of us do in similar circumstances. In the words of a country parson, describing his method of composing sermons: "I read myself full; I thought myself clear; I swung myself humble and then I let myself go!"

In "reading myself full," I found the literature on short-term group therapy presented a large variety of approaches, original proposals and solutions, which suggests a flexibility and readiness on the part of the writers to try the new and the different. However, as in most reports on psychotherapy, almost everyone seems to get good results with any and every method.

While any ideal psychotherapeutic approach should be determined by the patient's diagnosis, his life history, psychodynamics, individual needs, potentials, strengths and weaknesses, it is doubtful that we can fulfill each differentiated need in short-term group therapy. The varieties of brief group psychotherapy summarized in the following papers are in part attempts to meet particular needs at particular times. How much the methods used reflect the training, style and experimental interests of the writers is open to question. Therapists, no matter how much they deny it, often make unconscious choices in choosing patients to treat and methods to use. As Maskin (1960) points out, "Freud used hysteria as the model for his psychotherapeutic method, depression as the basis for his later theoretical conjectures. Adler's clinical demonstrations are rivalrous, immature character types. Jung's examples were constructed to a weary, worldly, successful, middle-aged group. Rank focused upon the conflicted, frustrated, rebellious artist aspirant. Fromm's model is the man in a white collar searching for his individuality. And Sullivan's example of choice is the young catatonic schizophrenic." Perhaps the wish to apply appropriate therapeutic means to the different kinds of individual necessities in the group setting accounts for the tendency to incorporate multiple treatment approaches in any one plan for therapy, so that distinct demarcations are often unclear.

REVIEW OF LITERATURE ON SHORT-TERM GROUP THERAPY

There are also many instances in the literature where good results were noted without any treatment description at all. By far in the minority were the papers which tell of uncertain results. Nevertheless, two points stand out in covering the literature: 1) that most of the papers, even those most overly optimistic in the assumption that the good results would last, contained something worthy of being pursued; and 2) that the group therapist's theoretical understanding and practical experience in psychoanalysis leads to more judicious interventions, no matter what the form of treatment.

To summarize some of this literature on brief group psychotherapy, I will divide the papers into rough categories of the techniques or type of groups used. The largest single group of papers concerned themselves with parents and their problems with children, ranging from so-called normal children through crippled children, emotionally disturbed children, etc. To cite some examples: Barnes (1952) describes the educational and therapeutic implications in working with parent study groups around the problems of the normal, preschool child. He led such a parent study group in a non-clinical setting with twenty members for twenty sessions. The leader saw the setting as a guidance situation. The group discussed the handling of aggression, discipline, sex education, toilet training, feeding, sleep disturbances, operations and illnesses, fantasies and the role of the father. As a result of this experience, parents' irritation with their children lessened, they handled their children better than before and some members sought psychotherapy.

Crocker (1955) conducted two mothers' discussion groups which focused on child behavior and development problems and met for six sessions. Meyer and Power (1953) describe the family case worker's contribution to parent education, working with small groups, meeting eight to fifteen times for two hour sessions. Here too, the parents became more relaxed and more tolerant with their children. Einstein (1952) also promoted better understanding in six lecture-demonstrations with mothers where films were used. Shapiro (1956) reports much the same with his discussion groups.

Yates and Lederer (1961) found that small, short-term group work helped parents of mongoloid children develop an increased ability to accept and express feelings toward their children.

Boles (1959) reported on the treatment of cerebral palsied children and their parents in simultaneous group therapy. There were thirteen families in this project, the children ranging in age from five to twenty-four. Six children, aged five to twelve were placed in one group, the remaining seven in another. Both groups were treated in activity group therapy with emphasis on rhythm, communication and socialization. The older group was provided with games, dancing and discussion, the members being encouraged to move from isolated play toward group involvement. The parents at group sessions numbered from four to fifteen. At early sessions they discussed practical problems and their feelings about them. They expressed their resentment at what they felt to be the injustices done them. After eight, once-a-week, two and a half hour sessions, the insights obtained by the parents and their children had an interactive effect, so that there was less neurotic entanglement, more independence and greater freedom to seek individual life satisfaction.

Kirby and Priestman (1957) treated a group of mothers and

schizophrenic daughters for one and a half hours once-a-week for sixty-two weeks. There were six daughters aged seventeen to twenty-two in the group with their mothers. Here it was found that group therapy, through dilution, ventilation and insight, improved the relation between mothers and daughters.

Rice (1952) describes a different sort of set-up. Here there were five groups of parents who met once or twice a week with two co-leaders, for from six to twenty-six sessions. The parents were chosen with a view to homogeneity in intellectual level and social standards, and the importance of including fathers in parent group therapy was stressed. The aim of therapy, namely, improved inter-personal relations between parents and children and between the parents themselves was achieved.

Lebovici (1958) reported on the use of short-term group therapy with parents whose children are in treatment. In this form of therapy the dynamic mechanisms are understood in the sense of the transferred relation but are neither verbalized nor interpreted. Greving and Grunwald (1953) also worked with parents in a discussion group, while Millman (1952) concentrated on the rehabilitation of parents of physically disabled children using a non-directive approach.

The foregoing papers describe discussion groups whose borders are not always sharply defined. Sometimes counseling and guidance takes place, sometimes attempts at clarification. The therapist tries to remove misconceptions and misinformation, thereby helping participants organize their disordered thinking. At no time is unconscious material gone into.

As to the question of whether or not this is psychotherapy, Grunwald (1954) and Scheidlinger (1953) attempt to clarify the distinctions between the concepts of social group work and group psychotherapy. Slavson (1960) does so too, outlining the differentiated principles and practices of counseling, guidance and psychotherapy. In the main, the group counselor or leader neither interprets transference nor delves into unconscious material. He does not introduce topics. In a genrally positive atmosphere, the members achieve increased self-acceptance and a more objective understanding of their reality situations. Though "therapy" as analysts know it, is not practiced, many therapeutic results are obtained. Lerner (1955), dealing with male alcoholic inmates at a city jail in teaching-counseling groups, comes to the same conclusion, as does Kotkov (1949, 1956) with his guidance technique in the treatment of out-patient white, male veterans, twenty to forty years of age. And Lawrence and Kiell

(1961) in their treatment of college students in a guidance group, concur that favorable changes in outlook and functioning took place.

Next we come to a series of articles on non-directive group therapy with children. Fleming and Snyder (1947 and 1952) report on the social and personal changes following non-directive play therapy using the Rogerian approach. A fixed time limit of twelve weeks was arbitrarily set as the length of treatment. The group speeded up the development of rapport with the therapist and hastened the development of insight. There was marked improvement in four out of seven children so treated.

Fisher (1933) matched two groups of children suffering from reading disability. Both groups took part in a remedial program, but one of the groups was treated by non-directive therapy for one hour a week. After six months both groups were retested. It was found that the treated group had improved 39 per cent more than the control group.

Koenig (1949) worked with third to sixth grade elementary school children in a play therapy group. Their problems ranged from withdrawn to aggressive behavior and included inattention, truancy and stealing. The children were encouraged to express their inner conflicts through the use of arts, handicrafts, music and puppetry. At the end of treatment, improvement was noted in eight patients. Friedlander (1953) also reports on a variety of group therapy patterns, this time in a child guidance service, with groups of children ranging from five to ten years old.

As was remarked before, failures, partial failures and partial successes, contradictory and confusing outcomes are rarely reported, except in the case of juvenile delinquents. It is interesting that they present as serious a problem for the therapist as they do for society as a whole. For example, Gersten (1951) tells of his experience with juvenile delinquents over twenty weekly sessions in which no changes in attitude or behavior were achieved. He was, nevertheless, encouraged by changes in various test procedures. In his first experiments, Gersten conducted the first five meetings by the interview method. Handicrafts were introduced at the sixth session. Because of the increasing interaction, the remaining meetings were conducted by the activity-interview method.

A year later Gersten (1952) was more optimistic. In further group therapy with institutionalized juvenile delinquents he found greater progress in adjustment, higher levels in intellectual performance and more emotional stability as a result of treatment by activity group therapy in three groups of twenty-one boys over twenty sessions. This time he adopted an approach between authoritarianism and complete permissiveness in a non-threatening atmosphere. The introduction of craft materials after six sessions had the effect of lessening inhibition and increasing spontaneity.

The difficulty of working with juvenile delinquents is also reflected in Feder's (1962) work with two-short-term discussion groups of institutionalized adolescent boys after sixteen therapy sessions and two groups of control subjects who received no therapeutic contact. The subjects were boys fourteen to seventeen years of age. Those with poor reading ability, mental deficiency, psychosis or serious organic involvement were excluded. There were twenty boys in each group, a total of eighty subjects.

The groups, similar in age, intelligence, social class, race and ward placement, were open-ended, changing as participants left the institution; were made up of from five to seven members; met twice a week from ninety minutes sessions and were treated with an approach roughly modeled after that of Slavson.

It was found that the discussion groups promoted therapeutic readiness but did not facilitate institutional adjustment. This research suggests that aggresisve and antisocial behavior cannot be changed within two months by the techniques investigated. Shellow et al (1958) found that it took about a year to alter the delinquent's attitude toward authority figures. Still, Feder's study indicates that in less than two months, group therapy can motivate delinquent boys to recognize that therapy might be of some help to them. Franklin (1959), working with seventeen year old delinquent boys in a training school setting, reports some positive results by using a form of resistance analysis and playing a somewhat provocative role; while Berg (1960) describes an experimental camp program in which ten boys, previously in individual casework treatment, were bunked together for three weeks with their therapist acting both as group leader and caseworker.

Philip and Peixotto (1959), also treating delinquent boys, reported that forty-three, in brief group therapy, showed a significant reduction of hostility when compared with a control group. And if any positive results at all can be attributed to brief therapy with this extremely difficult age group, it speaks well for the whole subject of brief group therapy.

Next is a group of papers dealing with short-term group therapy of patients with homogeneous organic disease. Adler (1953) conducted numerous groups of tuberculous displaced persons in the course of a year, one for eight months, the others for from six to eight weeks. Treatment was found to alleviate anxiety, further better understanding of the illness, improve interpersonal relations, and lead to a more realistic outlook. The therapist was active, setting topics for discussion, and directing the expression of feelings about leaving the hospital.

Hoch and Denis (1955) were co-therapists of medical and surgical patients in a general hospital who revealed psychogenic components in their illness. Here short-term group therapy proved to be effective in helping members to recognize their emotional conflicts and to accept medical and psychiatric treatment.

Moll and Shane (1952) also were obliged, in a general hospital setting, to try to treat patients in the course of twenty hours. They used a modified, non-directive approach, in which the therapist, though essentially passive and indirect, took an active role in order to speed discussion and to help focusing. Because tension was the main block to psychological unity, certain measures were used to reduce it: 1) 3 grains of sodium amytal by mouth one and a half hours before the meeting; 2) analyzing the resistance; 3) films and tape recordings. These therapeutic methods were found to be effective.

Chafez et al. (1955) working with three groups twice a week for six weeks, found that patients with Parkinson's disease made a better adjustment to their chronic illness when the therapist was actively participating, supporting their need to belong and clarifying the medical aspects of their illness. On the other hand, Graham (1960) records that non-directive, structured group discussion with the physically disabled brought results in the limited time available. And Lubin and Slominski (1960) discovered that four months of weekly individual counseling sessions followed by three months of group counseling meetings with adult male cerebral palsied patients had the effect of lessening feelings of isolation, enabling members to express previously hidden feelings and practice social skills.

Benaim (1957) obtained similar results working with a group of eighteen male, hospitalized patients, aged sixty to seventy-five who were diagnosed as manic-depressive, cerebrally arteriosclerotic, schizophrenic and psychosomatic. Wilson (1954) tried a six months experiment with manic-depressive psychotics, who at first could only emphasize their own symptoms but were later able to talk about possible causes. As mutual understanding and closeness developed, symptoms disappeared proving, in some measure, at least,

that manic-depressive patients can relate to each other and participate constructively in a group.

Semon and Goldstein (1957) had some success with chronic
schizophrenic patients in groups, each group having fifty hours of
treatment. Two methods of treatment were used with contrasting
styles of leadership: active-participant and active-interpretive. The
groups showed improved interpersonal functioning under both
methods of treatment. But Illing and Brownfield (1960) got uncertain results after one hundred meetings with schizophrenic patients suffering from delusions, despite increased group interaction
and work adjustment. And Partridge (1960) had some success with
short-term group therapy which focused on preparing hospitalized
schizophrenics for leaving the hospital.

Keeler (1960), working with hospitalized non-psychotic adults,
found that in a period of three to four weeks, group therapy expe-
dited individual therapy and generally improved patients' interpersonal relationships. Pine et al (1958) summarized their article
on short-term group psychotherapy in the treatment of psychiatric
patients in a hospital setting as follows: "It is useful in the treatment of individual patients by increasing their motivation, reducing their dependency ties, serving as a stimulus both in emotional
expression and psychotherapy, and aiding in adjustment to hospital
living. In more general ways, it has shed many new lights on hospitalization so that the functioning of medical staff and other personnel has been given a greater impetus for more interaction with
the patient. Within the total milieu program, short-term group psychotherapy serves as a basic hospital experience which helps patients gain some understanding of their problems. . . . Due to limitation of time with consequent restriction of goals to be obtained,
the therapist serves as a catalytic agent who stimulates and extends
group discussion. In thus promoting group interaction, the therapist
is aware of the need for rechanneling transference relations but
does this with little or no directing or interperting."

Kotkov (1956), using dynamically oriented short-term group
psychotherapy with hospitalized patients, emphasizes the need to
set realistic goals in a step by step treatment program. Feder (1962)
and Hiler and Berkowitz (1960) also discuss the importance of
goals in brief group therapy.

Rudolf (1955) did a follow-up survey three years after his experience with adult, female, mental defectives selected for brief group
therapy because of their prolonged misbehavior. Out of the five
members one patient showed no improvement but the other four

made reasonably good social adjustment outside the institution. None of these patients had been in the institution for less than six years. This, I think, speaks well for the possibilities of working with mental defectives in groups, so long as the language and techniques used are kept simple.

The use of short-term group therapy with soldiers, veterans and prisoners is described in the following papers: Hulse (1948) found he could reduce considerably the number of AWOL's in less than ten days of group therapy among soldiers in a holding unit. Whereas Illing (1952), treating service patients in an army hospital for from seven to ten days, reports he used such short-term therapy only because of necessity; that it was effective within limits and of limited value. Kotkov (1955) also treated veterans in short-term group therapy, but as out-patients, and he describes quite good results after sixteen sessions.

Illing (1951), after a period of short-term group therapy with prisoners writes, "All told, the purpose of this type of psychotherapy was achieved by the very fact of its existence, and for a period of months. Expressions from the group during this period indicate that even the members became, no matter how vaguely, aware of the benefits they seemed to derive from 'blowing off steam.' "

Kleines and Kallejian (1955) experimented with preventive group therapy in an industrial setting, where the leader functioned as teacher, information-giver and discussion guide, while Lulow (1951) tried to prevent behavior disorders in a group of nursery school children by lectures and discussions with a group of their mothers and teachers. Hinckley (1953) combined college mental hygiene with group therapy, while Calvin (1962) working with college students, and Amster (1954) with university and parent groups of non-patients, also applied group psychotherapy principles with good results.

Friedman and Gerhart (1947) introduce us to their "question-box" method of group psychotherapy, in which ward patients are invited to place unsigned questions in a box, and subsequent sessions are taken up with answering the anonymous questions. After twenty-four meetings 14 per cent stated they learned nothing from the experience, and 86 per cent felt they had profited by learning certain fundamentals of mental hygiene concepts.

A second type of spectator group psychotherapy is described by Bassin and Smith (1962), in which the silent patient is allowed to participate when and how he wishes, benefiting from the secure, empathic, non-evaluative atmosphere to an extent that he can have the freedom and safety to re-examine some positive and social values his ego defenses have prevented him from perceiving and internalizing.

Brief group treatment adjunctive to intensive insulin subcoma treatment is presented as effective by Bell and Barnett (1955) in one paper, and in an article published four years later, Barnett (1959) disclosed that, after six years of experience with this method, one-fifth of the patients improved markedly, one-half improved moderately, one quarter improved minimally and one patient in twenty showed no improvement.

Bindelglas and Gosline (1957) found that chlorpromazine and reserpine facilitated relatedness, lessened isolation, decreased hostility and improved social awareness in the course of group psychotherapy with psychotic female patients. And Faure (1960) reports that the results of group therapy, adjunctive to prolonged sleep induced by chlorpromazine and barbiturates, varied from good to excellent: the anxiety neurotics and acute psychotics making the best responses; chronic schizophrenics being able to achieve brief contact without lasting effect. Winkleman (1959) also found trifluoperazine effective as an aid to short-term group therapy.

Kosofsky (1957) did not have complete success with a short-term group of obese patients while Kotkov (1951) felt he did. Zucker (1961) treated three groups of drug addicts and at the end a number showed behavioral improvement. Hinckley and Hermann (1951) conducted group therapy for as little as ten hours as a preliminary to private treatment, excluding patients with weak egos and balancing the groups between the inhibited and the active, the passive dependent and aggressive, with the goals of treatment reasonable asymptomology and external adjustment. Little material was found in the literature to suggest the value of terminal group treatment following individual treatment.

Two dozen papers illustrate various kinds of homogeneous groups, though therapeutic approaches differed considerably. All reported need for support and considerable improvement on getting that support from the group and the group leader. Boas (1950) treated anorgastic women; Guy et al (1954), adults suffering from atopic eczema; Kotkov (1953) had a group of wayward adolescent girls; Yonge and O'Connor (1954), a homogeneous group of mentally defective delinquent youngsters. Tucker (1956), experimented with chronic, psychotic, soiling patients; Kraus (1959) with chronic psychotics matched by age, sex, diagnosis, education and previous treatment, with a control group. Linden (Linden, 1953, 1954, 1955,

1956, 1959) made extensive studies in short-term group therapy of aged patients, with gratifying results. After an average of fifty-four hours, twenty-three of fifty-one patients were ready to leave the hospital. In a control study of patients who received no group therapy, only thirty-seven out of two hundred and seventy-nine patients were ready to leave.

Directive therapy was practiced by Backus and Dunn (1947) with patients having speech disorders, by Orange (1955) with psychotics, and by Brunner-Orne and Orne (1954) with alcoholics. Miller et al (1960), however, resorted to reflex conditioning in their treatment of alcoholics. Singer (1952) claimed good results with posthypnotic suggestion in conjunction with group treatment and psychodrama, and Peberdy (1960) also reported good responses to hypnotherapy in about twenty sessions.

The didactic or tutorial method in group therapy is primarily re-educational. But the technique occasionally incorporates other forms of group therapy. Klapman (1959, 1954, 1951), the leading protagonist of didactic group therapy with psychotics, provides patients with a constant source of discussion and study, and after three months of treatment could claim a uniform improvement. But Carmichael (1953) using Klapman's method in groups of fifteen to twenty-five patients, felt that the approach was rather superficial. For large groups of fifty or more, he used repressive-inspirational group therapy. Parrish (1961) used discussion techniques and psychodrama in working with teen-age, emotionally disturbed girls.

Those who have organized heterogeneous groups in short-term therapy are in a definite minority. Only between 5 and 6 per cent of the papers on short-term group therapy reported the use of a heterogeneous membership. Laffal and Sarason (1957) tell how the diversity of patients and the transiency of group membership on a locked service necessitated a limited goal approach and the dealing with varying levels of pathology at the same time. Treatment was aimed at advancing each member one step forward in the direction of adequate adjustment.

Karson and Wiedershine (1961) attempted an objective evaluation of dynamically oriented group psychotherapy. Unfortunately they do not state explicitly diagnostic categories nor details of treatment method. They do say, however, that twenty-five sessions produced no personality changes, while fifty sessions did, though most patients with somatic complaints usually expressed relief from symptoms between the sixteenth and eighteenth meetings.

Group therapy in the course of, or as a byproduct of training, is described in four papers. In the first, Braunthal (1952) reports how a casework training course became a group therapeutic experience. Ganzarain et al (1958, 1959) claimed group therapy took place in the course of psychiatric training of medical students. In both of these papers the students showed considerable gains over a control group in scholarship and personality development. Markowitz (1962) and Markowitz and Liff (1962 a, b) also report success in an experiment in the use of frustration as an instrument in group therapy with trainees in a therapy training center.

The writer has had experience over the past fifteen years with psychiatrists in a psychoanalytic training institute. In the third year of their didactic courses, the candidates participate in an elective experience of psychoanalytically oriented group psychotherapy, lasting twenty to forty sessions, each meeting lasting one and a half hours with the therapist; there are also alternate meetings from which the therapist absents himself. These students are all in individual analysis or have completed their personal analysis with various members of the faculty. Analysts and analysands generally report that the group therapeutic experience expedites or facilitates the individual analysis, which is regarded as the central treatment process.

Analytic group psychotherapy, generally used more in private practice than elsewhere, is characterized by the introduction of psychoanalytic techniques in the group setting (Wolf and Schwartz, 1962). Treatment involves free association, the analysis of fantasies, dreams, resistance, transference and working through. The patient's life history, his present interactions in and out of the group and his plans for the future are explored. The introduction of a short-term patient into a long-term group in psychoanalytic therapy, or the attempt to conduct analytic treatment with exclusively short-term members, might be disquieting for most patients, stirring up more than can be dealt with in the time allotted. It might be possible to use analytically oriented short-term therapy with selected patients, namely, those with reasonably good egos, intelligence, less resistance, good motivation, flexibility, non-chronicity, psychic youth, and some history of the quick and ready use of provided abstractions.

The literature presents several papers where analytic therapy was the method of choice. Greenbaum (1954) tried it with alcoholics, as did Clapham and Sclare (1958) with asthmatic patients, both with encouraging results. Schwartz (1960) attempted "classical" analytic group psychotherapy with adolescent delinquent boys in residential treatment, with, he feels, good success. Epstein and Slavson (1962), also working with delinquent, institutionalized adolescent boys, describe a "breakthrough" in treatment by the application of a modified form of analytic group psychotherapy, when there was a "reversal from projection of blame upon the environment to self-understanding and self-confrontation."

Papanek (1960) treated a heterogeneous group of seven patients in Adlerian-oriented, analytic group psychotherapy. This group was mixed as to diagnosis, emotional background, sex and age. There were two borderline schizophrenics, one severe anxiety state, two passive-aggressive characters, one normal personality with mild anxiety and one narcissistic character. Improvement was reflected in symptom relief and better functioning, in the greater activity of previously withdrawn patients, and in more meaningful and frequent participation. The quality and quantity of verbalization changed after the first fifteen sessions. From the thirtieth to the last (41st) meeting, new attitudes became increasingly more apparent. These changes were confirmed by projective tests.

COMPOSITION OF SHORT-TERM GROUPS

On the whole it is evident that much diligent and imaginative research has already been attempted in the difficult field of short-term group psychotherapy, proving at least the possibilities it provides for some kind of successful treatment. Though on the basis of these presentations one could not make categorical rules for the formation or treatment of short-term groups, they do open the way for more and more speculation and experimentation in both these areas. It seems safe to say that the probabilities are that short-term group therapy seems most effective when practiced in homogeneous groups.

We have just reviewed many different possibilities for the formation of homogeneous groups, but by no means exhausted them. The concept of homogeneity could be extended to include the impulse ridden, the actor-out, who would demand one type of treatment of us, and the superego ridden, resistive, over-controlled obsessive-compulsive, who would demand another. These last, one might say, would need affect-producing therapy to help them over their emotional blocks, while the former would need to learn to incorporate controls.

Then there are the depressed patients, who would probably respond to encouragement to ventilate their resentment against figures of the past, or against individuals not present in the group. If guilt followed, the therapist might attempt to lessen the force of the overly critical superego. Thus, in brief therapy, we might be able to reassure the patient as to the appropriateness of his protest, without involving or locking horns with either other members of the group, or with the therapist.

Another type of homogeneous group might include members with relatively good egos, where an analytic approach might be successfully tried. Still another group, characterized by ego weakness, might profitably use an exclusively ego-building technique.

Then again there might be homogeneous groups of orally dependent, pre-oedipally mother-attached patients, of over-eaters and under-eaters. Or we might combine a group of anally fixated psychic incontinents with a number of overly clean patients, obsessively defended against their anality, to see if, in their interaction, the former do not acquire some controls, while the latter yield up some of their defenses. The same could be tried with a group of phallic patients mixed in with impotent patients, to help the former recognize their compensatory defenses and offer the latter (as well as the former) some relief from their castration anxiety.

Spinning these possibilities could go on indefinitely. Their multiplicity makes it clear that improved testing methods are needed, not only to expose the pathology of the patient, but also the positive facets of his personality and character structure. If a central clearing house were available and a more comprehensive picture of people seeking treatment, short- or long-term, each therapist would probably find his own type of patient to group together, his own starting point for brief group therapy and his own exploration of treatment methods. One therapist might lean toward working with certain age groups, another with family groups. Some might prefer unisexual groups to heterosexual groups; others might want like-character structures, or id or superego ridden groups, or groups with similar pathology, psychodynamics, symptoms, history or kinds of transferences. Whatever it is the therapist wishes to pursue, he must have some base of operation, because, in brief therapy, time is not on our side. Limited time can be used as a spur to acceleration of treatment and that is all. That is why adequate testing and diagnosis must be our first concern.

Tests might prove, for example, that some patients would do better in group therapy combined with an individual experience; some might need group therapy combined with shock, or hypnosis or drug treatment. Others might react best to co-therapist treatment:

a man and woman; two women or two men. The variations and combinations could be endless, depending on the latitude and freedom we allow ourselves to investigate before and not after treatment has begun.

Another technical question to be considered is the number of patients needed in each group for the best results in brief group therapy. Until proper research has been done, this will also be a matter of random choice, each therapist postulating from his own experience. The same would be true of the minimal number of sessions we might think necessary for any improvement at all.

In speculating about this, let me go again to my own experience. I arrange my present practice under the following rough formulations: my groups are heterogeneous and open-end. They are usually made up of eight to ten patients. Those who meet with me once a week for one and a half hours, average about thirty-three sessions a year with the therapist and I would say roughly sixty-six alternate sessions when patients meet with each other, in the absence of the therapist. In other words, if an insurance contract covered a patient for, let us say, thirty paid sessions, that patient could conceivably and actually receive one year's treatment under my present conditions of practice.

These conditions, however, need not be rigid. For one reason or another, a group might suddenly become five in number, or even two. I have found that therapy, for those who remain involved, might change course for awhile but does not slacken perceptibly. On the contrary, much comfort is to be gained from the simple fact that the group does not disappear because others, for whatever reason, have had to leave. By the same token, those groups who meet with me twice a week, do not necessarily progress twice as fast as those with one therapist-led session a week. Which might lead one to speculate on how a group might work which met with the therapist every two weeks but continued alternate meetings regularly, on their twice a week schedule, throughout the year. In such cases connection with the therapist and the group could be maintained over practically a two year period with the same number of paid sessions.

In other words, the challenge of short-term group therapy is not one of time alone. Therapists are not being asked to break the four minute mile. We need to remind ourselves that the real challenge is to increase our flexibility to include the many different kinds of patients who need our help. To that end we need to study what happens to us, the therapists, to our approach and our conduct when we know beforehand that our treatment is to be limited in time. And we have to find out what effect the same knowledge will have on the patient. Will he be more guarded, more restive or more cooperative and persistent? Or will these effects vary again with each patient and each therapist? It is not possible to answer these questions definitely now. Some of us may have to experiment with groups of ten up to, perhaps, groups of twenty-five. Some may find several sessions a week work better for them and the patients they treat, while others will prefer sessions stretched over a greater length of time. It is no cause for discouragement that answers are not immediately forthcoming. On the contrary, it would suffice if our wills and wits were sharp enough to begin asking the right questions. That again is part of the struggle toward an open system where every new possibility and approach can be considered. Therapists are only human. It is natural that their own theories and values will limit what they hear, see and think. But, being human, they also have the capacity to grow and expand enough to incorporate change when that change is called for.

GOALS IN SHORT-TERM GROUP THERAPY

This would be a good point, then, to begin a discussion of the goals of therapy. From the long-term point of view, our goals are reconstructive and perhaps perfectionistic in character. In short-term group therapy, the chances are we may be obliged to address ourselves to the patient's immediate need, hoping only that he will be able to continue on his own when the period of therapy is over. To use the analogy of the sinking boat again, instead of a thorough repair or reconstruction job, the short-term group therapist may have to content himself with plugging the holes or leaks with putty realizing that the process may have to be renewed at certain intervals, if the boat is to be kept afloat. The therapist may have to settle for patchwork therapy, simply to enable the patient to survive. This may be a lesser goal but it is still part of professional, therapeutic responsibility to try to meet it. And the sacrifice of more ambitious dreams in specific cases should not play too much havoc with the therapist's self-image. Reducing or even removing neurotic symptoms and anxiety, where it is possible, and leaving the patient more hopeful about himself and his future development, is a result not to be ashamed of.

An experience in a therapeutic group should help combat feelings of loneliness and isolation, as the patient discovers shared difficulties. It should be able to activate people socially, so they can achieve better interpersonal relations and more socialized personalities, because of the group interaction. At the same time, we could expect a corresponding sublimation of antisocial trends; growth of mutual empathy and acceptance of others, even though different. Some emotional re-education should also prove feasible, as long as communications are positive and reality bound. Short-term group therapy should also be expected to orient the patient more appropriately to reality, to help him to make more realistic choices and to test his misperceptions against reality. The patient's self-image ought to be improved through the feedback reactions of his peers and the authority figure. If these may be accomplished in short-term group therapy, even when there is little or no insight in the analytic sense, the therapist can claim achievement of which he can be proud.

The techniques by which we might achieve such goals are as varied as the patients themselves are likely to be. Some have already been indicated from the literature. Others are still in the realm of speculation. It is safe to say, however, that the trend of treatment would be toward the reparative rather than the reconstructive and that though the method may not be that of traditional analysis, it will be enough so, in character, to make it desirable to have analytically trained therapists. I make this assumption—I would even call it recommendation—on the theory that the analytically trained person will know enough about defenses, repression, internal conflicts, oedipal and otherwise, interpretation, dream analysis, etc., to know when to intervene and when not to.

For example, in most cases of short-term therapy, it might be wiser to strengthen defenses rather than to break them down. It would probably be wiser not to probe too hard for repressed feelings, nor analyze dreams on any but the most positive and perhaps superficial level. It also would probably be foolhardy to think in terms of inducing a transference neurosis. If transferences were to be dealt with at all, it might be only to indicate how they operate compulsively in the current dilemmas of the patient.

TECHNICAL APPROACHES

How then to proceed with treatment? Here I would like to describe in some detail Feinberg's ego-building technique as a possible starting point for speculation (Feinberg, 1959). I have chosen this particular example because of the universality of the split-ego problem, in which the patient's ego is in repression, while he ambivalates between submission and rebellion against the incorporated negative parental ego. This makes the ego building technique particularly relevant in the treatment of everyone, as long as the therapist focuses on the liberation, development and growth of the repressed positive ego. As in long-term therapy with the borderline patient or the diegophrenic, the initial attempt is not to achieve a synthesis of the various conflicting, ambivalent attitudes. Instead, the positive ego is accented and the negative ego de-emphasized. Insight therapy is not offered, support of the weak ego being the concentration point. The borderline patient is expected to have ambivalent transferences until his own ego develops enough for him to be able to establish a positive transference. In brief therapy, as in long-term therapy, the group can provide the patient with good auxiliary egos to support his weakened, positive ego and also give him the testing ground necessary for him to strengthen his original ego.

Feinberg's ego building technique was used exclusively in a group setting. He describes this technique as a group experience, in which each patient listens to his co-patients discuss as many of his positive qualities as they can discover. Group members are asked by the therapist to express what they honestly like about the co-patient under examination. They are specifically instructed not to say anything derogatory. The therapist stands by to interrupt the reactions to any one member, if the group's responses seem to be running out. He then explores how the individual patient, under scrutiny, feels. Following this, he asks the appraisers how they feel after having told their co-patient wherein and how they think he is praiseworthy. The therapist may then use these latter associations to see if what was said was projective: to learn from each of the observers whether they thought *they* had the characteristics they had ascribed to the member under examination.

At the next meeting, the therapist asks for feedbacks from the scrutinized patient. And, at each meeting, one or more other patients have the opportunity to be explored, in like manner, by members of the group.

These are some of the reactions Feinberg reports: Mr. X says immediately, on having collected positive observations from his co-patients: "I feel good. I felt I did some of these things but I wondered if anybody else felt that way about it. It does make me feel good, of course, and I believe you were all sincere." His last remark might make some stop and wonder, but I quote it, for what it is worth. "Some of you should take this 'hot seat.' The impact is terrific!"

At the next meeting, Mr. X reported further, "As I worked alongside my colleagues, I had the feeling my colleagues may have the very same thoughts that you people had. It gave me a great deal of confidence."

In other groups, Feinberg asked if a discussant had a different feeling, when he played the role of a negative critic rather than a positive one. In each case the discussant said he himself felt better for praising than for criticizing negatively. Eventually, every patient agreed he felt the same way. Feinberg concludes from this that the ego-building approach has a definite therapeutic value even for the praisers.

Feinberg notes further that what a member says about another (when he concentrates on his style, clothes, the colors he chooses, etc.) rather than on what he *does* as a person (the way he meets people, his keenness, his acuity, etc.) may reveal resistances in the very evasiveness and superficiality of observation. This is where the skill of the group leader comes into play. It is the therapist's function to see that the observations are maintained on an honest, sincere and meaningful level, even though the discussion is limited to the positive qualities of the persons under scrutiny. The therapist, Feinberg says, should also join in with his positive comments. He should also continually probe for reactions from all concerned.

In his summing up, Feinberg concludes that his technique is intended to: 1) enable each participant to feel himself part of an accepting group; 2) to help build up each patient's ego; 3) to reduce negative opinions about oneself; 4) to help patients feel responsible toward each other; 5) to give each a chance to feel the pleasure of finding somthing good in the other and telling him about it; 6) to enable each patient to get a frank evaluation of himself by others; 7) to afford a basis for scientific investigation of what values an individual has for others, what values people look for in others and whether these values have projective meanings; and 8) a fine way of building group cohesion.

I think one would have to say that Feinberg's technique, as described here, seems to be based on an over-simplified view of ego functions, the origin of ego strengths and weaknesses and how weak egos are restored. More sophisticated studies (Back, 1948) (Cameron, 1957) (Fabian, 1954) (Fried, 1955) (Freud, Anna, 1937) (Green, 1954) (Hartman, et al. 1946) (Mann, 1955) (Redl, 1951, 1957) (Rosenblatt, 1961) (Slavson, 1959) (Sterba, 1934, 1944) (Woodward, 1951) (Federn, 1952) reveal that insight into inadequate ego function can be extremely elaborate and diversified, and therapeutic intervention must be equally intricate, if the ego is to be effectively rehabilitated.

However, I think Feinberg's study can be of considerable value, if it only serves to underline the trend *some* therapists have developed to confront their patients mainly with their pathology; as if, somehow, in doing so, their sickness would be eliminated. Many times, the only concrete result obtained is that the patient feels humiliated and defeated.

From the point of view of short-term therapy, Feinberg's technique might be a little too rigidly structured in both the vertical and horizontal vectors, though he encourages much peer interaction within the highly selective activity. Since most patients suffer from depreciated self-esteem and feel they must protect themselves from aggression, humiliation and punishment, this repetitive, structured, supportive therapy on both vertical and horizontal levels may help them incorporate gradually the external, positive view. The general attention to one's positive resources should be individually encouraging, should help one develop a sense of belonging and sustain a wish to return to the group meeting as a place where one is appreciated and wanted. Group morale ought to be high and if the patient can eventually incorporate a less critical superego and a more adequate self-image, this should also lead to a more flexible readiness on his part to engage with the environment in search of more gratifying interpersonal experience.

It is impossible within the scope of this discusion to point out all the circumstances or types of patients where Feinberg's technique, if used exclusively, would not work. But to cite again from the literature: Illing (1952) emphasizes the need for ventilation, for "blowing off steam" against each other and against the therapist in a group of prisoners. Hulse (1948) also found that when working with soldiers, they benefited tremendously when they could ventilate their gripes. Mann (1955) is another who makes a case for the necessity to work through defensive hostility before group members are able to accept one another. He feels that when patients are forced to be close, they develop anxiety and defensive hostility and that unless there is a working through of this aggression, no genuine interest in helping anyone else can develop. If this working through of hostility does not take place, he feels, each patient will maintain a protective shell that will leave him isolated and uninvolved. Back (1948), Riecken (1952), Theodorson (1962), as well as Heinicke and Boles (1953) agree that expression of hostility is a necessary part of interpersonal relatedness even when working with non-patient groups.

The role of the therapist, then, in short-term treatment seems to take on even more importance. He would be wise, I think, to make it clear to all patients at the outset, and even perhaps at subsequent meetings, that the number of therapy sessions available to them is limited. From that point on his technique will be largely up to him, chosen, we hope, from a wide base of experimental work done and being done. His role will vary with his degree of commitment to therapy in general and analysis in particular; his choice of therapeutic devices; the kinds of patients he chooses to treat, in the kinds of groups he decides to organize.

If he believes he can practice analytically reconstructive treatment in a short-term therapy group, his intervention may be active, penetrating and insightful. If he believes he must avoid the development of a transference neurosis, he will stay out of the interaction except to sponsor patients' responses to one another. If he believes in eliciting strong positive transferences, which he thinks he can manipulate in the patient's interest, to effect constructive change, he will make the group leader-centered, in a firm, convincing way, with the use of suggestion, guidance, counseling and even hypnosis. Only certain therapists are capable of playing the role this requires, and only certain patients are able to accept the therapist in this role.

If the therapist believes his essential responsibility is to get the patient to face and accept reality—that is, that he, the therapist, as well as the patient, have only partial powers—he will try repeatedly to confront the patient with the actualities of partipotence. In the main, what the therapist does will depend on his convictions, his experimental interests, his flexibilities, the patient's diagnosis and the therapist's impressions of the patient's needs and responsiveness to a certain kind of intervention.

Of course, this is true of all therapy, long or short, group or individual. But the short-term group therapist will have to tailor these precepts; focus them more directly and control them more in operation. He will always have to keep in mind the reality that his goals are limited, as his time with the patient is limited. He will probably find that he has to preplan the course of his responses; that he must center them mostly toward the reality needs of his patients rather than toward working out and working through their irrational, inappropriate or archaic needs.

The short-term group therapist will have to encourage group members to support one another in the adoption of constructive, sublimating alternatives to their various pathologies. He will emphasize reality not unreality; the rational not the irrational; partial rather than absolute satisfaction; compromise rather than total victory; partipotence not omnipotence; reason not unreason.

Unless the therapist is attempting to do short-term analytic group psychotherapy, he will avoid deep interpretations and unconscious material. He will tend not to emphasize history, genesis and the past as much as the present and future possibilities. He will, in all likelihood, be more inclined than in other forms of psychotherapy to set limits, to advise, teach, counsel and encourage the positive.

It may be important for many patients in short-term group treatment for the therapist to assume a firm, authoritative position. For some, let us say with the phobic patient, we may even have to assume a Stekelian position, saying to him in effect: "You will have to go out and do exactly what you are most afraid of doing." Even if this is effective with only a percentage of patients, such an approach would be useful in that degree.

In terms of trying to meet the more immediate problem and offering instant relief, the therapist might be obliged to say to another patient: "Your difficulty lies in your relationship to your wife," leaving out his original problem with his mother and father. We may have to deal with the symptom rather than with what is behind the symptom. If a man needs his wife to be a good mother figure, and he is sick enough, we may have to call in his wife and encourage her to coddle her husband a little more than she has; to give him more the experience of being loved. In the same way if a woman feels her husband is no longer interested in her, we may have to invite her husband to a session and urge him to be more expressive of his loving feelings toward his wife without analyzing and working through the patient's need of the father and the husband's resistance to the projected demands of his parents invested in his wife.

Perhaps several women, deprived of the satisfactions of maternity, ought to be placed in a therapeutic group with men who need mothering. Maybe a number of women who were abandoned by their fathers should be placed in a treatment group with men who have a need to father their wives and daughters. While the analyst may object that this is simply complementing neurotic needs, perhaps it is the best that can be done for now. Such intervention does not ask us to be less than analysts. It rather demands of us the flexibility to meet a larger challenge, to be more efficient, more selective, to use our training in a new and more social way in a society which daily grows more complex. We must also recognize that one of the reasons group therapy is successful is because it

has demonstrated that one's peers, even when they are other patients, can also be reparative. Insurance companies may still look on
group therapy simply as a way to handle greater numbers of patients. That may be why they provide such low fees for group as
against individual treatment. They can be educated as to the real
reparative value of peer relationships in group therapy. But I doubt
if that will happen until group therapists themselves believe in the
importance of the horizontal vector in effecting constructive change
to the point of including the still controversial alternate meeting
into their scheme of therapy.

The fears some therapists have, even with their long-term groups,
that patients will not be able to operate properly and constructively
except under the expert eye of the therapist, might seem to have
more justification in short-term group therapy. I will go so far as to
admit that with certain types of patients, this may be true. But in
the great majority of cases, I think every patient should at least be
presented with the opportunity of trying to work things out with his
peers, in both those situations where the therapist is around as well
as when he is not present.

Harlow (1961, 1962) has done some very interesting work with
newborn rhesus monkeys, which seems to prove that the sooner the
infant monkey is allowed free play with other infants, the more
quickly he matures, and conversely, the longer he is allowed to
cling to the mother or the surrogate mother, (the terry-cloth, non-
responsive mother), the more hopelessly tied to her he remains and
the more incapable of infant-to-infant affection. Harlow finds that
the infant monkey does not even need a mother substitute; that
plenty of playmates will do just as well. In other words, the mother-
infant relationship may be dispensable, but infant-to-infant relations are absolutely essential for the development of wholesome adjustment in all areas later on in the monkey's social life.

Rosenblatt (1961) presents a slight variant of Harlow's thesis.
He says that ". . . the waning of maternal behavior in cats is related
to the growth of play in the kittens. It appears . . . as though the
play of kittens among themselves and with the mother throws the
mother out of her maternal mood, or contributes to this process."
If Rosenblatt's studies have bearing on peer and hierarchical vectors, then the extent to which there is positive interaction among
the co-patients, to that degree the bind of patients to the therapist
in the vertical vector will decrease. Harlow elaborates on this. He
says, "Before the infant will leave the mother, the curiosity responses must become strong enough to override the fear responses

and the mother must not block the infant's exploratory efforts, or, on the positive side, the real mother may encourage them."

The implications for group therapy seem significant. If the therapist, as parental surrogate, encourages his patients to look at, talk to and listen to each other, their infantile ties to parental figures, including the therapist, will diminish and the members' incentive, social curiosity and exploratory responses to the non-maternal environment will grow. On the other hand, if the therapist discourages patient interaction, overprotects the members, and encourages their relationship to him, he may well reduce incentive, social curiosity and so infantilize his patients.

I believe the alternate meeting can be as valuable a tool in short-term group therapy as it is in long-term treatment, to convince the patient that the therapist has confidence in the patient's ability to get on by himself and give him the opportunity to prove to himself that he can relate to his peers pleasurably as well as productively.

There is one other practical point which would make the alternate meeting particularly valuable in short-term group therapy. That is, it might suggest the possibilities of keeping contact, if only for discussion purposes after the term of treatment has come to an end. There will be many patients who will feel they have been dropped, no matter how often they have been advised that the treatment is limited in time. For these patients it might even be essential to give them some base from which they can continue, at least with the group or part of it, if not with the therapist. And it is not impossible that a group which does continue in this way, might find some way to resume therapy with the therapist, if they want it enough.

Agreeing to the alternate meeting as a part of the treatment program will call for changes of attitude on the part of many therapists, as will the thought of doing short-term therapy in the first place. And that is understandable. It is not an easy matter to change one's attitude especially toward a lifetime work. It is not easy to leave traditional and tried methods to one side while we explore new roads. I would suggest in regard to short-term therapy that one thing we do is discard the name, which has a connotation of insufficiency and inadequacy and substitute instead the concept of accelerated therapy. That might help overcome resistances to the undertaking of treatment, where we know results must fall short of the very best. If we set our minds to a goal of acceleration, we may very well find it also helps sharpen our tools in long-term treatment.

FUTURE PROSPECTS

It might also help to remember that even Freud practiced short-term analysis when the occasion warranted it. It is impossible to even begin to guess at the number of Americans who went to him for didactic analyses during the summer. And then there is the famous anecdote of his analytic sessions with Gustave Mahler at the end of which a cure was pronounced. This session, you will remember, began in a hotel in Leyden and continued during a four hour stroll through the town. Mahler had had no previous experience with psychoanalysis, but Freud reported he had never come across anyone who understood it more quickly. At any rate, the desired result seemed to have been obtained. Mahler reportedly recovered his potency and enjoyed a happy marriage until his death (Jones, 1955).

Naturally, the rewarding results of these excursions into brief therapy did not mitigate Freud's interest in methods designed for deeper treatment. They were by no means mutually exclusive. Nor does the therapist today have to fear that finding ways of making short-term group therapy practical, mean that eventually he will be asked to give up his devotion to deeper goals in treatment. If he did that, he would be like the lady with the two chickens whom a famous comedian tells about. One of the chickens was healthy, the other sickly. So this serious-minded lady killed the healthy one to make chicken soup for the sickly one.

There are some things the therapist may have to give up within himself, however. He may have to think in less perfectionistic terms and seek more limited goals for himself and for his patients. Whatever it is he has to do, revising his prejudicial attitudes will provide the first requisite for developing short-term methods: the freedom to look for and find new treatment forms and new therapeutic devices.

Many psychoanalysts will raise serious objections. In general, the analyst's therapeutic view is long-term and perfectionistic. It is understandable that he may feel that his skills are particularly unsuited to accelerated therapy and that he will not be easily satisfied with only modest changes in his patients. But it is unrealistic to resist all other forms of psychotherapy other than insight therapy, where the principal focus is on unconscious dynamics. This insistence on only deep therapy can often prolong treatment beyond what is required by the patient. We know that in cases where the patient is bound in a transference neurosis, analysis can often become interminable. In accelerated group therapy, especially when the alternate meeting is part of the therapeutic plan, therapists may come to realize that patients are not as fragile as we would sometimes think them; that they do not and will not collapse in an early confrontation with reality.

That reality is calling on today's therapists to devise some form of accelerated therapy to take care of the increased demand for psychiatric services. Group therapists and group analysts are particularly equipped to rise to that call. I believe this to be a social need, and I believe it is our responsibility to meet this need, instead of remaining entrenched in what we have learned so far and experienced so far. I do not believe that fulfilling this need will replace long-term therapeutic practice in any sense whatsoever, except perhaps, that our skills will be so sharpened, that we will achieve results more quickly, even there. If, for any reason, short-term or accelerated therapy makes us more mechanical or more superficial in our approach toward the patient as a human being, it will be because we have allowed it to happen. Some therapists, to be sure, might find it more lucrative to practice on a short-term, guaranteed basis, and give up entirely the challenges, frustrations and pleasures of long-term therapy. But, if that happens, as with testing, the fault will lie in the user of the method and not in the method itself.

If, however, we tackle this problem head on, we may find we are helped in all phases of our work. Eventually we should have access to wider choices from a greater variety of patients; experience with a greater variety of group formations and expanded bases for experimentation and research. And the likelihood is that the more expert we become in short-term group therapy, the more demand there will be from the public for deep therapy. Brief psychotherapy, when well-done, can whet the appetite for deeper therapy, not replace it.

Undoubtedly, accelerated group therapy will impose a great load on today's already overloaded therapist, and he may, like Icarus, plummet into the sea as he reaches for the sun; but only if there is too much wax in his wings or if he insists on the largest and hottest sun as his goal. Certainly, as with Icarus, there is danger in any daring new experiment. But we need to go beyond the given, until, through successive failures, we find our answers. Though Icarus' solution was inadequate, at least he tried to fly. Man, the problem-solving animal, is even now flying into cosmic space. We therapists, on the other hand, are trying to find some earthbound answers for the earthbound, and I, for one, can see no reason why we should be overwhelmed by either the possibilities or the burden. We may not find the best solutions for short-term group therapy, certainly not immediately, but I am certain that our struggles will gradually be repaid by more and more successful solutions. In science, we start with hypothesis, speculation and experimentation. The generic word for that process is—hope.

QUESTIONS AND ANSWERS

Question: Are there any special kinds of symptoms or syndromes that respond better to short-term than to long-term methods?

Dr. Wolf: With present methods of practice, I think most of us have found certain symptoms or syndromes responding to treatment more quickly than some others. We have also encountered cases where deep probing or prolonged treatment was contra-indicated.

In my own experience, patients who have responded in the shortest time have been neurotically depressed, who showed improvements as soon as they could ventilate negative feelings without guilt or fear of reprisal. I have also had considerable success with very young, teen-age paranoid personalities; with patients suffering from duodenal ulcer and with those suffering from transient, situational personality disorders and social problems. These patients would probably fare as well under a manifestly short-term therapeutic program.

The problem which will continue to baffle us concerns patients who, heretofore, had required the longest term treatment: patients with systematized delusions; extremely severe masochists and very obsessive-compulsive patients.

In short-term group therapy it might be necessary to simplify diagnostic categories. We might, for example, classify patients as feeling hopeless, helpless or confused, and direct our efforts to bringing them hope or giving them help or clarity. For the hopeless we might try a form of repressive-inspirational therapy in an effort to revive their hope. For the helpless we might try to instill a sense of their having more resources than they think they have, using perhaps, some variant of the ego-building technique I described earlier. And the confused would probably require some form of reeducation, clarity and direction toward reachable goals. In all likelihood we are most apt to find an interlocking of all three in patients—helplessness, hopelessness and confusion—and the best we can do as therapists is to ask ourselves continually what capacities we have for partly undoing the disturbance.

Question: Since it is manifestly impossible within the confines of a short-term psychotherapy program to arrive at the definitive psychodynamics in many cases, is it possible to present a general formulation of dynamics that may be meaningful to the average patient?

Dr. Wolf: I don't think it is possible to present a general formulation of psychodynamics that will be truly meaningful to the average patient in short-term therapy. To do this in any but the most superficial, intellectual way calls for insight, in the analytic sense, and insight is not always within the capacity of the patient even in long-term treatment. What's more, insight, contrary to TV programs and newspaper columns, requires working through to be of any real help, and working through requires time. Many people have come to believe that a magical panacea resides in remembering and that remembering alone can lead to insight and cure. I believe there are many patients who would do better to suppress their pathology and concentrate more on their constructive possibilities. We may find when our treatment time is limited, that repression and suppression have their healthy side.

Question: Are goals in short-term therapy limited to symptom relief, or are reconstructive personality changes possible?

Dr. Wolf: This naturally means that we will have to revise some of our goals with patients. With some we may be limited to symptom relief. With others—those with relatively good egos, for example—we may try for reconstructive personality changes. But in the main, I believe, we will have to be satisfied with helping a patient back to leading the life he led before he broke down. And I think this is no goal to be ashamed of.

Question: Are there qualitative differences in techniques in short-term as compared to long-term treatment?

Dr. Wolf: The most important qualitative difference in technique between short-term and long-term group therapy would be that in short-term therapy the development of a transference neurosis would be avoided and more emphasis placed on repressive-inspirational treatment coupled with ego-building techniques. As in long-term therapy with the diegophrenic, we would not try to achieve a synthesis of conflicting ambivalent attitudes, but would try instead to accent the positive ego and deemphasize the negative ego. We would not offer insight therapy, but would concentrate on supporting the weak ego. In this we would also have the help of the group, which can provide the patient with good auxiliary egos to support his weakened positive ego, and at the same time give him the testing ground necessary to strengthen his repressed ego.

Question: Psychotropic drugs deal with target symptoms. Are there any special psychotherapeutic techniques that can also deal with target symptoms?

Dr. Wolf: I think all these answers are still too much in the realm of speculation to speak of any definitive psychotherapeutic methods for treating target symptoms.

Question: Is a transference neurosis desirable in short-term therapy? How may it be managed most constructively, if it does develop?

Dr. Wolf: As I said before, I believe that in short-term therapy it would be wise to avoid the development of the transference neurosis. The best way I know of doing this is to confront the patient as often as possible with the reality of the situation and, more important, to place the patient in a group that has alternate meetings— that is—meetings without the therapist. This would encourage separation from the attachment to the therapist as mother. In general it can be said that the group is usually a good safeguard against the development of a transference neurosis and that the accelerated group, where everyone is aware of the time limitations would be an even better one.

Question: Are there ways of managing resistance in short-term therapy that differ from long-term therapy?

Dr. Wolf: While in long-term therapy we try to break down resistances, in accelerated therapy I think we might have to reinforce them, discouraging those who would uncover more unconscious material than they can handle.

Question: Since there are many patients who develop intensive dependency relationships and who consequently tend to make therapy an interminable affair, how can we deal with such patients in a short-term approach? Are there ways of by-passing dependency, or resolving it, or directing it at therapeutically corrective foci other than a never-ending therapeutic situation?

Dr. Wolf: In spite of all precautions, there will always be patients who will develop dependency relationships, who will want to make therapy an interminable affair. Here again, I think group therapy with alternate meetings works against this tendency. As does the contant reminder that the contractual association with the therapist is specific, limited and cannot be unilaterally changed. Though dependency is always a knotty problem with very sick patients, I believe it will be easier to handle if therapists do not try to break down resistances, uncover unconscious material and penetrate detachment, but concentrate instead on getting patients to accept themselves as they are and to be content to have learned a little more and to feel a little better.

Question: Are there ways of breaking through characterologic detachment to involve the patient therapeutically in a few sessions without stirring up too great anxiety?

Dr. Wolf: If detachment is extremely severe, we will, of course, have to find ways of breaking through it, but on the whole I would suggest not trying too hard. The patient who comes to therapy has already broken through detachment to some extent. If closeness causes too much anxiety to be coped with in short-term treatment, we ought rather to respect his detaching himself somewhat, and we ought to let him know we accept him where he is and respect him for where he is.

Question: How does one utilize dreams in short-term therapy? Does one employ them in any way other than that in long-term therapy?

Dr. Wolf: When it comes to the question of dreams, I think it would be foolhardy to explore unconscious dynamics at any depth in short-term therapy. Dreams, however, can continue to be one of our most valuable therapeutic tools. They can serve as guides to what is going on unconsciously in the patient, to know more about him—about what his growing edge may be—and as a form of communication between him, the therapist and the group. In interpreting the dreams, I think it would be wisest to emphasize the positive and realistic elements in them, sublimation, and in some cases, perhaps to teach the patient to repress frightening elements, or to face them or even to remake them.

Question: How valuable are drugs in short-term therapy?

Dr. Wolf: Psychotropic drugs can be very valuable for the acutely disturbed, for the anxious, the confused, the depressed, for target symptoms, for the psychotic, for the insomniac. They should, of course, not be prescribed routinely or generally.

Question: What supportive approaches are helpful in short-term therapy?

Dr. Wolf: The best supportive approach I can suggest at this time is again a variant of the ego building technique.

Question: Are there techniques that may encourage reconstructive changes in the therapy and post-therapy period?

Dr. Wolf: In short-term therapy we may be forced to be a bit more manipulative—a tendency always dangerous to encourage in a therapist. In this situation, however, it may be therapeutically necessary if we see a chance for reconstructive changes. At times we might have to try to reeducate patients to another way of life—perhaps encourage them to move to a less troublesome community; to change jobs or to get more education.

Question: Is it helpful to see related family members in short-term therapy? If so, for what purposes?

Dr. Wolf: I think it might be very helpful at times to see related family members of patients in short-term therapy. Understanding the family better might help us understand the patient better and more quickly. We might, perhaps, discover in the family the more pathological member who is most disturbing to the whole group. We might be able to facilitate communications among family members or convince them to help therapy along by supplying some of the patient's needs.

Question: Can psychological testing or other psychological approaches contribute to short-term treatment?

Dr. Wolf: As I have indicated above, I think psychological testing can be very useful as a preliminary to group therapy. Anything that will help us to know the patient better would be useful. Hopefully, the tester will assist the therapist in guessing at what might be the critical issue to be dealt with at this moment: Is it homosexual panic? Is it guilt in reference to the father or mother? Is it competition with women or men? What are the strengths and weaknesses of the patient? These are the clues we need from the tests and not analytic interpretations.

Question: What environmental resources may be enlisted to help a patient during short-term therapy?

Dr. Wolf: Strictly speaking, the utilization of social and environmental resources belongs in the province of the social and community agencies. I am certain that the services they offer—such as clubs, social activities, welfare, medical and educational—would be invaluable to patients in short-term group therapy. The difficulty would be in searching them out in each community and for this a central agency in each city would be of immeasurable help to both patient and therapist. This would also be true for patients who have completed their term of treatment.

Question: Would you advise group therapy following individual therapy?

Dr. Wolf: In response to this question about group therapy as a terminal experience, I think group therapy ought to be a terminal experience for every form of individual treatment whether psychoanalytic or psychotherapeutic. It ought to be made a testing experience to see how far we have gone in individual therapy.

IX

Hypnosis in Short-Term Therapy

================================ LEWIS R. WOLBERG, M.D.

(Editor's Note: Hypnosis may play a valuable part in a short-term approach if it is blended with other indicated technics. Ways of accomplishing this are suggested in the present chapter.)

"THE YEAR WAS 1897 and the place was St. Petersburg. The occasion was the premier of the twenty-four-year-old composer's (Rachmaninoff) First Symphony. It was a complete fiasco, and Rachmaninoff himself described how he sat in rapt horror through part of the performance and then fled from the concert hall before it had ended. At a post-concert party which had been arranged in his honor for that evening he was further shaken and ill at ease, but the crowning blow came the next morning when the reviews appeared. In *The News* Cesar Cui wrote: 'If there was a conservatory in hell Rachmaninoff would get the first prize for his symphony, so devilish are the discords he places before us.' This combination of events was too traumatic for a personality as sensitive as Rachmaninoff's. He was seized with a fit of depression and apathy from which he could not rouse himself. For two long, black years it lasted. Finally, friends persuaded him to see one of the pioneers in the field of auto-suggestion, a Dr. Dahl.

"Rachmaninoff, in his memoirs (*Rachmaninoff's Recollections*, told to Oskar von Riesemann) tells the story: 'My relations had told Dr. Dahl that he must at all costs cure me of my apathetic condition and achieve such results that I would again begin to compose. Dahl asked what manner of composition they desired and had received the answer, 'A Concerto for pianoforte, for this I had promised to the people in London and had given it up in despair. Consequently I heard the same hypnotic formula repeated day after day while I lay half asleep in my armchair in Dr. Dahl's study. 'You will begin to write your Concerto. . . . You will work with great facility. . . . The Concerto will be of excellent quality. . . .' It was always the same, without interruption. Although it may sound incredible, this cure really helped me. Already at the beginning of the summer I was composed once more. The material accumulated and new musical ideas began to stir within me—many more than I needed for my Concerto. By autumn I had completed two movements (the Andante and the Finale). . . . These I played that same season at a charity concert conducted by Siloti . . . with gratifying success. . . . By the spring I had finished the first movement (Moderato). . . . I felt that Dr. Dahl's treatment had strengthened my nervous system to a miraculous degree. Out of gratitude I dedicated my Second Concerto to him.' "*

Whatever else was accomplished for Rachmaninoff by Dr. Dahl, dissolution of his symptoms and restoration of his creativity were apparently helped through the instrumentality of hypnosis. Today we are not satisfied with a mere retrieval of homeostasis as a treatment goal. We strive, in addition, to resolve damaging conflicts and to fortify the personality structure itself. Hypnosis is consequently employed conjunctively with other short-term technics for the purpose of catalyzing the total treatment process. This is not to say that hypnosis should never be employed for symptom removal, symptom relief or symptom substitution in the case of emergencies, or where the patient is motivated only for the elimination of disabling complaints. But such usage must be recognized as goal limited; more substantial personality changes, if they occur at all, being a fortuitous by-product.

RATIONALE FOR THE USE OF HYPNOSIS

An appraisal of the therapeutic values of hypnosis is burdened by a number of human obstacles. First, there are psychiatrists who with little experience but great conviction, inveigh against the use of hypnotic technics. Echoing Freud's doubts, expressed at the end of the nineteenth century, they denounce the method as an irrational use of suggestion which by-passes and hence neglects resistance, contaminates transference thereby reviving regressive needs and expectations, and temporarily banishes symptoms only to have them return in their original or substitutive form. Under these circumstances, hypnosis, they allege, serves as a contaminant of good therapy. Second, there are professional persons with considerable experience in hypnosis who warn against its dangers, vividly describing cases in which sexual and hostile outbursts, and even psychotic break-downs have occured. Third, there are individuals employing hypnosis who find its effects to evanescent and innocuous to influence treatment in the least for the good or the bad. Fourth, there are those who are so over-enthusiastic about hypnotic therapy

* The above are notes by Martin Bookspan from the record album Vox Box, containing Rachmaninoff's Piano Concerto #2 in C Minor, Op., reprinted by permission of Vox Productions, Inc.

that they employ it for every imaginable ill and even recommend it to bolster normal functions. Finally, there are investigators who deny that there is such a state as hypnosis, who contend that it is a kind of role-playing feigned to please the operator, or who insist that hypnosis is merely suggestion with unessential adornments of "mumbo-jumbo." The literature is deluged with writings from all of the foregoing groups, making an evaluation of hypnosis for the therapist who seeks to use it precarious to say the least.

Ambivalence about results is, of course, not unique to hypnosis. It invests practically every branch of psychotherapy. Psychoanalysis, particularly, has had more than its share of unfavorable publicity both from the pens of untutored theoreticians and from sophisticated "turncoat" psychoanalysts. The ineffectuality and danger of drug therapy, psychosurgery, group therapy and other forms of treatment are periodically promoted in both scientific and popular writings. Such reporting has its favorable aspects, since it focuses attention on some of the weaknesses of our current modes of treatment. Yet, by exaggerating the shortcomings of current technical operations, and by concentrating on failures rather than successes, great harm may be done to many persons in need of help who might benefit from the careful application of the method under attack.

A number of patients, warned against hypnosis by their physicians or psychiatrists, and plagued with symptoms that do not yield to traditional technics, in desperation finally consult a practitioner of hypnosis in defiance of such warnings. Apart from the usual resistances to treatment, the therapeutic effort is handicapped by haunting doubts and guilt feelings at having defied a respected authority, adding to convictions of hopelessness and to a negative placebo effect.

Moreover, a further complication adulterates the therapeutic application of hypnosis, namely, the expectation of magic on the parts of patient and therapist. Hypnosis is allied in the minds of some patients with such super-normal phenomena as telepathy, clairvoyance, precognition, divination, and manifestations of survival after death. This association is undoubtedly fostered by the traditional confusion of hypnosis with sorcery, by what may be considered as weird outpourings in the trance that seemingly defy laws of nature, and by extraordinary productions in the literature describing "trance revelations," automatic writing, crystal gazing and trance speaking. The notion that hypnosis is a wondrous substance that can somehow bring about rapid cure is an aspect of the desire for wizardry that most patients possess in applying to a healer who will, they hope, relieve their suffering. It inevitably results in disappointment, because hypnosis can do no conjuring tricks to outwit an enemy that for years has defied control or even detection. And the therapist himself may, in the early stages of his experimentation with hypnosis, expect that it will do the impossible. When resistance start fighting back, neutralizing the suggestions given the patient in the hypnotic state, he may lose faith in the power of hypnosis to contain or resolve the patient's illness.

A further confusion impairing the full acceptance of hypnosis as a treatment mode is the dilemma investing its exact nature. If one scans the literature, hypnosis is equated with dependency, masochism, homosexuality, transference, pre-genital fixations and "what-not." Its point of origin is held out to be the forebrain, the thalamus, the reticular formation, the neurons or the synapses. The evidence presented for these affiliations, from laboratory experiments, and the content of verbalizations, phantasies, dreams and behavioral manifestations is impressive. Should the reader be biased in any special direction, or awed by the reputation of the author, he may well endorse such findings. But caution is essential in assigning to hypnosis any permanent place in the catalogue of causation. We are no more certain about where hypnosis fits in the electronics or chemistry or neurophysiology of brain function, than we are about consciousness or sleep. We are no further advanced in divining hypnotic psychology or psychodynamics or sociology than we are in fathoming non-hypnotic cognitive, affective and behavioral processes. It would seem only prudent to expose hypnosis to the conditions of scientific method, the six-fold steps of observation, analysis, understanding, predication, experiment and replication. Yet in applying these operations we must recognize that hypnosis, like other behavioral sciences, lacks a conceptually simplified paradigm around which we may crystallize our ideas of theory. No matter how sophisticated our experiments or how brilliantly we seem to have verbalized our hypotheses, great caution must be exercised to prevent the metamorphosis of our data into dogma, and our ideas into ideologies. The complex and multiple variables in hypnosis, the arduousness of controlling the circumstances of experiment, the fallibility of the observer and his prejudicial myopia, and the difficulty of establishing proper controls make modesty essential in ascribing predictive reliability to any observed events in the trance state.

To the objection that we should not employ a rubric the precise nature of which is still unknown, one may reply that most of medicine is rooted in the soil of empiricism. It is only through constant observation and experiment that we are able to establish specificity for some of our therapeutic tools. We still employ the others without knowing why they work, simply because they do happen to work. And we utilize hypnosis, though exactly what it is and precisely how it operates are not entirely clear.

ARE THERE DANGERS IN HYPNOSIS?

Of even greater importance in appraising hypnosis are accounts of precarious effects in its employment that have been given publicity in both the lay and professional press. From these the therapist may assume that in hypnosis he has a tiger by the tail, that he can through its treachery unleash psychotic forces in the patient that may become irreversible.

Some time ago, I started a research project that was designed to study the presumed perils of hypnosis. Questionnaires, most of which were returned, were sent to almost 2,000 professional persons in two categories: the first, members of two professional organizations in hypnosis; the second, persons who had no affiliation with these organizations. Included were questions as to whether the respondent, if he utilized hypnosis, had witnessed any untoward effects, a number of symptoms being specifically listed. Questions were also asked about whether the respondent had experienced any of the same consequences in patients he had treated without hynosis. The questionnaires returned from general practitioners, psychiatrists, dentists, and psychologists who indicated that they did not employ hypnosis in their practices showed approximately the same percentage and kinds of untoward responses as a result of nonhypnotic procedures as did the group who practiced hypnosis. Counting noses in this way is not the best kind of scientific methodology; but certainly a sample of this size bears some relationship to fact. My feeling in studying the questionnaires was that a caseload of emotionally unstable persons is bound to show signs of disturbed reaction to therapeutic procedures of any kind that are unsettling or that have a frightening meaning for the patient, whether these be hypnosis, psychoanalysis, or any other type of therapy.

Hypnosis in itself is a harmless procedure. However, if it connotes in the patient's mind something vicious, or if the therapist conducts himself in an anti-therapeutic way during hypnosis, the patient may respond with anxiety. While hypnosis may lower repressive barriers and facilitate a return to consciousness of repudiated psychic content, there is no reason to fear that the patient will automatically be hurt by this even though his ego is fragile. I have employed hypnosis with benefit in countless numbers of borderline and psychotic persons, and I have found the effects to be soothing to these patients rather than upsetting. But what may disturb the patient are activities, attitudes and feelings in the therapist that come through to the patient and that are not in the interests of good therapy.

A patient was referred to me in a state of anxiety which was fostering a disorganization close to a psychotic break. He had been in therapy with a psychiatrist who had employed hypnosis, and the family and patient were under the impression that this technic was responsible for his upset. The patient was an obsessive-compulsive individual who had always made a marginal adjustment utilizing his compulsive defenses. Shortly after his marriage he began to develop an intensive fear of pointed objects, particularly knives, and he went to great lengths to avoid these, even to the point of locking all instruments and cutlery with a lethal potential in a drawer, giving the key to his wife, and warning her not to tell him of its whereabouts. What was behind this maneuver was a fear that he would lose control, and, taking command of the weapon, plunge it into his wife's chest. Underlying this fear and impulse was a feeling that he was trapped by his wife the way he had felt trapped by his mother. Encapsulated in a confining marriage which he interpreted as robbing him of the little independence he had finally achieved, he envisaged liberation through violence, and then, in guilt, he had repressed his impulse. What disturbed his wife and made her insistent that the patient see a psychiatrist were the precautions he took to avoid getting at the key awarded to her safe keeping. Since she might talk in her sleep, the patient demanded that his wife sleep in another room. Then he feared that he might walk in his sleep to her bedroom, and that the stimulus of his presence would bring out the unwelcome information. In precaution he insisted on placing pails of water in the doorway so that he would trip and awaken from sleepwalking during any lethal mission.

In therapy, the psychiatrist had decided to desensitize the patient to knives, and, employing hypnosis, he had suggested to the patient that he would while picturing himself in a pleasant atmosphere imagine himself touching, then holding, then utilizing a knife to prepare food for a meal. Thereafter he suggested that the patient try to use knives for other household purposes. After this was successfully accomplished, the therapist forcefully suggested to the patient during hypnosis that he would prove to himself that he would never use a knife destructively by placing a paring knife under his pillow and sleeping on it. On the evening following this suggestion the patient telephoned the therapist in anxiety asking if it was necesasry to go through with the hypnotic order, and he had received an unequivocal command to do so. During a fitful evening, the patient found himself fingering the knife and responding with terror at his impulse to proceed with it to his wife's bedroom. The next morning he experienced an attack of panic from which he could not seem to extract himself. My therapy was essentially reassuring in nature, and hypnosis was employed to help allay his anxiety with beneficial effect.

A therapy is as good as the operator who implements it. A scalpel is a tool which in the hands of a skilled surgeon can be a healing instrument. But in the hands of an unskilled person who tries to do surgery the damage can be infinite. Employed by an untrained and unskilled therapist, hypnosis can be useless and even upsetting to patients.

Hypnosis expedites a powerful relationship between operator and patient that influences both participants. On the part of the patient, at bedrock there may be symbolically reanimated a relationship to an idealized parent who will give the patient the support and gratifications he believes were lacking in his own childhood. This, in essence, is identical to what happens in any physician-patient relationship, where the patient, upset, tense, in pain and fearful turns to the healing figure who will bring an end to his misery. During hypnosis this effect is intensified. In essence, the patient, reaching for a protective parental agency, invests the hypnotist with omnipotent and omniscient qualities. This is complicated by the fact that sooner or later he may project onto the operator the kinds of attitudes, and relive with him some of the experiences, that he had with his parents or siblings during vital formative periods of his life. This transferential drama can both expedite and negate the therapeutic process, and its management constitutes the essence of depth therapy. In the usual course of short-term therapy, with or without hypnosis, these unrealistic projections are not, except in very sick patients, too much of a problem, and they tend to be neutralized when they are not encouraged by formal analytic technics like free association, focusing on the past, therapist passivity and the use of the couch. One may, nevertheless, observe evidences of transference during and following hypnosis from slips of speech, dreams, attitudes and feelings which the short-term therapist will by-pass unless they interfere with his therapy. The realistic relationship with the therapist more or less is superimposed upon the transference relationship keeping it in check.

Important, too, is the fact that hypnosis may mobilize in the therapist some neurotic attitudes and feelings toward the patient.

The patient in trance represents in his mind a different kind of individual than in the waking state. Passive and immobilized, at least seemingly so, the patient may stimulate in some therapists omniscient, grandiose, sadistic and sexual fantasies. Where the therapist himself has unresolved problems in interpersonal relationships, he may project these by the way he talks, his emphasis on certain kinds of content, and a display of unusual behavior toward the patient. The patient in hypnosis will generally respond to such maneuvers with anxiety. Many therapists are able to do good therapy with their patients in the waking state, but when they attempt to employ hypnosis, they lose their objectivity and consequently their therapeutic effectiveness.

What is important then for each therapist to establish is the utility for him of the hypnotic method. He will have to employ a kind of applied research approach in order to assess his results. Does he feel comfortable in utilizing hypnosis? Does hypnosis make him feel powerful, sadistic, anxious or sexually stimulated? Does he sense a change in his feelings toward the patient? Is he able to remain objective about the material produced by the patient? Can he apply the same dynamic criteria to the behavioral responses of the patient in hypnosis as he would to patients with whom he works without hypnosis? Does hypnosis have a personal meaning that makes him over-value its effects? These questions can only be answered when the therapist utilizes hypnosis with a variety of patients and carefully observes his own responses as well as those of his patients. Where his patients consistently display aggressive, sexual or masochistic inclinations during or following a trance, he may find the source within himself. If the therapist cannot control his own emotions as a hypnotist, hypnosis as an adjunct is not for him.

Assuming that counter-transference is not too much of a problem, each therapist will still have to experiment with hypnosis to see how it may be blended with his own technics, his personality and unique ways of working with his patients. The induction of hypnosis may be learned easily, often within a few minutes, but much time will be needed to test the effects of hypnosis on one's therapeutic results.

CAN HYPNOSIS REMOVE SYMPTOMS?

It sounds logical to expect that hypnosis can banish symptoms at least temporarily without explaining their origin or purpose. In some cases this expectation will be fulfilled. Authoritative suggestions, particularly during hypnosis, may modify or remove symptoms of a hysterical nature provided that these have no great functional value for the individual, having both fulfilled their neurotic purpose and exhausted the secondary gain. Other symptoms which are the product of tension may be automatically alleviated as a result of the resolution of tension during hypnosis. By and large the time honored dictum that symptoms removed by hypnosis must return in the same or substitute form, or that the psychic equilibrium will be upset precipitating a psychosis, is purely fictional. Relief may be permanent and advantage may be taken of the symptom-free interlude to encourage a better life adjustment.

Repeatedly witnessed is the phenomenon of an individual who blighted by a symptom, whether this be a functional paralysis, a facial tic, obesity, impotence or any other frailty, becomes so immersed in misery and in his own realistic failure to fulfill himself that he is handicapped in his ability to function. Announcing to such a person that one will have to delay dealing with his inmmediate complaint until he works through factors in his development is both illogical and unfair. To attempt to bring about as much relief in as short a period of time as possible constitutes a measure of thoughtfulness that can help the working relationship immeasurably. Should one succeed in relieving the symptom, a restoration of functioning may redeem the individual's self-respect and improve his interpersonal relationships in the interests of a better total adjustment.

In the chapter on "The Technic of Short-Term Therapy" mention is made of how resolution of one aspect of the individual's problem may initiate a chain reaction that can reverberate through the entire personality structure influencing other of its dimensions. I have witnessed some surprising examples of how a few hypnotic sessions may alter even the most serious patterns in the spectrum of psychiatric pathology. How this came about and why are beyond my ken. The fact that they happened is testimony to an inherent plasticity in human beings which sometimes takes advantage of hypnosis to unbridle dormant healing forces.

One patient, a preacher from a distant state who had dedicated his life to helping the poor and distressed, had six years prior to his initial interview with me, at the age of forty, become obsessed with homosexual yearnings that had sent him prowling the streets for physically attractive men. To his horror he found himself entering toilets to observe the genitals of strangers. Self-castigation, prayer and the imposition on himself of harsh disciplines failed to palliate his conscience or to halt in the least his forays into sin. A pillar of the community, he knew he was jeopardizing his reputation and security with conduct that could only bring disgrace to himself and to his wife and son. The homosexual desire had descended on him following a gradual loss of sexual interest in his wife. Except for sporadic mutual masturbation with a male companion during early adolescence, his sexual proclivities had been exclusively toward females. His choice of a wife was a good one, and his early sexual adjustment with her, he claimed, was excellent. He was unable to understand the evil powers that had overwhelmed him, threatening his reputation, security and feelings of integrity as a man of god. In search for some answer he had explored journals of Medicine, and, in one of them, he had come across an article on hypnosis written by me, which intrigued him so that he had saved as much money as his paltry earnings would allow, accumulating sufficient funds to permit a trip to New York for three days. One consultation with me in which I induced hypnosis would, he was sure, take him off the road to ruin and put him firmly back on the heterosexual path. I scarcely shared his confidence in my talents or his exuberant assurance that things so easily would be put to right. Nevertheless, I could not, in view of his great sacrifice in coming to New York, bring myself to deflate his optimistic balloon. I had scarcely any time to do more than to listen to a sketchy account of his story and to induce hypnosis, during which I told him that I had the impression that he was not as sick as he imagined, that, in view of his past good adjustment with his wife, he had sufficient strength to stop himself from homosexual explorations. There must be reasons why his interest in his wife had waned. Perhaps he had become angry at her for certain reasons, and had bottled up his resentment. Since he had given up so much to come to visit me, he inwardly wanted heterosexuality and he would soon find his desire for his wife returning. He would begin to have dreams in which he would recognize why he turned away from his wife, and dreams of feeling close to her physically. He would be able to practice self-hypnosis regularly and give himself suggestions to observe himself and to work on the sources of his trouble, as well as to restore his faith in himself as a man. Prior to termination of the session, I briefly instructed him in self-hypnosis. Regular weekly letters for a few months gave me details of his practice and recounted dreams which indicated fear of and hostility toward female figures. These in later dreams gradually became more benign. Sexual phantasies of a heterosexual nature returned. Difficult at first, he found it progressively easier to restrain himself from homosexual excursions.

In a few months sexual contact with his wife was reestablished with steadily increasing satisfaction. Follow-up letters over an eight year period, and one follow-up visit, have indicated changes in his overall adjustment which would have been registered as a striking success had prolonged therapy been the prescribed approach. I am not certain as to what had happened to alter the patient's complex intra-psychic mechanisms, whether changes were sponsored by placebo factors, by the healing influences of self-observation or both. Whatever the mechanism, the interlude with hypnosis played a signal part in his improvement.

I have had many experiences with chronic obsessive-compulsives who were tearing themselves to pieces with their miserable phantasies, who, after unsuccessful long-term psychotherapy and psychoanalysis, had responded to a few hypnotic sessions which were focused on teaching the patient how to push his mind away from his obsessions toward more peaceful and productive preoccupations. Here self-hypnosis, in quite a number of patients, had proved to be an instrument of value. In follow-up studies, some of these patients, who had been considered hopeless, had shown astonishing changes in their total personality structure and in their reality adaptation that had proceeded far beyond my clinical expectations.

From the above accounts one should not assume that hypnosis is a substitute for long-term treatment in cases suited for this approach. Where it is indicated and done well, long-term treatment may promote a depth of personality change that is excitingly rewarding. Resistances may be attended to in a consistent and efficient way, and new potentials may be released to enhance adjustment. At the same time one should not minimize what can be done for people on a short-term basis, particularly for those whose problems do not lend themselves to long-term exploration, or who, because of personality needs may become hopelessly mired in an interminable therapeutic quagmire. In such persons hypnosis may contribute substantially to the short-term effort.

Not all symptoms will yield themselves to hypnotic influence. Those that serve an important purpose in the psychological economy, and those consequent to tensions that resist influence, will cling to the patient with a desperation that defies the concerted skills of the hypnotist. Most patients can easily neutralize a hypnotist's intentions by resisting suggestions even in the deepest trance state. But if a patient is a very good hypnotic subject, and the hypnotist is a skilled operator, though obviously a poor therapist to do this, he may cleverly confuse issues and trick the patient into compliance. The patient may then expose himself to dangers he has avoided through his symptoms, which may liberate uncontrollable anxiety and break down his psychological reserve.

The semantics of suggestion giving are important. A patient commanded to yield a symptom may either resist as a carry-over of resentments toward over-disciplinary parents, or, rarely, if he is an exceptionally good subject, he may comply temporarily. Ultimately his anxiety will force him to restore his symptomatic controls. On the other hand, if the patient is told that he will have a desire to yield his symptoms, that this desire will grow so strong that it will make him want to do what is necessary to give it up, and that he will enjoy the experience of being symptom-free, he may respond most appropriately. For example, if a patient has a facial tic, he may be told in hypnosis: "You will find that you will feel so much more relaxed, and so much easier and so much better, that it will not be necessary for you to have this particular symptom. You will be able to go through the day without even thinking about your tic, and feeling good that it is not there. This is because it will not have any meaning for you. When you get to the point where you want to give up your facial tic, then you will find that it will not be there anymore." Improvisations of suggestions along similar lines may be made for such tendencies as overeating in obesity, under-eating in malnutrition, smoking, insomnia, enuresis, impotence and other symptoms. These suggestions may be quite effective.

INDUCTION METHODS IN SHORT-TERM THERAPY

Hypnosis is extremely easy to induce and all methods seem to work equally well provided the operator applies himself confidently and acts as if he expects the patient to enter into hypnosis without question. If the therapist accepts the fact that all people are hypnotizable in varying degrees, and that the acceptance of suggestions bears little relationship to the depth of trance, he will be able to approach the patient with a feeling he can help him irrespective of the patient's resistances or expressed doubts. The confidence of the therapist is communicated to the patient in the therapist's bearing and intonations, and, if the paient feels that the therapist has faith in what he is doing, he will usually respond satisfactorily.

I have found that giving the patient some literature he can study in advance helps to answer some of his questions, though he will still have doubts about his ability to be hypnotized in the early stages of therapy. The mimeographed pages I give my patients are these:

Questions You May Have About Hypnosis

1. *Exactly what is hypnosis?* Hypnosis is a state of altered consciousness that occurs normally in every person just before he enters into the sleep state. In therapeutic hypnosis we prolong this brief interlude so that we can work within its bounds.

2. *Can everybody be hypnotized?* Yes, because it is a normal state that everybody passes through before going to sleep. However, it is possible to resist hypnosis like it is possible to resist going to sleep. But even if one resists hypnosis, with practice the resistance can be overcome.

3. *What is the value of hypnosis?* There is no magic in hypnosis. There are some conditions in which it is useful and others in which no great benefit is derived. It is employed in medicine to reduce tension and pain which accompany various physical problems, and to aid certain rehabilitative procedures. In psychiatric practice, it is helpful in short-term therapy, and also, in some cases, in long term treatment where obstinate resistances have been encountered.

4. *Who can do hypnosis?* Only a qualified professional person should decide whether one needs hypnosis or could benefit from it. In addition to his other experience, the professional person requires further training in the technics and uses of hypnosis before he can be considered qualified.

5. *Why do some doctors have doubts about hypnosis?* Hypnosis is a much misunderstood phenomenon. For centuries it has been affiliated with spiritualism, witchcraft and various kinds of mumbo jumbo. It is a common tool of quacks who have used it to "cure" every imaginable illness, from baldness to cancer. The exaggerated claims made for it by undisciplined persons have turned some doctors against it. Some psychiatrists too doubt the value of hypnosis because Freud gave it up sixty years ago, and because they themselves have not had too much experience with its modern uses.

6. *If hypnosis is valuable, shouldn't it be employed in all psychological or psychiatric problems?* Most psychological and psychiatric problems respond to treatment by skilled therapists without requiring hypnosis. Where blocks in treatment develop, a therapist skilled in hypnosis may be able to utilize it effectively. But only a qualified professional person can decide whether this is necessary or desirable.

7. *Is the use of hypnosis endorsed by the proper authorities?* Both the American Medical Association and the American Psychiatric Association have qualified hypnosis as a useful form of treatment

in the hands of skilled doctors who have had adequate training, and who employ it in the context of a total treatment program.

8. *Can't hypnosis be dangerous?* The hypnotic state is no more dangerous than is the sleep state. But unskilled operators may give subjects foolish suggestions, such as one often witnesses in stage hypnosis, where the trance is exploited for entertainment purposes. A delicately balanced and sensitive person exposed to unwise and humiliating suggestions may respond with anxiety. On the whole, there are no dangers in hypnosis when practiced by ethical and qualified practitioners.

9. *I am afraid I can't be hypnotized.* All people go through a state akin to hypnosis before falling asleep. There is no reason why you should not be able to enter a hypnotic state.

10. *What does it feel like to be hypnotized?* The answer to this is extremely important because it may determine whether or not you can benefit from hypnosis. Most people give up hypnosis after a few sessions because they are disappointed in their reactions, believing that they are not suitable subjects. The average person has the idea that he will go through something different, new and spectacular in the hypnotic state. Often he equates being hypnotized with being anaesthetized, or being asleep, or being unconscious. When in hypnosis he finds that his mind is active; that he can hear every sound in the room; that he can resist suggestions if he so desires; that his attention keeps wandering, his thoughts racing around; that he has not fallen asleep; and that he remembers everything that has happened when he opens his eyes, he believes himself to have failed. He imagines then that he is a poor subject, and he is apt to abandon hypnotic treatments. *The experience of being hypnotized is no different from the experience of relaxing and of starting to go to sleep.* Because this experience is so familiar to you, and because you may expect something startlingly different in hypnosis, you may get discouraged when a trance is induced. Remember, you are not anaesthetized; you are not unconscious; you are not asleep. Your mind is active; your thoughts are under your control; you perceive all stimuli; and you are in complete communication with the operator. The only unique thing you may experience is a feeling of heaviness in your arms, and tingliness in your hands and fingers. If you are habitually a deep sleeper, you may doze momentarily; if you are a light sleeper, you may have a feeling you are completely awake.

11. *How deep do I have to go to get benefits from hypnosis?* If you can conceive of hypnosis as a spectrum of awareness that stretches

from waking to sleep, you will realize that some aspects are close to the waking state, and share the phenomena of waking; and some aspects are close to sleep, and participate in the phenomena of light sleep. But over the entire spectrum, suggestibility is increased; and this is what makes hypnosis potentially beneficial, provided we put the suggestibility to a constructive use. The depth of hypnosis does not always correlate with the degree of suggestibility. In other words, even if you go no deeper than the lightest stages of hypnosis and are merely mildly relaxed, you will still be able to benefit from its therapeutic effects. It so happens that with practice you should be able to go in deeper, but this really is not too important in the great majority of cases.

12. *How does hypnosis work?* The human mind is extremely suggestible and is being bombarded constantly with suggestive stimuli from the outside, and suggestive thoughts and ideas from the inside. A good deal of suffering is the consequence of "negative" thoughts and impulses invading one's mind from subconscious recesses. Unfortunately, past experiences, guilt feelings, and repudiated impulses and desires are incessantly pushing themselves into awareness, directly or in disguised forms, sabotaging one's happiness, health and efficiency. By the time one has reached adulthood, he has built up "negative" modes of thinking, feeling and acting which persist like bad habits. And like any habits they are had to break. In hypnosis, we attempt to replace these "negative" attitudes with "positive" ones. But it takes time to disintegrate old habit patterns; so do not be discouraged if there is no immediate effect. If you continue to practice the principles taught you by your therapist, you will eventually notice change. Even though there may be no apparent alterations on the surface, a restructuring is going on underneath. An analogy may make this clear. If you hold a batch of white blotters above the level of your eyes so that you see the bottom blotter, and if you dribble drops of ink onto the top blotter, you will observe nothing different for a while until sufficient ink has been poured to soak through the entire thickness. Eventually the ink will come down. During this period while nothing seemingly was happening, penetrations were occurring. Had the process been stopped before enough ink had been poured, we would be tempted to consider the process a failure. Suggestions in hypnosis are like ink poured on layers of resistance; one must keep repeating them before they come through to influence old, destructive patterns.

13. *How can I help in the treatment process?* It is important to mention to your therapist your reactions to treatment and to him,

no matter how unfounded, unfair or ridiculous these reactions may seem. Your dreams may also be important. If for any reason you believe you should interrupt therapy, mention your desire to do so to your doctor. Important clues may be derived from your reactions, dreams and resistances that will provide an understanding of your inner conflicts, and help in your treatment.

14. *Wouldn't hypnotic drugs be valuable and force me to go deeper?* Experience shows that drugs are usually not necessary. Often they complicate matters. If you should require medications, these will be employed.

15. *What about self-hynosis?* "Relaxing exercises," "self-hypnosis" and "auto-hypnosis" are interchangeable terms for a reinforcing process that may be valuable in helping your therapist help you. If this adjunct is necessary, it will be employed. The technic is simple and safe.

The actual hypnotic method I employ in short-term therapy is a simple one, and it amalgamates itself easily with other technics. It also lends itself readily to self-relaxation and self-hypnosis. The procedure essentially is contained in the following transcription which the therapist may, of course, modify, if he desires, according to the special needs of his patient.*

The patient is made comfortable, leaning his head against the back of a chair with his feet on an ottoman, or he may lay on a couch.

Four steps are employed: (1) deep breathing exercises, (2) progressive muscle relaxation, (3) visualization of a relaxed scene, and (4) counting slowly from 1 to 20. The pace of suggestions should be slow with occasional hesitations between suggestions. The following is from a recording.

"Now just settle back and shut your eyes. Breathe in deeply through your nostrils right down into the pit of your stomach. D-e-e-p-l-y, d-e-e-p-l-y, d-e-e-p-l-y; but not so deeply that you are uncomfortable. Just deeply enough so that you feel the air soaking in. (*As the patient inspires as indicated by a heaving of the chest, the operator may say "in" and with expiration "out" for several breathing cycles.*) In . . . and out. D-e-e-p-l-y, d-e-e-p-l-y. In . . . and out. And as you feel the air soaking in, you begin to feel yourself getting t-i-r-e-d and r-e-l-a-x-e-d. Very r-e-l-a-x-e-d. Even d-r-o-w-s-y, d-r-o-w-s-y and relaxed. Drowsy and relaxed.

* The technic is detailed more fully in: Wolberg, L. R.: Hypnoanalysis, 2nd ed. N. Y., Grune & Stratton, 1964. For short-term therapy the abbreviated technic described here should be ample.

"Now I want you to concentrate on the muscle groups that I point out to you. Loosen them, relax them while visualizing them. You will notice that you may be tense in certain areas and the idea is to relax yourself completely. Concentrate on your forehead. Loosen the muscles in your forehead. Now your eyes. Loosen the muscles around your eyes. Your eyelids relax. Now your face, your face relaxes. And your mouth . . . relax the muscles around your mouth, and even the inside of your mouth. Your chin; let it sag and feel heavy. And as you relax your muscles, your breathing continues r-e-g-u-l-a-r-l-y and d-e-e-p-l-y, deeply within yourself. Now your neck, your neck relaxes. Every muscle, every fiber in your neck relaxes. Your shoulders relax . . . your arms . . . your elbows . . . your forearms . . . your wrists . . . your hands . . . and your fingers relax. Your arms feel loose and limp; heavy and loose and limp. Your whole body begins to feel loose and limp. Your neck muscles relax; the front of your neck; the back muscles. Wiggle your head if necessary to get all the kinks out. Keep breathing deeply and relax. Now your chest. The front part of your chest relaxes . . . and the back part of your chest relaxes. Your abdomen . . . the pit of your stomach, that relaxes. The small of your back, loosen the muscles. Your hips . . . your thighs . . . your knees relax . . . even the muscles in your legs. Your ankles . . . your feet . . . and your toes. Your whole body feels loose and limp And when I lift your arm, it will feel very relaxed, v-e-r-y, v-e-r-y, r-e-l-a-x-e-d. Heavy and relaxed. *(The left arm may be lifted slightly and released to see if it falls without assistance. If the patient controls it, the operator may say: 'Make it loose and floppy; relax.' He may continue until the arm relaxes.)* And now as you feel the muscles relaxing, you will notice that you begin to feel heavy and relaxed and tired all over. Your body begins to feel v-e-r-y, v-e-r-y tired . . . and you are going to feel d-r-o-w-s-i-e-r, and d-r-o-w-s-i-e-r, from the top of your head right down to your toes. Every breath you take is going to soak in deeper and deeper and deeper, and you feel your body getting drowsier and drowsier.

"And now, I want you to imagine, to visualize the most relaxed and quiet and pleasant scene imaginable. Visualize a relaxed and pleasant quiet scene. Any scene that is comfortable. It can be some scene in your past, or a scene you project in the future. It can be nothing more than being at the beach watching the water break on the shore. Or a lake with a sail boat floating lazily by. Or merely looking at the blue sky with one or two billowy clouds moving slowly. Any scene that is quiet and pleasant and makes you feel drowsy. *(Some patients find it difficult to visualize a pleasant scene. Some begin to do so, but it is interrupted by unpleasant images. If the patient reports this at the end of the session, the operator may reassure him that he will be able to do this more easily soon. In the meantime he may merely visualize a blank wall or curtain, and if any unpleasant obtrusions occur to push these out of his mind.)* Drowsier and drowsier and drowsier. You are v-e-r-y weary, and every breath will send you in deeper and deeper and deeper.

As you visualize this quiet scene, I shall count from one to twenty, and when I reach the count of twenty, you will feel yourself in deep. One, deeper and deeper. Two, deeper and deeper and deeper. Three . . . drowsier and drowsier. Four, deeper and deeper. Five . . . drowsier and drowsier and drowsier. Six . . . seven, very tired, very relaxed. Eight, deeper and deeper. Nine . . . ten, drowsier and drowsier. Eleven, twelve, thirteen; deeper and deeper. D-r-o-w-s-i-e-r and d-r-o-w-s-i-e-r. Fourteen, drowsier and drowsier and drowsier. Fifteen . . . sixteen . . . seventeen, deeper and deeper. Eighteen . . . nineteen . . . and finally twenty.

I want you, for the next few minutes, to continue visualizing a quiet and wonderfully relaxed scene, and, as you do, you will get more and more and more relaxed. Your body will begin to get heavier and more relaxed, and you will get drowsier and drowsier. When I talk to you next, you'll be more deeply relaxed. (*Pause for a half minute or so before proceeding.*)

Following this I usually continue on to deepen the trance: The patient's arms are gently placed on the corresponding arms of the chair, or at his sides if he is on a couch.

"Now I'd like to have you concentrate on your left arm. I am going to stroke the arm and as I stroke it, the muscles get firm and rigid and the arm gets stiff. (*The arm is stroked from the shoulder to the finger tips while suggestions are continued.*) Every muscle, every fiber in the arm stiffens, and the arm will feel as if it is glued right down to the arm of the chair (or couch). The arm feels so s-t-i-f-f and f-i-r-m and h-e-a-v-y as if it is glued right down to the chair, and any attempts to lift it only make it feel heavier and stiffer. Heavy and stiff (*firmness in the operator's voice during these suggestions is often helpful*). Heavy and stiff, and when I t-r-y to l-i-f-t t-h-e a-r-m i-t i-s g-l-u-e-d r-i-g-h-t d-o-w-n o-n t-h-e c-h-a-i-r. (*The operator may lightly attempt to lift the arm. Generally it will be firmly fastened to the chair due to stiffness. If the patient fails to show stiffness, or if he voluntarily lifts his arm, he is willfully resisting. Only rarely will this situation be met. In the event it does occur, the therapist may simply say: 'Don't resist voluntarily; just let things happen as they will.' He can then proceed with further suggestions.*)

"Feel your eyes firmly glued together. Your eyes feel tight, tight, and when you try to lift them, they feel as if they are glued together. Tight, tight, tight.

"Now what I'd like to have you do is to picture things in your mind as I describe them, and, as you do, indicate it by lifting this finger an inch or so in the air. (*The operator touches the index finger of the patient's left hand.*) For example, imagine yourself walking outside on the street, and, when you see yourself walking on the street, indicate this by lifting up your finger. (*Patients will usually respond well to this suggestion. If they do not life the finger it means they either are resisting or find it difficult to visualize themselves walking. At any rate, the therapist encour-*

*ages the patient to try to think about seeing himself walking on the
street, and as soon as he does this to lift his finger. If he still fails to react, he may be asked to visualize himself coming into the treatment room
and looking at the therapist. If he lifts his finger at the accomplishment
of this, the previous suggestion may be given him.)*

"Visualize yourself walking into an alley-way between two buildings.
See yourself stepping into this alley-way. And you walk right into an
open courtyard. See yourself walking into this courtyard, and right in
front of you you see a tall church—the steeple, spire and bell. As soon
as you see that, indicate it to me by lifting your finger. *(When this happens, the operator may say 'Good' and proceed.)* Now watch the bell.
Now watch the bell. It will begin to move from one side to the next,
from one side to the next, and, as it does, you get the sensation of a
clanging, clanging, clanging in your ears. As soon as that happens, as
soon as you see the bell move, lift your finger. *(It is obvious that sufficient latitude in suggestions is given so that the patient will not consider as a failure his inability to hallucinate the bell ringing.)*

"Turn away from the church building now and see yourself walking
back through the courtyard into the alley. Over on the right hand side
of the alley, on the ground, you see a pail with steaming hot water. Lift
your finger when you see this.

"Now see yourself taking your right hand and waving it through the
steam. As you do this, your hand will get tingly and tender and sensitive
as if it has been soaked in steam. When you see yourself doing this,
lift your finger.

"In contrast to your sensitive right hand, your left hand is going to
get numb and insensitive. As a matter of fact, you are now going to
imagine yourself wearing a thick heavy leather glove on your left hand,
and as soon as you see yourself in your imagination wearing a thick
heavy leather glove on your left hand, indicate it by lifting your finger.
*(As soon as the patient does this, he may be shown the contrast in sensa-
tion between his right and left hands. I have prepared for this purpose
a box containing a bottle of rubbing alcohol, a hypodermic needle and
some cotton pledgets. Prior to touching the skin, I wipe the needle with
alcohol.)* Now I am going to show you the difference between the sensitive right hand and the left hand enveloped in a glove. I am going to
touch your left hand with a sterilized needle, and it will feel as if I am
touching it through a thick, heavy leather glove. You will feel touch,
but no pain; touch but no pain. *(The space on the dorsum of the left
hand between the thumb and index finger may be lifted by the operator
and wiped with alcohol. Then it is touched with the needle.)* Touch, but
no real pain. On the contrary, the other hand, the right hand, will be very
sensitive and tender and painful even to the slightest touch. *(The back
of the hand is wiped with alcohol once, then quickly pricked several
times with the needle. This exercise in most cases results in the patient's
experiencing a difference in the two hands which impresses him greatly.*

Sometimes he will imagine that the operator is deceiving him by using a sharp and a blunt needle.)

"Now relax and rest for a minute or so, going deeper, d-e-e-p-e-r, d-e-e-p-e-r, and in a minute or so I shall talk to you, and you will be more deeply relaxed. *(After a pause the therapist continues with therapeutic suggestions that are designed to the patient's needs.)* "There are four things we are going to accomplish. I call them the 4 s's: symptom relief, self-confidence, situational control and self-understanding. First, your various symptoms *(these may be enumerated)* are going to be less and less upsetting to you. You will pay less and less attention to them, because they will bother you less and less. You will find that you have a desire to overcome them more and more. As we work at your problem, you will feel that your self-confidence grows and expands. You will feel more assertive and stronger. You will be able to handle yourself better in any situations that come along particularly those that tend to upset you *(these may be enumerated)*. Finally, and most importantly, your understanding of yourself will improve. You will understand better and better what is behind your trouble, how it started and why your symptoms developed. Whenever you feel your symptoms coming on, you will be able to understand what is bringing them about, and you will be able to do something constructive about this, more and more easily. You will continue working on what is behind your problem. *(After therapeutic suggestions have been given, the patient may be aroused.)* I shall now count slowly from 1 to 5. At the count of 5, lift your eyes. O-n-e . . . t-w-o . . . you are coming out of it . . . t-h-r-e-e . . . more and more awake . . . f-o-u-r . . . f-i-v-e. Lift your eyes and feel relaxed."

The patient will, after coming out of hypnosis, generally voice doubts that he has been hypnotized, and the therapist may then repeat pertinent aspects from item ten in the "Questions You May Have About Hypnosis" above. The patient will, nevertheless, usually have been impressed with his reactions. He may ask if the therapist really touched his left hand with a needle. The therapist may then tell the patient that he did and that the patient experienced hypnotic anesthesia. He may then be told that he will probably be able to go in deeper with practice.

The following questions are commonly asked and answers to them may be along indicated lines:

I do not believe I was hypnotized because my mind was wandering. I could hear everything you said. "Hypnosis is no bludgeon that knocks a person out. It would be totally without value if the subject couldn't hear what was said. You are supposed to be aware of everything, even hypersensitive to stimuli. You are in contact with me at all times. Your mind, if you go in deeper, will bounce around from one thought to another."

Shouldn't I be deeper? "It is true that in the deepest states of hypnosis some things are not remembered, but deep states of hypnosis, while useful for stage tricks and the like, are not necessary in most forms of therapeutic hypnosis. As a matter of fact in your particular case a light form of hypnosis may be advantageous. If a deeper form is necessary, we will attempt to achieve it by training you to enter the deeper states in later sessions. It takes time for a person to learn how to enter into a deep trance, and we will go as deep as necessary with your cooperation."

I could have opened my eyes, if I wanted to. "Of course you could because you are not out of control. But the fact is that you didn't want to open them."

I am afraid hypnosis will not help me because I wasn't able to do everything you suggested. "In the next few sessions I am going to suggest that you observe a number of different kinds of phenomena. You will be able to observe some, but not all of them. It is not necessary for you to be able to observe everything that I bring to your attention. All hypnotized people are capable of doing certain things in the trance and not others. What you have experienced is perfectly normal."

I do not believe I was hypnotized because I was in full control at all times and could have resisted suggestions. "Hypnosis is a cooperative enterprise and I have no desire for you to lose control of yourself. Indeed, I am aiming to give you better control of yourself and your functions, so you will get stronger. If you have a desire to resist suggestions, there are reasons for this resistance, and I shall try to help you to understand them. In the next few sessions you will develop greater confidence in your ability to enjoy the experience of hypnosis which will be of value to you in overcoming your problems."

When you tell me to do things should I do them voluntarily? "It is not necessary for you to do things deliberately. If you make your mind passive, things will happen in the natural course of events. Just relax and enjoy the experience of watching how things come about as the result of suggestion. It is not necessary to try too hard."

The patient should, following clarification of his doubts, be questioned as to how he felt emotionally, and he may be asked what went through his mind both as he started entering the hypnotic state and while he was in hypnosis. Notes may be made of the patient's experiences which can be mentioned in the course of subsequent inductions. Each patient reacts to hypnosis in his own unique way, and when he is presented with a picture of his experiences in his own terms, this facilitates the induction process.

SELF-HYPNOSIS

In short-term therapy self-hypnosis may be a valuable technic to help alleviate tension, to promote symptom relief and even to help foster a better understanding of inner conflicts. The technic is simple, harmless and non-habituating, contrary to what one may imagine.

If self-hypnosis is to be employed, I suggest to the patient during hypnosis that he will be able to relax himself through suggestions. I usually give the patient the following mimeographed sheet which I ask him to study and to use as a guide.

Relaxing Exercises

These exercises may be performed the first thing in the morning before getting out of bed. They may be repeated during the day if possible. They should always be done at night prior to retiring; relaxing suggestions will eventually merge into sleep. The total time for each session should be at least twenty minutes.

After shutting your eyes, proceed with the following steps:

1. Deep slow breathing for about ten breaths.
2. Progressive muscle relaxation from forehead, face, neck, to finger tips; from chest to toes, visualizing and purposefully loosening each muscle group.
3. Visualizing a wonderfully relaxed scene or simply a blank white wall.
4. Slow counting to self from 1 to 20 while visualizing the relaxed scene (or white wall).
5. Relaxing or sleeping from one to two minutes during which visualization of the relaxed scene continues.
6. Make the following suggestions to yourself (using the word "you").
   a. *Symptom relief* (disturbing symptoms, like tension, etc. will get less and less upsetting).
   b. *Self-confidence* (self-assuredness will grow).
   c. *Situational control* (visualize impending difficult situations and successful mastery of them).
   d. *Self-understanding* (make connections if possible between flare-ups of symptoms and precipitating events and inner conflicts).
7. Relax or sleep for several more minutes.
8. During the daytime arouse yourself by counting from one to five.

At night do not arouse yourself; continue relaxing until sleep supervenes.

If sleep begins developing during the 4th step before the count comes to an end, interrupt counting and proceed immediately to suggestions (6th step above). Then continue with count and go as deeply as you wish. A racing of the mind and a tendency to distraction are normal. When this occurs, force your attention back to the exercises.

Remember, you will not really be asleep during these exercises. You will be aware of your thoughts and of stimuli on the outside. If, for any reason, before you finish you want to bring yourself out of the relaxed state, tell yourself that at the count of five you will be out of it. Count from 1 to 5 and say to yourself: "Be wide awake now, open your eyes." If negative thoughts crop up, by-pass them, and continue with the steps outlined above. *Results are rarely immediate.* It takes a while to neutralize negative suggestions you have been giving yourself all your life. So be patient. Persistence is the keynote to success.

Typical questions posed by patients practicing self-hypnosis are these, the answers to which are indicated:

Q. Can I lie in any position when I do the exercises?

A. Yes, you can assume any position that makes you most comfortable.

Q. I don't realize it, but I find thoughts coming into my mind that have nothing to do with what I am supposed to think.

A. This is quite normal. As you get more deeply relaxed, a whole chain of thoughts are likely to crowd in. Try to notice the kinds of thoughts they are and jot them down so we can discuss them.

Q. I start counting to 20, but before I get to 11 my mind wanders off the count.

A. If this happens consistently, give yourself the therapeutic suggestions at the count of 9 or so.

Q. I start relaxing, and, before I get to the count, I am asleep.

A. You are just too good a subject. Just watch next time for the point in the routine where you fall asleep, and then give yourself the therapeutic suggestions before you reach that point, continuing on with the routine after the suggestions. If you fall asleep then, it doesn't matter.

Q. I am left with a headachey feeling. I feel a little woozy.

A. This comes when a good subject comes out of it too fast. Slow down the count at the end, telling yourself that when you come out of it, your mind will be clear, with no headaches. Also try counting to 10 instead of to 5.

Q. I went deep, but my mind would blank for ten minutes and I wasn't really asleep.

A. This is not unusual in good subjects. Continue practicing the routine.

Q. What do I do if I am interrupted? Do I come out of it, and then go through the whole thing from the beginning, or do I take off from where I was interrupted?

A. It is best to start all over again.

Q. The count is annoying to me, I want to get there faster.

A. When you get to the count, tell yourself that at five you will be sufficiently relaxed to absorb suggestions. If you are, you needn't count further.

Q. Can I set the alarm say in a half hour, since I fall asleep?

A. Yes.

Q. I just don't seem to find the time to practice.

A. This is a form of resistance; your inner saboteurs are fighting back. You certainly can practice just before going to bed, and perhaps in the morning before you get up.

Q. I don't feel physically relaxed enough.

A. This may mean that you are not deep enough. Ask yourself if you have any resistances to practicing. If so, see if you can understand them. If not, take a longer time practicing, trying it exclusively at night before you go to bed.

Q. Do I touch the various parts of the body in muscle relaxation?

A. No, just visualize them.

Q. I find it difficult to visualize any kind of relaxed scene, nothing comes to my mind.

A. Practice looking at a blue sky in your imagination, with one or two billowy clouds floating lazily by. Or simply picture a blank white wall.

Q. When I picture a relaxed scene, awful thoughts come into my mind. (*This is an obsessional patient with obsessive thoughts as a symptom.*)

A. Keep pushing them away and keep on with the routine. Everytime a bad thought comes in, tell yourself to stop, and then try to substitute another, more pleasant thought.

Q. I find it difficult to word the suggestions correctly.

A. Write them out in advance and memorize them. Then you can repeat them while relaxed.

Q. When I attempt self-hypnosis, any outside influence is overpowering, like a door slamming.

A. This is common in hypnosis since perceptions may be heightened. Among your therapeutic suggestions include desensitizing yourself to noises.

Q. I don't go deep enough.

A. Even in light relaxation, suggestions can be effective.

Q. I give myself suggestions, but I feel no effect.

A. A lifetime of problems will not yield in a few weeks. Practice must be constant and consistent. You may not see the effects on the surface, but underneath changes are occurring. If you hit a rock ninety-nine times, nothing may show on the surface. The hundredth time it may crack into little pieces. So keep on practicing.

One may anticipate that the patient will try to incorporate self-hypnosis into his neurotic design in a subversive attempt to defeat himself. He may spontaneously get inklings of his destructive motifs or the therapist may sense an impending debacle from his verbalizations. Triumph over these trends is won by dealing with them actively as resistances.

EFFECTS OF HYPNOSIS ON THERAPEUTIC PROCESS

1. *Effect on rapport.* Perhaps the chief influence of hypnosis is the effect it has on the relationship with the therapist. Reproduced for the average patient in the trance is the protective child-parent alliance, where needs are gratified and fears become allayed. The sicker the patient the more he reaches for these comforting bounties. This contingency is, of course, an aspect of every helping process; but whereas in the usual interviewing situation considerable time may be needed to register change in the relationship, in hypnosis one may observe a transformation almost immediately. Quickly the patient will respond with hope, trust and a quieting of inner tension. In this soil plantings of therapy can take root, greatly advantageous in short-term therapy. Expanded also are the placebo effect and emotional catharsis about which more will be said later. The influence on rapport is particularly helpful in mistrustful, hopeless or detached patients who may hold themselves aloof, refusing to enter into a working relationship except perhaps after many months of testing of the therapist, an extravagance one cannot provide in short-term treatment.

2. *Effect on suggestibility.* Suggestion permeates all therapies no matter how indirective their intent. Hypnosis expands the sug-

gestive reservoir in each patient, with an exaggerated susceptibility to those suggestions that are acceptable. The rapport between patient and therapist reinforces the authoritative position of the therapist and accents the power of therapeutic suggestions. These may be in the interest of providing for the patient supportive aid, helping to ameliorate or remove symptoms, or to substitute for them less disabling ones. The patient may be guided to adjust himself more adaptively to his life situation; he may be reassured regarding needless fears and guilt feelings; he may be persuaded to abandon destructive habits, attitudes and modes of thinking; and he may be encouraged to develop more assertiveness and self-confidence. By these measures he may rapidly be brought to an emotional equilibrium, releasing spontaneous impulses toward a more healthy emotional adjustment. Among the conditions which seem favorably influenced by this use of hypnosis are anxiety and tension states, certain hysterical conversion symptoms, some obsessive-compulsive reactions, and habit disorders, like insomnia, enuresis, over-eating, nail biting and smoking.

3. *Effect on emotional catharsis.* The opening up of pockets of guilt, fear and conflict are important in psychotherapy. Hypnosis may expedite this process remarkably. During induction accumulated charges of emotion often liberate themselves impulsively, or upon the exploration of sensitive areas. The ability of the patient to tolerate explosive feelings during hypnosis appears to be greater than in the waking state, and more fluid expressions of emotion may continue post-hypnotically.

4. *Effect on verbalization.* Where the patient exhibits blocks in his capacity to communicate, hypnosis may be notably effective in breaking through this obstruction. The resolution of his resistance during the trance may persist in the waking state.

5. *Effect on motivation.* In instances of defective motivation, particularly where the patient is dubious about the results of psychotherapy and has little or no desire for it, the induction of hypnosis may foster an alleviation of tension and convince the patient that he can derive something meaningful from his visits to the therapist. In cases where the sole purpose for treatment is to relieve symptoms and emotional suffering, the soothing impact of hypnosis may promote a climate for insight approaches which would have been resisted if originally attempted.

6. *Effect on exploratory technics.* By alleviating excessive anxiety which blunts the desire to explore its sources hypnosis may help

insight technics. The influence of hypnosis on repressive processes, facilitating the return to awareness of repudiated psychic aspects, is of great benefit in dealing with unconscious conflict. Hypnosis is particularly valuable in handling resistance, both by detecting it in early stages and by promoting its resolution. In the trance state, dreams may be stimulated, revived and explored, and memories that have been shunted from consciousness may sometimes be restored. In employing hypnoanalytic technics, such as regression, one may remove amnesia in stress reactions, and lift repressions in conversion and dissociative reactions.

7. *Effect on transference.* Hypnosis catalyzes transference, which, contrary to what may be imagined, does not need to get out of hand. It may be explored if this seems essential. It may be encouraged by pointed suggestions or it may be resolved rapidly by reassurance, interpretation and focusing on reality. A transference neurosis is usually avoided in short-term therapy, and, if it threatens to erupt, and is being sponsored by hypnosis, further hypnotic inductions should be avoided.

8. *Effect on the working-through process.* Hypnosis and self-hypnosis are of importance in enabling the patient to convert his insight into action, and in helping him to master his anxieties that shadow the reconditioning of his behavior. Since in short-term therapy the working-through of established patterns cannot occur within the limited span of formal treatment, the patient will have to continue the self-exploratory and working-through phases on his own. Self-hypnosis can be beneficial here. Suggestions in self-hypnosis may also consolidate essential shifts in philosophical outlook toward a recasting of values.

9. *Effect on termination.* Self-hypnosis, by transferring responsibility to the patient, may be fruitful in termination. The patient is provided with a means by which he may actively participate in perpetuating and extending the gains he has achieved in therapy. There is no reason to fear habituation to and dependency on self-hypnosis; the patient can easily halt it whenever he feels he has achieved maximal benefits.

It goes without saying that hypnosis must be intelligently used within the context of a comprehensive treatment plan and with due regard for its indications and limitations. Applied indiscriminately, hypnosis not only serves no therapeutic purpose, but its failures tend to discredit it as a scientific procedure and to relegate it to a position of undeserved oblivion.

QUESTIONS AND ANSWERS

Question: I am interested in how hypnosis can help the dream process; can you say more about this?

Dr. Wolberg: Hypnosis may stimulate dream remembering in patients who claim they do not dream, or in those who know they dream, but forget their dreams. Suggestions are given the patient that he will be able to remember his dreams, or that he will find himself dreaming during self-hypnosis and recall this when he is awake. A patient came to me for hypnosis to help him recover a dream that kept eluding him, but which he felt was very significant. It had first appeared, he claimed, years ago during his psychoanalysis, but he had forgoten it. Try as hard as he could, he was not able to bring it back. Years had gone by and he had stopped his analysis, but periodically he had the impression that the dream returned, only to vanish with daylight. The situation intrigued me enough to consent to utilize hypnosis, during which I told him that if he had a spontaneous dream, he would remember it. On awakening he revealed that a most remarkable thing had happened to him while he was relaxing. The forgotten dream had come back to him in detail. It was the memory of an actual experience that had occurred when he was four which involved a good deal of sexual content. The dream relieved the patient tremendously and it provided a starting point for more therapeutic work. Where dreams do not readily occur, hypnosis may help stimulate them. In instances where insights are fragmented, it may serve to weld unrelated segments together into a meaningful fabric.

Question: Would you say the hypnotic relationship is the key factor in producing the hypnotic effects?

Dr. Wolberg: Yes. In hypnosis the person often feels soothed due to the relationship that is set up. He feels a flow, a bond between himself and the hypnotist which comforts him and, in this protective milieu, he is able to face up to certain experiences and feelings from which he fled before. This situation prevails, of course, in any kind of psychotherapy, but it takes a great deal longer to develop this bond in the usual psychotherapeutic relationship. It is often established immediately with hypnosis. In many instances the very induction of hypnosis will release a flood of emotional feelings with ensuing relief. This has temporary therapeutic value in reducing his tension. It does not cure because the basis for generation of burdensome emotions is still there. Nevertheless, it helps the patient to get things off his chest, to develop and consolidate a relationship with the therapist. The fact that he begins to reach into deeper layers of feeling, helps liberate repressed ideas and memories, sometimes quite spontaneously.

Question: Why did Freud give up hypnosis?

Dr. Wolberg: Freud turned away from hypnosis for a number of reasons. First, he believed not enough people could be deeply hypnotized to recover significant amnesic data. Second, he minimized the permanence of suggestions given the patient by the therapist, and he presented material to indicate that when a patient lost confidence in the therapist his symptoms returned. Third, he believed that hypnosis by-passed resistances which remained intact and continued to sponsor problems. Actually, when we examine his writings we see that what Freud was inveighing against was not hypnosis as a phenomenon, but the suggestive use to which it was being employed. You must remember that hypnosis in Freud's time was restricted to the search for traumatic memories. Since the memories Freud considered significant could not be brought back, or, if memories did occur, these were often found to be fictions, Freud assumed hypnosis was no good. Actually, it merely had failed in the fishing expedition for memories. We do not employ hypnosis in this way any longer. Freud himself predicted that hypnosis would eventually return as a respectable form of treatment, particularly as a means of shortening treatment methods.

Question: What about the contention of many analysts that hypnosis is only effective as long as the dependent relationship between the therapist and the patient continues, and that as soon this relationship is over the patient relapses?

Dr. Wolberg: This is the original idea Freud voiced in the early nineteen hundreds. He said that as long as a positive relationship exists, a patient retains his gains; the moment a negative element enters, gains are lost. Now obviously, if gains are exclusively predicated on the basis of positive transference, the moment this ends and negative transference enters, the improvement will cease. But not all gains in hypnosis are due to positive transference, that is if the therapist has been doing his job. The basis for Freud's early premise does not take into account the broad extensions of therapeutic hynosis to which we are now dedicated.

Question: Why do some psychiatrists continue to say that when you remove a disturbing symptom any underlying anxiety will come out, or some other symptom will arise to take its place?

Dr. Wolberg: Again they are repeating folklore. A hypnotist is not so powerful an agency that he can eliminate symptoms by forceful suggestions if these symptoms are important in the patient's psychic economy. And if he is fortunate enough to help the patient overcome a symptom, the patient may never restore it; in fact the elimination of his symptom often promotes a better general adjustment. The exceptions are the removal of certain symptoms by force in some borderline patients who happen to be peculiarly susceptible to the hypnotist. This is a rare occurrence and when it happens it is a manifestation of poor technic.

Question: Some practitioners suggest that schizophrenics or borderline psychotics should never be hypnotized. I'm wondering if in your experience you have some ideas about contraindications for hypnosis.

Dr. Wolberg: Some therapists are unable to treat schizophrenic patients, with or without hypnosis. There are some who are not able to treat drug addicts. There are some who find that they cannot get along with neurotic children, or with psychopaths, or with alcoholics, or with obsessive-compulsives, or with homosexuals. Difficulties will be rampant where the therapist does not like the patient or feels uncomfortable with him. All of us have our likes and dislikes, our personal prejudices, and our particular areas of interest. We find that we can work better with some patients and not so well with other patients. I know some therapists who do remarkably well with schizophrenics, and they are able to work on various levels with them, even analytic. Why? Because they like their patients and the patients know it. They want to help their patients. Patients perceive this and can make a better relationship with such empathic therapists. Under such conditions one can work with schizophrenics, borderline cases, obsessive-compulsives, homosexuals and so on, on hypnotic or non-hypnotic levels. I personally treat psychotics, psychopaths, borderline patients and homosexuals, even paranoids, with hypnosis and I consider my results to be good. Now if a patient feels a therapist does not like him or is not too sympathetic, he will interpret hypnosis as an attack on him, and he is apt to blow up. So the inability to treat certain patients with hypnosis has nothing to do with the fact that they fit into designated diagnostic categories. Of course, if any therapist uses hypnosis with hostile intent, or if he humiliates or frightens a patient with it, the latter will get upset; a patient with a weak ego may respond with disintegrative tendencies. I have found that even though unconscious conflicts may come up in hypnosis as repression is released, and even if the patient gets momentarily disturbed, if I have a good relationship with him, he can pull himself together easily. His calm is restored with reassurance or with suggestions to repress and to forget. The exposure he

has experienced to traumatic material tends to strengthen him ultimately. One can observe how he will go back to this material voluntarily, as if he wants to resolve it. Dreams also show a progressive
mastery in coping mechanisms.

Question: Doesn't hypnosis upset paranoid patients and really
make realistic their idea that they are being influenced?

Dr. Wolberg: Yes, if the therapist does not have the proper relationship with them. Paranoids are difficult, but one may work with
them if one has their confidence. I have treated a number of paranoid patients with hypnosis, and several whose chief delusion was
that somebody was trying to hypnotize them. I cannot say that my
results were brilliant, but utilizing hypnosis to get them to relax,
and to want to take phenothiazines, has benefitted them above and
beyond the drug effect.

Question: Do you use hypnosis in alcoholics?

Dr. Wolberg: Yes, but hypnosis alone is not particularly successful with alcoholics. That does not mean it should not be used.
There are some psychiatrists who claim that it constitutes a prime
source of help. I find that antabuse and Alcoholics Anonymous are
the prime agencies. On top of this, psychotherapy with or without
hypnosis may be effective.

Question: Have you had any success with sexual difficulties in a
short-term therapeutic approach?

Dr. Wolberg: Sexual difficulties, interestingly, for some reason,
seem to clear up rapidly in hypnotherapy. At least they do for me.
Impotence responds more easily than frigidity. I teach self-hypnosis
to patients with sexual disorders. In the case of impotence, there is
generally involved a lowered confidence in oneself and an equation
of low self-worth with poor performance. In any kind of biological
function, whether this involves sleeping, eating or sexuality, utilizing it for any purpose other than for its biological aim is bound to
bring trouble; particularly if the person is trying to prove himself
through the exercise of his function. I try to get my patients to accept the fact that they must approach sexuality for whatever pleasures they can derive from it, not caring whether they succeed or
fail. I try to get them to see the rationale of resuming a sexual relationship, not caring whether they succeed or fail. I encourage them
to employ self-hypnosis to recondition themselves in accepting a
different attitude toward sex. I may want to talk to the wives or
husbands to enlist their cooperation, and to get details of other
problems in their relationships. One case I treated not long ago was
a man who had been impotent for fifteen years. It started off in the

usual way. He was tired one evening and his wife was irritated at him when he approached her sexually. She used this opportunity to goad him into trying to function "like a real man." When he was unable to retain an erection she reviled him for his inability to perform. This reinforced his feelings of ineffectuality; he then began to approach sex with anxiety, wondering whether it would work or not. His wife did not help matters any with her depreciatory attitudes. In desperation, he tried other women, but his anxiety was too strong to enable him to function. Finally, he gave up sex completely, but years later, on reading an article on hypnosis, he decided to explore its possibilities. We had eight sessions during which I taught him self-hypnosis, enjoining him to practice daily and warning him that it might require a good deal of time before results registered themselves in a better performance. He required almost three months of constant work on himself to restore his potency. It is important, therefore, to encourage patients not to give up if results are not immediate.

Question: Have you used hypnosis on adolescent delinquent type boys?

Dr. Wolberg: Yes. I have employed it with adolescent delinquents and they were intrigued with it. They usually make excellent subjects, since the delinquent is looking for a powerful authority figure. He wants to identify with somebody who is stronger than himself whose disciplines and injunctions he cannot challenge. Hypnosis creates the impression of this powerful authority. Of course, one should not trust this illusion, nor relax with the patient's temporary improvement. He will challenge the hypnotic authority after a while. But, nevertheless, hypnosis is a way of establishing a relationship with a delinquent or psychopath that holds him in position for therapeutic work.

Question: How do you account for the fact that a patient may be given a suggestion in hypnosis and doesn't follow it until years later?

Dr. Wolberg: I believe such a patient really did not brush off the suggestion entirely. It may have been too much for him; or it may not have had any particular meaning for him at the time. A suggestion given a person prematurely is often repudiated by him. Years later he may come around to it, having worked it through the layers of his defenses. He gradually suspects that the suggestion may have a validity for him. Then he tests it and finds that it does have a validity. Of course, certain suggestions and interpretations can be wrong; then they never have too much meaning for the patient.

Question: Isn't this why some psychiatrists say that their apparent immediate failures become delayed successes?

Dr. Wolberg: Probably, but they must be better than I am, because some of my immediate failures continue to be such.

Question: Why do so many psychiatrists resent hypnosis? I mean, even the word seems like a red flag.

Dr. Wolberg: There are a great many reasons for this. A good deal of the prejudice is traditional. To some, the word "hypnosis," itself, has meanings equated with mandrake root, snake oil or blood-letting. Because Freud abandoned it originally—he never really considered it useless—some psychiatrists, for whom God is a secondary divinity, carry on the fight. Hypnosis has also a Svengali-like significance to many therapists. In therapy you are supposed to have a cooperative relationship, not a master-slave relationship which weakens the mind of the subject and makes him dependent. Now, of course, this is all nonsense, but it is surprising how firmly some psychiatrists cling to these false convictions. There are psychiatrists who try hypnosis and are unable to get results with it simply because personality-wise they are not suited for this technic. Others use it over-enthusiastically expecting that it will perform miracles, and then turn against it when it fails to come up to their expectations. Some psychiatrists are afraid to experiment with hypnosis, because their tutelary divinities frown on it or insist they must be neurotically driven to want to employ it. The unfortunate thing is that professionals most hostile to hypnosis pose as authorities and do extensive propagandizing against hypnosis verbally or in writing. If they happen to hold prestige positions, the damage they do is great. You actually come across psychiatrists who have never hypnotized a single patient, and yet write papers on its bad effects.

Question: Since the hypnotic state is not a loss of consciousness, but rather a heightened state of consciousness, in view of this, I wonder if you would comment on the possibility of developing insight with or through hypnosis.

Dr. Wolberg: Let us say that hypnosis is altered consciousness, selectively heightened in certain instances and selectively lowered in others. If you focus a patient's attention on specific aspects of his experience in hypnosis, he will get a heightened awareness of some of its elements. He may be able to enlarge on things he was not able to talk about before and this heightened awareness may persist in the waking state. One may be able to get a person to dream which may increase his insights. One may be able to get him to perceive himself in certain roles with people, and to be able to work out certain kinds of emotional responses while he is in hypnosis that he couldn't understand before.

Question: Shouldn't hypnosis, then, be used in all cases?

Dr. Wolberg: Hypnosis may expedite the learning process. But one does not have to use hypnosis for this. Most people are able to work on their problems without hypnosis. It should be used for special reasons and only as part of an integrated treatment program.

Question: Wouldn't you say that hypnosis almost has an indication for accelerating the transference neurosis?

Dr. Wolberg: Hypnosis can accelerate a transference neurosis. But, if this is not desirable, one can try to prevent it from coming up, or from getting out of hand. A patient may begin to experience certain transferential feelings during hypnosis and afterwards. One may negate this by adopting a casual everyday attitude toward the patient, by minimizing and not talking about depth material, and by keeping verbalizations on a realistic level. In short-term therapy we would want to keep a transference neurosis down in contrast to prolonged therapy where the analytically trained therapist may want to encourage it.

Question: Will hypnosis remove resistance?

Dr. Wolberg: Yes, in some cases it can. As you know, resistance reflects a reluctance on the part of the individual to relinquish primary or secondary gains of his neurosis, inducing him to cling stubbornly to difficulties he has, even though they foster maladjustment. He may find more security in his neurotic tendencies than he does in normal values, and he will be confronted with anxiety whenever he tries to give up some of his neurotic problems even though these are arduous to sustain. Consequently, in working therapeutically with any patient, we may expect that he will manifest resistance to change in some form. And this includes therapy with hypnosis. His resistance may even take the form of his no longer being hypnotizable.

Question: If hypnosis is a regressive manifestation, shouldn't a completely psychoanalyzed individual lose his ability to be hypnotized?

Dr. Wolberg: Since there is no such thing as a completely psychoanalyzed person, the question answers itself. But even assuming that we could find a monster of complete normality, I am sure he would be able to be hypnotized. I would consider this ability an inborn characteristic like sleep.

Question: Are there any EEG changes during the trance?

Dr. Wolberg: Changes have been reported. As one goes into a trance, he proceeds through a continuum from the waking to the sleep state, with various physiological changes throughout the body, including the brain, corresponding to shifting levels of awareness, from waking to sleep. As the trance gets deeper and is almost to a point of sleep, one will get EEG changes that are characteristic of the sleep state. These shift as the level of awareness lightens and moves towards the waking state, the waves thereupon resembling those in consciousness.

Question: There is very little work reported with children. Can hypnosis be used in psychoneurosis of children?

Dr. Wolberg: One can utilize hypnosis with children and sometimes very effectively. It depends upon whether one knows how to work with children. Generally, it is mostly used in emergencies. For instance, a child of three was sent to me because he was virtually starving to death. He gagged with food until his diet became completely liquid, which he often would regurgitate to the distress of his mother. I consented to use hypnosis and, following the consultation during which I induced a trance, I never again saw the patient. Because I was so deeply involved with so many other matters at the time, I never followed the case up, assuming that the parents had decided against treatment. Five years later, the pediatrician who had referred the patient telephoned me and said, "Since you did such a wonderful job with that child who gagged, maybe you can help another one of my patients." I vaguely remembered the old referral. Having the name and address of the patient's mother, I wrote her inquiring about what had happened. Her written reply was accompanied by a photograph of a plump little boy of eight. In the letter she revealed that when her son came out of my office into the waiting room, he had asked his mother for a potato, the first time he had asked for such a dish. And he had been eating potatoes since. "And, doctor," she continued, "you do not know this, but while you were in your office with my son, I walked over to your door and put my ear to it to listen to what was going on. I heard you say, 'You will want to eat, you will have a strong desire to eat because you want to, not because anybody else wants you to. And, doctor, *I* gained twenty-four pounds." So you see, suggestions can be effective even through a closed door.

X

A Clinical Psychologist Looks at Short-Term Therapy

================ MOLLY HARROWER, PH.D.

(Editor's Note: Dr. Harrower describes a research project in which she has been engaged during the past fifteen years, in which she tested, with various psychological instruments, 2,131 patients referred by 276 therapists prior to treatment. A follow-up study was done to determine how the pre-test profile related to the outcome of therapy, long-term and short-term. In general, the greater the psychological endowment as revealed by projective tests the fewer the failures reported by the therapists. The longer the treatment process the more satisfaction most of the therapists in this survey expressed with results; utilizing present-day methods of therapy, "disturbed" patients proved to be relatively unsuited for brief approaches. Judgments of what has been done for a patient on a short-term basis must, of course, consider the fact that the effects of brief therapy may not be fully felt until sufficient time outside of therapy has occurred for proper "working-through." This is indicated by Dr. Harrower's report that at the time of termination no improvement may be detectable by projective tests. However, testing ten years subsequent to the original re-testing has shown marked improvement and suggests that there is a factor that is operative over the therapeutically empty time interval. An interesting short-term therapeutic use of psychological tests is described.)

THE WELL-TRAINED CLINICAL PSYCHOLOGIST traditionally wears three hats, or can offer his services to the public or his colleagues in the mental health field in three distinct areas. He is a psychodiagnostician, a research worker and a psychotherapist.

The first named activity—psychodiagnosis—may be considered his unique province. There is no overlap in this with other professions. The research orientation, on the other hand, derives from his basic training as a psychologist, rather than a *clinical psychologist*, and insofar as he tackles clinical problems, experimentally, he does so by virtue of a training in psychology as a science. Finally, his activities as a therapist are, of course, by no means unique. He is, as a matter of fact, a relative newcomer as an active participant in the psychotherapeutic field.

When we ask, therefore, what the psychologist has to contribute to the all-important topic of short-term therapy, our first question has to be "Which hat is he wearing?" Shall he be asked to consider short-term therapy from the point of view of the psychodiagnostician, the research worker or the practicing psychotherapist? We might also ask can these approaches be combined; does a psychologist have something unique to offer, by virtue of his tri-partite training, to this important problem?

I shall concern myself today with three questions: (1) Have any psychodiagnostic, or psychological types, been shown to correlate with success or failure in a patient's response to short-term therapy? (2) Are there any methods of short-term therapy which depend specifically on psychological techniques? (3) Have any surveys been made which threw light on the extent to which brief therapeutic methods of the present day are considered satisfactory by those who use them?

I will start with the description of one such survey, in which I have been actively engaged for many years. In describing this, I shall be wearing my psychodiagnostic and my research hat, one on top of the other, and discussing my questions Nos. 1 and 3. (Harrower, 1965)

In the course of fifteen years in practice as a psychodiagnostician, 2,131 patients were referred to me for psychodiagnostic evaluation, prior to entering into some form of psychotherapeutic endeavor, be it long-term or short-term therapy. Two hundred and seventy-six therapists, utilizing various methods, and trained in various ways, were the referrants. Five years ago I started on an ambitious follow-up program to attempt to discover what had happened to these patients. I was interested in knowing how the pre-therapy test profile related to the outcome of therapy as judged by the therapist. I was interested in knowing to what extent the patient, reported as improved by his therapist, would indicate that improvement, if retested psychodiagnostically. I was interested, among many other things, in discovering how many patients had actually been treated by full-term analysis, psychotherapy, counseling or various forms of short-term treatment.

I do not need to go into the details of some of the initial stages of this research. Suffice it to say, questionnaires were sent out concerning 1,600 patients to approximately 200 of the 276 therapists. After a period of three years, 1,493 questionnaires had been returned, a startlingly high percentage.

From this group, 622 case records (a battery of six projective tests) were selected for intensive study on the basis of the fact that the information given by the therapist in these cases was sufficiently detailed and indicated that the patient had been followed for at least four years subsequent to termination of treatment.

The questionnaire for each patient dealt with the following questions: How long has this patient been in treatment? What type of therapy was employed? On a four-point scale, would the patient be rated as having shown "Good Improvement," "Moderate Improvement," "Slight Improvement" or "No Improvement" at all? Half a page was left for additional material concerning the patient's progress, to be supplied by the therapist.

Before turning to the results of this survey, it is necessary for me to confront you with a major problem that faced the psychologist as a psychodiagnostician in this particular investigation. I mentioned earlier that a reasonable type of question to ask, and a profitable question to have answered, would be: Are there any psychological types, any special kind of test profiles which have been associated with the patient having responded favorably or noticeably unfavorably to short-term therapy? A somewhat startling admission has to be made at this point that there are no, or let me say prior to this investigation, there were no well-documented psychological types, based exclusively on the performance on the projective tests. Let me restate this to make the omission stand out more clearly. For many years, psychologists have been able to speak of different levels of intellectual achievement. There are, broadly speaking, groups or types of intellectual performance: the "Very Superior," "Superior," "High Average," "Average," "Below Average," and so on, which have been standardized on the Bellevue-Wechsler Scale. But there never have been devised comparable standardized measurement for the tests such as the Rorschach, the Szondi, the Figure Drawing, the Sentence Completion, and the Thematic Apperception Test.

Before any meaningful correlations could be sought between test findings and results of psychotherapy, long-term or brief, some standardized psychological or projective categories had to be determined.

To this end, the 622 records were studied and, again, to cut a long story short, there finally emerged two scales of what we may call non-intellectual or personality endowment, as reflected by scores on a battery of five projective techniques. One of these scales, which we have called the "Homogeneous Scale," showed individuals whose performance on the five tests were approximately equal.

They could have excellent performance on *all* tests or, conversely, (at the bottom of the seven-point scale) extremely poor performances on *all* tests. But such persons appeared to function homogeneously, and one level of performance could be utilized to describe the totality of their tests.

Such a classification took care of 358 test records, but there remained 264 which somehow could not be fitted into the scale. Finally, a second scale, which reflected the *inhomogeneity,* or the *heterogeneity,* of the individual's test performance was formed. Here, two factors were combined; *positive assets,* running side by side with varying degrees of disorganizing or disruptive and frankly *pathological material.* This scale again ran the gamut from the "Gifted" individual with one area of minor problems, to the "Very Disturbed" individual whose pathology had, so to speak, eaten up or colored the entire psychological output.

It is not possible here to give examples for each point on our scale, but we may contrast the "Very Superior" group, the top end of the Homogeneous Scale, with the "Impoverished" group, the lowest rung of this ladder.

It will be seen that when we are dealing with the "Very Superior" group of Personality or Projective endowment, we find an extremely rich Rorschach record, many responses, many good M and Color Responses, virtual absence of F– and a wide range of content. We find artistic Drawings, a Szondi showing no undue loading, TAT stories that are full without overinvolvement of the individual in his productions (see Fig. 1).

Conversely, at the end of this Scale, the "Impoverished" individual has a Rorschach record with fewer than ten responses, a meager range of psychic reactivity, pathetic little Drawings, TAT stories which are shallow or evasive (see Fig. 2).

Now that we are, as psychodiagnosticians, equipped with some measurable categories, so that we do not need to rely on psychiatric pigeon-holing in the description of our test data, we may go back again to the results of the questionnaire. Six hundred and twenty-two cases were rated by their therapists in the following way: 134 were described as showing "Good Results;" 212—"Moderate Improvement;" 129—"Slight Improvement;" 147—"No Improvement" at all.

And what relationship did our descriptive categories bear to the outcome of therapy? A significant one. Namely, the greater the psychological endowment, that is, the higher scores obtained on the projectives, the fewer failures in psychotherapy were found. The following table shows these relationships for both scales, and when a bi-serial coefficient of correlation was calculated, using success and failure as criteria, the coefficient was found to be .438 significant beyond the point .01 level of confidence. Thus, we are entitled to say that the chances of failure to respond to therapy increase as the position on the Scale worsens.

TABLE I.—Homogeneous Scale

Descriptive Evaluation of Total Performance	No. in Group	% of Cases Failing to Respond to Any Type of Therapy
Very Superior	5	0
Superior	17	0
Within Normal Limits +	71	10
Within Normal Limits	73	14
Within Normal Limits —	83	21
Mediocre	74	27
Impoverished	35	54
Total	358	

Heterogeneous Scale

Descriptive Evaluation of Total Performance	No. in Group	% of Cases Failing to Respond to Any Type of Therapy
Gifted—Problems	45	13
Potential—Problems	67	19
Gifted—Disturbed	13	31
Potential—Disturbed	51	31
Disturbed—Potential	46	30
Disturbed / Very Disturbed	42	50
Total	264	

And how about the kind of therapy? Here we are forced to say that at the present time, using present-day methods of short-term psychotherapy, it would seem as if there is much less satisfaction on the part of the therapist concerning the results he obtains than there is with the more classical forms of treatment which require a longer time.

Table II demonstrates these results, which are statistically significant, namely, therapists using Classical Analysis, and to a lesser degree Modified Analysis, feel greater satisfaction as a result of their therapeutic work than do those employing short-term therapy or

TABLE II.

	Classical Analysis	Modified Analysis	Psychotherapy Supportive Re-Educational Counseling	Brief Therapy Narcoplexis	"Other"	Total
Maximum	67	20	29	12	6	134
Moderate	67	41	72	20	12	212
Slight	28	14	56	19	12	129
No Improvement	24	11	75	25	12	147
Total	186	86	232	76	42	622

other forms of psychotherapeutic endeavor. Chi square = 66.5664 (.001).

Again, contrasting Charts I and II, brings home very clearly that, at the present time, utilizing the present methods of Brief Therapy, and *taking into account the individual's intellectual and non-intellectual endowment* that failures to respond to therapy occur many times more frequently amongst those patients who receive Brief Therapy than (in this contrasting group) those who use Classical Analysis.

How was Brief Therapy defined in this particular study? In terms of the amount of time in therapy, it was described as therapy of nine months duration or less. In some of our specialized tables, we divided it into therapy of three months and less, as opposed to between three and six months. Also included under Brief Therapy were patients where the method was so described, even if an exact time limit had not been set, provided, again, this brief treatment did not exceed six months in duration.

It is important to emphasize that those cases which we had included in this category were only those in which the therapist considered the treatment to be at an end. We did not include, for instance, 131 cases seen from three to twenty times, since, though the treatment was undoubtedly brief, the therapist did not consider it had been brought to any kind of conclusion. Nor have we included here a group of 193 patients seen from one to three times, even though in some of these instances therapists were willing to state that some change in the patient, or therapeutic results, had been achieved.

It should also be pointed out, lest it be felt that Brief Therapists were more critical of their own work than were those who were engaged in Classical Analysis, that almost all therapists reported utilizing different methods with different patients, achieving some successes and some failures in each form of treatment.

Let us go back now to a question asked earlier, namely, are there indications in some psychological pre-therapy test records that short-term therapy should, under no circumstances, be used? In answering this, our new psychological categories are definitely helpful. Take, for example, that group of individuals described as "Disturbed," whose test scores are, therefore, virtually identical. If we now include in this description of these patients their intellectual endowment as well, as measured by the Bellevue-Wechsler Intelligence Test, we can think of them as reasonably similar prospects for psychotherapeutic intervention. Of the forty-two patients whom we can describe in this way, twenty-three were rated as showing "No Improvement," six as showing "Maximum Improvement." The average length of time in therapy, however, for the Improved group was four times as long as that of the Unimproved.

In our desire to further short-term therapeutic techniques, it may be considered inappropriate to emphasize these findings, despite their statistical significance. On the other hand, the need to develop briefer forms of treatment remains just as acute even if, at the present stage of our knowledge, many therapists are dissatisfied with their results utilizing present-day methods and a limited number of sessions.

Let me turn before closing to a brief consideration of my second question, namely, "Are there therapeutic methods which are derived essentially from psychological techniques?" In answering "yes" to this, I shall again be wearing two hats, namely the psycho-diagnostician's on top of the therapist's.

Several methods of utilizing psychological techniques, or psycho-diagnostic tests, in a therapeutic way, have been reported. (Bellak, L., et al, 1949; Harrower, M., 1956 b) I will speak briefly of the one which I developed, and with which I have had considerable experience. Projective counseling, or projective therapy, is a method whereby a patient is confronted, at the appropriate moment in his treatment, with some of his own test productions; some of his answers to the Rorschach; some of his TAT stories; some of his answers to the Sentence Completion. (Harrower, 1956 a) The patient's test material is used in much the same way as are his dreams. He can free associate to them or, if the moment of timing is right, he may achieve startling insights into some of his own problems by what he, himself, has said in the supposedly neutral situation of the tests. This technique has been used with individuals in group counseling sessions, and perhaps most effectively in marital counseling, where the partners gain insight into each other, as

ANALYSIS   CHART I.—Scales of Personality Endowment Derived from Scores on Seven Projective Techniques

(Allowing for correlation with I.Q.)

Failure = O
Maximum = +   HOMOGENEOUS SCALE

HOMOGENEOUS SCALE — WECHSLER SCALE

Personality Endowment	Very Superior	Superior	High Average	Average	Below Average
Very Superior	+				
Superior	+++ ++	++ ++			
Within Normal Limits [+]	+++ ++ +++	+++ ++	+		
Within Normal Limits	+++ ++	+++ +++		+	
Within Normal Limits [—]	O	++ O	+		
Mediocre	+	+	+ O	+ O	
Impoverished	O	O	+ O		

HETEROGENEOUS SCALE — WECHSLER SCORES

Personality Endowment	Very Superior	Superior	High Average	Average	Below Average
Gifted With Problems	++ ++	+ OO	++		
High Potential With Problems	++ O	+ OO		+	
Gifted With Disturbance	+ O				
Potential With Disturbance	+++ OO	+++ ++	++ OO	OO	+
Disturbed With Potential	O	+			
Disturbed	O	+++ OO		O	
Very Disturbed					

BRIEF THERAPY   CHART II.—Scales of Personality Endowment Derived from Scores on Seven Projective Techniques

Failure = O   (Allowing for correlation with I.Q.)

Maximum = +

HOMOGENEOUS SCALE

WECHSLER SCALE

Personality Endowment	Very Superior	Superior	High Average	Average	Below Average
Very Superior		+			
Superior		+			
Within Normal Limits [+]	+ OO	+ OO	+ O	+	
Within Normal Limits	OO	+ OOO	OO		
Within Normal Limits [−]	+ OO	+ OOO OO		+	
Mediocre	+++ OO	OOO OOO	OOO OOO	+ OO OOO	OO
Impoverished	OO	OOO OO	OO OO	OOO	O

HETEROGENEOUS SCALE

WECHSLER SCORES

Personality Endowment	Very Superior	Superior	High Average	Average	Below Average
Gifted With Problems	+++ O	+			
High Potential With Problems	+ O	+ OOO OO	OOO	+ O	
Gifted With Disturbance	OO				
Potential With Disturbance		OO		O	+
Disturbed With Potential	O	OO	OOO	OOO	
Disturbed		OO	OO	O	
Very Disturbed		O	OO OO	OO	

well as to their own problems, by comparing and contrasting their experiences and spontaneous answers to one and the same psychological stimulus.

An example of how this technique is utilized in an individual case may be illuminating. The patient was a girl in her early twenties. An adopted child, she was seen therapeutically as a result of an immediate crisis, although there had been a background of difficulties with her parents extending over many years.

"She had been expelled from her college dormitory, was supposed to have been hopelessly snarled in bad company, associating particularly with—and this is important in the light of the history—a near-blind musician who was with a band known to be using 'dope.' The patient, herself, was also suspected of taking drugs, although this subsequently proved to be untrue. It was true, however, that she was lying flagrantly in an attempt to ward off her parents' knowledge that she had lost the part-time job necessary for keeping her in college.

"While some of the accusations by over-anxious parents and distressed college officials turned out to be exaggerations, it was true that she was completely unable to arouse herself in the morning, would appear 'doped,' and would have to be dragged out of bed by physical force before she could start the day. Moreover, this inertia carried over into her daily occupation so that she became actually unable to hold her part-time job. A vicious cycle was thus set up whereby she lied and was then afraid to apply for any job.

"Despite the fact that her parents considered her to be of mediocre intelligence and treated her as such, the Wechsler-Bellevue indicated an I.Q. of 138. Moreover, the Rorschach, the Figure Drawing, the Sentence Completion and the Most Unpleasant Concept Test all provided rich material for direct use in projective counseling. There was no question of an underlying psychosis; although a free flow of associative material was maintained, she was never engulfed by uncontrollable moods or fantasies. In terms of attacking the problem with as much dispatch as possible, one aspect of the Szondi was the most arresting and suggestive. This was the 6-s responses which this patient gave, and which provided a clue to the central immobilizing tendencies and their probable dynamics. It was clear that release of this rigidly repressed aggression must take place before any movement could be expected.

"Free associations to the selected answers from the Rorschach almost at once activated memories that converged upon the central theme; namely, her hatred for, and fascination of her father. A highly significant answer was 'a long-nosed wolf.' Although not apparent to the patient at first, and followed by evasive associations, this key clue ultimately brought the patient to the consideration of her father's nose (and the whole problem of his being a Jew), of his angry, 'animal,' wolf-like expression and from here to the key source of her terror—her father's angry eyes. Her own inability to retaliate in the face of his anger had, to use her own words, 'driven her underground.' She smoldered but never dared to retaliate. Once, associating to a Sentence Completion and contemplating retaliation, she envisaged herself plunging a pair of scissors into her father and killing him.

"Associations to 'eyes' which she had seen in the Rorschach brought this patient quickly to fascinating material. More than anything else, it was 'those blazing eyes' which had terrified her. From this she came to understand that her present attachment to an individual who was virtually blind was closely related to the original fear of the penetrating, all-seeing eyes of her father. It was necessary, and safe, to love only some one who could not see. From this it was but a small therapeutic step to a discussion of her inability to open her eyes, and her attempt to shut out the world through continued sleep.

"Alternately terrified and attracted by her father, she came close to Oedipal material when free-associating to her drawings. She had drawn the man without a face but with a stick and commented, 'I wish he would actually hit me rather than hitting me verbally.' In this particular case, no further probing or suggestions were given along these lines since the patient's adjustment in terms of her everyday life was so spectacular that deeper material was not touched on.

"The interrelation of the material from the Sentence Completion and Most Unpleasant Concept was used to attack an obviously phobic area for this patient, namely, the 'spider.' On the Most Unpleasant Concept test a 'spider' had been drawn, and several of the sentences in the Holsopple-Miale Sentence Completion showed her concern: 'She couldn't bear to touch . . . the spider,' and again, 'Closer and closer there comes . . . a big spider.' While the first completion is not unusual, the second alerts one to the pathological aspects of this idea for the patient. The 'spider,' when she associated to it, led her back along a direct path to the point at which, terrified and yet fascinated by her father, she had gathered spiders to burn them in effigy, believing thereby she could destroy him. Then, terrified by her own daring and cruelty, she would swing to the other extreme and attempt to keep a spider in view at night in a web outside her window. Her profound feelings of hatred of her father, with their ambivalent aspects, were again made known and became at this point an all-important step in her capacity to adjust more realistically to the family situation." (Harrower, et al 1960).

Such an account may give the "feel" of how projective material is used in a form of short-term therapy.

Returning now in conclusion to the three questions asked initially, we may say: having as psychodiagnosticians, determined and standardized projective types reflecting personality endowment, we find that the "better" the personality picture, the better the results in both long-term and short-term therapy. Moreover, there are

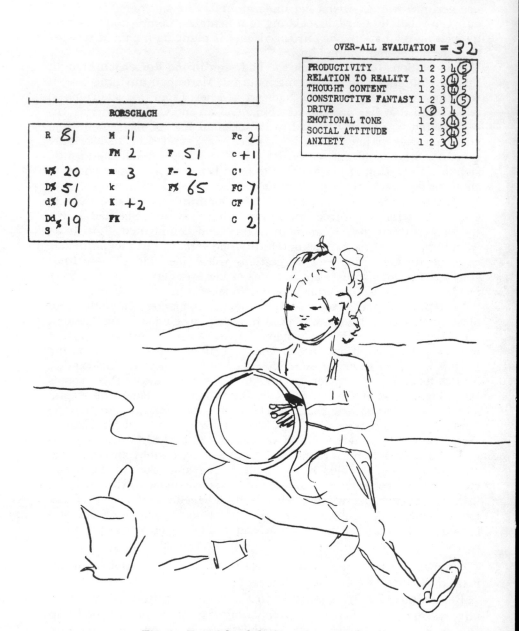

OVER-ALL EVALUATION = 32

PRODUCTIVITY	1 2 3 4	⑤
RELATION TO REALITY	1 2 3 ④ 5
THOUGHT CONTENT	1 2 3 ④ 5
CONSTRUCTIVE FANTASY	1 2 3 4 ⑤
DRIVE	1 ② 3 4 5
EMOTIONAL TONE	1 2 3 ④ 5
SOCIAL ATTITUDE	1 2 3 ④ 5
ANXIETY	1 2 ③ 4 5

RORSCHACH

R 81	M 11		Fc 2
	FM 2	F 51	c +1
W% 20	m 3	F- 2	C'
D% 51	k	F% 65	FC 7
d% 10	K +2		CF 1
Dd% 19 S	FK		c 2

Fig. 1—Example of the Very Superior Group

OVER-ALL EVALUATION = 14

PRODUCTIVITY	① 2 3 4 5
RELATION TO REALITY	1 ② 3 4 5
THOUGHT CONTENT	1 ② 3 4 5
CONSTRUCTIVE FANTASY	① 2 3 4 5
DRIVE	1 ② 3 4 5
EMOTIONAL TONE	① 2 3 4 5
SOCIAL ATTITUDE	1 2 ③ 4 5
ANXIETY	1 ② 3 4 5

RORSCHACH

R 10	M		Fc
	FM 3	F 4	c 1
W% 60	m	F- 1	C' 1
D% 40	k	F% 50	FC
d%	K		CF
Dd%	FK		C
S			

MAN

Fig. 2—Example from the Impoverished Group

certain types for whom short-term therapy seems definitely counter-indicated, namely the "Disturbed" group. As psychological thera-pists we have seen that certain therapeutic methods may be the direct outgrowth of the projective material which the patient pro-duces. Finally, as research oriented psychologists a large scale sur-vey has indicated that therapists, are, at the moment, better satis-fied with their results in long-term than short-term therapy.

Short-term therapy, as now conceived of, may not produce im-provement, detectable by the projective tests, *at the time of its termination*. However, one experimental study, reported elsewhere (Harrower, 1958), has demonstrated that if patients are tested for a third time, ten years subsequent to the original re-testing, marked improvement may be shown. This suggests that there is a factor which we are not taking into account which may occur during the therapeutically empty time interval.

XI

The Contribution of Social Casework to Short-Term Psychotherapy

================ ARLENE WOLBERG, M.S.S.

(Editor's Note: Short-term casework methods have been used for many years in the social work field and have been proven successful. How casework may be incorporated into a psychotherapist's armamentarium is indicated in this chapter. There is a great deal of misunderstanding about the field of social work both inside and outside the field. Mrs. Wolberg attempts to clarify some of the existing misconceptions. She illustrates how the social worker who is properly trained can cooperate with the psychiatrist in a variety of ways: working conjunctively with a patient or with members of the patient's family; operating as a specialist in the use of community resources for special problems; doing environmental manipulation along with counseling. It is suggested that the worker who is qualified by special training can do psychotherapy with members of the family or with the patient when this is appropriate.)

DOES THE SOCIAL WORK FIELD employ techniques which can help the psychotherapist in shortening clinical treatment procedures? Can the psychotherapist employ casework methods in his practice? Can the social worker, whose profession involves helping the individual solve problems on a conscious level in a social situation, work effectively with the psychotherapist? Answers to these questions require knowledge of social work and a concept of the training and professional skills of social workers.

WHAT IS SOCIAL WORK?

Social work covers a broad area. It includes a wide spectrum of services not all of which will be of interest to the psychiatrist dealing with patients in treatment. There are, however, a number of specialties in social work that have pertinence to the psychotherapist's function and understanding of what may enhance his work with certain patients. These specialties include group work and casework. Not all social workers are skilled in these areas by virtue of their specialization in other divisions of the social work field.

Originally there were seven separate national social work organizations, each reflecting the provincial interests of what were considered to be seven broad specializations. These were: The American Association of Medical Social Workers (1918); The National Association of School Social Workers (1919); American Association of Social Workers (1921); The American Association of Psychiatric Social Workers (1926); The American Association of Group Workers (1946); The Association for the Study of Community Organization (1946); Social Work Research Group (1949). Perhaps this arrangement of organization influenced the thinking of the educators in the field, for after 1944 there was an agreement among the schools of social work that the curriculum be divided into eight content areas: social casework; social group work; community organization; public welfare; social research; medical information; psychiatric information; and social administration. More recently (1952), with the establishment of the Council on Social Work Education, ideas on training have been revised and the curriculum is now based on three major subject areas: human growth and behavior; social services (policy and programs) and social work practice methods (social casework, social group work, community organization, social work administration, social work research, social work consultation, social practice or field work). The specialties are now designated by five categories: community organization, group work, research, consultation and casework. All social workers who attend schools of social work receive a basic or generic education and then they may specialize during their field work practice. On October 1, 1955 after about three years of planning and negotiations, the seven organizations finally founded the National Association of Social Workers, which, for the first time, united all social workers in one professional organization.

An important aspect of social work is community organization. The community organizer works to develop such agencies in the field of health and welfare as planning boards, national and international professional organizations that have to do with the setting of standards in a field, the development of new resources, community chests, social security systems and health insurance programs, community welfare councils and race relations programs.

Group workers are found in agencies dedicated to changes in society which will enhance the socialization process of individuals or that aim to promote the social adjustment of people in the various age groups. Such work may be done in leisure time organizations, summer camp and residence programs, rehabilitation centers, gangs, and other "street" groups, old age homes and settlement houses.

Research has been used only recently in social work, some attempts being made at evaluation. Studies of group phenomena are also taking place by making observations of: family life; relationships between children and parents; the "indigent"; gangs or street corner groups; interactions in rehabilitation centers.

Consultation is used in social work practice both within the field of social work itself, and with other disciplines and with volunteers. Social workers advise groups and organizations in programs which have social aims for the elimination of problems such as poverty, child care, adoption, school practices, and mental health prevention. The field of social work is itself a potent force in the prevention of mental and emotional disorders in that it encompasses the development of programs which provide a basic economic standard for all people. Social workers emphasize that basic security needs, nondiscriminative practices and democratic community plans are of utmost importance to the health and welfare of all of the citizens in a society. The social work consultant often brings to the health team information which give a new dimension to the work of the other professions. Social workers have, in the past ten years, contributed to the knowledge of physicians, psychologists, the clergy, school personnel and others to increase their awareness of the way in which social components affect their various professional practices, particularly information regarding family and other group phenomena which affect the adjustment of the individual in his relations with society.

The caseworker, who functions principally in clinics, family agencies and hospitals, is especially indoctrinated with the knowledge of dynamic psychology and its clinical meaning in terms of health and illness. This includes mental and emotional problems, but relates to physical illness as well. Other social workers do not have this "dynamic" orientation.

Casework, essentially a counseling, planning and problem solving method, has been designated as identical with psychotherapy by a number of authors. This affiliation has interfered with the proper understanding of the aims of the social work field. Counseling is a method which is used by a variety of professionals—lawyers, physicians, clergymen, psychologists, and social workers. There are differences in the objectives of counseling, however, among these different professions. Thus when a physician gives aid to a person as compared to when a social worker does so, he has medical aims in mind, while the social worker works toward social goals employing sociological techniques in attempting to influence attitudes. Every physician is thus a counselor, as is every social worker, although what they seek to accomplish may differ. In counseling a psychiatric patient, the social worker utilizes environmental manipulation, explores attitudes and feelings, and discusses plans to enhance the patient's adjustment. Social workers aim primarily at helping the individual mobilize his own capacities to act in a productive way. The aims of group work are the same as those of casework, but traditionally group workers have had no training in concepts related to depth psychology. Casework has been practiced in the one-to-one relationship. This may be a false distinction in terms of describing the techniques of social work; it is now felt by many that casework may be practiced in groups as well as in the one-to-one relationship and that group workers should have the specialized clinical practice or family agency practice that caseworkers have had, so that they may be more informed as to the psychodynamic and psychopathological implications in the individuals with whom they deal. In the past ten years many group workers have acquired a clinical orientation through private means by attending seminars, given, for example, by the American Group Psychotherapy Association, and some have gained admission to that organization by virtue of their shifting their base of operation from group work settings to the clinic and hospital.

The social work and psychiatric literature of the past twenty years in the United States has revealed a great diversity of opinion as to the nature of casework and the difference between this method and psychotherapy. In fact, ever since dynamic psychology made an impact on the field of social work, there have been attempts to reconcile the natures of casework and psychotherapy. A great deal of conceptual floundering has resulted. Among the reasons for this are the following: First, social work is not understood as a field and parenthetically because of this it is not sufficiently appreciated by the community. Social work emphasizes the individual's adjustment in groups: in the family, at work, in school, in society, and in leisure time activities. This kind of emphasis impinges upon political, educational, economic and social values. Many professionals feel that social workers should not bring such values into the field of health and welfare. Accordingly, when social workers join forces with other professionals, their objectives often become so circumscribed as to rob their work of its potential effectiveness. For example, home visiting, which is frequently an essential component of good casework, is often frowned upon by some of the psychiatrically oriented professionals. Advice giving, an ingredient of adequate performance in specific problems in social casework, is also considered taboo by some, particularly in agencies influenced by psychoanalytic thinking. Such attitudes, obviously, are deterrents to the development of adequate social work programs.

A second factor is that social work, like all professions which depend upon applied techniques, has had its share of troubles in attempting to adapt information from other fields for use in the process of casework. Many dislocations have resulted from the misuse of concepts appropriate to another discipline, but not applicable to the casework field.

A third factor is that social workers are usually placed on the lowest rung of the economic ladder in the mental health professions. This may be because their education is not as systematically organized as that of the psychiatrist or the psychologist, or possibly because they have worked largely in social agencies which, like public schools, suffer from financial starvation and low status.

Fourth, the field has not been as highly developed as have the fields of medicine and psychology. The National Social Work Organization has only relatively recently come into being to foster the professionalization of social workers and to safeguard their economic life.

Fifth, the early trend toward specialization in social work, and the fact that it was slow to be recognized as an entity separate from other fields, has prevented the development of multi-service agencies which could become centers for the meeting of a variety of social needs. Financing and planning in the field of social work was thus often oriented around limited parochial goals. This, in some cases, has been a deterrent to public community support.

A bewildering period in the history of social work in the United States occurred some years ago when the field was arbitrarily divided into "functional" and "diagnostic" schools, based not on social work principles or theory, but on the differences in two psychological systems which were being absorbed into the social work field, i.e. those of Rank and Freud. Confusion was rampant in working with psychoanalysts as consultants who focused on the clinical aspects of problems. Social workers, with the exception of psychiatric and medical social workers, usually do not have a "clinical" orientation. This was not understood by the medically trained psychoanalyst. In the course of this "clinical" emphasis, many social agencies became transformed into clinics. This was to be regretted, for the original agency was often as important, from the point of view of social need, as was the clinic which replaced it.

The many difficulties investing their functioning as social workers induced some to enter private practice. This trend took two
forms: some social workers sought psychoanalytic training and set
themselves up as practitioners of psychoanalysis; others continued
to do social work, but had as their clients the "middle-class" population who could afford to pay for casework help, excluding the
"poor" and jobless and the blue and white collar workers who were
unable to pay private fees. One of the lessons of the Second World
War was that social dislocation and emotional illness are no re-
spectors of class, and that members of all strata of our society suffer from psychiatric disorders, family disintegration and other difficulties. Casework was therefore accepted in some families of higher
socio-economic levels, and this encouraged the development of private practice for social workers.

Social service programs are sorely needed in our society; often
it is social casework rather than psychotherapy which is the treatment of choice. Vast numbers of persons who have emotional problems are not motivated for psychotherapy and cannot be helped
in a clinical setting. Their needs are for a problem-centered discussion of social situations and opportunities to form meaningful life
relationships with others. Social work, including casework, depends
in great part on manipulating the environment, or in helping the
individual to rearrange or alter the environment so that constructive learning may take place. Social work is not interested in "cur-
ing" an emotional disorder, but in giving the individual a corrective social situation in which to function, thereby creating an atmosphere where new learning and change may take place. The
idea of the corrective experience comes from the "diagnostic" school
of social work and is based upon the proposition first promulgated
by Freud that the interpersonal experience in psychoanalysis is "corrective." Expanding this concept and adapting it to social casework
meant that not only the interpersonal situation could be corrective,
but also the total situation, if changed, could be "corrective."

An example of this is the case of Stephen R., whose aunt, a social
worker, took a hand in helping him and the other members of his family. Stephen is a tall, handsome, blue-eyed blond boy of fourteen. His
father and mother were both diagnosed schizophrenic, each having had
two periods of hospitalization in mental institutions. Stephen is the only
boy in a family of four children; the girls are ages 23, 16 and 10. The
oldest girl has been living and working in New York City for the past
four years. She had great difficulty in breaking away from home due to
her father's need to maintain a sado-masochistic relationship with her,

and incidentally, to have her supplement the family income by her work as a telephone operator.

Stephen's 16 year old sister, A, was born with a facial defect which made her look bizarre. Her eyes were set far back in her head to give her the appearance of a Cro-Magnon woman, and restricting her visual field so that she had to move her head in a wide sweep whenever she wanted to cover a range for vision.

Stephen's mother was phobic. She refused to allow her children to be away from home. When Stephen reached school age, his mother insisted that he come directly home after school. He could never engage in sports, since she feared that he would be hurt. As a consequence, Stephen and his sister, A, were thrown together as companions, and finally he developed with her an "exclusive" relationship. He scarcely spoke to another person. The mother, withdrawn and "vegetable-like," scarcely conversed with anyone either. She favored the girls, however, and did communicate with them more than with Stephen. The father, also withdrawn, was often away from home for weeks at a time so that his contacts were chiefly to give the children orders or to berate them. Feeling inadequate and frustrated, he tended to be competitive with the children, discouraging them if they acted independently.

With his wife, the father maintained a passive dependent relationship, never attempting to undo any of the damage she was inflicting on the children by cutting them off from their peers. The mother had the idea that Stephen and his sister A should sleep in the same bed. On one occasion when the aunt visited the family, the father asked: "Do you think it will be harmful for Stephen and A to sleep in the same bed?" The aunt answered: "Yes." But the father countered with the statement that his wife said it would be "all right," so nothing could be done about it. The mother was thought of by the children as strong-willed and they did not dare to challenge her.

The father had a Master's degree in English. He worked first as a school teacher, but he was unable to continue because his paranoid feelings were aroused when he had to have an extended relationship. Having a fear of authority figures, he could not let himself hold a position of authority. His first schizophrenic break occurred when he was 25 years of age, at the time he had been promoted to head the English Department in the High School where he taught. He became a door-to-door salesman and this seemed to stabilize him; but even at this job, when he was promoted to manager of a district, he had to give up the position due to intense anxiety. He was unable to be close with members of his family, yet he was the most active parent. He would, for example, shop for food when he was at home. He did all the managing, paid all the bills, took the children to the dentist, and on excursions on very rare occasions. He reverted to detachment and withdrawal as defenses, often staying for weeks at a time with his mother who was neurotically attached to him. This involved a fifty mile trip. She gave him money to supplement his paltry earnings which amounted to less than $2500 a year.

Two years ago in August, Stephen's father died of hypertension and kidney disease at the age of 50. Stephen's mother refused to remain in their modest home which was being financed at the rate of $75 per month. Selling it, she bought a trailer which she had placed on the property of her father and mother, a retired couple who lived on a small pension.

Stephen's aunt became involved with the family in a professional way when she invited the children to visit New York City to attend the World's Fair. Their father had promised to bring them to New York City, but he had died before he could make good on his promise. Their aunt, the father's sister, who lived in New York City, decided to have the children in her home so that they could visit the World's Fair and see the "sights" in New York. While the children were visiting, their oldest sister spent a great deal of time with them. It was obvious to the aunt and to the oldest sister from the first contact that Stephen was a disturbed child. He was withdrawn and never spoke unless spoken to except to his sister A. Whenever he was asked to speak, he seemed to resent this. Stephen's 10 year old sister C is an extremely attractive little girl who functions best of all the children. Stephen, however, appeared to have a great deal of hostility toward her.

The aunt, as a social worker, decided to try to intervene to help these children, particularly Stephen and his sister A. She arranged for them to see a series of specialists: psychologists, psychiatric social workers in a family agency, an internist, a dentist, and in addition for A, a neurologist and plastic surgeon.

Stephen's psychological examinations revealed that he had a verbal I.Q. of 132, a performance I.Q. of 94 and a full scale I.Q. of 115. The psychologist summarized her findings as follows:

Intellectual Capacity and Functioning:

The quotient of 132 on the verbal section of the test indicates very superior intelligence. There is even distribution in the interest scatter except for Stephen's problem in repeating more than four digits backward. Logical reasoning is excellent. Information is above the average of his age group. The high verbal score indicates Stephen's basic intellectual potential.

There is a marked discrepancy between verbal achievements and performance. Except for a better than average result on Picture Completion, the other subtests in this area do not exceed the average level. This is due to comparatively slow work on digit symbols and on block design. The impression is that Stephen becomes easily anxious when faced with a task that requires speed and accuracy.

He then seems to work laboriously but loses sight of the main objective and becomes entangled in details. This increases his anxiety and further interferes with the correct solution of the problem. It also can be assumed that at times depressive moods may interfere with effective work.

Emotional Structure:

The projective tests indicate a youngster who spends a great deal of energy by keeping up a facade of indifference designed to shield him from closeness to others. He feels that he has to protect himself from emotional stimulation which easily could arouse aggressive impulses that might overwhelm him. Strong tension and anxiety generated by these impulses are manifested in depressive moods, in a tendency to withdraw, a pessimistic outlook and fear of impending danger. Ego boundaries are fragile and strong defenses have to be employed to cope with emotional stimuli. Intellectualization, withdrawal, evasion and denial are the defenses he uses most intensively. His anger with and fear of the many females with whom he is surrounded is clearly evidenced in the tests. He is very much aware of the emotional disturbance in his mother and the mental deterioration of his grandmother. The latter process appears to be an especially frightening experience for Stephen. Fear of mental illness and of death is expressed in some of his test responses. Interpersonal relationships are poor, and at the present time he is especially guarded and concerned about getting hurt. The tremendous effort in maintaining control and rallying of defenses must necessarily detract from the great amount of energy which otherwise might be used for emotional growth and intellectual functioning. In spite of the intense, aggressive impulses which he cannot channelize and the tremendous anxiety which they generate, Stephen has managed to keep his fragile equilibrium. He may be at a crossroad while struggling with the conflicts and needs of adolescence. One of his responses to the Rorschach blots seems to reflect the image he has formed of himself: 'Some kind of bird—it could not fly because the body is too big for it's wings.'

A change of environment could be very decisive for Stephen's future and could help him to trust himself and others sufficiently to be able to face his needs and to accept therapy."

The social worker aunt felt that psychotherapy in this case would be a mistake and that what was needed here was a special residence situation where Stephen could be removed from his home and from his sisters and mother; yet he would have peer contacts and an opportunity for counseling if and when he could use these. The aunt sought the help of a family social agency and Stephen was placed in a residence home where there were "normal," i.e., not psychotic children, and where he could go to school in the community. A social worker in residence at the home sees him once a week for counseling. Stephen is an isolated child in the residence home. He talks to the social worker only at her request, volunteering nothing. Recently he has spoken a few words spontaneously to the house mother. It was observed that he did not send his clothes to the laundry like other boys did. He never gave clothes to the cleaner. The house mother finally told him that he was allowed to have clean clothes and that all the children, boys and girls alike, may send all their dirty clothes to be cleaned. Stephen was amazed to hear this. He also was astonished that the people in the residence home took so many showers. He is being offered help with school work by the counselor, but he is not able yet to accept help. He is not being forced to discuss his feelings. He has recently begun to play chess with one of the boys in the residence home and has joined the chess club at school. He also has begun to engage in athletics. It is the purpose of casework, here, to give Stephen an environmental situation which is different from the one he has known in the hope that at the end of a year or two he will have learned that there are people with whom he can have a relationship which will not be fraught with anxiety and trauma. Considerable personality change may be brought about by a shift in the environment where the personality distortions are not too deeply structuralized. Desirable effects from such environmental change have even been noticed in children institutionalized in a mental hospital. (Wolberg, 1959)

During holidays, arrangements are made by the aunt and Stephen's oldest sister for him to spend time in New York City where he goes to shows, visits museums, and has the opportunity for a relationship with a male counselor who takes trips with him in the city visiting camera stores, factories, and other places of interest to boys and men.

The "corrective environmental experience" may mean providing a "reaching out relationship" which is carried on over a period of months in which the detachment of the client is respected, but during which time frequent contact is maintained by telephone and through other means. In certain instances the experience may refer to the kind of situation in which the social worker acts as a "model", and the client observes how the worker reacts, with the hope that the client will pattern himself after the worker. This technique is illustrated in the pamphlet "Diagnostic and Functional Schools of Social Work" wherein Lucille Austin (1950), representing the "diagnostic school," described the Adams case, an "experience" between a child, a worker, and a mother. In this group-of-three, the mother was primarily an observer, the idea being that the parent, through observer-participation and through identification with the worker whom she used as a "model" would learn the difference between appropriate and inappropriate handling of the child. The worker presumably established a "good relationship" with the mother in one or two interviews. The child, through the experience with the social worker, learned how he had been thwarted and frustrated by the parent. He realized that in a different kind of situation it was not necessary for him to act the way he did with his parent.

Often the social worker does no more than help the individual to find a situation similar to one he has lost through no fault of his own so that he may regain his "lost object."

Mrs. A., a 45 year old widow, is an example of such an effort using a short-term treatment approach. Shortly after the death of her husband, she sought help. In taking her history, it was apparent that the woman herself had led a "helping" life; she had taken care of a very neurotic mother for twenty years. During this time she had maintained a sexual and social liaison with a married man whom she finally married, the man having obtained a divorce from his wife who was a hospitalized mental patient. Four years after the marriage the husband died suddenly of a heart attack. Mrs. A. "fell apart," nurturing a depression which persisted for months. She sought the advice of a friend who was prominent in philanthropic work who counseled Mrs. A. to see a psychiatrist. At the initial interview with the psychiatrist, it was apparent that Mrs. A. was not motivated for psychotherapeutic treatment, but she did want someone with whom she could talk, someone "to lean on." All her life she needed a person who was the center of her world. First it was her mother, then her husband, and now it could be any other person who would listen to her and help her. She simply needed to be attached to someone. The psychiatrist enlisted the help of a social worker who planned a series of ten interviews with the purpose of exploring her interests to find if she could transfer her need to "help" to a social situation like working with a blind person. The psychiatrist decided to see Mrs. A. once a month to check on drug therapy prescribed by him, and the social worker was to see the patient once each week. The management of the case turned out to be difficult because of the patient's dependency and her persistence in hanging on either to the worker or the doctor as a figure from whom to draw strength and life. She was not willing to go out into the world to find a consuming interest. The social worker was finally able to arrange for her to take care of a middle aged woman who was recovering from an eye operation and who would need retraining for approximately one year. Mrs. A. was able to accept this task when she was assured that the woman would be willing to live in Mrs. A.'s apartment during the rehablitation process. Mrs. A.'s depression suddenly lifted and she was able to resume her interest in things.

Fifteen sessions were devoted in all to this one case during which time
the social worker was able to steer Mrs. A. toward a course in practical
nursing.

Social casework is not primarily a psychological method. Unlike
psychotherapy, it has sociological dimensions. If we must make
comparisons, the social work field is more like the fields of law and
education than like psychology or medicine. In order for the psychotherapist to understand what the social worker has to contribute
to a psychiatric program, it is helpful to distinguish between what
the social worker does and how the psychotherapist works.

Recognizing that there are specializations in the field of social
work, such as group work, psychiatric social work, family social
work, child welfare work, and so forth, there are at least six ways
in which any well trained social worker can be of help in short-
term psychotherapeutic practice. The first way is by contributing a
social diagnosis through collecting data about the patient that enables one to understand his social adjustment in the family, at
work, and in the other groups to which he belongs. The second
way is by application of what the social worker calls "the reaching
out process"—a method used to establish and maintain a relationship with certain types of patients by employing many avenues of
communication simultaneously, such as home visits, telephone
calls, written notes, and group or social rehabilitation meetings.
The third way is working as a counselor in the one-to-one situation,
giving the patient or his relatives an opportunity for expression of
their thoughts, feelings and attitudes, and offering practical advice
designed to initiate changes in attitudes and behavior. The fourth
way is by employing a group casework process with individuals who
have intense anxiety in the one-to-one relationship. The fifth way is
working as a specialist in problems encountered by the psychotherapist that have sociological implications, such as juvenile delinquency, alcoholism, mental retardation, school absenteeism, old
age, adoption, foster care, social security, public welfare, drug addiction and vocational problems. The sixth way is helping the patient to use a variety of community resources to enhance his adjustment, or coordinating a general plan for the patient and his
family in the constructive use of community resources.

Social workers have long been used to employing brief methods
in casework. The "functional" (Rankian) school, in particular, developed short-term counseling techniques which proved helpful to
individuals who had family difficulties based on emotional problems. According to this school any prospect of change gives rise to

feelings of *ambivalence:* The patient wants the change and does not want it. Anxiety is often experienced as anger, which is handled by *projection.* One of the skills of a "helping person" is to accept the ambivalence and the projective mechanisms so that the individual may express neurotic feelings and eventually allow his "good feelings" to come through by way of *identification.* Identification had a somewhat different connotation to Rank than to Freud. Rank did not mean that the individual must incorporate the values of the other person as in the superego concept. He felt that aggression was evoked by experience and the individual was always angry at a person who was "different" or who had different ideas. Accordingly he had to fight that person or oppose him. Only after he had resolved his anger and oppositional feelings toward the other person for being different could he learn to identify with the other. Agreements as well as differences were pounded out in this struggle. The ability of the individual to work through the ambivalence depended upon the way in which he had been able to handle his "separation anxiety," the first experience of which took place at the time of the birth trauma. Rank felt that each time the individual gave up an old situation for a new one, he experienced "separation anxiety," i.e. he was loathe to separate from the old one and enter the new. This aroused ambivalence and anxiety. If the patient's "will" (motivation) was at odds with his "mind" (reason) conflict resulted, the intensity of which was related to the degree to which the original birth trauma anxiety was resolved.

The Rankian school makes particular use of establishing time limitations in "helping." It also emphasizes the importance of the function of the setting in which the "helping process" takes place. Individuals may be aided in their social adjustment and in their ability to mobilize their own capacities if the aims of casework are circumscribed and brief goals agreed upon jointly by the client and the social worker in advance, and if the particular agency is set up to handle the specific problem for which the client seeks help. Dependency and other neurotic attitudes, it is claimed, will not be encouraged or fostered when brief contacts are maintained. Casework is conducted in the following way: after careful study of the "total situation," one area of the difficulty is selected as the focus of the "helping process." The problem sector chosen for consideration is one which, in the estimation of the worker, can be managed in a way that will arouse the least defensiveness in the client. Thus intensive intrapsychic and characterological defenses are reduced and operate at a minimum. An important consideration in selecting a phase of the problem is that the client show some indication of motivation for constructive activity. Supporting this motivation is the task of the social worker. The diagnostic skill of the worker depends upon his ability to understand the psychodynamics and the psychopathology of the individual's relatedness to others. Histories are taken with the focus on social manifestations of the central problem. Definite time schedules are a part of the "contract" between the worker and the client. Goals and purposes are stated and agreements verbalized. The principle of establishing the nature of the roles of the helper and the one being helped, and the formal verbal definition of the goals of the interpersonal transactions had, of course, been employed by both Freud and Adler in psychoanalysis. Rank was the first to apply this principle in casework. Many of these principles of Rankian casework can be applied in psychotherapy.

An illustration is the case of John W. whose mother brought him to the social agency with the request for help in finding a boarding school for disturbed children. Her son, she said, had a reading disability and needed special education. After exploring the situation, the social worker felt the client was not focusing on an area which would lead to the most appropriate solution of the problem. It was obvious to the worker that the mother wished to be rid of the child so that she would not be confronted daily with her mismanagement and feelings of guilt. Denial, projection and repression were operative as major defenses. "Acting out" with the child was also a problem since the mother took him from doctor to doctor to have him "helped," "reasoned with," and finally "examined physically to prevent injury to his genitals." Recognizing these mechanisms, the worker recommended a different course for the mother. The child, she suggested, should obtain remedial reading lessons. A place might be found for him in an after school group which emphasized both physical games and social relationships. The mother agreed to the remedial reading class, but refused to let the child belong to a social group. Exploration of the resources of the public school for remedial reading help had to be accepted as a compromise. The worker then estimated that five sessions would be the amount of time required to meet the goal of helping mother and child establish a relationship with the remedial reading teacher. If in the course of these five sessions, the mother would verbalize in any way her wish for help, time would be allotted her in order to lay the groundwork for this step. However, the mother, irate at the suggestion of therapy for herself, expressed her anger toward the social worker. After the prescribed five sessions, she continued to display resentment. This, more or less, was helpful since it syphoned off the mother's aggression and helped prevent expressions of paranoid feelings in the exchanges with the remedial reading teacher. In this instance, the social worker did not attempt to explain the projection of anger in either its manifest or latent meaning. She was content to work with the mother toward relieving the child's reading problem and helping her to establish a relationship with the school. Follow-up of this case showed that the child had achieved improvement and that the mother did seek psychiatric treatment later at the suggestion of her family doctor who had discussed the case of the child with the teacher.

Fern Lowery (1948) wrote a paper concerning the functional approach, underlining the following skills that were required to do short-term casework: (1) the ability to evaluate the nature of the problem in the first interview so as to know whether the agency could help and whether the individual was able to use the resource; (2) the ability to understand the relation of the request to the underlying problem; (3) the ability to estimate the quality of the client's reactions in asking for and in accepting help; (4) the ability to understand the meaning of the client's past relationships; (5) the capacity to note the ease or difficulty the client displays in revealing factual data; (6) sensitivity in detecting responsiveness or withdrawal of the client during the first encounter; (7) the ability to determine how consistent the client's factual story and feelings are with his reality situation; (8) the ability to grasp the meaning of the problem and to utilize this insight to help the client work out a plan. The worker, Lowery alleged, needed skills also for evaluating the rationalizations of the client, for interpreting the significance of illogical behavior, for clarifying goals and purposes, and for explaining inconsistencies. The above skills were part of the diagnostic capacities of the social worker. History taking, the method of collecting information, included learning about the client's social stability, his relationships within the family group, his job experience, his ability for economic management, the chronicity of seeking assistance, and the influences of past experiences upon the present sense of personal adequacy—these were the most important clues for a quick evaluation of the present situation. One asked such questions, also, as how has the client managed himself in the past? Why did this happen today instead of a year ago, or a year from now? In coming for help the individual was doing something active in his own behalf. The worker, Lowery insisted, should not "move in" or "take over," but should "assist" so as to enhance the client's "activity." During the brief contact in casework, one should attempt to take care of the immediate situation with the thought of helping the client's future life. Thus even help of short duration should take into account the overall picture and be related to the "total situation." In this sense, casework is always an "enabling" process. Lowery's contribution is a significant one, since her principles still apply today, and can be used in psychotherapy as well.

SOCIAL CASEWORK AND PSYCHOTHERAPY

It was primarily the psychiatric social worker who had experience in clinics and thus was exposed to psychoanalytic orientation. In these instances the social worker often acted as a co-therapist with the psychiatrist or the psychoanalyst under his supervision.

An example of this kind of work is the case of a 44 year old woman, Mrs. C., who was seen for a total of thirty sessions, once a week over a period of seven months. She had been married only six months at the time she applied at the psychiatric clinic for treatment. Dissatisfied with what she termed her "incomplete sexual adjustment" she was seeking help at the suggestion of her husband who was in psychotherapeutic treatment and had become unhappy with the marriage. At the initial interview with the psychiatrist, she complained that she had never experienced a vaginal orgasm. Her first sexual experience occurred at the age of thirty, and from that time until her marriage she had had five unsatisfactory sexual contacts, all with men younger than herself. She confessed feeling guilty over recurring thoughts during her marriage about her last boyfriend. She had no complaints other than her frigidity. She said: "I have anxiety about my husband's cardiac condition and am coming to therapy primarily to do everything to make our marriage a success." The diagnosis made at the initial interview was "personality disorder with frigidity." Asked about her preference regarding a therapist, she said that she wanted a female analyst about thirty years old. The doctor felt she would do well with a caseworker since it was obvious that the patient was not sufficiently motivated to work out her basic personality problems; rather it appeared that she merely wanted to be relieved of certain symptoms.

Mrs. C's family history indicated that she was born and reared in a small New England town. She was the youngest of four children, with two sisters, five and ten years older than herself and a brother seven years older. She was one of a pair of twins, but both her twin and her mother died of an infectious disease when the patient was one year old. She described her father, a Protestant minister, in glowing terms as a "wonderful, kind man loved by the whole town." Her home to her was a cultural mecca in which music, art and literature were enjoyed. There was no further elaboration about her sisters and brother or her feelings toward them. Her father, she said, had remarried, and she described her stepmother as a "wonderful mother to the children and a wonderful wife to her husband." The marriage turned out to be a very happy one.

Her father and stepmother had died eight years ago and the patient felt a great loss, particularly at the death of her father.

During her first interview with the social worker, she displayed an over-pleasant manner. She was medium of stature, with graying sandy-colored hair. She wore a hearing aid which was well concealed; her face was plain and she used little makeup. Her attitude was one of utmost cooperativeness though she seemed ingratiating. One had the feeling that she was going into this therapeutic situation as if she were tackling spring house cleaning—a necessary job to be done, "so why not pitch into it and get the task over with."

Beginning the interview with a long, circumstantial history of her masturbatory activities, she led up to her sexual relationship with her husband. She spoke with little apparent conscious guilt. Interspersed in this account were comments of thinly veiled hostility toward her husband, such as "I worry about his heart during intercourse." "My husband thinks his penis is too small." "My husband and I never discuss his dying." She outlined numerous complaints which her husband had about her which he told her he hoped would be eliminated by treatment. He objected, for example, to her twirling her hair, picking at her face and monopolizing conversations. She expressed considerable concern over whether these habits could be eliminated, and she agreed with him that they must be annoying to live with. He had suggested that twirling her hair was connected with masturbation, and she wondered whether this were true; if so, would the social worker get to the reason for it. She was delighted with the choice of "therapist" since she had wanted a young woman to help her. She felt, she insisted, completely at ease. Throughout the interview, and at subsequent ones, she displayed an almost manic push of speech. She rambled rapidly so as to be almost irrelevant. This rapid speech combined with a happy, smiling, elated manner, was suggestive of an underlying personality problem. When the social worker asked her to describe her mood during the session, she replied: "I am sad that I met my wonderful husband too late."

A brief summary of her husband's clinic record described him as a warm, attractive man of superior intelligence. He had a severe reality problem inasmuch as he had had two coronary occlusions with resultant anginal pains. In addition, he had bleeding peptic ulcers. His chief psychological complaint was that he had reacted to his physical problem by refusing to expose himself to gainful work. His purpose in seeking treatment at the clinic was to discuss this problem with a trained person. He was assigned to a psychiatrist.

At the second session, the patient brought in a series of dreams all carefully written down together with her associations to them. One of her dreams was: "There was a house with an attic, a second floor room and a big attractive downstairs room. The landlord decided to shut off the second floor room and the only entrance to the attic was by an upright ladder from the large room below. He erected this ladder." Her written associations were: "I immediately thought the second floor was my clitoris, and the downstairs room my vagina. The closing off of the main entrance, and the erection of the ladder meant that I intend the clitoris reaction to come from the vagina rather than directly from outside. The focus of interest has become the vagina, or I want it to be so."

The social worker made no attempt to interpret this dream or others that she later presented which were usually elaborately written. She did not ask for further associations. Instead she tried to direct the patient toward current problems and feelings. In effect, the patient's dreams served four major purposes: one, they stimulated her childhood recollections (there were frequent references to childhood incidents); two, they kept the social worker informed of the patient's anxiety and how she was handling this; three, they revealed the nature of the transference with the social worker; and four, they served as a stimulus for the patient's associations which were used in interpretations. In other words, while dreams gave the social worker data, they were not probed or dealt with except to refer to the current relationship with her husband.

During the next session, the patient began a pattern of alternately discussing her husband and father. Whenever she mentioned a feeling or attitude toward her husband, she would immediately compare it with attitudes toward her father. If she mentioned her father first, she would then compare these feelings with those toward her husband. Since hostility toward her husband was so thinly disguised, the social worker directed questions around this area. Why had she married her husband? "He thinks it's to take care of him. I wouldn't want to leave him alone. I'd take care of him. I felt no one would take him away from me because he is so sick. I have given up trying for the best things. I couldn't have an orgasm; I feared failure."

At the following session, she began talking about what she called her "jealousy of attractive women," relating her feeling of inadequacy to having had a pretty older sister. Then she launched into feelings of dislike for her stepmother. She felt that her stepmother had been hypocritical in many of her dealings with the townspeople. Immediately thereafter she confessed that she did not believe that the social worker was as pretty as she had thought she was during the first interview. At this point she presented three dreams: one, "A play was being rehearsed between a boy and a girl. The manager thinks it is immoral and separates them. I thought it was silly of him"; two, "I went to the ladies' room and discovered it was the men's room"; three, "I am in bed and holding the landlady in my arms." The first dream seemed to the social worker to be an ego acceptable resistance dream. This led her to ask the patient if she felt that therapy might cause difficulty between her husband and herself. Did she believe that the social worker was critical of her behavior? The patient replied that she had actually felt that the social worker might come between her and her husband as her stepmother had come between her and her father. This was both the first and last transference reference that was mentioned during the entire casework treatment.

During the next session she brought in lists of complaints about her husband. She realized that she was repulsed by his numerous illnesses. She spoke of fearing that she might choke him while he dozed under the influence of sleeping pills. Similarly she verbalized feelings of hostility toward her father. She felt that her father had caused her sexual repressions because of his religious and puritanical values. He imposed his values upon all the members of his household.

Following these five sessions, the patient remained away from therapy for three weeks due to infectious mononucleosis. Upon her return, she continued to exhibit the same rapid speech, and in one session she presented a variety of subjects. She talked about her husband's losing his job and expressed the notion that he was testing her to see if she was worried or not. She presented two dreams. In the first her husband had turned into a fly. In the second, half an orange, stuck on the wall, was attracting and sucking in flies. She then talked about her husband's resemblance to his degenerate half-brother who had raped his own daughter. Realizing, as she talked, the irrationality of any such connection, she then read off a list of what she considered shameful acts which she had committed in her childhood. She finished with a discussion of her father's demands for compliance from everyone around him.

In this and the following sessions in which there were always numerous areas for interpretation, the worker emphasized only those areas involving her relationship with her husband—their social relationships as well as their sexual life. The patient's dreams usually dealt with her sexual problem. They were interpreted to mean that she seemed to have some fears regarding her own sexual aggressiveness, as if she might destroy her husband in some way. She picked this up enthusiastically, recalling a fear that she might injure if not break off her husband's penis were she not to control herself in intercourse. At this point the major content and direction of casework changed from expressions of hostility toward her husband and father to one of talking about her intimate sexual feelings. This shift was ushered in by a discussion of a homosexual relationship she had had when she was twenty-seven years old. This consisted of mutual masturbation with a woman with whom she had shared an apartment. She revealed this with much guilt, and the worker responded with reassurance and some educative material explaining the prevalence of certain kinds of masturbatory experiences.

The content of the next two months of therapy, eliminating circumstantial details, brought out many fearful obsessive thoughts. She spoke of having been frightened for years of being raped by men, and of occasional thoughts that someone would put a hypodermic needle into her in the subway and cart her away to a white slave market. It was with some anxiety and guilt that she discussed her feelings of repulsion when her father had once kissed her on the mouth. Treatment of these obsessive thoughts consisted of discussing them as symptoms of a great fear of men sexually, and of her father in particular. Such fears she was told often preclude any real sexual relaxation and enjoyment. She confided her feelings of distaste for her husband's sexual advances. She then spoke for the first time of her notion that she might have injured herself through masturbation. She feared also that she might learn to be happy sexually without men. She had some nightmares, but the anxiety was not too intense as illustrated by these dreams: "I am supposed to shoot a gun at someone. A snowball comes out." "My husband, a woman and I live together. I see an auto crash over a bridge. Actually I expected to see the crash, but apparently there was none, and the occupants were unharmed." "I fell off a cliff and nothing happened." These dreams seemed to indicate a greater control over her feelings and fears of violence.

Shortly after this she began to experience orgasms. In the session before her first orgasm, she revealed a dread that she would urinate if she were to relax and enjoy intercourse. She recalled her disgust at her first discovery that men both urinate and have sex with the same organ. The following session she burst into the room saying: "I had a terrible week. I had an awful fight with my husband because he was nagging me. I had three orgasms." She then described the following dream which was the only one she could remember during the interval between sessions: "There is a scene in the mountains with a church, the building, hangs precariously on a cliff." The rest of the discussion in the session was spent in describing the pleasure of her sexual accomplishment, the feeling of freedom which she now experienced, and the ability she had displayed in arguing with and expressing resentment openly toward her husband; this seemed to have released her in her feelings. She could see that her anger did not really injure her husband or herself.

With the removal of the symptom of frigidity, the patient felt that the goals in treatment were accomplished, although her relationship with her husband was far from a good one. She continued however with the casework treatment for two more months focusing on her attitude toward her husband.

A slowing of speech was apparent and her dreams seemed to indicate a further reduction of her habitual fears. The following dreams illustrate this: "I am in a railroad station. I went to the ladies' room. There were five men there (this is the number of men with whom she had sexual contact). I accepted them as having some right to be there." The second dream was: "I am fifteen and at home kissing a boy. I felt that my stepmother would not disapprove." At this point she no longer assumed a protective role toward her husband; she began to make realistic demands of him. The effect of this change was that he did find a job. His severe anginal attacks greatly decreased. At the same time she no longer restricted her own activities by martyrizing herself for him.

She resumed attendance at concerts and the threatre, and went back to her piano playing, perfecting it to a point where she gave a recital.

Shortly before the termination of treatment she presented the following dream: "I am in a church with my father. I realize that I don't have the right handle to my umbrella, so I go into a new house where I find the right handle. Then I discover that I am not in church, but in a political meeting, and that the man is not my father but my husband. I am very happy about the whole thing." During the last month of treatment, the patient seemed to be handling her problems of daily living assertively, rarely requiring help. At her suggestion, and with the agreement of the caseworker, she felt that it would be a good time for her to stop coming to sessions and to try things on her own. A three year follow-up via telephone showed the outcome to have been favorable.

In speculating what happened here it would appear that somehow in meeting her requisites for a younger woman therapist, the caseworker was able to establish a relationship with the patient which was not too frightening, one in which she could talk about the situation without developing overwhelming anxiety. She was thus able to accept what the worker said to her with a minimum of anxiety and could therefore focus on her symptom of frigidity which was the only aspect of her problem that she was willing to discuss. She was not motivated for psychoanalysis, but came in primarily because her husband was complaining about her habits. Her wish was to be relieved of the burden of guilt she felt in having so much hostility toward her husband, and as her guilt abated through talking with the social worker she was able to go on with the marriage. The worker never suggested areas for her to explore, and never made interpretations that would force her to look deeper into her unconscious. Only those problems which she herself raised were discussed. In terms of what was accomplished, it seemed that she worked through to a manageable degree, by what might be called "conscious insight" her sexual disgust for and her hostility to her husband. She also appeared to have touched upon enough of her oedipal conflict, insofar as she verbalized that her feelings for her father were interfering with her relations with men, to enable her to get along with her husband with some degree of relaxation.

From this example it is apparent that while psychotherapeutic principles were employed, there were some differences in techniques as compared to conventional depth therapy. The relationship between the caseworker and the patient was kept on a positive level; transference was not permitted to build up to irrational proportions. The reality situation was focused on at all times; the content of the interviews were of her own choice and related to stress factors with which she wished to deal. No attempts were made to open up facets that she herself did not clearly see and present. While no encouragement was given her to bring in dreams, she did this on her own, and her dreams were utilized as guidelines to more conscious feelings. She was given reassurance and explanations.

There are obviously some similarities between casework as performed in this instance and psychotherapy, but there are also distinctive differences. For example, working with children who "act out," the psychotherapist is interested in the process as it involves the fantasy life and intrapsychic dynamics, while the caseworker emphasizes the social implications of the acting out process. The caseworker will discuss with an "acting out" child methods by which the behavior can be controlled on a conscious level, in the playground or at home. With Mrs. C the caseworker reiterated or confirmed what the patient already knew; she was very angry at her husband and did fear that she would lose control of her sadistic impulses and cause trouble by acting out. She was acting out daily with her husband in small ways, but her emphasis was on control. An interesting differentiation can be made in relation to the problem of school absenteeism. In casework the problem is approached from the point of view of the child's adjustment to school. The child is encouraged to verbalize his feelings at school concerning his teachers and peers. He is urged to talk about what he may be thinking or feeling just before he *wants* to perform an impulsive kind of behavior so that he may be able to see that he was angry about something or afraid. He will learn through exploration and education that he can control some of his behavior if he talks about it. He is urged to *talk out* rather than to *act out*. It is hoped that when the child sees results from this conscious effort, he will be helped; his tension and guilt will be relieved and he will tend to repeat the new pattern rather than the old one. In the case of children the parents are approached and the dynamics of the problem clarified; help may be given to them or to other members of the family who seek advice. In contrast, psychotherapy tackles the problem of *why* and inquires into the roots of the repetitive behavior. The problem is approached through discussion of mechanisms of defense, their relation to anxieties and fantasies, and their connection to past experiences with parental figures. Casework gives encouragement, suggestions, education and reassurance. Defenses are dealt with by discussing the relationship between a particular defense and some anxiety the patient may have been experiencing about some incident in the present. This is done on an explanatory level rather than by relating the experience to feelings about the therapist which are reminiscent of incidents from the past. When rational means do not produce results and the behavior is repetitive in spite of casework help, then psychotherapy with its exploration of intrapsychic dynamics may be required. There are many authors who make no distinction between this casework approach and a psychotherapeutic process—they are considered identical.

SELECTION OF A QUALIFIED WORKER

It is apparent from the above examples that casework techniques may be employed with certain patients which, though non-directive, are focused on one sector of a problem, and this approach may be utilized by a psychiatrist or by a psychiatric social worker to whom the psychiatrist refers the patient. If the psychiatrist in private practice wishes to select a social worker in private practice with whom to work, he should examine the experience and the education of the social worker. The worker should have graduated from an acceptable school of social work and have an M.S. or an M.S.S. degree. If the problem is a special one, such as drug addiction delinquency or alcoholism, the worker should have had special experience in these areas. There is a great deal of information that is uncoded and unorganized in the field of social work, and five or six years of experience in a specialty makes the worker extremely useful in the field. For example, in home placement there is information about the kinds of unmarried mothers who will be good mothers as opposed to unmarried mothers who will not. There is no substitute for experience. The social worker who is called in on a case should have a broad range of knowledge such as knowing the importance of the self help organizations like Alcoholics Anonymous, Recovery, Cyanon and others. Often a social agency would be better for a patient than a social worker in private practice, and in that case the psychiatrist should choose an agency that has high standards of practice and a function that is relevant to the patient's problems—i.e., adoption, senior citizens, child care, family welfare, marriage, and foster care.

In the event that the psychotherapist wishes to secure the services of a social worker, there are several ways in which he can do so. He may use the directory published periodically by the National Association of Social Workers. He may inquire at the local public health service, the public welfare agency, or the family agency, if there is one. The family court will have information about social workers as will the local mental health association. In the absence of other agencies, one may inquire at the State Department of Mental Health regarding social work resources in one's community.

BIBLIOGRAPHY

ACKERMAN, N. W.: "The Psychodynamics of Family Life." New York, Basic Books, 1958.

ADLER, J.: "Therapeutic group work with tuberculosis displaced persons." Internat. J Group Psychother., V. 3, No. 3:302-308, July, 1953.

ALEXANDER, F.: "The brief psychotherapy council and its outlook." Proc. Brief Psychotherapy Council, 2:14, 1944.

—: "Principles and techniques of briefer psychotherapeutic procedures." Res. Publ. Ass. Nerv. Ment. Dis., 31:16-20, 1951.

— AND FRENCH, T. M., et. al.: "Psychoanalytic Therapy," New York, Ronald Press Co., 1946.

ALSEN, V.: Die Kurtzanalyse; Versuch einer Charakterisierung an Hand eines praktischen Beipiels. (Short-term analysis: an orientation based on a specific case) Z. Psychotherap. med. Psychol., 2(6): 245-258, 1952.

AMSTER, F.: "Application of group psychotherapy principles to non-structured groups." Internat. J. Group Psychother., V. 4, No. 3:285-292, July 1954.

AUSTIN, L.: In: "A Comparison of Diagnostic and Functional Casework Concepts." New York, Family Service Association of America, 1950.

AVNET, H. H.: "Psychiatric insurance: Financing Short-term Ambulatory Treatment." N. Y. Group Health Insurance Company, Inc. 1962.

BACK, K. W.: "Interpersonal relations in a discusion group." J. Soc. Issues, V. 4:61-65, 1948.

BACKUS, O. L. AND DUNN, H. M.: "Intensive group therapy in speech rehabilitation." J. Speech Disorders, V. 12:39, 1947.

BARNES, M. J.: "The educational and therapeutic implications in working with parent study groups around the problems of the normal pre-school child." Am. J. Orthopsychiat., V. 22:268, April, 1952.

BARD, P. AND MOUNTCASTLE, V. B.: "Some forebrain mechanisms involved in expression of rage, with special reference to suppression." The Frontal Lobes, ARNMD, 27:362-404, 1947.

BARNETT, G. J.: "Group psychotherapy as an adjunct to insulin subcoma treatment." Internat. J. Group Psychother., V. 9, No. 1:62-70, January 1959.

BASSIN, A. AND SMITH, A. B.: "Verbal participation and improvement in group therapy." Internat. J. Group Psychother., V. 12, No. 3:369-372, July 1962.

BATTEGAY, R.: "Group therapy with alcoholics and analgesic addicts. Internat. J. Group Psychother., V. 8, No. 4:428-434, October, 1958.

BELL, J. AND BARNETT, G.: "Intensive insulin sub-coma treatments combined with group therapy in a mental hygiene clinic." Dis. Nerv. Syst., V. 16:38, 1955.

BELLAK, L.: "The use of oral barbiturates in psychotherapy." Am. J. Psychiat. CV, Pp. 169-176, 1949.

BELLAK, L., PASQUARELLI, B. A., AND BRAVERMAN, S.: "The use of the thematic apperception test in psychotherapy." J. Nerv. & Ment. Dis., 64:110, 1949.

BENAIM, S.: "Group Psychotherapy within a geriatric unit, an experiment." Internat. J. Soc. Psychiat., V. 3:123-128, 1957.

—: "Use of hydroxydione in psychiatry." Brit. Med. J., 20:801-4, 1959.

BERG, B.: "Combining group and casework treatment in a camp setting." Social Work, V. 5:56, 1960.

BERG, G. C.: "A case showing some implications of short therapy." M 1944, 20:1-19. Abs VC Q 18:129, 1949.

BINDELGLAS, P. M. AND GOSLINE, E.: "Differential reactions of patients receiving group psychotherapy with concomitant somatic and drug therapies." Internat. J. Group Psychother., V. 7, No. 3:275-280. July, 1957.

BOAS, C.: "Group therapy with anorgastic women." Internat. J. Sexology, August, 1950.

BOILEAU, V. K.: "New techniques of brief psychotherapy." Psychol. Rept., 4:627-45, (10 references), 1958.

BOLES, G.: "Simultaneous group therapy with cerebral palsied children and their parents." Internat. J. Group Psychother., V. 9, No. 4:488-495. October, 1959.

BONIME, W.: "Some principles of brief psychotherapy." Psychiat. Quart., 27:1-18, 1953.

BOS, C.: "Short-term psychotherapy." Canad Psychiat. Assoc. J., 4:162-5, July, 1959.

BRASHER, G. W. J.:"A short study of psychoanalysis." Practitioner, London, 133:733-740, 1934.

BRAUNTHAL, H.: "A casework training course as a group therapeutic experience." Internat. J. Group Psychother., V. 2, No. 3:239-244. July, 1952.

BREUER, J. AND FREUD, S.: "Studies on Hysteria." New York, Basic Books, Inc., 1957 (Published in German, 1895).

BRILL, N. Q. AND STORROW, H. A.: "Prognostic factors in psychotherapy." J. A.M.A., 183:913-6, (13 references), 1963.

BROWNE, S. E.: "Short psychotherapy with passive patients, an experiment in general practice." Brit. J. Psychiat., 110:233-9, (19 references), 1964.

BRUNNER-ORNE, M. AND ORNE, M. T.: "Directive group therapy in the treatment of alcoholics: technique and rationale." Internat. J. Group Psychother., V. 4, No. 3:293-302, July, 1954.

BULLARD, D. M. JR. et al.: "The relative value of tranquilizing drugs and social and psychological therapies in chronic schizophrenia. Psychiat. Quart. 34(2):293-396, (TZ 1943), Apr., 1960.

BURDEN, A. P.: "Principles of brief psychotherapy." J. Louisiana Med. Soc. 115:374-8, (7 references), 1963.

CALVIN, A. D.: "Social reinforcement." J. Social Psych., V. 56:15-19, 1952.

CAMERON, J. L.: "Some implications of ego psychology for group psychotherapy of chronic schizophrenia." Internat. J. Group Psychother., V. 7, No. 4:355-362, October, 1957.

CARMICHAEL, D. M.: "Potential of group practices in mental hospitals." Internat. J. Group Psychother., V. 3, No. 3:309-314, July, 1953.

CARNCROSS, H. L.: "Activity in analysis." R. 13:281-293, 1926.

CATTELL, J. P.: "Psychopharmacological agents: a selective survey." Am. J. Psychiat., 116:352, 1959.

CATTELL, J. P., et al.: "Limited goal therapy in a psychiatric clinic." Am. J. Psychiat., 120:255-60, 1963.

CHAFETZ, N. B., BERNSTEIN, N., SHARPE, W., AND SCHWAB, R. S.: "Short term group therapy of patients with Parkinson's disease." New England J. Med., V. 253-961, December 1955.

Chicago Institute for Psychoanalysis: "Proceedings for the Brief Psychotherapy Council Held under the Auspices of the Institute for Psychoanalysis, Chicago." Chicago 1942-1944, 71p. Rv. Foxe, A.N.R. 31:354-355, 1944.

CLAPHAM, H. I. AND SCLARE, A. B.: "Group psychotherapy with asthmatic patients." Internat. J. Group Psychother., V. 8, No. 144-54, January, 1958.

COLEMAN, M. D.: "Recent progress in psychiatry," N.Y.S. J. Med., p. 3542, December 15, 1963.

COLLINS, R. T.: "Occupational psychiatric therapy." Curr. Psychiat. Ther., 2:192-5, 1962.

Council on Drugs, A.M.A.: "Evaluation of a tranquilizing agent—Diazepan (Valium)." J.A.M.A., 189:371-372, 1964.

CROCKER, O.: "Family life education: some new findings." J. Soc. Casework, V. 26:106, 1955.

CYTRYN, L. et al. "The effectiveness of tranquilizing drugs plus supportive psychotherapy in treating behavior disorders of children: a double-blind study of eighty outpatients." Amer. J. Orthopsychiat. 30:113-29, (Cz 239), 1960.

DELATTRE, J.: "Psychotherapie psychoanalytique de longeur restreinte." Evolut. Psychiat., (Paris) no. 4:757-73, (9 references), 1958.

DUBOIS, P.: "Zur Psychopathologie der Angstzustande." (On the psychopathology of anxiety states.) Berlin klin. Wschr. 1909, 33.

EINSTEIN, G.: "Family education as part of a public relations program in a casework agency." Mental Hygiene, V. 36:245 April, 1952.

EPSTEIN, N. AND SLAVSON, S. R.: "Further observations on group psychotherapy with adolescent delinquent boys in residential treatment; Subtitled: I. "Breakthrough in group treatment of hardened boys." Internat. J. Group Psychother., V. 12, No. 2:199-210, April, 1962.

ERLICH, R. E. AND PHILLIPS, P. B.: "Short term psychotherapy of the aviator." Aerospace Med., 34(11):1046-47, Nov., 1963.

FABIAN, A. A.: "Group treatment of chronic patients in a child guidance clinic." Internat. J. Group Psychother., V. 4, No. 3:243-252 July, 1954.

FAURE, H.: "Sleep-induced group psychotherapy." Internat. J. Group Psychother. V. 10, No. 1:22-37 January, 1960.

FEDER, B.: "Limited goals in short-term group psychotherapy with institutionalized delinquent adolescent boys." Int. J. Group Psychother. 12:503-7, 1962.

FEDERN, P.: "Ego Psychology and the Psychoses." New York, Basic Books, 1952.

FEINBERG, H.: "The ego building technique." Group Psychother., V. 12, No. 3:230-235, September, 1959.

FENICHEL, O.: "Brief Psychotherapy." (Presented at Los Angeles, October, 1944), (Tr:DRand ASt) OF-CP 2:243-259.

FISHER, B.: "Group therapy with retarded readers." J. Educ. Psych., V. 44:354, 1933.

FLEISCHL, M. F.: "The understanding and utilization of social and adjunctive therapies. Am. J. Psychotherapy, 26:255-265 1952.

FLEMING, L. AND SNYDER, W. V.: "Social and Personal Changes Following Non-Directive Group Play Therapy." Am. J. Orthopsychiat., January, 1947.

FRANKLIN, G. H.: "Group psychotherapy with delinquent boys in a training school setting." Internat. J. Group Psychother., V. 9, No. 2:213-218 April, 1959.

FREUD, A.: "The Ego and the Mechanisms of Defense." London, Hogarth Press, 1937.

FREUD, S.: "Freud's psychoanalytic method." In: Collected Papers. London, Hogarth Press, Vol. I, 1924(a). (Published in German, 1904.)

—: "Freud's papers on technique." In: Collected Papers. London, Hogarth Press, Vol. II, 1924(b). (Published in German, 1910-1919.)

—: "Fragment of an analysis of a case of hysteria." In: Collected Papers. London, Hogarth Press, Vol. III, 1925. (Published in German, 1905.)

—: Collected Papers. London, Hogarth Press, Vol. V, p. 283, 1933.

—: "Transference, psychoanalytic therapy." In: A General Introduction to Psychoanalysis. New York, Horace Liveright, Inc. 1935. (Published in German, 1918.)

—: "Analysis terminable and interminable." In: Collected Papers. London, Hogarth Press, Vol. V, 1950. (Published in German, 1937.)

—: "Analysis terminable and interminable (1937)." In: Collected Papers. London, Hogarth Press, Vol. V, p. 316, 1952.

FRIED, E.: "Ego functions and techniques of ego strengthening." Am. J. Psychother., V. 9, No. 3:407-429 July, 1955.

FRIEDLANDER, K.: "Varieties of group therapy patterns in a child guidance service." Internat. J. Group Psychother., V. 3, No. 1:59-65, January, 1953.

FRIEDMAN, J. H. AND GERHART, L .W.: "The question-box method of group psychotherapy." Mental Hygiene, V. 3, No. 2:246-256 April, 1947.

FROHMAN, B. S.: "Die aktive Analyse in der praxis." (Active analysis in the practice of the therapist.) Psa. Prx. 3:170-173, 1933.

FROHMAN, B. S. AND FROHMAN, E. P.: "Brief Psychotherapy." Philadelphia, Lea and Febiger, 1948.

FRUMKES, G.: "Types of activity in psychoanalytic techniques." 38-305-317, R. 1951.

FUERST, R.: "Efficacy of brief contact: comments on case D." In: Alexander, F. and French, T., Psychoanalytic Therapy. New York, Ronald Press, p. 161-162, 1946.

FULTON, J. F.: "Frontal Lobotomy and Affective Behavior." New York, Norton, 1951.

GANZARAIN, R., DAVANZO, H. AND CINZALETTI, J. et al.: "Group psychotherapy in the psychiatric training of medical students." Internat. J. Group Psychother., V. 8, No. 2:137-153 April, 1958.

GANZARAIN, R., DAVANZO, H., FLORES, O. AND DROBNY, E.: "Study of the effectiveness of group psychotherapy in the training of medical students." Interat. J. Group Psychother., V. 9, No. 4:475-487 October, 1959.

GERARD, M. W.: "Techniques." Proc. Brief Psychotherapy Council, 40-41, 1942.

GERSTEN, C.: "An experimental evaluation of group therapy with juvenile delinquents." Internat. J. Group Psychother., V. 1, No. 4:311-318 November, 1951.

GERSTEN, C.: "Group therapy with institutionalized juvenile delinquents." J. Genetic Psych., V. 80:35, 1952.

GIBBS, J. J. et al.: "A controlled clinical psychatric study of chlorpromazine," J. Clin. Exp. Psychopath, 18(3):269-83, (Tz 1292), September, 1957.

GITELSON, M.: "Brief psychotherapy: symposium organized by the Chicago Institute for Psychoanalysis." Proc. Brief Psychotherapy Council, 60-61, 1942.

GLOVER, E.: "Active therapy and psychoanalysis." J. 5:269-311, 1924.

GOOLISHIAN, H. A.: "A brief psychotherapy program for disturbed adolescents." Am. J. Orthopsychiat., 32:142-8, 1962.

GRAHAM, F. W.: "Group psychotherapy in the rehabilitation of the physically disabled." Med. J. Australia, 537-538, October 1, 1960.

GREEN, S.: "The evolution of ego adequacy." J. of the Hillside Hosp., V. 3, No. 4, 1954.

GREENBAUM, H.: "Group psychotherapy with alcoholics in conjunction with antabuse treatment." Internat. J. Group Psychother., V. 4, No. 1:30-41, January, 1954.

GREVING, F. T. AND GRUNWALD, H.: "Group counseling: A new family service." Better Times, Bull. of the Welfare and Health Council, New York City, V.35:1, November 20, 1953.

GRUNWALD, H.: "Group counseling in a casework agency." Internat. J. Group Psychother., V. 4, No. 2 April, 1954.

GUTHEIL, E. A.: "Basic outlines of the active analytic technique." 20:53-72, (Stekel) R 1933.

—: "Psychoanalysis and brief psychotherapy." J. Crim. Psychoapth., 6:207-230, 1944.

—: "Current trends in psychotherapy." J. Med. Soc. N.J., 52:580-585, 1955.

GUY, W. B., SHOEMAKER, R. J. AND McLAUGHLIN, J. T.: "Group psychotherapy in adult atopic eczema." A.M.A. Arch. Derm. & Syph., V. 70:767, 1954.

HADER, M.: "Psychotherapy for certain psychotic states in geriatric patients." J. Am. Geriat. Soc. 12(5):607-17, June, 1964.

HALEY, J.: "Control in brief psychotherapy." A.M.A. Arch Gen. Psychiat., 4:139-53, February, 1961.

HARLOW, H. F.: "The Development of Affectional Patterns in Infant Monkeys in Determinants of Infant Behavior." Foss, B. M., Ed., New York, John Wiley & Sons, 1961.

—: "Development of Affection in Primates." In: Roots of Behavior, Ed. Bliss, E. L. New York, Harper & Bros., 1962.

—: As reported anon, in "Expert says mother may not be best." Med. World News, V. 3, No. 23:62-63, November 9, 1962.

HARRIS, M. R.; KALIS, B. L.; AND FREEMAN, E. H.: "Precipitating stress: an approach to brief therapy." Am. J. Psychother., 17:465-471, 1963.

HARROWER, M.: "Projective Counseling. A Psychotherapeutic technic." Am. J. Psychother., 10:74-86, 1956(b).

—: "Projective tests and psychotherapy." In: Wolff, W., Contemporary Psychotherapists Examine Themselves." Springfield, Charles C Thomas, pp. 184-191, 1956(a).

—: "Personality Change and Development." New York, Grune & Stratton, 1958.

—: "Psychodiagnostic Testing; an Empirical Approach. Based on a follow-up of 2,000 cases." Springfield, Ill., Charles C Thomas, 1965.

HARROWER, M., ROMAN, M., VORHAUS, P. AND BAUMAN, G.: "Creative Variations in the Projective Techniques." Springfield, Ill., Charles C Thomas, 1960.

HARTMAN, H., KRISE, E. AND LOWENSTEIN, R.: "Comments on the Formation of Psychic Structure." In: Psychoanalytic Study of the Child, V. 2, 1946.

HEILBRUNN, G.: "Results with psychoanalytic therapy." Am. J. Psychother., 17:427-435, 1963.

HEINICKE, C. AND BOLES, R. F.: "Developmental trends in the structure of small groups." Sociometry, 16:7-38, 1953.

HILER, E. AND BERKOWITZ, A.: "Expanding goals of short term group psychotherapy." Dis. Nerv. Syst., V. 27-573, 1960.

HINCKLEY, R. G. AND HERMANN, L.: "Group Treatment in Psychotherapy." Minneapolis, University of Minnesota Press, 1951.

HINCKLEY, R. G.: "College mental hygiene and group therapy." Internat. J. Group Psychother., V. 3, No. 1:88-96, January, 1953.

HENDIN, H. C., LENNARD, H. L., AND BERNSTEIN, A.: "Psychotherapy as a system of action." Am. J. Psychiat., 117:903-9, April, 1961.

HOCH, P. H.: "Drugs and psychotherapy." Am. J. Psychiat., 116:305, 1959.

HOCH, E. AND DENIS, M.: "The role of group psychotherapy in a general medical and surgical hospital." J. Maine Med. Asso., V. 46:192, 1955.

HOLLENDER, M. H.: "Selection of patients for definitive forms of psychotherapy." Arch. Gen. Psychiat., 10:361-369, 1964.

HULSE, W. C.: "Group Psychotherapy with Soldiers and Veterans." Military Surgeon, V. 103, No. 2:116-121, August, 1948.

ILLING, H. A.: "The prisoner in his group." Internat. J. Group Psychother., V. 1, No. 3:264-277, September, 1951.

—: "Short-Contact Group Psychotherapy." Internat. J. Group Psychother., V. 2, No. 4:377-388, October, 1952.

ILLING, H. A. AND BROWNFIELD, B.: "Delusions of schizophrenic patients in group psychotherapy." J. Soc. Ther., V. 6:35, 1960.

JACKSON, D. D.: "Interactional psychotherapy." In: Stein, Morris I., Ed. Contemporary Psychotherapies. New York, Free Press of Glencoe, 1961, pp. 256-71.

JONES, E.: "The Life and Work of Sigmund Freud." Vol. 2, New York, Basic Books, 1955.

JONES, M.: "Intravenous insulin in the treatment of schizophrenia." Lancet, 2:361, 1940.

KALIS, B. L., HARRIS, M. R., PRESTWOOD, A.R. AND FREEMAN, E. H.: "Precipitating stress as a focus in psychotherapy." Arch. Gen. Psychiat. 2:219, 1961.

KALINOWSKY, L. B.: "Problems of psychotherapy and transference in shock treatments and psychosurgery." Psychosomat. Med., 18:399, 1956.

— AND HOCH, P. H.: "Somatic Treatments in Psychiatry." New York, Grune & Stratton, 1961.

KAPLOWITZ, D.: "Techniques effecting change in analytically oriented psychotherapy." Am. J. Psychother., 14:677-90, October, 1960.

KARSON, S. AND WIEDERSHINE, L. J.: "An objective evaluation of dynamically oriented group psychotherapy." Internat. J. Group. Psychother., V. 11, No. 2:166-174, April, 1961.

KEELER, M. H.: "Short-term group therapy with hospitalized non-psychotic patients." N. Carolina Med. J., 21:228-31, June, 1960.

KELMAN, H.: "Analysis once a week." (Read at the Association for the Advancement of Psa, March 11, 1945) Psa., 5:16-27 1945.

—: "The Short-therapies—an evaluation." Am. J. Psychiat., 7:3-17, 1947.

KING, P. D.: "Controlled study of group psychotherapy in schizophrenics receiving chlorpromazine." Psychiat. Dig. 24(1):21-passim, (Tz 2693) March, 1963.

KIRBY, K. AND PRIESTMAN, S.: "Values of a daughter (schizophrenic) and mother therapy group." Internat. J. Group Psychother., V. 7, No. 3:281-288 July, 1957.

KLAESI, J.: Uber die therapeutische Anwendung der "Dauernarkose" mittles Somnifen bei Schizophrenen." Ztschr. f. d. ges. Psychiat. u. Neurol., 74:557, 1922.

KLAPMAN, J. W.: "Clinical practices of group psychotherapy with psychotics." Internat. J. Group Psychother., V. 1, No. 1:22-30, April, 1951.

—: "Psychoanalytic or didactic group psychotherapy?" Psychiat. Quar. V. 28:279-286, April, 1954.

—: "Group Psychotherapy: Theory and Practice." (Sec. Ed.) New York and London, Grune & Stratton, 1959.

KLEINES, M. A. AND KALLEJIAN, V. J.: "The group psychotherapist in industry: a preventive approach." Internat. J. Group Psychother., V. 5, No. 1:91-98 January, 1955.

KOENIG, F. JR.: "A group therapy experiment in a city elementary school." Understanding the Child, V. 18:40, 1949.

KOSOFSKY, S.: "An attempt at weight control through group psychotherapy." J. Indiv. Psych., V. 13, No. 1:68-71, May, 1957.

KOTKOV, B.: "Technique and explanatory concepts of short term group psychotherapy." J. Clin. Psychopath., V. 10:304-316, 1949.

—: "Experiences in group psychotherapy with the obese." Internat. Record of Med., V. 164:10, 1951.

—: "Group psychotherapy with wayward girls." Dis. Nerv. Syst., V. 14:308, 1953.

—: "The effect of individual psychotherapy on group attendance: a research study." Internat. J. Group Psychother., V. 5, No. 3:280-285, July, 1955.

—: "Goals of short-term psychotherapy." J. Nerv. & Ment. Dis., V. 123:546-552, 1956.

KRAUS, A. R.: "Experimental study of the effect of group psychotherapy with chronic, psychotic patients." Internat. J. Group Psychother., V. 9, No. 3:293-302 July, 1959.

KRIS, E. B.: "Intensive short-term treatment in a day care facility for the prevention of rehospitalization of patients in the community showing recurrence of psychotic symptoms." Psychiat. Quart., 34:83-88, 1960.

LAFFAL, J. AND SARASON, I.: "Limited goal group psychotherapy on a locked service." Dis. Nerv. Syst., V. 18:63, 1957.

LAFORGUE, R.: "Sur le caractere actif ou passif de la therapuetique psychanalitique." Z. 13:476, 1927.

LAWRENCE, R. M. AND KIELL, N.: "Group guidance with college students." Internat. J. Group Psychother., V. 11, No. 1:78-87, January, 1961.

LEBOVICI, S.: "Group psychotherapy in France." Internat. J. Group Psychother., V. 8, No. 4:471-472, October, 1958.

LERNER, A.: "Self-evaluation in group counseling with male alcoholic inmates." Internat. J. Group Psychother., V. 5, No. 3:286-288, July, 1955.

LESHAN, L. AND LESHAN, E.: "Psychotherapy and the patient with a limited life span." Psychiatry, 24:318-23, 1961.

LESSE, S.: "Psychotherapy and ataraxics; some observations on combined psychotherapy and chlorpromazine therapy." Am. J. Psychother., 10(3):448-59, (Tz 984) July, 1956.

—: "Combined use of psychotherapy with ataraxic drugs." Dis. Nerv Syst., 18(9):334-8, (Tz 1296) September, 1957.

—: "Psychotherapy in combination with ataractic drugs." Am. J. Psychother., 14:491, 1960.

—: "Psychotherapy in combination with anti-depressant drugs." J. Neuropsychiat. 3(3):154-8, (Pt. 77) February, 1962.

—: "Psychotherapy in combination with anti-depressant drugs." Am. J. Psychother., 16:407-28, July 1962.

LINDEN, M. E.: "Group psychotherapy with institutionalized senile women: study in gerontologic human relations." Internat. J. Group Psychother., V. 3, No. 2:150-170, April, 1953.

—: "The significance of dual leadership in gerontologic group psychotherapy: studies in gerontologic relations, III." Internat. J. Group Psychother., V. 4, No. 3:262-273, July, 1954.

—: "Transference in gerontologic group psychotherapy: studies in gerontologic human relations, IV." Internat. J. Group Psychother., V. 5, No. 1:61-79, January, 1955.

—: "Geriatrics." In: Slavson, Sr. R., Ed. The Fields of Group Psychotherapy. New York, International Universities Press, 1956 (83-86 as reported by Ross, M.: "Recent contributions to gerontological group psychotherapy." Internat. J. Group Psychother., V. 9, No. 4:442-450, October, 1959.

LINN, L.: "The use of drugs in psychotherapy." Psychiat. Quart., 38(1):138-48, 1964.

LORR, M. et al.: "Meprobamate and chlorpromazine in psychotherapy; some effects on anxiety and hostility of outpatients." Arch. Gen. Psychiat. (Chicago), 4(4):381-9, (Tz 2088), April, 1961.

LOWERY, F.: "The Social Service Review." Chicago, University of Chicago Press, June, 1948.

LOWY, S. AND GUTHEIL, E. A.: "Active analytic psychotherapy" (Steckel). In: Progress in Psychotherapy. New York, Grune & Stratton, 1956, pp. 136-143.

LUBAR, G. H.: "Procedures in Active Psychoanalysis." New York, Pamphlet Publishing Company, 1948.

LUBIN, B. AND SLOMINSKI, A.: "A counseling program with adult male cerebral palsied patients." Cerebral Palsy Rev., V. 2, 13, 1960.

LULOW, W. V.: "An experimental approach toward the prevention of behavior disorder in a group of nursery school children." Internat. J. Group Psychother., V. 1, No. 2:144-153, June, 1951.

Medical News: "Outpatient drug therapy proves successful in treating mental and emotional disorders." Medical News, 188:25-26, 1964.

MACLEOD, J. A. AND MIDDELMAN, F.: "Wednesday afternoon clinic: a supportive care program." Arch. Gen. Psychiat. 6:56, 1962.

MAHER, B. A. AND KATKOVSKY, W.: "The efficacy of brief clinical procedures in alleviating children's problems." J. Indiv. Psychol., 17:205-11, 1961.

MANN, J.: "Some theoretic concepts of the group process." Internat. J. Group Psychother., V. 5, No. 3:235-241, July, 1955.

MARKOWITZ, M.: "An experiment in frustration as a tool in the training of group psychotherapists." (In manuscript, 1962.)

MARKOWITZ, M. AND LIFF, Z. A.: "The impact of a group process experience in the training of group psychotherapists." Paper read at the 19th Annual Conference, Am. Group Psychother. Assoc., Barbizon-Plaza Hotel, New York, January 26, 1962(a).

—: "Report on the laboratory course of the group psychotherapy training program." (Mimeographed, 1962(b).)

MASKIN, M.: "Adaptations of psychoanalytic technique to specific disorders." In: Masserman, J. H., Ed. Science and Psychoanalysis, V. 3. New York, Grune & Stratton, 1960.

MASLAND, R. P. JR.: "Office management of the disturbed teenager." Rhode Island M. J., 44:361-3, 369, 1963.

MASSERMAN, J. H.: "Motion pictures on animal behavior." Psychological Cinema Register, State College, Pa., 1936 to 1950.

—: "Behavior and Neurosis." Chicago, University of Chicago Press, 1943.

—: "Psychological medicine and world affairs." In: Harris, N. G., Ed. Modern Trends in Psychological Medicine. London, Butterworth, 1948.

—: "Faith and delusion in psychotherapy." Am. J. Psychiat., 110:324, 1953(a).

—: "Psychoanalysis and biodynamics." Internat. J. Psychoanalysis Supplement, 1953(b).

—: "Practice of Dynamic Psychiatry." Philadelphia, W. B. Saunders, 1955.

—: "Experimental psychopharmacology and behavioral relativity." In: Hoch, P. and Zubin, J., Eds. Problems of Addiction and Habituation. New York, Grune & Stratton, 1958.

—: "Ethology, comparative biodynamics and psychoanalytic research." In: Masserman, J. H., Ed. Science and Psychoanalysis, Vol. III. New York, Grune & Stratton, 1959, pp. 20-80.

—: "Principles of Dynamic Psychiatry." Philadelphia, W. B. Saunders, 1961.

—: "Drugs, brain and behavior: an experimental approach." J. Neuropsychiat., 3 Supp. 1, S 104-113, 1962.

MASSERMAN, J. H. AND PECHTEL, C.: "Neuroses in monkeys: a preliminary report of experimental obsevations." Ann. New York Acad. Sci., 56:253-265, 1953(c).

MASSERMAN, J. H., PECHTEL, C. AND SCHREINER, L. H.: "The role of olfaction in normal and neurotic behavior in animals." Psychosom. Med., 15:396, 1953(d).

MEERLOO, J. A. M.: "Emergency-psychotherapy and mental first aid." Internat. Rec. Med., 171:101-10 (9 references), 1958.

MENG, H.: "Uber Psychohygiene des Volks und der Volker" (On mental hygiene of the people and the nations). Gesundh. u Wohlif, 1937.

MENNINGER, K.: "The Vital Balance." New York, Viking Press, 1963, p. 73.

MEYER, M. S. AND POWER, E. J.: "The family caseworker's contribution to parent education through the medium of the discussion group." Am. J. Orthopsychiat., V. 23:62, 1953.

MILLER, L. C.: "Short-term therapy with adolescents." Am. J. Orthopsychiat., 29:772-9, 1959.

MILLER, E. C., DVORAK, B. A. AND TURNER, D.W.: "A method of creating aversion to alcohol by reflex conditioning in a group setting." Quart. J. Studies on Alcohol, V. 21, No. 3:424-431, September, 1960.

MILLMAN, B.: "Group therapy with parents; an approach to the rehabilitation of parents of physically disabled children." J. Pediatrics, V. 41:113, 1952.

MOLL, A. E. AND SHANE, S. G.: "Short term group psychotherapy." Treatment Services Bull., Dept. Veterans Affairs (Ottawa, Canada), V. 7:7, 1952.

MORSELLI, E. A.: "Le emozioni subcoscienti e il metodo rapido di cura nelle sindromi emotive di guerra." (Subconscious emotions and the fast method of cure in syndromes caused by war.) Quad. Psichiat., 689-96, 1919.

MULLER, M.: "Die Insulin—und Cardiazolbehandlung in der Psychiatrie." Fortschr. D. Neurol., Psychiat. u. ihrer Grenzgeb, 11:361, 1939.

MURPHY, W. F. AND WEINREB, J.: "Problems in teaching short-term psychotherapy." Dis. Nerv. Sys., 17:568-569, 1948.

NOYES, A. P. AND KOLB, L. C.: "Modern Clinical Psychiatry" (6th ed.). Philadelphia, W. B. Saunders, 1953, p. 508 (Modified Psychoanalysis).

ORANGE, A. J.: "A note on brief group psychotherapy with psychotic patients." Internat. J. Group Psychother., V. 5, No. 1:80-83, January, 1955.

OSTOW, M.: "The effects of the newer neuroleptic and stimulating drugs on psychic function." In: Sarwer-Foner, G. J., Ed. The Dynamics of Psychiatric Drug Therapy. Springfield, Ill., Charles C Thomas, 1960.

—: "The Use of Drugs in Psychoanalysis and Psychotherapy." New York, Basic Books, 1962.

PAPANEK, H.: "Projective test evaluation of changes effected by group psychotherapy." Internat. J. Group Psychother., V. 10, No. 4:446-455, October, 1960.

PARRISH, M.: "Group techniques with teen-age emotionally disturbed girls." Group Psychother., V. 14:20, 1961.

PARTRIDGE, W.: "Deadline for family care." Mental Hosp., V. 11:21-4, 1960.

PAVLOV, I. P.: "Conditioned Reflexes," London, Oxford University Press, 1927, p. 291.

PEABODY, G. A.: "Campus psychiatry." Curr. Psychiat. Ther., 1:1-7, 1961.

PEBERDY, G. R.: "Hypnotic methods in group psychotherapy." J. Ment. Sci., V. 106, No. 444:1016-1020, July, 1960.

PHILIP, B. R. AND PEIXOTTO, H. E.: "An objective evaluation of brief group psychotherapy on delinquent boys." Canad. J. Psychol., 13(4):273-80, 1959.

PINE, I., GARDNER, M., AND TIPPETT, D. L.: "Experience with short term group psychotherapy." Internat. J. Group Psychother., V. 8, No. 3:276-284, July, 1958.

PRIBRAM, K. H., MISHKIN, M., AND ROSVELD, H. E.: "The behavioral effects of selective partial ablations of the frontal lobe in monkeys." (Private communication.)

PUTNAM, M. C.: "Psychotherapy in a guidance center for infants and preschool children." Proceedings of the Second Brief Psychotherapy Council, Institute for Psychoanalysis, Chicago, January, 1944.

RADO, S.: "Adaptational development of psychoanalytic therapy." In: Psychoanalysis of Behavior: Collected Papers, V. I. New York, Grune & Stratton, 1956(a).

—: "Adaptational psychodynamics: a basic science." In: Psychoanalysis of Behavior: Collected Papers, V. I. New York, Grune & Stratton, 1956(b).

—: "Recent advances in psychoanalytic therapy." In: Psychoanalysis of Behavior: Collected Papers, V. I. New York, Grune & Stratton, 1956(c).

—: "The relationship of patient to therapist." In: Psychoanalysis of Behavior: Collected Papers, V. I. New York, Grune & Stratton, 1956(d).

—: "Psychotherapy: a problem of controlled intercommunication." In: Hoch, P. and Zubin, J., Eds. Psychopathology of Communication. New York, Grune & Stratton, 1958.

—: "Obsessive Behavior." In: Arieti, S., Ed. American Handbook of Psychiatry. New York, Basic Books, Inc., 1959.

—: "Achieving self-reliant treatment behavior: Therapeutic motivations and therapeutic techniques." In: Psychoanalysis of Behavior: Collected Papers, V. II. New York, Grune & Stratton, 1962(a).

—: "Psychoanalysis of Behavior: Collected Papers, V. II." New York, Grune & Stratton, 1962(b).

—: "Psychotherapy: A problem of controlled intercommunication." In: Psychoanalysis of Behavior: Collected Papers, V. II. New York, Grune & Stratton, 1962(c).

—: "Rage, violence and conscience." In: Psychoanalysis of Behavior: Collected Papers, V. II. New York, Grune & Stratton, 1962(d).

REDL, F.: "The concept of ego disturbance and ego support." Am. J. Orthopsychiat., V. 21:273-284, April, 1951.

REDL, F., AND WINEMAN, D.: "The Aggressive Child." Glencoe, Ill., Free Press of Glencoe, 1957.

REISTRUP, H.: "Lidt om psykoanalyse." (A few remarks on psychoanalysis.) Ugeskr. Laeg., 100:1147-1154, 1938.

RHEINGOLD, H. L.: In discussion of H. F. Harlow's "The development of affectional patterns in infant monkeys." In: Foss, B. M., Ed. Determinants of Infant Behavior. New York, John Wiley & Sons, 1961.

RICE, K. K.: "The importance of including fathers." Internat. J. Group Psychother., V. 2, No. 3:232-238, July, 1952.

RIDENOUR, R. H.: "Brief psychotherapy with 'Thorazine.'" Med. Ann. DC, 26(5):234 passim (Tz 1202), May, 1957.

RIECKEN, H. W.: "Some problems of consensus development." Rural Sociol., V. 17:245-252, 1952.

ROSENBAUM, C. P.: "Events of early therapy and brief therapy." Arch. Gen. Psychiat., 10:506-512, 1964.

ROSENBLATT, J. S.: In discussion of H. F. Harlow's "The development of affectional patterns in infant monkeys," In: Foss, B. M., Ed. Determinants of Infant Behavior. New York, John Wiley & Sons, 1961.

RUDOLF, G. DE M.: "An experiment in group therapy with mental defectives." Internat. J. Soc. Psychiat., V. 1, No. 1:49-53 (Summer), 1955.

SAGER, C. J., RIESS, B. F., AND GUNDLACH, R.: "Follow-up study of the results of extra-mural analytic psychotherapy." Am. J. Psychother., 18:161-173, 1964.

SAUL, L. J.: "On the value of one or two interviews." Psych. Quart., 20:613-615, 1951.

SCHEIDLINGER, S.: "The concepts of social group work and group psychotherapy." Socal Casework, V. 34:292, 1953.

SCHMIDEBERG, M.: "Short-analytic therapy." Nerv. Child, 8:281-290, 1949.

SCHOENBERG, B. AND CARR, A. C.: "An investigation of criteria for brief psychotherapy of neurodermatitis." Psychosom. Med. (7 references), 25:253-63, 1963.

SCHREINER, L. H., RIOCH, D. M., PECHTEL, C. AND MASSERMAN, J. H.: "Behavioral changes following thalamic injury in cat." J. Neurophysiol. 16:234-246, 1953.

SCHULMAN, J. L.: "One-visit psychotherapy with children." Progr. Psychother. 5:86-93, 1960.

SCHULTZ, J. H.: Uber kleine Psychotherapie in der allgemeinen Praxis und Kurzverfahren in der Psychotherapie." (On minor psychotherapy in general practice and short procedures in psychotherapy.) ZPt., 11:69-84, 1939.

SCHWARTZ, E. K.: "Recent observations on group psychotherapy with adolescent delinquent boys in residential treatment." Internat. J. Group Psycother., V. 10, No. 2:195-212, April, 1960.

SEMON, R. G. AND GOLDSTEIN, N.: "The effectivness of group therapy with chronic schizophrenic patients and an evaluation of different therapeutic methods." J. Consulting Psych. V. 2, No. 4:317-322, 1957.

SHAPIRO, I.: "Is group parent education worthwhile? A Research Report." Marriage and Family Living, V. 18:154, 1956.

SHEELEY, W. F.: "Emotional disorders in the family psychiatrist's office." Southwest Med. 43:375-77, 427-35 (35 references), 1962.

SHELLOW, R. S., WARD, J. S. AND RUBENFELD, S.: "Group therapy and the institutionalized delinquent." Internat. J. Group Psychother., V. 8, No. 3: 265-275, July, 1958.

SIEGEL, Z.: "Kleine Analysen aus der allgemeinen Praxis." (Brief analysis from general practice.) Fortschr. Sexualw. Psychoan., 2:412-432, 1926.

—: "Zwei Falle aus der Praxis der kleinen Analyse." (Two cases from the practice of "minor analysis") Psa. Prx., 3:77-82, 1933.

SIFNEOS, P. E.: "Phobic patient with dyspnea: short term psychotherapy." Am. Pract., 9:947-52, 1958.

—: "Dynamic psychotherapy in a psychiatric clinic." Curr. Psychiat. Ther., 1:168-74 (5 references), 1961.

SINGER, W. B.: "Post-hypnotic suggestion in group therapy." J. Clin. Psychol., V. 8:205, 1952.

SLAVSON, S. R.: "Current trends in group psychotherapy." Internat. J. Group Psychother., V. 1, No. 1:7-15, April, 1951.

—: Section II: "Group Therapy for Children in Latency." Internat. J. Group Psychother., V. 2, No. 1:77-82, January, 1952.

—: "A bio-quantum theory of the ego and its application to analytic group psychotherapy." Internat. J. Group Psychother., V. 9, No. 1:3-30, January, 1959.

—: "When is a 'therapy group' not a therapy group? An outline of the principles and practices of counseling, guidance and psychotherapy." Internat. J. Group Psychother., V. 10, No. 1:3-21, January, 1960.

SPEERS, R. W.: "Brief psychotherapy with college women: technique and criteria for selection." Am. J. Orthopsychiat., 32:434-44, 1962.

SPLITTER, S. R.: "Treatment of the anxious patient in general office practice." J. Clin. Exper. Psychopath., 21(2):106-13 (Cz 171), June, 1960.

STERBA, R. F.: "The fate of the ego in analytic therapy." Internat. J. Psychoanal., V. 16, 1934.

—: "Formative activity of the analyst." Internat. J. Psychoanal., V. 25, 1944.

—: "A Case of brief psychotherapy by Sigmund Freud." Psychoanl. Rev., 38:75-80, 1951.

STONE, L: "Psychoanalysis and brief psychotherapy." Psychiat. Quart., 20: 215-236, 1951.

TANNENBAUM, S. A.: "Three brief psychoanalyses." Am. J. Urol., 15:145-151, 1919.

TERHUNE, W. B.: "Brief psychotherapy with executives in industry." Progr. Psychother., 5:132-9, 1960.

THEODORSON, G. A.: "The function of hostility in small groups." J. Soc. Psychol., V. 56:57-66, 1962.

TOMPKINS, H. J.: "Health insurance and psychiatric therapy." Am. J. Psychiat., 120:345-349, 1964.

TRAINING BULLETIN MED. 103: War Department Technical Bulletin, October 10, 1944.

TUCKER, J.: "Group psychotherapy with chronic psychotic soiling patients." J. Consulting Psych., V. 20:430, 1956.

URBANTSCHITSCH, R.: "Uber die Abkurzung der Behandlungsdauer psychoanalytischer Kuren." (Concerning the abbreviation of the duration of treatment of psychoanalytic cures.) 76:51-55, WMW, 1926.

VISHER, J. S.: "Brief psychotherapy in a mental hygiene clinic." Am. J. Psychother., 13:331-42, 1959.

WALKER, R. G. AND KELLEY, F. E.: "Short term psychotherapy with hospitalized schizophrenic patients." Acta Psychiat. Scand., 35:34-56, 1960.

—: "Short-term psychotherapy with schizophrenic patients evaluated over a three-year follow-up period." J. Nerv. Ment. Dis., 137(4):349-52, October, 1963.

WEINSTOCK, H. I.: "Hospital psychotherapy in severe ulcerative colitis." Arch. Gen. Psychiat., (Chicago) 4:509-12, 1961.

WENDT, C. F.: "Psychotherapie im abgekurzten Vefahren." (Brief Psychotherapy.) Berlin, Springer, 1948.

—: "Poliklinische Kurztherapie." (Polyclinical therapy of short duration.) Med. Klin., 46:946-948, 1951.

WHITAKER, C. A., WARKENTIN, J. AND JOHNSON, N.: "The psychotherapeutic impasse." J. Orthopsychiat., 20:641-647, 1950.

WILLOUGHBY, R. R.: "The efficiency of short psychoanalysis." ASP, 26:125-130, 1931.

WILSON, D.: "Group psychotherapy and manic-depressive psychosis." Am. J. Psychiat., 110:911, 1954.

WINKLEMAN, N. W. JR.: "Some thoughts concerning trifluoperazine and its place in ataractic therapy." In: Trifluoperazine: Further Clinical and Laboratory Studies. Phila., Lea & Febiger, 1959, pp. 78-81.

WOLBERG, A.: "The borderline patient." Am. J. Psychother., V. 6:694-710, 1952.

WOLBERG, L. R.: "The Technique of Psychotherapy." New York, Grune & Stratton, 1954.

—: "Study of Hypnosis." London, Proc. Dent. Med. Soc., 1957.

—: "Child institutionalization as a psychotherapeutic procedure." In: Glueck, S., Ed. The Problem of Delinquency. Boston, Houghton Mifflin Co., 1959, pp. 755-762.

—: "Hypnoanalysis," 2nd ed. New York, Grune & Stratton, 1964(a).

—: "The evaluation of psychotherapy." In: Hoch, P. and Zubin, J., Eds. The Evaluation of Psychiatric Treatment. New York, Grune & Stratton, 1964(b), pp. 1-13.

WOLF, A.: Discussion of G. Bychowski's "Psychic structure and therapy of latent schizophrenia." In: Schizophrenia in Psychoanalytic Office Practice. New York, Grune & Stratton, 1957, pp. 135-139.

WOLF, A. AND SCHWARTZ, E. K.: "Psychoanalysis in Groups." New York, Grune & Stratton, 1962.

WOLMAN, B. B.: "Group psychotherapy with latent schizophrenics." Internat. J. Group Psychother., V. 10, No. 3:301-312, July, 1960.

WOLPE, J.: "Psychotherapy by Reciprocal Inhibition." Stanford, Calif., Stanford Univ. Press, 1958.

WOODWARD, W.: "Spontaneous personality synthesis in group therapy." Internat. J. Group Psychother., V. 1, No. 2:123-125, June, 1951.

YATES, M. AND LEDERER, R.: "Small short term group meeting with patients of children with mongolism." Am. J. Ment. Def., V. 65:457, 1961.

YONGE, K. A. AND O'CONNOR, N.: "Measurable effects of group Psychotherapy with defective delinquents." J. Ment. Sci., V. 100:944, 1954.

ZUCKER, A. H.: "Group psychotherapy and the nature of drug addiction." Internat. J. Group Psychother., V. 11, No. 2:209-218, April, 1961.

AUTHOR INDEX

SUBJECT INDEX